MANAGING THE
TESTING
PROCESS

Rex Black

PUBLISHED BY
Microsoft Press
A Division of Microsoft Corporation
One Microsoft Way
Redmond, Washington 98052-6399

Library of Congress Cataloging-in-Publication Data
Black, Rex, 1964–
    Managing the Testing Process / Rex Black.
        p.   cm.
    ISBN 0-7356-0584-X
    1. Computer software--Testing.   2. Computers--Testing.   I. Title.
    QA76.76.T48B553 1999
    005.1'4--DC21   99-27358
                                                                        CIP

Printed and bound in the United States of America.

1 2 3 4 5 6 7 8 9   MLML   4 3 2 1 0 9

Distributed in Canada by Penguin Books Canada Limited.

A CIP catalogue record for this book is available from the British Library.

Microsoft Press books are available through booksellers and distributors worldwide. For further information about international editions, contact your local Microsoft Corporation office, or contact Microsoft Press International directly at fax (425) 936-7329. Visit our Web site at mspress.microsoft.com.

Macintosh is a registered trademark of Apple Computer, Inc. Intel is a registered trademark of Intel Corporation. Microsoft, Microsoft Press, MS-DOS, Outlook, Visual Basic, Windows, and Windows NT are either registered trademarks or trademarks of Microsoft Corporation in the United States and/or other countries. Other product and company names mentioned herein may be the trademarks of their respective owners.

The example companies, organizations, products, people and events depicted herein are fictitious. No association with any real company, organization, product, person or event should be inferred.

Acquisitions Editor: Ben Ryan
Project Editor: Wendy Zucker
Manuscript Editor: Mary Renaud

CONTENTS

Acknowledgments

I start by thanking the fine folks at Microsoft Press who helped hammer my thoughts into a book that can actually help you do something. Special thanks go to Mary Renaud, Wendy Zucker, Ben Ryan, and Erin O'Connor. I also thank the three excellent professionals who reviewed this manuscript and gave me the benefit of their time and insight. Dr. Boris Beizer, Reynolds MacNary, and Jay Nelson brought their own special talents, unique perspectives, and broad experience to their critiques.

In the course of learning how to manage test projects, I have worked with many talented professionals. At the risk of omitting somebody and in random order, I'd especially like to thank the following people for their help over the years:

Dr. Shahram Zaman, Dr. Art Gooding, Dr. Richard Baker, Kyle Marple, Tom Bohner, Jim Magdich, Troy Sukert, Bill Schoneman, Bob Petersen, Jeff Fields, Dave Desormeau, Jerry MacMillan, Armand Aghabegian, Bob Hosale, Neal Pollack, Chris Baker, Greg Cummings, Shawn Panchacharam, Summer Chien, Dr. Bertrand Chen, Kefetew Selassie, Craig Rittenhouse, Terry Newgard, Gary Hochron, Greg Scala, Dr. Alonzo Cardenas, and Dr. Shoichi Minagawa.

Of course, my appreciation goes out to all my past and current colleagues, subcontractors, employees, clients, and employers.

In the realm of "without whom," I thank my parents, Rex Sr. and Carolynn, for their love and support over the years and, most important for this book, my wife and business partner, Laurel Becker. Writing this book took me away from a lot of things in my life, but I especially appreciate my wife's support in terms of her own time given up with me. This book is dedicated to her.

Please attribute all errors, omissions, mistakes, opinions, and bad jokes in this book solely to me.

Introduction

So you are responsible for managing a computer hardware or software test project? Congratulations! Maybe you've just moved up from test engineering or moved over from another part of the development team, or maybe you've been doing test projects for a while. Whether you are a test manager, a development manager, a technical or project leader, or an individual contributor with some level of responsibility for your company's test and quality assurance program, you're probably looking for some ideas on how to manage the unique beast that is a test project.

This book contains what I wish I had known when I moved from programming and system administration to test management. It will show you how to develop some essential tools and apply them to your test project, and it will also offer techniques that can help you get and use the resources you need to succeed. If you master the basic tools, apply the techniques to manage your resources, and give each area just the right amount of attention, you can survive managing a test project. You'll probably even do a good job, which may make you a test project manager for life, like me. Read this book at your own risk.

THE FOCUS OF THIS BOOK

I've written *Managing the Testing Process* for several reasons. First, in what some have termed the "software crisis," many projects suffer from a gap between expectations and reality when it comes to delivery dates and quality, a gap that is acutely experienced by the individual contributors who are creating and testing the software, by senior project managers, and by customers. Similarly, computer hardware development projects often miss key schedule and quality milestones. Effective testing and clear communication of results as an integrated part of a project risk-management strategy can help.

Second, I perceived a gap in the literature on software and hardware testing. I have read books targeting the low-level issues of how to design and implement test cases as well as books telling sophisticated project managers how to move their products to an advanced level of quality using concepts and tools such as ISO 9000, Total Quality Management, software quality metrics, and so forth. But I believe that test managers like us need a book that addresses the basic tools and techniques, the bricks and mortar, of test project management.

The tips and tools offered in this book will help you plan, build, and execute a structured test operation. As opposed to the all-too-common ad hoc and reactive test project, a structured test operation is planned, repeatable, and documented. What you learn here will allow you to develop models for understanding the meaning of the myriad data points generated by testing so that you can effectively manage what is often a confusing, chaotic, and change-ridden area of a software or hardware development project. It will also show you how to build an effective and economical test organization.

To that end, I've chosen to focus on topics unique to test management in the development environment. Because they're well covered in other books, I do not address two related topics:

◆ Basic project management tools such as work breakdown structures, Gantt charts, status reporting, and people management skills. It goes without saying that these tools must be part of your repertoire.

◆ Computer hardware *production* testing. If your purview includes this type of testing, I recommend books by W. Edwards Deming, Kaoru Ishikawa, and J. M. Juran as excellent resources on statistical quality control as well as Patrick O'Connor's book on reliability engineering. (Full bibliographic details for books discussed in the text and notes are available in the appendix.)

Software production, in the sense of copying unchanging "golden code" to distribution media, requires no testing. But it is also the case that both hardware and software production often include minor revisions and maintenance releases. You can use the techniques described in this book to manage the small test projects involved in such releases.

The particulars of testing software, as opposed to hardware, are well documented, which might make it appear, at first glance, that this book is headed in two directions. I have found, however, that the differences between these two areas of testing are less important from the perspective of the *test project* than they are from the perspective of *test methodology*. This makes sense: hardware tests software, and software tests hardware. Thus you can use similar techniques to manage test efforts for both hardware and software development projects.

CANON OR COOKBOOK?

When I first started working as a test engineer and test project manager, I was a testing ignoramus. Ignorance, of course, often leads to unawareness that the light you see at the end of the tunnel is actually an oncoming train. "How hard could it be?" I thought. "Testing is just a matter of figuring out what could go wrong and trying it."

As I soon discovered, however, the flaws in that line of reasoning lie in three key points:

- The tasks involved in "figuring out what could go wrong and trying it"—that is, in designing good test cases—are quite hard indeed. Wiser individuals than I have written better books than this on the art of test case engineering. Unfortunately, my professors didn't introduce me and my undergraduate computer science colleagues to the likes of Boris Beizer or Glenford Myers. As a student, I read half a dozen books on software engineering, none of which devoted more than a couple of pages to testing. Perhaps this explains how I failed to understand the difficulty of writing good test cases. It may also explain a number of other curiosities about the state of the art in the computer business.

- Testing does not go on in a vacuum. Rather, it is part of an overall development project—and thus testing must respond to real project needs, not to the whims of hackers playing around to see what they can break. In short, test projects require test project management.

◆ The prevalence of the "how hard can testing be" mind-set only serves to amplify the difficulties that testing professionals face. Once we've learned through painful experience exactly how hard testing can be, it sometimes feels as if we are doomed—like a cross between Sisyphus and Dilbert—to explain, over and over, on project after project, why this testing stuff takes so long and costs so much money.

Implicit in these points are several complicating factors. One of the most important is that the level of maturity of an organization's test processes can vary considerably: testing can be considered an annoying afterthought or a critical step in delivering quality products. In addition, the motivating factors—the reasons why management bothers to test—can differ in both focus and intensity. I have learned that managers who are motivated by bowel-wrenching fear do not see testing in the same light as managers who want to produce the best possible product. Finally, test practitioners have been left largely to their own devices by academia and have been forced to create processes by trial and error, leading to still more variability in test project management.

These factors make it difficult to develop a "how to" guide for planning and executing a test project. As academics might say, test project management does not lend itself to the easy development of a canon. "Understand the following ideas and you can understand this field" is not a statement that can be applied to the field of testing. And the development of a testing canon is certainly not an undertaking I'll tackle in this book.

But do you need a canon to manage test projects properly? I think not. Instead, consider this analogy. I am a competent and versatile cook, an amateur chef. I will never appear in the ranks of world-renowned chefs, but I regularly serve passable dinners to my family. I have successfully prepared a number of multicourse Thanksgiving dinners, some in motel kitchenettes. I mastered producing an edible meal for a reasonable cost as a necessity while working my way through college. In doing so, I learned how to read recipes out of a cookbook, apply them to my immediate needs, juggle a few ingredients here and there, handle the timing issues that separate dinner from a sequence of snacks, and play it by ear.

An edible meal at a reasonable cost is a good analogy for what your management wants from your testing organization. This book, then, should serve as a test project manager's "cookbook," describing the basic tools you need and helping you assemble and blend the proper ingredients.

The Tools You Need

Five basic tools underlie my approach to test management:

- *A thorough test plan.* A detailed test plan is a crystal ball, allowing you to foresee and prevent potential crises. Such a plan addresses the issues of scope, quality risk management, staffing, resources, hardware logistics, configuration management, scheduling, test phases, major milestones and phase transitions, and budgeting.

- *A well-engineered test system.* A good test system ferrets out, with wicked effectiveness, the bugs that can kill a product in the market. It also possesses internal and external consistency, is easy to learn and use, and builds on a set of well-behaved and compatible tools. I use the phrase "good test system architecture" to characterize such a system. The word "architecture" fosters a global, structured outlook on test development within the test team. It also conveys to management that creating a good test system involves developing an artifact of elegant construction, with a certain degree of permanence.

- *A state-based bug tracking database.* In the course of testing, you and your intrepid test team will find lots of bugs, a.k.a. issues, defects, errors, problems, faults, and other less printable descriptions. Trying to keep all these bugs in your head or in a single document courts immediate disaster because you won't be able to communicate effectively with one another or with the development team—and thus won't be able to contribute to increased product quality. You need a way to track each bug through a series of states on its way to closure. I'll show you how to set up and use an effective and simple database that accomplishes this purpose. This database can also summarize the bugs in informative charts that tell management about projected test completion, product stability, system turnaround times, troublesome subsystems, and root causes.

◆ *A comprehensive test tracking spreadsheet.* In addition to keeping track of bugs, you need to follow the status of each test case. Does the operating system crash when you use a particular piece of hardware? Does saving a file in a certain format take too long? Which release of the software or hardware failed an important test? A simple set of worksheets in a single spreadsheet can track the results of each individual test case, giving you the detail you need to answer these kinds of questions. The detail worksheets also roll up into summary worksheets that show you the big picture. What percentage of the test cases passed? How many test cases are blocked? How long do the test suites really take to run?

◆ *A simple change management database.* How many times have you wondered, "How did our schedule get so far out of whack?" Little discrepancies such as slips in hardware or software delivery dates, missing features that block test cases, unavailable test resources, and other "minor" changes can hurt. When testing runs late, the whole project slips. You can't prevent test-delaying incidents, but you can keep track of them, which will allow you to bring delays to the attention of your management early and explain the problems effectively. This book presents a simple, efficient database that keeps the crisis of the moment from becoming your next nightmare.

I've implemented these basic tools using Microsoft Windows–based applications such as Microsoft Excel, Microsoft Word, and Microsoft Access; and I've used them to manage multiple projects simultaneously from a laptop computer in hotel rooms and airport lounges around the world. Simple and effective, these tools comply with industry standards and bring you in line with the best test management practices and tools at leading software and hardware vendors. I use these tools to organize my thinking about my projects, to develop effective test plans and test suites, to execute the plans in dynamic high-technology development environments, and to track, analyze, and present the results to project managers.

THE RESOURCES YOU NEED

In keeping with our culinary analogy, you also need certain ingredients, or resources, to successfully produce a dish. In this testing "cookbook," I will show you how to assemble the resources you need to execute a testing project. These resources include some or all of the following:

◆ *A practical test lab.* A good test lab provides people—and computers—with a comfortable and safe place to work. This lab, far from being Quasimodo's hideout, needs many ways to communicate with the development team, the management, and the rest of the world. You must ensure that it's stocked with sufficient software and hardware to keep testers working efficiently, and you'll have to keep that software and hardware updated to the right release levels. Remembering that it is a *test* lab, you'll need to make it easy for engineers to keep track of key information about system configurations.

◆ *Test engineers and technicians.* You will need a team of hardworking, qualified people, arranged by projects, by skills, or by a little of both. Finding good test engineers can be harder than finding good development engineers. How do you distinguish the budding test genius from that one special person who will make your life as a manager a living hell of conflict, crises, and lost productivity? Sometimes the line between the two is finer than you might expect. And once you have built the test team, your work really begins. How do you motivate the members of the team to do a good job? How do you defuse the land mines that can destroy motivation?

◆ *Contractors and consultants.* As a test manager, you will probably use "outsiders," hired guns who work by the hour and then disappear when your project ends. I will help you classify the garden-variety high-tech temporary workers, understand what makes them tick, and resolve the emotional issues that surround them. When do you need a contractor? What do contractors care about? Should you try to "keep" the good ones? How do you recognize those times when you need a consultant?

◆ *External test labs and vendors.* In certain cases, it makes sense to do some of the testing outside the walls of your own test lab—for instance, when you are forced to handle spikes or surprises in test workloads. You might also save time and money by leveraging the skills, infrastructure, and equipment offered by external resources. But this isn't a trivial exercise. What can these labs and vendors really do for you? How can you use them to reduce the size of your test project without creating dangerous coverage gaps? How do you map their processes and results onto yours?

Of course, before you can work with any of these resources, you have to assemble them. As you might have learned already, management is never exactly thrilled at the prospect of spending lots of money on equipment to test stuff that "ought to work anyway." With that in mind, I have also included some advice about how to get the green light for the resources you really need.

USING THIS BOOK

Nothing in this book is based on Scientific Truth, double-blind studies, academic research, or even flashes of brilliance. It is merely about what has worked—and continues to work—for me on the dozens of test projects I have managed. You might choose to apply these approaches "as is," or you might choose to modify them. You might find all or only some of my approaches useful.

Along similar lines, bear in mind that this is not a book on the state of the art in test techniques, test theory, or the development process. Rather, it is a book on test management, for both hardware and software, as I have practiced it. In terms of the development process—"best practices" or your company's practices—the only assumption I make is that you as the test manager are involved in development projects with sufficient lead time to do the necessary test development. Although it might seem odd that I would write a book about managing a process without defining every aspect of that process, I would argue that a more detailed definition would restrict the usefulness of this book. The tools and tips explained here apply to organizations from the most ad hoc, disorganized, and process-free operations all the way up to successful, organized, best-practices commercial hardware and software companies. You will find these tools easier to apply in an environment that is process-friendly, but in many ways the tools are likely to be at their most useful when you are forced to implement them to impose order on chaos.

Of course, to some extent, I can't talk about test management without talking about test techniques. Because hardware and software test techniques differ, you might find some of my terminology unclear or my usage unfamiliar. I have included a glossary to help you decipher the hardware examples if you're a software tester, and vice versa. In addition, because the test manager is usually both a technical leader and a manager, it's important to be sure that you understand and use best practices, especially in terms of test techniques, for your particular type of testing. The appendix includes a list of books that can help you brush up on these topics if needed.

This book is drawn from my experiences, good and bad. The bad experiences—which I use sparingly—are meant to help you avoid some of my mistakes. I'll try to keep the discussion light and anecdotal; the theory behind what I've written, where any exists, is available in books listed in the appendix.

I find that I learn best from examples, so I have included lots of them. Because the tools I describe work for both hardware and software testing, I base many examples on one of these two hypothetical projects:

- Most software examples involve the development of a Java-based word processing package named SpeedyWriter, being written by Software Cafeteria, Inc. SpeedyWriter has all the usual capabilities of a full-featured word processor, plus network file locking, Web integration, and public-key encryption. SpeedyWriter includes various JavaBeans from other vendors.

- Most hardware examples refer to the development of a server named DataRocket, under development by Winged Bytes, LLP. DataRocket provides powerful, high-capacity file and application services as well as Web hosting to LAN clients. It runs multiple operating systems on an unnamed CPU. Along with third-party software, Winged Bytes plans to integrate a U.S.-made LAN card and a Taiwanese SCSI controller.

As for the tools discussed in this book, the companion CD contains templates that you can use to bootstrap your own implementations of the tools. As you read the various chapters, you might want to open and check out the corresponding templates from the CD to gain a deeper understanding of how the tools work. And once you've read the book, you might find the templates on the CD useful as stand-alone objects.

Finally—in case you haven't discovered this yet—testing is not a fiefdom in which one's cup overfloweth with resources and time. I have found that it's critical to focus on testing what project managers really value. Too often in the past I've ended up wrong-footed by events, spending time handling trivialities or minutiae while important matters escaped my attention. Those experiences taught me to recognize and attend to the significant few and ignore the trivial many. The tools and techniques presented here can help you do the same. About a quarter of computer test organizations are disbanded in their first two years; this book will help keep you in the remaining three-quarters.

Although it's clearly more than simply hanging onto a job, success in test management means different things to different people. In my day-to-day work, I measure the benefits of success by the peace of mind, the reduction in stress, and the enhanced professional image that come from actually managing the testing areas in my purview rather than reacting to the endless sequence of crises that ensue in ad hoc environments. I hope that these tools and ideas will contribute to your success as a computer test professional.

1

Defining What's on Your Plate: The Foundation of a Test System

Testing requires a tight focus. It's easy to try to do too much. Before you start to develop a test system—and, obviously, after you have taken the time to learn the product reasonably well—you need to figure out what you *might* test, then what you *should* test, and finally what you *can* test. Determining the answers to these questions will help you focus your test efforts.

What you might test are all those untested areas that fall within the purview of your test organization. On every project in which I've been involved, some amount of the test effort fell to organizations outside my area of responsibility. Testing an area that is already covered by another group adds little value, wastes time and money, and can create political problems for you.

What you should test are those untested areas that directly affect the customers' experience of quality. Customers can—and do—use buggy programs and computers and remain satisfied nevertheless; either they never encounter the bugs or the bugs don't significantly hinder their work. Your test efforts should find the critical defects that will limit your customers' ability to get work done with your product.

What you can test are those untested, critical areas on which your limited resources are best spent. Can you test everything you should? Not likely, given the schedule and budget restrictions you will probably face.[1] In reality, you must make tough choices, using limited information, on a tight schedule. You also need to "sell" the test project to your managers to get the resources and the time you need.

What You *Might* Test: The Extended Test Effort

In a typical development project in a typical hardware or software company, a lot of testing goes on outside the test organization. This arrangement not only can make sense technically but also can keep your workload manageable as your team and your test system develop. This section uses two lenses to examine how groups outside the formal test organization contribute to testing: the first lens is the level of focus—the *granularity*—of a test; the second is the type of testing performed within various test phases. Perhaps other organizations within your company could be (or are) helping you test.

From Microscope to Telescope: Test Granularity

Test granularity refers to the fineness or coarseness of a test's focus. A highly granular test case allows the tester to check low-level details, often internal to the system; a less granular test case provides the tester with information about general system behavior. Test granularity can be thought of as running along a spectrum ranging from structural (white-box) to behavioral (black-box and live), as shown in Figure 1-1.

---

1. See *Testing Computer Software*, by Cem Kaner, Jack Falk, and Hung Quoc Nguyen, and *The Art of Software Testing*, by Glenford Myers, for discussion about the difficulty of achieving "complete" testing, however one defines "complete."

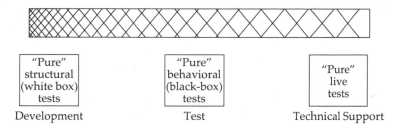

"Pure" structural (white box) tests	"Pure" behavioral (black-box) tests	"Pure" live tests
Development	Test	Technical Support

FIGURE 1-1   *The test granularity spectrum.*

Structural (White-Box) Tests

Structural tests (also known as white-box tests, glass-box tests, code-based tests, and design-based tests) find bugs in low-level operations such as those that occur down at the levels of lines of code, chips, subassemblies, and interfaces. These structural tests are based on *how* a system operates, and they tend to identify simple, isolated bugs. For example, a structural test might reveal that the file-close logic in our hypothetical product Speedy-Writer fails to check a flag indicating whether the file has changed since the last save, thus causing extraneous file-save operations.

Structural testing involves a detailed knowledge of the system. For software, most structural tests are developed by looking at the code and the data structures themselves; hardware structural tests compare chip specifications to readings on oscilloscopes or voltage meters.[2] Structural tests thus fit well in the development area. For test staff who are separated from low-level details, structural testing can be difficult unless the test team includes experienced developers or engineers.

Behavioral (Black-Box) Tests

Behavioral tests (also known as black-box tests) are often used to find bugs in high-level operations, at the levels of features, operational profiles, and customer scenarios. They are functional tests based on *what* a system should do. If DataRocket can achieve an effective throughput of only 10 Mbps across two 1-gigabit Ethernet connections acting as a bridge, behavioral network-performance tests can find this bug.

---

2. Such tests are structural if the chip is an indivisible unit used to assemble the system under test, as in a computer's CPU. But they are behavioral if the chip itself is the system under test. Such classifications, and the white-box/black-box dichotomy itself, can be slippery; see the sidebar "Is the White-Box/Black-Box Model Wrong?" on page 6.

A behavioral test, which is requirements-based, typically evaluates a hypothetical—and often challenging—scenario that could arise during actual use. But don't let the phrase "actual use" fool you into thinking that behavioral testing consists merely of playing with a computer to see what breaks. Neither should you let the description "requirements-based" serve as a justification for running tests to demonstrate that the system meets requirements (in contrast to the real purpose of testing, which is to find problems). Both of these views are dangerous, if common, misconceptions. Good behavioral tests, like good structural tests, are structured, methodical, repeatable sequences of tester-created conditions that probe suspected system weaknesses and strive to find bugs; behavioral tests, however, focus on the external interfaces of the system under test. Behavioral testing is the bread and butter of most independent test organizations.

Live Tests

Live tests involve putting customers, content experts, early adopters, and other end users in front of the system and encouraging them to try to break it. Beta testing is the most well known form of live testing. For instance, if the SpeedyWriter maintenance patch mechanism "starves" and crashes when more than one hundred customers try to download and apply an update simultaneously, live testing might be the only way to catch this bug. Live tests are completely behavioral in that users care only about what a program does, not about how it does it.

Live tests can follow general scripts or checklists, but they are often ad hoc. They don't focus on system weaknesses except for the "error guessing" that comes from experience. Live testing is a perfect fit for technical support, marketing, and sales organizations, whose members don't know test techniques but do know the product intimately. This understanding, along with recollections of the nasty bugs that have bitten them before, allows them to find bugs that developers and testers miss.

The Complementary and Continuous Nature of Test Granularity

The crew of a fishing boat uses a tight mesh net to catch eighteen-inch salmon and a loose mesh net to catch six-foot tuna. They might be able to catch a tuna in a salmon net or vice versa, but it would probably make them less efficient. Likewise, each test technique is most effective at finding certain kinds of bugs. Ideally, your company's overall test effort should include a mix of all three types.

Don't feel bound to declare your test group "the black-box bunch." If you can use structural tests effectively as part of what you're doing, add them to your test system. With some planning, you can reuse structural tests that have been created by the development team.

Remember that the concept of test granularity implies a spectrum, not a set of "either/or" categories. I have implemented test suites and cases that included both structural and behavioral elements. Mixing these elements can be useful in creating test conditions or assessing results. You can also mix planned test scenarios with ad hoc live testing. Use what works.

A STAMPEDE OR A MARCH? TEST EXECUTION PHASES

The test execution phase of the development process is often an undifferentiated blob. Testing begins, testers run some (vaguely defined) tests and identify some (vaguely reported) bugs, and then, at some point, project management declares testing complete. As their development processes mature, however, companies tend to adopt the industry-standard approach of partitioning test execution into a sequence of phases, often with groups other than the test organization responsible for one or two of the phases.

The following sections take a look at a number of possible test phases. I've identified most of these phases by the name that is most commonly encountered in software testing. When an alternative is given ("subsystem testing," for instance), the two terms are not really interchangeable; rather, the alternative is the analogous name from hardware testing.

Unit Testing

Unit testing involves the basic testing of a piece of code, the size of which is often undefined in practice, although it is usually a function or a subroutine. Not a test phase in a project-wide sense of the term, unit testing is the last step of writing a piece of code. The test cases can be structural or behavioral in design, depending on the developer or the organizational standard. Either way, this is white-box testing in the sense that the developer knows the internal structure of the unit under test and is concerned with how the testing affects the internal operations. As such, unit testing is almost always done by developers.

Component, or Subsystem, Testing

During the phase of component, or subsystem, testing, testers focus on bugs in individual pieces of functionality. This phase usually starts when the first component of the product becomes functional, along with whatever scaffolding, stubs, or drivers you need to operate this component without the

Is the White-Box/Black-Box Model Wrong?

The white-box/black-box model of testing is in widespread use. Glenford Myers's pioneering book *The Art of Software Testing,* for example, contrasts white-box and black-box approaches. Cem Kaner, Jack Falk, and Hung Quoc Nguyen, in *Testing Computer Software,* refer to test cases as following either a glass-box or a black-box paradigm; Jeffrey Voas and Gary McGraw make the same distinction in *Software Fault Injection.* The model is handy because its concepts are quite intuitive. In working with my clients, I've sometimes used it to make communication easier when explaining the kind of testing needed in particular projects or test phases.

This model is not ubiquitous, however. For instance, Bill Hetzel, in *The Complete Guide to Software Testing,* describes six types of test cases: requirements-based, design-based, code-based, randomized (especially in terms of the underlying data), extracted (from live data), and abnormal (or extreme). Hetzel does point out that requirements-based tests are black-box, that design-based and code-based tests are white-box, and that extracted tests are live (although the book's index contains no entries for the terms "white-box" or "black-box").

Some argue that the white-box/black-box model is an oversimplification—and a dangerous one at that. Boris Beizer, who once wrote a book called *Black Box Testing,* points out in his 1998 essay "The Black Box Vampire" that a better model is to think in terms of the structural/behavioral spectrum, with a fault model providing an orthogonal dimension. He argues that the white-box/black-box model makes testing look simpler than it is, encourages a potentially negative division of test work between developers and testers, feeds the mind-set that testers are less skilled than developers, and fosters a false belief that black-box testing is about demonstrating compliance with requirements.

Who's right? As one wag observes, "All models are wrong; some are useful."

rest of the system.[3] In our SpeedyWriter product, for example, file manipulation is a component. For DataRocket, the component test phase would focus on elements such as the SCSI subsystem: the controller, the hard disk drives, the CD-ROM drive, and the tape backup unit.

Component testing tends to emphasize structural (white-box) techniques. In addition, components often require support structures. Component testing is thus a good fit for development in such cases. If a component is stand-alone, however, behavioral (black-box) techniques can work. For example, I once worked on a UNIX operating system development project in which the test organization used shell scripts to drive each UNIX command through its paces using the command-line interface—a typical black-box technique. We later reused these component test scripts in system testing. In this instance, component testing was a better fit for the test organization.

Integration, or Product, Testing

Integration, or product, testing means that testers must look for bugs in the relationships and interfaces between pairs of components and groups of components in the system under test, often in a staged fashion.[4] At the project level, the project team is *integrating* the entire system—putting all the constituent components together, a few components at a time. SpeedyWriter's integration testing might start when developers integrate the file-manipulation component with the graphical user interface and continue as developers integrate more components one, two, or three at a time, until the product is "feature complete." For DataRocket, integration testing might begin when the motherboard is attached to the power supply, continuing until all components are in the case.

Not every project needs a formal integration test phase. If your product is a set of stand-alone utilities that don't share data or invoke one another, you can probably skip this. But if the product uses APIs or a hardware bus to coordinate activities, share data, and pass control, you have

---

3. See Myers, *The Art of Software Testing,* for a good discussion on support structures for component testing. Myers's discussion focuses on software, but it also extends to hardware.

4. The meaning of the terms "integration," "integration testing," and "product testing" can be very different depending on the environment in which you are working. See Boris Beizer's *Software System Testing and Quality Assurance* for a description of the integration process and the corresponding test activities. (Regrettably, this classic volume is now out of print, but you might find a copy in the library or in the possession of one of your test colleagues.)

a tightly integrated set of components that can work fine alone yet fail badly together.

The ownership of the integration test phase depends to a large extent on whether the techniques needed to perform it are structural and, if so, whether the test organization has sufficient internal system expertise to perform structural testing. The issue of resources also comes into play. If your product needs integration testing, plan to spend some time with your development counterparts working out the question of who should run this phase.

String Testing

String testing zeroes in on problems in typical usage scripts and customer operational "strings." This phase is a rare bird; I have seen it used only once, when it involved a strictly black-box variation on integration testing. In the case of SpeedyWriter, string testing might involve cases such as encrypting and decrypting a document or creating, printing, and saving a document.

System Testing

During this phase, testers use the entire system, fully integrated, to look for bugs in various system operations. Sometimes, as in installation and usability testing, these tests look at the system from a customer or end user point of view. At other times, the tests are designed to stress particular aspects of the system that may be unnoticed by the user but are critical for proper system behavior. For SpeedyWriter, system testing would address such concerns as installation, performance, and printer compatibility. For DataRocket, system testing would cover issues such as performance and network compatibility.

System testing tends toward the behavioral end of the test granularity spectrum. You can apply structural techniques to force certain stressful conditions that you would be hard-pressed to create through the user interface—especially load and error conditions—but you will usually be measuring the pass/fail criteria at an external interface. If a test organization exists, it will probably run the system tests.

Acceptance Testing

Thus far, the description of each test phase has revolved around looking for problems. Acceptance testing, in contrast, often tries to demonstrate that the system under test meets requirements. Although this phase of testing is not always performed, it is most useful in contractual situations, when successful completion of acceptance tests obligates a buyer to accept a system. In commercial software and hardware development, acceptance tests can be the final stage of testing that demonstrates a product's readiness for market, or they can be an alpha test of the software or hardware (sometimes referred to as "eating your own dog food"). In any of these situations, the meaning of a "successful" test is reversed: a successful unit, component, integration, or system test finds bugs, whereas a successful acceptance test demonstrates quality.

Acceptance testing involves live or "near live" techniques and often borrows the test tools and suites that have been developed during system testing. Because the objective is to demonstrate that the product will satisfy customers' needs, the focus is on typical product usage scenarios, not extreme conditions. Therefore, marketing, sales, technical support, beta customers, and even company executives are perfect candidates to run acceptance tests. (Two of my clients—one a small software startup and the other a large, publicly traded PC manufacturer—each use their CEO in acceptance testing; if the CEO likes the product, it ships.) Test organizations might provide test tools and other support for this phase; sometimes they also perform the acceptance tests.

Pilot Testing

Hardware development often involves pilot testing, either following or in parallel with acceptance tests. Pilot testing checks the ability of the assembly line to mass-produce the finished system. I have also seen this phase included in custom software development, where it demonstrates that the system will perform all the necessary operations in a live environment with a limited set of real customers. Unless your test organization is involved in production or operations, you probably won't be responsible for pilot testing.

Why Should You Use a Phased Test Approach?

As you've seen, a phased test approach marches methodically across the test granularity spectrum from structural to behavioral to live tests. Such an approach can provide the following benefits:

◆ Structural testing builds product stability. Some bugs are simple for developers to fix but difficult for the test organization to live with. You can't do performance testing if SpeedyWriter corrupts the hard disk and crashes the system after 10 minutes of use.

◆ Structural testing using scaffolding or stubs can start early. For example, you might receive an engineering version of Data-Rocket that is merely a motherboard, a SCSI subsystem, and a power supply on a foam pad. By plugging in a cheap video card, a 14-inch monitor, and a floppy drive, you can start testing basic I/O operations.

◆ You can detect bugs more efficiently, as mentioned earlier.

◆ You are able to compare metrics from your project against industry standards.

◆ Phases provide real and psychological milestones against which you can gauge the "doneness" of testing.

The last two benefits are explained in more detail in Chapter 4, which discusses defect metrics, and in Chapter 9, which explores the politics of test projects.

Test Phase Sequencing

Figure 1-2 shows the typical sequence of test phases. The phases are not drawn to scale—that is, the relative length of each phase and the degree of overlap between phases can vary considerably.[5] Some companies omit the test phases that are shown with dotted lines in the figure. There's no need to divide your test effort exactly into the seven test phases diagrammed in Figure 1-2; it's better to simply start with the approach that best fits your needs and let your process mature organically.

As you plan test sequencing, you should try to start each test phase as early as possible. Software industry studies have shown that the cost of fixing a bug found just one test phase earlier can be lower by several orders of magnitude, and my experience leads me to believe that the same argument applies to hardware development. In addition, finding more bugs earlier in

---

5. In particular, some might argue that the integration test phase—if it is a "phase" at all—starts the moment a developer integrates one component with another and doesn't end in any real sense until testing is over, since testing should always look for bugs that arise from the interaction of components and the interfaces between the components. Such an approach is the best practice, but I have found, especially when an independent test team runs integration tests, that this test phase cannot begin until a fairly sizable chunk of the product is integrated, primarily for logistical reasons.

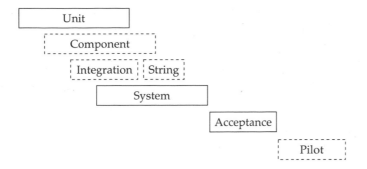

FIGURE 1-2 *Test phases in a development project.*

testing increases the total number of bugs one will find. And since the nasty, hard-to-fix problems often first rear their ugly heads in behavioral testing, moving into integration or system testing early buys the project more time to fix them. Finally, on unique, leading-edge projects, you'll need to test basic design assumptions. The closer to "real world" you make this testing, the more risk mitigation you achieve.

THE FIRST CUT

At this point, you have some ideas about how other organizations attack the division of the test roles. Now you can look into the testing that already goes on in your organization and locate gaps. If you are establishing a new test organization, you may find that folks who tested certain areas on previous projects believe that they needn't continue testing now that *you're* here. (Chapter 9 discusses how development groups can become "addicted" to the test team.) After identifying past test contributions, be sure to close the loop and get commitments from individual contributors (and their managers) that they will continue to test in the future.

WHAT YOU *SHOULD* TEST: CONSIDERING QUALITY

Once you've identified the areas of testing that might be appropriate for your test organization, the next step is to figure out what you should test. To do this, you must understand quality and the quality risks pertinent to these areas. I approach the topic of quality with some trepidation. If you're worried that I'm going to drag you through a lengthy discussion of ISO 9000, Total Quality Management,[6] Fagin inspections, or some other great idea for mature companies that won't help you take control of your test operation, you can rest assured—my approach to quality is pragmatic.

THREE BLIND MEN AND AN ELEPHANT: CAN YOU DEFINE QUALITY?

You have probably heard the old tale of the three blind men who come across an elephant. One touches the tail and declares it to be a snake. Another touches a leg and insists that it's a tree. The third touches the elephant's side and claims that it's a wall.

Defining quality can be a similar process. Everyone "knows" what it is, but disagreements abound. Have you debated with developers over whether a particular test case failure was really a bug? If so, weren't these debates in fact about whether the observed behavior was a quality issue? What, really, is quality? What factors determine its presence or absence? Whose opinions matter most?

J. M. Juran, a respected figure in the field of quality management, defines quality as "features [that] are decisive as to product performance and as to 'product satisfaction'…. The word 'quality' also refers to freedom from deficiencies…[that] result in complaints, claims, returns, rework and other damage. Those collectively are forms of 'product *dis*satisfaction.'"[7] Testing focuses on the latter half of this definition. I often call possible bugs *quality risks*, while referring to the observed symptoms of bugs as *failure modes*. At the most general level, the process of testing allows the test organization to assess the quality risks and to understand the failure modes that exist in the system under test.[8]

---

6. Some argue that Total Quality Management, in the sense in which this phrase was used in the 1980s and 1990s, is a dead letter. However, in a January 1999 article published in the journal of the American Society for Quality, Larry Todd Wilson and Diane Asay write: "Quality has won…. Whether or not your organization has succeeded in implementing a full total quality management program…our society has been infused with the language of the quality movement" (p.25). Perhaps TQM isn't quite dead yet.

7. J. M. Juran, *Juran on Planning for Quality,* pp. 4–5. This book is not a light read, but it offers a good discussion of the topic.

8. In *Quality Is Free,* Phillip Crosby argues that quality is precise conformity to requirements—nothing more and nothing less. But when was the last time you worked on a project with complete, unambiguous requirements?

After a product is released, customers who encounter bugs might experience product dissatisfaction and then make complaints, return merchandise, or call technical support. This makes the customer the arbiter of quality. Who are the customers, and what do they intend to do with the product?[9] For our purposes, let's assume that customers are people who have paid or will pay money to use your product and that they expect your product to do what a similar product, in the same class and of the same type, should reasonably do.

Testing should look for situations in which your product fails to meet customers' reasonable expectations in particular areas. For example, IBM evaluates customer satisfaction in terms of capability (functions), usability, performance, reliability, installability, maintainability, documentation/information, service, and overall fitness for use; Hewlett-Packard uses the categories of functionality, usability, reliability, performance, and serviceability.[10]

THE PERILS OF DIVERGENT EXPERIENCES OF QUALITY

As people use a product—a car, an espresso machine, a bar of soap—they form opinions about how well that product fulfills their expectations. These impressions, good or bad, become their *experience of quality* for that product. In a sense, during development you and your test team use the test system to try to gauge, in advance, customers' experiences of product quality. I refer to the extent to which the test system allows you to do this as the *fidelity* of the test system.

Figure 1-3 on the following page and Figure 1-4 on page 15 provide visual representations of two test systems. In Figure 1-3, test system A allows the tester to cover a majority of the product's quality risks and also to cover those areas that affect customer A's experience of quality. Test system B, shown in Figure 1-4, fails in both respects: it covers a smaller

---

9. Total Quality Management theory provides complex, formal methods of answering this question. Such methods are not only beyond the scope of this book; they are probably beyond your own scope as well. Unless you are a vice president in charge of quality, you aren't likely to have the organizational clout necessary to institute a company-wide quality program.

10. For more information, see Stephen Kan's *Metrics and Models in Software Quality Engineering*. This book provides a good discussion of software quality in general and also includes excellent material on implementing a metrics program using defect data. You can use Kan's ideas to enhance and extend the basic metrics I introduce in Chapter 4.

portion of the product's features, and, worse yet, the portion tested does not cover customer B's experience of quality.[11]

Two other scenarios are possible. First, suppose that you have a test system with the same coverage area as test system B but that the coverage area aligns with customer B's use of the product. In this case, your test team will do a fine job of catching key defects—at least from customer B's perspective. If most customers, including your most important ones, use the product the same way customer B does, then test system B, coverage limitations notwithstanding, is a good test system.

Second, suppose that you have a test system with the same coverage area as test system A but that the coverage area does not align with customer A's usage of the product. In this case, you fail to test the features that customer A expects to use. Since these features will probably reach the field buggy, customer A will be dissatisfied. If customer A is typical of your customer base—especially your important customers—you have a serious test coverage problem, even though the test system covers most of the product's features.

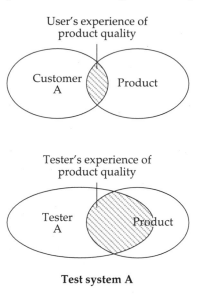

Test system A

FIGURE 1-3   *A high-fidelity test system.*

---

11. The phrase "test coverage" is often shorthand for structural coverage of the code or components in the system under test. Here, however, I use the term to encompass not only this type of coverage but also behavioral coverage of the operations, activities, functions, and other uses of the system to which the customer base as a whole is likely to subject it.

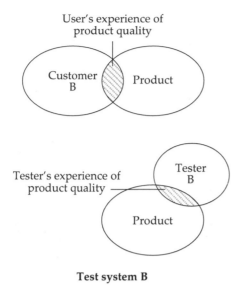

Test system B

FIGURE 1-4   *A low-fidelity test system.*

Figure 1-5 represents these scenarios. Of course, you can't test all of the quality risks and none of the customer uses, or vice versa. The two variables aren't really orthogonal; moving on one axis moves you in the same direction on the other axis, though to a lesser extent. Nonetheless, the point stands: it's good to chase potential bugs, but it's better to make sure that the features customers count on work as advertised.

FIGURE 1-5   *Test system coverage and its ability to assess customer-focused quality.*

THE CLASSICS AND BEYOND:
INFORMAL METHODS FOR ASSESSING QUALITY RISKS

Let's proceed to the "how" of customer-focused test development. You'll want to address as many quality risks as possible, subject to the constraint that you develop tests in a "customer priority" order. Later in this chapter we'll examine a formal approach for determining this priority, but you can begin with an informal method in which you outline the major quality risk categories and then refine and flesh out that list with the help of your test staff and those colleagues in your company who are especially "customer-aware."

The Usual Suspects

To develop the list of major categories, you can start by breaking down the test process into the classic phases of component testing, integration testing, system testing, and acceptance testing. Using the guidelines presented earlier in this chapter, you will have already determined which of these test phases you will run and which can be skipped because other colleagues are covering them. (Because we're focusing on test management rather than on the technical intricacies of test design, the following list doesn't define every quality risk in detail, especially some of the more complicated concepts such as states and data flows. If you need further information, you might find it helpful to consult some of the books on test design listed in the appendix.)

Component Testing

States. In some computer systems, especially telephony systems, the components or sets of components implement what computer science calls a *state machine*. Informally, a state machine is a system that moves through clearly defined states, while the response (the associated output and the subsequent state) to an input depends on the current state and the input. State machines present a variety of quality risks that are related both to the state machine as a whole and to the individual states.[12] Do the transitions from one state to another occur under the proper conditions? Are the correct outputs generated? Are the correct inputs accepted for each state?

---

12. State machines and state testing are complex topics. If you need pointers on designing structural or functional state-machine tests, you might begin by consulting Boris Beizer's *Black Box Testing* or *Software Testing Techniques*.

Consider an alarm card in the DataRocket server that sends SNMP information over the network if problems arise. This component spends most of its time in a quiescent state, but if it senses that the CPU is overheating, it transitions to a CPU Overtemp Warn state, during which it sends out alerts at regular intervals. If the problem does not clear up, the component transitions to a CPU Overtemp Critical state, at which point it initiates a system shutdown. You will need to verify that the transitions occur at the right points and that the component can't get "stuck" in a given state. For example, if the CPU returns to a normal temperature but the alarm card remains in a CPU Overtemp Warn state, the alarm card will continue to send (now spurious) alerts over the network and might do something dangerous, such as transitioning incorrectly to the CPU Overtemp Critical state.

Transactions.   Components that have transactions with the user or with other components present various risks. For example, creating a new file is a transaction in SpeedyWriter. Can you select the appropriate file template? How does the product respond to illegal file names?

Code Coverage.   An archetypal structural risk concerns the presence of untested code in a component. These untested areas often handle unusual or hard-to-create conditions, which makes it tempting to skip them. For instance, simulating the CPU Overtemp Critical condition described earlier might result in damage to the test configuration. But how else can you verify that the system shutdown will actually occur? If it is impractical—because of CPU placement, for example—to simulate the overheating using a hair dryer or a soldering iron, you might be forced to sacrifice one CPU to find out.

Data Flow Coverage.   Simply put, a data flow is the transfer of information—through parameters, shared (global) data space, or a stored database—from one component of the system to another. In my opinion, the risks associated with data flows haven't received nearly the attention they deserve—and it shows in today's software. Increasingly, programs allow you to import, export, and link data from other programs, creating complex data flows. Users sometimes report strange and counterintuitive failures while using these features. If SpeedyWriter, for example, includes a component that reads and writes Microsoft Word files, you will need to test this feature across multiple Word formats (versions) and with files that include more than just text. In the hardware world, signal-quality testing is a form of component-level data flow testing.

Functionality.   Each component exists to implement some set of functions, which are internal operations such as calculations and formatting. Functional quality risks are generally of two types: either the function is implemented incorrectly (usually only slightly so) or the function works—or appears to work—but has unpleasant side effects.

User Interface.   The quality risks in this area are similar to those encountered for functionality, but they also include questions of usability such as understandable prompts and messages, clear control flows, and appropriate color schemes and graphics. User interface testing during the component test phase often involves prototypes of the interface or the use of lots of stubs as placeholders. The testers might not be able to exercise the whole interface end to end, but each screen should be mocked up. (As Steve McConnell points out in his *Software Project Survival Guide*, these mock-ups offer an excellent opportunity to get real users in front of the interface. The screen mock-ups are best created during the requirements, design, or detailed design phase of development.)

Mechanical Life.   Any object that can be flexed or moved has a limit to the number of motions it can endure: keys on a keyboard break, hinges fatigue, buttons snap off, latches crack, and contacts fail.

Signal Quality.   Any circuit that processes data, whether digital or analog, is subject to the constraints imposed by signal quality. Lead times, lag times, rise times, fall times, noise, spikes, transients, and the like can be out of spec, causing a component to fail.

Integration Testing

Component or Subsystem Interfaces.   Every API, every function, every bus, every connector represents an opportunity for misunderstandings between the two (or more) component development engineers. These misunderstandings manifest themselves when two components that are otherwise correct fail together. In a sense, shared data files, and especially dynamic data such as configuration files and multiuser databases, are interfaces as well. In general, anywhere data or control is transferred from one component to another component (or components), either immediately or in a delayed fashion, an interface exists that can cause trouble.

Functionality.   In integration tests, you again encounter the "wrong action" and "right action, wrong side effect" risks, but here you should focus on functionality that requires the correct operation of two or more components or a flow of data between them.

Capacity and Volume. Think of software, a computer, or a network of computers as a system of pipes for bringing in information, operating on it, storing it, and sending it out. The capacities (static) and volumes (dynamic) of these pipes must match the requirements of the application and the expectations of the user. From a structural test perspective, every buffer, queue, storage resource, processor, bus, and I/O channel in the system has a theoretical limit and a (lower) practical limit. For a single-user program on a PC, this might be a simple, well-bounded set of risks. For SpeedyWriter, the effects of network traffic and the speed of the typist might be the only issues. For a network server like DataRocket, however, a variety of risks can apply. Can the network card handle realistic traffic levels? Can the disk subsystem deal with realistic loads? Is the data storage capability sufficient? In integration testing, you can begin to evaluate these risks.

Error/Disaster Handling and Recovery. Undesirable events happen. PCs lock up. Servers crash. Networks drop packets. Modem connections fail. Hard drives experience errors. Building air conditioners and heaters go out. Electrical grids have power surges, brownouts, and failures. It might be depressing, but you should construct a list of such situations and how they can affect your system. Be realistic, though; nuclear wars and aster-oid strikes *could* happen, but the odds are low—and who would care about your system's survival if they did? Try to focus on the mundane mini-catastrophes that will eventually afflict the system. You can start looking at these quality risks early in the integration test phase.

Data Quality. If your product stores, retrieves, and shares significant amounts of data—especially data that has delicate links, relationships, and integrity constraints—you should consider testing whether the product can handle that data reliably. For instance, I once used an expense reporting program that had a serious data quality bug. Because I needed to analyze data across multiple reports, all reports had to reside in the same file. If Microsoft Windows 95 crashed while the application had the file open, the application corrupted the file. The corruption was subtle; I could continue to use the file for quite a while afterward, but in the meantime the corrup-tion compounded itself. At some point, any attempt to add a new transac-tion caused the application to crash. The application did not include a file-repair utility. Because data storage and retrieval tend to be clustered in certain components or subsystems, you should start testing these areas as soon as these components are integrated.

Performance. Like capacity and volume issues, performance concerns apply to most subsystems or components in a product. For real-time and mission-critical applications, performance can be the most important quality risk, timely response under all possible circumstances being the *sine qua non.* Even for systems that are not real-time, important performance issues exist. Have you ever seen a product review in a computer magazine that didn't address performance? Performance is not only "how many per second" but also "how long"; consider the battery life of a laptop. As the system is integrated, you can begin to measure performance.

User Interface. As more pieces of "real" functionality are integrated into the system, you might be able to test them through the user interface. (If the user interface was a true throw-away prototype, however, you might not have this option.)

System and Acceptance Testing

Functionality. During system testing, you should consider functionality in terms of whole sequences of end user operations or an entire area of functionality. For example, with SpeedyWriter you might look at creating, editing, and printing a file or at all the possible ways of creating a file, all the editing options, and all the printing options.

User Interface. If you or the developers have had a chance to work with a prototype in earlier test phases, usability testing during the system test phase can focus on scrubbing out the irritating behaviors that crop up once everything is connected to the interface. Regrettably, however, the prototyping advocated earlier usually occurs only in the best projects; the system test phase is often the first time you will see the complete user interface with all the commands and actions available. In this case, you must address all usability issues at this stage. Either way, some usability testing should take place during this test phase.

States. State machines can exist at the system level as well as at the component level. For example, a voice mail system is a complex computer-telephony state machine.

Transactions. Transaction handling can also occur at the system level. DataRocket, for instance, handles transactions: printing a file, delivering a file (one chunk at a time), and so forth.

Data Quality. During the system test phase, you should revisit the data quality risks initially covered in integration testing, since the complexity of the data often increases once the whole product is integrated. For example, if SpeedyWriter supports embedded pictures and other nontext objects, this feature might not be dropped in until the end of the integration test. Working with such complex data makes problems more likely.

Operations.   Complex systems such as databases and servers often require administrators. These operators perform essential maintenance tasks that sometimes take the system off line. For DataRocket, consider the following quality risks: Can you back up and restore files? Can you migrate the system from Novell Netware to Microsoft Windows NT Server? Can you add an external RAID array? Can you add memory? Can you add a second LAN card?

Capacity and Volume.   You should revisit the capacity and volume risks that were covered in integration testing, but this time you'll want to use a more black-box approach. Rather than beating on individual buffers, queues, resources, and channels inside the product, look at the capacity and volume limitations from a user's point of view.

Reliability and Stability.   Quality risks in this area include unacceptable failure rates (mean time between failures, or MTBF), unacceptable recovery times (mean time to repair, or MTTR), and the inability of the system to function under legitimate conditions without failure. MTBF demonstrations provide a typical example of reliability testing in the hardware world. For hardware, the theory and practice of measuring reliability are well established, but this is not so for software. In the software world, reliability and reliability growth are hot fields in theory, but the models that currently exist provoke much controversy.[13]

---

13. Without embarking on a full discussion of the theory and the limitations of software reliability models, I should nonetheless mention three fundamental problems arising from the fact that software is different from hardware. First, the assumption of independence of errors does not hold for software. Boris Beizer offers a memorable analogy in his essay "Software Is Different": you don't expect your rear tire to blow out if you can't tune your car radio to a station, but similar bugs occur all the time in software. Second, hardware wears out with use, but software wears out only as a result of maintenance. Third, fixes to observed reliability problems in a hardware product during development tend to increase reliability, whereas fixes to similar software problems might actually decrease reliability. For a detailed discussion of software reliability, see Michael Lyu's *Handbook of Software Reliability*. In addition, the IEEE standards 982.1, 982.2, and 1061 provide models you can try.

Error/Disaster Handling and Recovery.   As in the case of capacity and volume, you should revisit error/disaster handling and recovery from a behavioral perspective. Focus on the external failures.

Stress.   This risk category is often an amalgam of capacity, volume, reliability, stability, and error/disaster handling and recovery. A single "stress test" suite can push the system in a way that provides information about all these areas.

Performance.   First broached during integration testing, performance is another risk category that you need to revisit during the system test phase. Once again, think about a behavioral approach.

Date and Time Handling.   The hot topic of the moment is the much-touted—dare I say hyped?—Year 2000 (Y2K) bug. Hyped or not, it's worth consideration. You might also need to take into account the fact that some countries—for example, Taiwan—base their calendars on events other than the birth of Jesus. Additionally, you should verify that your product can work properly in different time zones, or even in multiple time zones if it is a distributed system.

Localization.   Localization typically refers to problems associated with different languages. Even Romance languages, which use the Latin alphabet, often include special letters, such as the ñ in Spanish, that can generate a quality risk if your product includes sorting or searching capabilities. Languages such as Chinese, Japanese, Russian, and Greek create bigger difficulties. Besides the software considerations, computers in these environments use different keyboards and different printer drivers. And language is not the only custom that changes at the border and can affect your system. Can your product handle 220 volts and 110 volts, 50 hertz and 60 hertz? How about the unique dial tones and ring signals found in Europe and Asia? Beyond the technical considerations, you can encounter cultural issues, taboos, and "shorthands." For example, a graphic that is considered an acceptable way of communicating information in one culture might be seen as rude or obscene in another.

Networked and Distributed Environments.   If your product works in a networked or distributed environment, you have some special quality risks to consider. For example, what if your system spans time zones? Can the constituent systems talk to each other without becoming confused about central standard time and Pacific standard time? If your systems must communicate internationally, will the telephone standards affect them?

Configuration Options and Compatibility. Most PC software these days supports various configuration options. SpeedyWriter, for instance, might need to remember a customer's name, address, and company to generate letter outlines. DataRocket might allow various CPU speeds and multiprocessor settings. Configuration options today are also dynamic in a variety of ways that would have been unthinkable only a few years ago. On-demand loading and unloading of drivers (Plug and Play), libraries, and software; "cold," "warm," and "hot" swapping of devices; and power management can be seen as dynamically changing the configurations of both software and hardware.

In addition, when you look out past the internal variables, the PC world includes a bewildering variety of software, hardware, and network environments that can create problems for your system. Will the system talk to all the printers your customers own? Do network drivers cause your system to fail? Can your software coexist with leading applications? (Some might argue that the software and hardware compatibility programs offered by leading operating system vendors, such as Microsoft's "Designed for Windows 98," make such testing obsolete, but independent test labs still earn quite a bit of money doing these kinds of tests, as Chapter 10 discusses.)

Standards Compliance. In the hardware world, you need to consider legal and market standards such as UL, FCC, CE, and others that might be applicable for your target market. In the software and hardware worlds, your customers might require compatibility logos such as Microsoft's "Designed for Windows." Seemingly innocuous bugs related to standards can have serious repercussions: your company might even find the product legally or effectively barred from the market.[14]

---

14. Although standards are based on technical issues, politics and protectionism can come into play when the stakes are high. In her 1999 article "Standards Battles Heat Up Between United States and European Union," Amy Zuckerman writes that the "European Community...has reorganized to better use standards to take aim at what EC officials consider monopolistic high-tech manufacturers and consortia, mainly based in the United States" (pp. 39–42). If standards can affect your company's ability to sell its product in target markets, you should consider further research in this area. See also Zuckerman's book *International Standards Desk Reference: Your Passport to World Markets.*

Security.   Given your dog's name, your spouse's name, your children's names, and your birthday, I might be able to crack your computer accounts. On a larger scale, given a modem bank or a Web site, some asocial people with lots of time on their hands might be able to break into your network. If implementing security is a feature of your product—and it isn't for all products—you will need to think about testing it.

Environment.   Because hardware products must live in the real world, they are subject to environmental risks. What happens if you knock your laptop off the airplane's tray table? How do the shaking and bumping encountered during shipping affect a server? Can power sags and surges cause your system to crash and fail? What about the effects of temperature and humidity?

Power Input, Consumption, and Output.   All computers take in electrical current, convert some of it to heat or other electromagnetic radiation, and send the rest of it to attached devices. Systems with rechargeable batteries, such as laptops, might add some conversion and storage steps to this process, and some systems might use power in unusual modes such as 48 VDC, but ultimately the process is the same. This orchestration of electrical power can fail; insufficient battery life for laptops is a good example.

Shock, Vibration, and Drop.   All computers will be moved at some point. I have never worked with a system that was assembled on the floor on which it would operate. In the course of this movement, the computer will experience shocks, vibrations, and, occasionally, drops. The system test phase is the right time to find out whether the system misbehaves after typical encounters with the laws of gravity and Newtonian physics.

Installation, Cut-Over, Setup, and Initial Configuration.   Every instance of a product has an initial use. Does the installation process work? Can you migrate data from an old system? Are there unusual load profiles during the first few weeks of use? These loads can include many user errors as people learn the system. In a multiuser situation, configuration will also include the creation of the initial accounts. Think about the entire process, end to end; individual actions might work, but the process as a whole could be unworkable. Also consider the possibility that a user might want to uninstall the product. If you've ever uninstalled a Windows-based application, you know how problematic that can be. In addition, don't forget to check out the licensing and registration processes.

Documentation and Packaging.   If your product includes documentation, you have risks ranging from the possibly dangerous to the simply embarrassing. Consider instructions in DataRocket's manual, accompanied by an illustration, that lead a user to set the input voltage selector for 110 volts in a 220-volt environment. On the less serious side, think of some of the humorous quotations from technical documentation that circulate on the Internet. Do you want your company singled out for such honors? Packaging, likewise, should be appropriately marked. (Packaging is also a factor in shock, vibration, and drop testing for computers.)

Maintainability.   Even if your system is too simple to require an operator, you might still have maintainability risks. Can you upgrade software to a current version? Can you add memory to your PC? If your software works in a networked environment, does it support remote (possibly automated) software distribution?

Beta.   For general-purpose software and hardware, no amount of artificial testing can cover all the uses and environments to which your customers will subject your product. To address these risks, you need to consider a beta or early-release program of some sort.

Checking and Completing Your List

By the end of this exercise, you have an outline of the quality risks, broken down by phases and, within each phase, by test suite. Your list almost certainly suffers from two defects, however. First, it includes some unimportant risks that customers won't care about. Second, and worse, it doesn't include some critical risks that customers *will* care about very much. Your list is based on general categories of quality risks and your best educated guesses about how those categories apply to your product. It's a good start, but you need to refine it.

Peer Review

Assuming that you alone don't constitute the entire test team, you should review this list with your staff. Spending an hour or so working together on this list will improve it considerably; peer reviews often consist simply of an author going over his or her work in front of a group.

The basic process of a peer review can be described as follows:

◆ Circulate the draft document a few days in advance, and then schedule a conference room.

◆ Invite anyone on your team who can contribute, and try to draw everyone into the discussion. Broad participation is important.

◆ Take care to create a collegial review environment. If members of your test team are afraid to criticize your ideas, you won't learn anything interesting.

◆ Walk through the document, spending sufficient time on the important details while guarding against the natural tendency of meetings to become trapped in a "rat hole" or obsess on minor points. Take careful notes on comments and concerns.

◆ Try to avoid spending longer than two hours in any one session. Although the duration of the meeting will depend on the level of detail that must be covered, most people find it hard to focus on highly technical material for more than a couple of hours.

◆ After the review, revise the document and recirculate it to the participants to ensure that you have adequately captured their ideas in your notes.

Internal Experts

After getting your team's input, it's time to consult with your co-workers. I start with sales, marketing, and technical support because they know and serve the customers. Set up meetings with the managers; you'll probably be referred to others in the respective groups who have strong feelings about the product. I have found that most sales and marketing people are happy to explain what customers expect from the product and what the product should do.

Members of the technical support staff not only know the customers but also know the product—often better, functionally, than developers do. They have probably talked with customers who treated them to frank and detailed analyses of product quality risks as they relate to customer dissatisfaction. Ask the technical support staff which product failures—past, present, and future—they lose sleep over. Which bug caused the most unpleasant support call? Technical support often tracks the details of the customer calls in a database, which is a treasure trove for you. By analyzing this data, you can learn where the product breaks and how customers use it.[15]

Keep in mind the story about the blind men and the elephant; people have different ideas about what's important and what's trivial. Try to cover everyone's "important" list, but remind people about reasonable limits if they give you an extensive wish list. Also, if you encounter significant disagreements about the features and capabilities of the product, discuss these with the project manager; you might be in the middle of an unresolved dispute over product design.

External Sources

If your company's product or product line has a large number of customers, trade magazines can help you understand quality risks. For example, if you build Intel-based computers, you can read publications such as *PC Magazine*, *Byte,* and many others. The magazines often review hardware and software—not only yours but also your competitors'. Be sure to read these reviews, including the sections that describe how testing was performed. (The test tools used by these publications are sometimes available for use or adaptation. For instance, an engineer I worked with used a PC-based benchmarking program to create a CPU/memory subsystem stress test for a VME/Solaris server.) You can also join professional organizations, such as the Association for Computing Machinery, that publish journals on academic and commercial trends in the computer industry.

For some test areas, you might consider consulting experts. Reliability and security, for example, require specialized knowledge. If you want to measure the MTBF of the DataRocket server or the security of SpeedyWriter, you might need professional help. If the system under test serves a unique customer base or has unique quality risks—for instance, medical, banking, tax preparation, or accounting software—bringing in content experts and people who have experience developing similar systems makes sense.

The idea of surveying your customer base also bears consideration. If you are selling a product that includes a registration form, you might be able to add a section on quality and customer expectations that could help you to define the key quality risks. It might be a challenge to implement this quickly enough to help on a current project, but long-time benefits could accrue.

---

15. In some companies, the technical support manager and the test manager work in the same organization, often called Development Services. In some cases, the technical support manager *is* the test manager.

Proposing the Quality Risks

The last hurdle is ensuring that the project manager and the development managers buy into your list of quality risks. These individuals can suggest important additions and changes and might raise pertinent questions about the relative priorities; getting their input will improve the list. In addition, their inclusion in the process builds a level of comfort between you and these managers about what tests you plan to run. This mutual understanding prevents surprises and confrontations down the road as well as assuring the managers that you won't pull any "gotcha" maneuvers on them by running mysterious tests late in the game.

Finally, if your list contains any gross misunderstandings about what the product is designed to do, consulting with the project manager and the development managers will help you clear up the misunderstandings at this early stage. This avoids the lost time and the potential embarrassment of developing new tests for—and even reporting bugs against—"broken features" that don't exist.

After you and the other managers concur on the list of quality risks, you have the skeleton of a test system. Table 1-1 shows an example of such a list, generated for SpeedyWriter. The table is broken down by test phase, by general category of risk, and then by specific risks. A priority—from 1 to 5 in this example—is assigned to each risk.

Test Phase/General Risk	Specific Risk	Priority
Component Test Phase		
Code coverage	Error handling	1
	Importing/exporting	2
	General	5
Data flow coverage	Importing	2
	Exporting	2
	Hyperlinks	2
Functionality	File operations and dynamic data flows	1
	Editing	1
	Printing	1
	Tables, figures, references, fields, and complex objects	1
	Formatting	1
	Spelling, thesaurus, grammar, change tracking, and other tools	1
	Help	1

TABLE 1-1   *Prioritized quality risks for SpeedyWriter.*

Test Phase/General Risk	Specific Risk	Priority
Component Test Phase *(continued)*		
User interface	Microsoft Windows 95/98	3
	Microsoft Windows NT	3
	Solaris OpenWindows (Sun)	3
	Apple Macintosh	3
Integration Test Phase		
Component interfaces	Toolbar-to-function	1
	Menus-to-function	1
	Display/preview	2
	Printing	2
	Event handling	2
Functionality (regression from component test)		1
System Test Phase		
Functionality (regression from component test)		1
User interface	Microsoft Windows 95/98	1
	Microsoft Windows NT	1
	Solaris OpenWindows (Sun)	1
	Apple Macintosh	1
Capacity and volume	Maximum file length	3
	Maximum table size	3
	Maximum number of revisions	3
Error/disaster handling and recovery	Platform crash	3
	Network failure	3
	File space overflow	3
Performance	Microsoft Windows 95/98	1
	Microsoft Windows NT	1
	Solaris OpenWindows (Sun)	1
	Apple Macintosh	1
Date handling	Year 2000	4
	Other	4
Localization	Spanish	2
	French	2
	German	2
	Italian	5
	Chinese	5
	Japanese	5
Networked environment	Novell Netware	5
	Microsoft Windows NT	5
	PC NFS	5
Configuration options	Preferences storage/retrieval	1
	Available printer selections	1

(continued)

Test Phase/General Risk	Specific Risk	Priority
System Test Phase (*continued*)		
Standards	Microsoft Windows 95/98	1
	Microsoft Windows NT	3
	Sun Solaris	3
Security	Password-protect files	4
	PGP encrypt/decrypt files	4
Installation, setup, and initial configuration	Microsoft Windows 95/98	2
	Microsoft Windows NT	2
	Solaris OpenWindows (Sun)	2
	Apple Macintosh	2
Documentation		3
Beta		3

FAILURE MODE AND EFFECT ANALYSIS: A FORMAL METHOD FOR UNDERSTANDING QUALITY RISKS

The previous section outlined an informal approach to assessing quality risks. In this section we'll examine a more formal technique for defining quality risks using an approach called *failure mode and effect analysis* (FMEA). This formal approach allows you to map requirements, specifications, and project team assumptions onto specific quality risks and effects. You then rank these risks according to their risk priority and attack them in order.

If you intend to use the FMEA technique, you should also study D. H. Stamatis's book *Failure Mode and Effect Analysis,* which contains a thorough presentation of this technique. In the following discussion, I have modified Stamatis's format and approach slightly.

An FMEA Chart Template

Fundamentally, an FMEA is a top-down process for understanding and prioritizing possible failure modes (or quality risks) in system functions and features. It also provides a means of tracking closed-loop corrective actions.[16] (Although we are looking at the FMEA technique primarily from

---

16. A closed-loop corrective action occurs when, after discovery of a problem, steps are taken to prevent the recurrence of that and similar problems in the future. For example, if you find that your room is full of flies, you might notice that they're coming in through the open window, which you then notice has a torn screen. Closed-loop corrective action refers neither to swatting the flies nor to closing the window but rather to repairing the screen.

the point of view of test engineering and management, you might keep in mind that its *raison d'être* is its usefulness in cross-functional Total Quality Management.)

Figure 1-6 shows the top page of a sample FMEA chart for DataRocket. Let's go through each of the columns in detail.

System Function or Feature.   This column is the starting point for the analysis. In most rows, you enter a concise description of the system function. If the entry represents a category, you must break it down into more specific functions or features in subsequent rows. Getting the level of detail right is a bit tricky. With too much detail, you can create an overly long, hard-to-read chart; with too little detail, you will have too many failure modes associated with each function.

Potential Failure Mode(s)—Quality Risk(s).   For each specific function or feature (but not for the category itself), the entry in this column addresses the ways you might encounter a failure. These are quality risks associated with the loss of a specific system function. Each specific function or feature can have multiple failure modes.

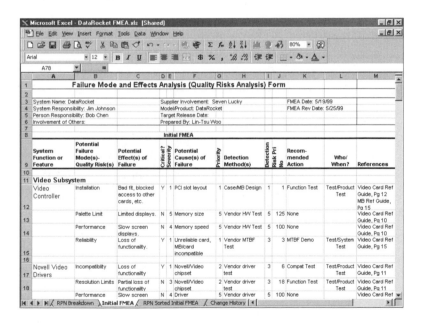

FIGURE 1-6   *A sample FMEA chart for DataRocket.*

Potential Effect(s) of Failure. Each failure mode can affect the user in one or more ways. It's best to keep these entries general rather than trying to anticipate every possible unpleasant outcome.

Critical? In this column, you answer yes or no to the question of whether the potential effect has critical consequences for the user. Is the product feature or function completely unusable if this failure mode occurs?

Severity. This column denotes the absolute severity of the failure mode in question, regardless of likelihood. I use a scale from 1 (worst) to 5 (least dangerous), as follows:

1	Loss of data or a safety issue
2	Loss of functionality with no workaround
3	Loss of functionality with a workaround
4	Partial loss of functionality
5	Cosmetic or trivial

Stamatis uses a reverse scale, in which larger numbers denote greater severity. But I prefer to use the scale shown here, which is more in line with the typical use of the term "severity" in the computer business.

Potential Cause(s) of Failure. This column lists possible factors that might trigger the failure—for example, operating system error, user error, or normal use. In my experience, this column is not as important as others when you are using an FMEA strictly as a test design tool.

Priority. While Stamatis uses the word "occurrence," I prefer the term "priority," by which I mean both the likelihood of occurrence (the odds of the typical customer encountering the problem) and the extent to which occurrences might affect the experience of quality for the overall customer base. In other words, priority rates how badly the failure mode will affect your company's ability to market this product during its expected life cycle, assuming that the failure mode remains in your product on release. Again, I use 1 (most dangerous) to 5 (least dangerous), which reverses Stamatis's scale. These numbers, in addition to being "soft," are difficult for test staff to estimate; you will need input from sales, marketing, and technical support.

Detection Method(s). This column lists a currently existing method or procedure, such as development activities or vendor testing, that can find the problem before it affects users, excluding any test suites you might create to catch it. (If you do not exclude the tests you might create, the next column will be skewed.)

Detection.   The number in this column represents the likelihood of detection by the methods listed in the previous column. In other words, if you are confident that current procedures will catch this failure mode, the column should indicate a low risk; if you believe that it would escape detection, it should indicate a high risk. I use a ranking from 1 (most likely to escape detection now) to 5 (least likely to escape detection now), which is, again, the reverse of Stamatis's scale. Like the Priority column, this column can be challenging for test staff; your development colleagues can help.

RPN (Risk Priority Number).   This column tells you how important it is to test this particular failure mode. The risk priority number (RPN) is the product of the severity value multiplied by the priority value (the expected customer impact) multiplied by the detection value (the likelihood of catching the defect without testing or other further actions). Because I use values from 1 to 5 for all three of these parameters, the RPN ranges from 1 (most dangerous quality risk) to 125 (least dangerous quality risk).

Recommended Action.   This column contains one or more simple action items for increasing the risk priority number (making it less severe). For the test team, most recommended actions involve creating a test case that influences the detection figure.

Who/When?   This column indicates who is responsible for each recommended action and when they are responsible for it (for instance, in which test phase).

References.   This column provides references for more information about the quality risk. Usually this involves product specifications, a requirements document, and the like.

Action Results.   A final set of columns (not visible in Figure 1-6) allows you to record the influence of the actions taken on the priority, severity, detection, and RPN values. You will use these columns after you have implemented your tests, not during the initial FMEA.

Populating an FMEA Chart

Stamatis recommends the use of a cross-functional brainstorming session to populate your FMEA chart. Gathering together senior technical representatives from each team—development, test, marketing, sales—you proceed to fill in the chart row by row. This is certainly the best way, but it requires a commitment from each group to send a participant to a meeting that could consume a significant part of a day.

If you can't get people to attend a cross-functional session, you might want to proceed with an FMEA anyway. To do so, you need written specifications, requirements, or other documents that describe how the system is supposed to work and what it is supposed to do. In this case, you should keep in mind the generic outline of quality risks described here, which will help you cover all the areas. It's definitely a poor second place to the cross-functional approach, but it works.

Caveats and Cautions

I have encountered a few pitfalls in using the FMEA method. In many cases, you can easily become distracted by quality risks that lie outside the scope of the test project. If you are working on SpeedyWriter, for example, you don't need to worry about operating system bugs or underlying hardware failures. For DataRocket, you needn't analyze possible low-level failures in drives or chips. If you find a bug related to a given failure mode, will the development team—or some other group—address it? If not, it's out of scope.

An FMEA document is large. If you develop it from specifications and requirements rather than from a brainstorming session, you will nonetheless need to solicit comments from the rest of the project team. How do you convince these busy people to spend a couple of hours reviewing a dense document? You can try circulating the document via e-mail; asking for responses, questions, and concerns; and then scheduling a final review meeting. If you still have difficulty getting participation, you might need to raise the issue with your manager. Be ready to move forward without outside feedback.

If you assign one person to go off and do the entire FMEA alone, you lose an essential benefit of the process: consensus on test priorities. It's preferable to divide the effort among multiple test engineers and then use frequent informal discussions to synchronize the effort, eliminate overlap, and keep the effort within the appropriate scope.

Finally, if you are able to use the cross-functional meeting approach, be sure that all participants understand what they're in for. The meeting will take time, possibly all day. Earlier I mentioned limiting technical review meetings to a couple of hours. In the case of FMEA reviews, however, I've often found it more productive to push ahead and try to conclude the FMEA work all at once. Attempting to restore context after a day or two off can be tough. If you need to break up the discussions into shorter meetings, try to keep the sessions daily until the chart is complete. Participants also need to agree on the scope of the meeting. You can use e-mail to clarify these issues and to introduce all the participants to the FMEA form you intend to use.

WHAT YOU CAN TEST: SCHEDULE, RESOURCES, AND BUDGET

Whether you use an informal approach or the more formal FMEA technique, you should now have a prioritized outline of quality risks. If you happen to work in an environment in which quality trumps time-to-market and budget, you can skip this section and instead send me an e-mail letting me know what it's like. If you work in the same world I do, you will need to develop a test schedule and a budget that allow you to test the scariest risks.

One of my first managers was fond of this saying: "Schedule, cost, and quality—pick two." This pithy remark means that although, for a given feature set, you can freely select the boundaries of any two of these variables, doing so determines the third variable. I call this rule, which is illustrated in Figure 1-7 on the next page, the "Iron Box and Triangle" of development. The clockwise arrow indicates refinement during the planning stage. These refinements balance schedule, cost, and quality. Once implementation begins, the feature set becomes more rigid, the schedule more painful to change, and the budget increases less likely. Within the fixed "box" enclosing the feature set in Figure 1-7, the two lines that are drawn to select the schedule and the cost determine the placement of the third line (quality) that completes the triangle.

Hence, your planning conundrum is this: you have only a rough idea of what your test project is about, but the window of opportunity that might allow a realistic schedule and an adequate budget is closing. (And even this scenario assumes that you are on the project team during the planning phase. It could be worse: if you have joined the team later, during implementation, you might have a fixed budget and schedule.) There's no perfect solution, but I have found an approach I can live with.

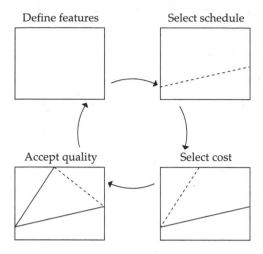

FIGURE 1-7   *How features, schedule, and cost affect quality.*

SHOEHORNING: FITTING A TEST SCHEDULE INTO THE PROJECT

Often software and hardware project schedules don't evolve according to any textbook approach. You might have to start with a ship date and a list of product features—the negotiability of both varies—and build the schedule from there. How can you construct a workable test schedule within these constraints?

Your best bet is to use a top-down approach. It's usually easier to start with big categories and then refine, especially at the early stages when you don't have a lot of details. Start by breaking the test effort into major categories such as these:

◆ Planning (the work discussed in this chapter and the next)

◆ Configuration (acquiring the necessary hardware and other resources and setting up the test lab)

◆ Development (building or deploying the test tools, creating the test suites and the test case library, putting the reporting tools in place, and documenting how the test system works)

◆ Test execution (running the tests, recording test status, and reporting results)

Next divide each category. Within the planning category, for instance, you might set up subtasks such as defining quality risks, creating the schedule and the budget, writing test plans, and selecting test tools. Other subtasks might include getting bids from third parties for their help or hiring test technicians, test engineers, and system administrators.

The subtasks in the configuration category depend on the hardware you need. Even though you probably don't know all the details at this point, your discussion of quality risks should have given you some ideas. Once you think through the quality risks, you will usually have a "10,000-foot perspective" on the test suites you must create, which should give you a pretty good idea of your hardware needs.

For development, you must deploy your test tools and then develop the test suites themselves. You might list separate major tasks for each test phase and then enter the test suites as individual tasks within each phase. Test suite development should proceed in priority order. Developing test suites is a full-time job; don't set up work on various suites as parallel tasks unless you have multiple test engineers or can give a single engineer twice as long to finish. Also be sure to add a task for the developers to document how the test system works.

For test execution, I've found that it usually works to estimate three test cycles per phase.[17] For simple projects, you can estimate one week per test cycle, three cycles per phase. Complex projects might require two or three weeks per cycle. Unless a given test suite runs longer than a week, it might not be worthwhile to break out the suites as separate subtasks in each cycle; after all, you might want to move the test suites around, running them later or earlier in the cycle, or even changing the cycle in which they run. But if you want a better feel for how long each cycle will take, you can go through the exercise of adding the suites as subordinate tasks.

In this first cut, try to capture the basic dependencies. For example, you must develop a test suite before you can run it, and you can't start a test cycle until you receive something to test. Although some dependencies that loom

---

17. If the idea of test cycles within a test phase is new to you, just think of the cycles as passes through some significant portion of the test suite against a fixed version of the product. We'll discuss test cycles more extensively in Chapter 2 ("Test Execution," page 52) and throughout Chapter 3.

far in the future won't jump out at you, your best effort will probably suffice. Remember that you will revise this schedule throughout your project, so you can add dependencies as they become apparent.

As you're creating the tasks, you should also assign resources, even if you can't be complete at this point. In addition, don't worry about staples such as desks, workstations, or telephones unless you have genuine concerns about getting an adequate budget for them. You should, however, take a stab at items such as these:

- Expensive resources such as networks, environmental test equipment, and test tools

- Resources that require long lead times, such as lab space that must be rented and set up or ISDN and T1 lines

- Missing resources such as people you need to hire

- External resources such as third-party labs

- Scarce resources such as your test engineers and technicians

Try to ensure that you will not be overutilizing resources that have limited "bandwidth" or availability—especially people.

With this minimum of planning, you can construct a draft schedule for your test project. You should perform a quick "sanity check" of your milestone dates against the constraints of the project. After you're comfortable with the schedule, review it with your staff. Later on you will need to add details, adjust durations, resolve resource conflicts, include more dependencies, and so on, but for now you have a workable rough estimate. Figure 1-8 shows an example of this approach as it might be applied to testing for SpeedyWriter.

Perhaps you're thinking, "C'mon, nothing that simple ever works." Indeed, most of my schedules contain more detail than this. My ability to schedule projects has improved—partly as a result of acquiring skills with the tools, although mostly as a result of experience—but I started with equally simple schedules and ran a number of test projects successfully. Scheduling— especially scheduling software—is not trivial, so I recommend keeping it simple to start; your schedules may be less precise but are likely to be more accurate. If you try to create complicated 300-task schedules, you can get lost in the minutiae.

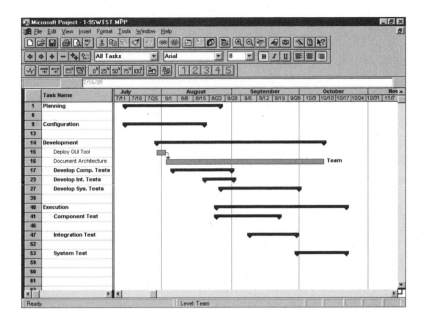

FIGURE 1-8   *A Gantt chart for SpeedyWriter testing.*

ESTIMATING RESOURCES AND CREATING A BUDGET

Given a schedule with fairly detailed resource allocations, you can hammer out a budget in an afternoon. Again, a top-down approach is useful. You first need to create a list of resources, starting with general categories such as the following:

- *Staff.*   This category includes permanent employees, contractors, and consultants.

- *Test tools.*   If you are testing software, you might need code coverage analyzers, scripting utilities, GUI test automation systems, low-level diagnostic programs, and so forth. Hardware testing can involve oscilloscopes, shock and vibration tables, thermal chambers, CD-ROM burners, and other equipment. Don't forget basic utilities for hardware and software testing.

- *Facilities and overhead.*   Items in this category can include travel allowances, lab space, workstations, and infrastructure such as cabling, routers, hubs, bridges, ISDN terminals, and so forth.

◆ *Test systems.* This category includes the hardware, software, engineering samples, and experimental prototypes.

◆ *External labs.* Include this category if you intend to use external labs for environmental testing, localization, performance, or other purposes.

Within each category, list the individual items you need. Use placeholders to indicate where you might add items or quantities later.

To transform this resource list into a budget, load it into a spreadsheet and line up columns to the right for each month of the project. For each item, enter a cost figure—a monthly figure for variable costs or a one-time figure for fixed costs. Don't forget "invisible costs" such as health care benefits, agency markups for staff, application software, support contracts, and training.

If you find it difficult to estimate costs for tools, facilities, infrastructure, or test systems, you can hit the Web or make some telephone calls. Estimating the cost of using an external lab might require an actual bid, although you can probably get a ballpark figure by calling the lab. For unknown items—the placeholders on your resource list—you'll simply have to make an educated guess. Pick a comfortable figure with some wiggle room, but don't be so conservative that you'll be shot down when you approach management.

At this point, you can compare each line item against your schedule. When do you start using the resource? How long do you use it? Are ramp-up and ramp-down times associated with the resource? Answering these questions will tell you which months must absorb charges for each item and what fraction of the charge applies in beginning and ending months. For fractions, keep it simple; halves and quarters are usually precise enough.

As you did for your schedule, you need to run a sanity check to ensure that all the numbers make sense. You can often involve your staff in the process, although you should check with your management before circulating a proposed budget; some companies don't allow individual contributors to see budget information. (If you give staff members printed copies of the budget, be sure to omit all salary information.) After coming up with the budget, sleep on it and then review it the next day. Ask yourself whether you've forgotten anything. If the budget contains a few gaping holes where you don't have enough information to even hazard a guess, be honest and indicate that. Figure 1-9 provides an example of a budget for SpeedyWriter, assuming the schedule shown in Figure 1-8.

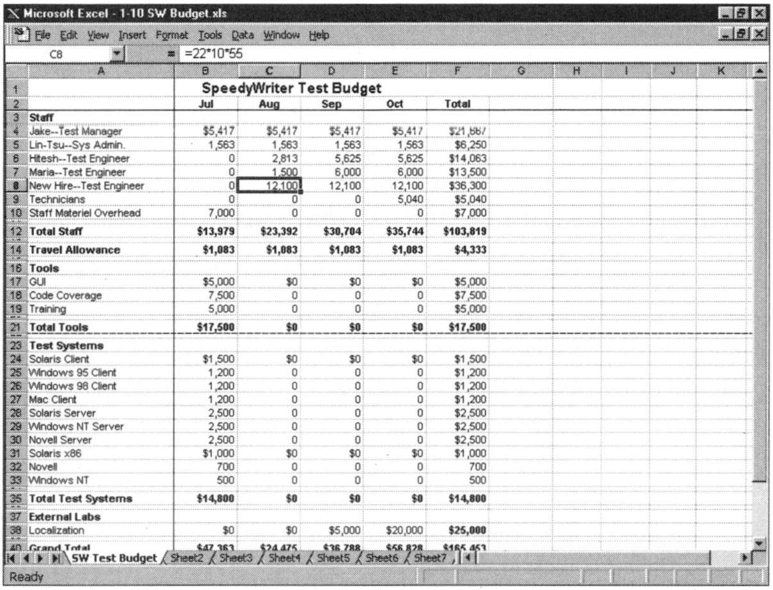

	A	B	C	D	E	F
1		**SpeedyWriter Test Budget**				
2		**Jul**	**Aug**	**Sep**	**Oct**	**Total**
3	**Staff**					
4	Jake--Test Manager	$5,417	$5,417	$5,417	$5,417	$21,667
5	Lin-Tsu--Sys Admin.	1,563	1,563	1,563	1,563	$6,250
6	Hitesh--Test Engineer	0	2,813	5,625	5,625	$14,063
7	Maria--Test Engineer	0	1,500	6,000	6,000	$13,500
8	New Hire--Test Engineer	0	12,100	12,100	12,100	$36,300
9	Technicians	0	0	0	5,040	$5,040
10	Staff Materiel Overhead	7,000	0	0	0	$7,000
12	**Total Staff**	**$13,979**	**$23,392**	**$30,704**	**$35,744**	**$103,819**
14	**Travel Allowance**	**$1,083**	**$1,083**	**$1,083**	**$1,083**	**$4,333**
16	**Tools**					
17	GUI	$5,000	$0	$0	$0	$5,000
18	Code Coverage	7,500	0	0	0	$7,500
19	Training	5,000	0	0	0	$5,000
21	**Total Tools**	**$17,500**	**$0**	**$0**	**$0**	**$17,500**
23	**Test Systems**					
24	Solaris Client	$1,500	$0	$0	$0	$1,500
25	Windows 95 Client	1,200	0	0	0	$1,200
26	Windows 98 Client	1,200	0	0	0	$1,200
27	Mac Client	1,200	0	0	0	$1,200
28	Solaris Server	2,500	0	0	0	$2,500
29	Windows NT Server	2,500	0	0	0	$2,500
30	Novell Server	2,500	0	0	0	$2,500
31	Solaris x86	$1,000	$0	$0	$0	$1,000
32	Novell	700	0	0	0	700
33	Windows NT	500	0	0	0	500
35	**Total Test Systems**	**$14,800**	**$0**	**$0**	**$0**	**$14,800**
37	**External Labs**					
38	Localization	$0	$0	$5,000	$20,000	**$25,000**
40	**Grand Total**	**$47,363**	**$24,475**	**$36,788**	**$56,828**	**$165,463**

FIGURE 1-9 *A first draft budget for SpeedyWriter testing.*

NEGOTIATING A LIVABLE TEST PROJECT

With your quality risks list, schedule, and budget, you have a concise package that you can take to management. By speaking management's language, you can address three key questions that will arise:

- What kind of risk management are we buying?
- How long will it take?
- What will it cost?

Although each company has a different process for approving a test program, every project I've worked on has required some degree of discussion, explanation, and negotiation. Be flexible. If management insists on reduced costs or a faster schedule (or both), eliminate tests in reverse priority order. If cost is the major concern but you are able to add a few weeks to the schedule, perhaps you can get by with one less employee. Outsourcing can also reduce costs when done wisely, as you'll see in Chapter 10. Make the case for what you believe needs to be done, but be prepared to do less.

At the end of this negotiation, you should have an approved budget and schedule and a mutual understanding of the scope and deliverables for your test project. Now it's time to move on to creating a detailed plan, building a test system, and putting the resources in place to carry out the project.

2

Plotting and Presenting Your Course: The Test Plan

This chapter offers a practical approach to writing one or more test plans for your project. We'll walk through a sample template that can help you develop a solid test plan—and we'll also look at the issue of getting the plan approved once you've drawn it up.

Why Write a Test Plan?

In the previous chapter, you came up with working definitions for the efforts that might be required in a test project. Given a budget, resource commitments, and a schedule, can you claim that you have a test plan? You can, and some people do. In my experience, however, you need more detail to successfully manage a test project. Below the high-level, quick-and-dirty outlines and estimates featured in Chapter 1 lurks another layer of complexity, right above the specific details of test suites—and it pays to consider this complexity in advance.

Writing a test plan allows you to collect your thoughts, your ideas, and your memories. Undoubtedly you've learned a great deal throughout the course of your career. Writing a thorough test plan gives you a chance to crystallize that knowledge into a concrete way of tackling the tasks ahead.

A test plan is also an opportunity to communicate with your test team, your development colleagues, and your management. The most intense discussion of what testing is all about may well occur when you hold a test plan review. I find that I appreciate the chance to have a forum focused solely on testing before a project enters the often-chaotic test execution periods, in which everyone can become so oriented toward minutiae that they lose sight of the big picture.

In some organizations, the test plan encompasses the entirety of the test effort, all the way down to defining the individual test cases that the team will run. But I strongly recommend creating two distinct documents: first a test plan and then an accompanying document detailing the test suites. The difference between a test plan and a test suite is a matter of strategy versus tactics: strategy consists of your overall plan for hunting down and identifying as many bugs as possible; tactics are the specific steps you will take to do this. This chapter focuses on the test plan itself; Chapter 3 discusses the process of creating test suites and test cases.

HOW MANY TEST PLANS?

Let's suppose that you are working on SpeedyWriter. As the test manager, you have responsibility for the component, integration, and system test phases, with an aggressive beta testing program included in the system test phase. You thus have three distinct test subprojects to plan and manage. Do you write one plan or three? I favor using separate plans for test subprojects that are distinct in one or more of the following ways:

◆ *Different time periods.* If the test development and test execution tasks for the subprojects start and end on different dates, it is likely that you will have the information needed to plan the earlier subprojects well before you get the necessary information for the later subprojects. If you try to write only one test plan, you'll probably be forced to leave large sections of it marked "TBD" ("to be determined"), which can make the overall plan hard for people to understand.

◆ *Different methodologies.* Detailed discussions of code coverage instrumentation and platform-independent automated GUI test tools don't really go together. Likewise, in the case of hardware, discussions of thermal chambers, accelerometers, and business application compatibility testing can create a rather eclectic mix of topics in your plan.

◆ *Different objectives.* If you're trying to accomplish three different goals—for example, finding bugs in functional units, testing the integration of functional units, and checking the business function of the integrated whole—why not focus your thinking on each goal in turn?

◆ *Different audiences.* Your test plan is not only your chance to inform your colleagues, your testers, and your managers of your vision; it is also a chance to discover their perspectives. This input is especially valuable to the extent that it gives you a better idea of how to focus your test efforts. If you write one lengthy test plan that addresses every issue, you might have trouble getting people to read it, not to mention getting them to participate in a three- or four-hour review. On the other hand, if you segment your planning, you are better able to create documents that speak to the specific concerns of the individuals involved.

One advantage of preparing a single document is that you can do a lot of cutting and pasting for cases in which test subprojects share certain facets such as test tracking, bug reporting and management, and revision control. Having the same information spread across multiple documents leaves you open to the possibility of inadvertent discrepancies or contradictory statements. If this is a concern, however, you can create separate documents that address these common topics and include them by reference.

USING DRAFTS TO STIMULATE DISCUSSION

You can expect to release several versions of any test plan you write. Don't be surprised to find yourself posing questions to the readers as you write the first drafts. I use brackets in my plans (as opposed to colored fonts, which don't show up as well in hard copy) to indicate questions and open issues. My first drafts are always full of bracketed questions and statements like these:

[Need to figure out what the hardware allocation plan is.]

[Need the Configuration Management team to define the revision numbering schema and the packaging.]

[TBD]

Although this might seem like "copping out," identifying and documenting open issues are among the most useful aspects of the planning exercise. Writing the plan forces you to think through the entire test operation and to confront issues that you might otherwise miss. You can then use the first few drafts of the plan as a method of bringing these issues to the attention of your peers and your management.

That said, you should of course spend some time thinking about the problems you raise. Rather than simply asking a question, you might also be able to include a suggested answer or a set of possible answers. A test plan that consists largely of notations about matters that are "to be determined" or issues that await resolution by someone else doesn't add a lot of value.

A TEST PLAN TEMPLATE

The template presented here is one that I often use for developing test plans. It isn't a tool for cutting and pasting a test plan in little time with little thought; rather, it is a logical set of topics that need to be carefully considered in any well-planned test effort. You should, of course, feel free to add or delete topics as your needs dictate. The following sections examine the parts of the test plan template one by one.[1]

OVERVIEW

The overview section of a test plan allows you to introduce readers of the plan to your test approach. Sometimes managers one or two levels above you don't really have a good idea of what testing buys them. In the overview, you can present a concise explanation of your goals, methodologies, and objectives. Although this section should be fairly brief, it's often useful to include simple pictures or charts. You might want to illustrate concepts such as the architecture of the system under test, the decomposition or segmentation of the system for unit or integration testing, or how this test effort fits into other test efforts that may precede, run concurrently, or follow.

---

1. This template is consistent with IEEE standard 829 in that it includes all the information listed in that standard.

BOUNDS

In this section, you set bounds for the test plan by discussing what you will and will not test, by defining important terms and acronyms related to the testing you plan to perform, and by determining where the test efforts associated with this test subproject will take place.

Scope

Webster's defines scope, in the context of a project or an operation, as the "extent of treatment, activity, or influence; [the] range of operation." When you describe the scope of your project, you are essentially drawing a boundary that separates what you will and will not pay attention to during the course of the project. I often use an "Is/Is Not" table to define the scope of testing, with the Is column listing the elements that are included within the

---

Test Plan Template
    Overview
    Bounds
        Scope
        Definitions
        Setting
    Quality Risks
    Proposed Schedule of Milestones
    Transitions
        Entry Criteria
        Stopping Criteria
        Exit Criteria
    Test Configurations and Environments
    Test Execution
        Resources
        Tracking and Management of Tests and Bugs
        Bug Isolation and Classification
        Release Management
        Test Cycles
    Risks and Contingencies
    Change History
    Referenced Documents

scope of a particular test phase and the Is Not column specifying elements that are not covered by this test effort. Here's an example of such a table, used to describe the scope of system testing for SpeedyWriter.

Is	**Is Not**
◆ Installation/deinstallation	◆ Time and motion study
◆ Web browser compatibility	◆ OS/2 or UNIX
◆ Beta program	◆ File conversion
◆ Error handling and recovery	
◆ File sharing	
◆ Network compatibility	
◆ Performance	

This compact form allows you to present a precise statement of scope. It's usually unnecessary to define each bulleted item at this point; the details about each aspect of testing belong in the test suite.

DEFINITIONS

Testing, like other disciplines in the computer world, has its own terms and phrases. You might find it useful to include a table of definitions in your test plan. Such a table can help to clarify terminology for those who are not experienced in the field of testing, and it can also help to ensure that everyone on your test team is operating from the same set of definitions.

You might want to use the glossary contained in this book as a starting point for compiling your own list. You should edit the definitions as necessary, deleting phrases that do not apply to your project. Remember that extraneous verbiage can cause your readers to tune out and miss key points.

SETTING

This section of the test plan describes where you intend to perform the testing. The description might be as simple as "our test lab." In some cases, though, you might have testing spread hither and yon. I once managed a test project in which work took place in Taipei and Lin Kuo, Taiwan; in Salt Lake City, Utah; and in San Jose and Los Angeles, California. In cases like this, you should consider presenting a table that shows how work will be allocated among the various participants. (For more information on managing distributed test efforts, see Chapter 10.)

QUALITY RISKS

If you followed the process discussed in Chapter 1, you should already have the material you need for this section. You can either summarize the quality risk documents you've prepared or simply reference them in the test plan. If you suspect that many of your readers won't look at the reference documents, it makes sense to summarize the quality risks here, given that your purpose is to communicate as well as to plan. But if you know that people support your test planning process and will take the time to read your outline of quality risks or your FMEA chart, you can save yourself some work by referencing them.

PROPOSED SCHEDULE OF MILESTONES

Most plans should contain a schedule for the test project's major milestones. You can extract these from the schedule Gantt chart. Keep the focus on the high-level milestones and deliverables that are visible to management. Table 2-1 provides an example of such a schedule for SpeedyWriter.

TRANSITIONS

For each test phase, the system under test must satisfy a minimal set of qualifications before the test organization can profitably spend time in test

Milestone	Date
Test Development and Configuration	
Test plan complete	8/9/99
Test lab defined	8/12/99
Test lab configured	8/26/99
FMEA complete	8/16/99
Test suite complete	9/5/99
Test Execution	
System test entry	9/2/99
Cycle 1	9/2/99–9/16/99
Cycle 2	9/19/99–10/3/99
Cycle 3	10/6/99–10/13/99
System test exit	10/13/99

TABLE 2-1   *A proposed schedule of major milestones for SpeedyWriter system testing.*

execution. For instance, it makes little sense to start extensive user-scenario testing of SpeedyWriter if the application cannot open or save a file or display text on the screen. Likewise, the DataRocket server can't undergo environmental testing—especially thermal testing—if you don't have even a prototype case. This section of the test plan should specify the criteria essential for beginning and completing various test phases (and for possibly halting a phase midway through). These three sets of criteria are usually referred to as entry, exit, and stopping criteria, respectively.[2]

As you write criteria for test phases and transitions, be aware of what you're actually saying: "If someone outside the test group fails to comply with these rules, I'm going to object to starting this phase of testing, ask to stop this phase of testing, or suggest that we not move this project forward." While these are technical criteria, make no mistake that invoking them can create a political firestorm. Don't write them down unless you're serious, and, if you do commit them to paper, remember to refer to them during test execution.

Entry Criteria

Entry criteria spell out what must happen to allow a system to move into a particular test phase. These criteria should address questions such as the following:

◆   Are the necessary documentation, specifications, and requirements available that will allow testers to operate the system and judge correct behavior?

◆   Is the system ready for delivery, in whatever form is appropriate for the test phase in question?[3]

---

2. Alternatively, the criteria for completing a test phase are sometimes called "stopping criteria," and the criteria for halting a phase before completion can be termed "suspension criteria."

3. In the component test phase (assuming that the test organization is involved at that point), you must usually accept whatever development is ready to provide as long as it includes sufficient scaffolding or harnesses to run your tests. Once you reach the system test phase, however, you should ask for customer packaging, especially in the case of software, whose installation process has a significant impact on whether the system works at all.

◆ Are the supporting utilities, accessories, and prerequisites available in forms that testers can use?

◆ Is the system at the appropriate level of quality? Such a question usually implies that some or all of a previous test phase has been successfully completed, although it could refer to the extent to which code review issues have been handled.

◆ Is the test environment—lab, hardware, software, and system administration support—ready?

Stopping Criteria

Stopping criteria define those conditions or events that would lead you to suspend test execution. For example, the test environment could become (or turn out to be) unready; or the system might have so many bugs, or such severe bugs, that it makes no sense to continue testing. Once these problems are fixed, testing can resume.

Exit Criteria

Exit criteria address the issue of how to determine when testing has been completed. For instance, one exit criterion might be that all the planned test cases and the regression tests have been run. Another might be that project management deems your results "OK," by whatever definition they use to decide such questions. (See Chapter 9 for discussion of the political considerations that can be involved in such decisions.) Some people recommend using hard-and-fast, bug-related exit criteria such as "no open severity 1 bugs," "ten or fewer open severity 2 bugs," and so forth. I disagree, however. Basically, whether or not to ship a product is a business decision, and some amount of flexibility is required. Even so, the point is usually moot: I have never seen a test manager given that much clout.

TEST CONFIGURATIONS AND ENVIRONMENTS

This section of the test plan should document which hardware, software, networks, and lab space you will use to perform the testing. For a PC application or utility, this task can be as simple as listing the half-dozen or so test PCs, the two or three test networks (assuming that networking is even an issue), and the printers, modems, terminal adapters, and other accessories you might require from time to time.

Suppose, however, that you are testing a system with significant custom hardware elements (such as a new laptop or a server), one with many hardware elements (such as a network operating system or a network application), or one with expensive hardware elements (such as a mainframe, a high-availability server, or a server cluster). In these complex cases, using a simple table or a spreadsheet might not be sufficient. Chapter 6 introduces a logistics database that can help you stay on top of complicated situations such as these; see "A Spider's Web of Connections: Managing Test Hardware and Software Configuration Logistics." Chapter 7 extends this concept to include managing lab space and equipment; see "Selecting and Planning a Lab Area" and "Managing Equipment and Configurations." This database also models human resources and network needs. You can include the reports produced from this database in this section of the test plan.

You can present a scheme for hardware allocation in any of several locations: in this portion of the test plan, in a later section (under the Resources heading), or in a separate document. Whatever the location, it is extremely important that you prepare this allocation plan. Failing to establish a detailed plan for allocating hardware is tantamount to assuming that the hardware you need will magically make itself available, properly configured and ready for testing, at the very moment you need it. If you lead a charmed life, such things probably happen to you all the time, but they never happen to me. I always worry about hardware allocation and work to have a plan in place around the time I'm finishing the test plan.

What goes into a test hardware allocation plan? You should usually list the test purpose or use, the systems needed (including the quantities and revision levels), the infrastructure, the time period, the location, and any other hardware necessary for a particular test. Table 2-2 on page 54 shows a sample hardware allocation plan for DataRocket's integration test and system test phases.

Test Execution

This portion of the test plan addresses important factors affecting test execution. For example, in order to run tests, you often need to receive items from the outside world, primarily resources (or funding for those resources) and systems to test. In the course of running tests, you will gather data that you must track in a way presentable to your team, your peers, and your managers. Also, you will run through distinct test cycles in each test phase.

Note, though, that you don't need to write in detail about every process and activity involved in test execution.

Resources

Here you should spell out the people, tools, systems, software, hardware, networks, and other resources you need. You might find some overlap with the portion of your plan that covers test configurations; to avoid redundancy, you can reference that section.

Tracking and Management of Tests and Bugs

This section deals with the systems that help you track and manage test execution and the bugs that are discovered during this process. Test tracking refers to the listing you use to manage all the test cases in your test suites and to the way you document progress through that listing. (If you don't list the tests you plan to run, how will you gauge your test coverage later on?) Bug tracking has to do with the process you use to manage the bugs you find in the course of testing. Since these systems form your principal communication channels inward to your own team, outward to other teams such as development, and upward to your management, you should define them well here. (Chapters 4 and 5 deal with these topics in more detail. Even if you choose not to use the approaches described there, you may find some ideas in those chapters that will help you complete this section of the plan.)

Bug Isolation and Classification

This section of the test plan should explain the degree to which you intend to isolate bugs and the method you will use to classify bug reports. Isolating a bug means to experiment with the system under test in an effort to find connected variables, causal or otherwise. You need to be explicit about bug isolation because otherwise the test organization can end up involved in debugging, a developer task that can consume lots of your testers' time with very little to show for it in terms of test coverage. (See "Drawing a Line in the Sand: The Boundary Between Isolation and Debugging" in Chapter 4.)

Classifying a bug report assigns the underlying bug to a particular "bucket" that indicates how the bug should be communicated and handled. For example, you might use classifications such as the following:

- *Requirements failure.* The bug report concerns a failure of the system to meet its requirements. The appropriate party will resolve the problem.

Test Usage	System	Network	When	Where	Other
Integration Test Phase					
Component interfaces/signal quality	Engr proto [2]	Novell Netware, Network File System, Microsoft Windows NT	9/15–10/15	Engr lab	MS mouse, MS kbd, VGA mon, USB mouse, USB mon, USB kbd, 3COM LAN, USR mdm, Epson prn, Quantum HD, oscilloscope
Mechanical life	Engr proto [2]	None	8/1–10/1	Engr lab	None
Stress, capacity, volume	Engr proto [1]	Novell, NFS, NT	9/15–10/15	Test lab	MS mouse, VGA mon
Performance	Engr proto [1]	Novell, NFS, NT	9/15–10/15	Test lab	MS mouse, MS kbd, VGA mon, Quantum HD, IBM HD
System Test Phase					
MTBF demonstration	Vld proto [4]	Novell	10/17–1/17	Engr lab	MS mouse, MS kbd, VGA mon, MUX
Functionality	Vld proto [2]	Novell, NFS, NT	10/17–12/1	Test lab	MS mouse, MS kbd, VGA mon, USB mouse, USB mon; USB kbd, USR mdm, Epson prn, ISDN T. adptr
Stress, capacity, volume	Vld proto [1]	Novell, NFS, NT	10/17–12/1	Test lab	MS mouse, VGA mon
Performance	Vld proto [1]	Novell, NFS, NT	10/17–12/1	Test lab	MS mouse, MS kbd, VGA mon, Quantum HD, IBM HD
Compatibility	Vld proto [3]	N/A	10/24–12/1	System Cookers, Inc.	MS mouse [3], MS kbd [3], VGA mon [3]
Environmental	Vld proto [2]	N/A	10/24–12/1	System Cookers, Inc.	MS mouse [2], MS kbd [2], VGA mon [2]

TABLE 2-2 *A hardware allocation plan for testing DataRocket.*

◆ *Nonrequirements failure.* The bug reported is not covered by the system requirements, but it impedes usability of the system. The appropriate party will resolve the problem.

◆ *Waiver requested.* The bug report does indeed describe a failure, but the developers request a waiver because they believe that the problem will not impede usability of the system.

◆ *External failure.* The bug report addresses a failure that arises from a factor or factors external to or beyond the control of the system under test.

◆ *Test failure.* The developers believe that the test has returned a spurious or invalid error.

Release Management

Every new release of a software or hardware component should have a release (revision) number or identifier attached. This identifier is essential for determining which version of the system contains a bug, which version fixes that bug, which pieces are compatible with other pieces, and which versions you have tested.

In addition, you must be able to count on receiving new releases in a certain format. You should specify for each test phase—and therefore in each test plan—a specific process and format for delivering new releases. For example, for software delivered during component and integration test phases, this format might be as simple as a tar or zip archive sent via e-mail or posted to the network. Once you enter system testing, however, software releases should arrive in the same format and with the same installation process as the initial customer release.

You must also consider (for both software and hardware) whether you will accept new revisions in the middle of a test cycle. The key issues here are regression testing and the implications of the revision for the validity of your previous test cycle results. Will you have to do a complete reset and start the test cycle over if a driver, a configuration file, or an application build shows up midway? These unexpected arrivals can cause real problems, especially toward the end of the system test phase, if you are receiving new releases every few days or even every few hours. Without a completely automated regression test system that can repeat every test flawlessly in a day or so, you will never be able to eliminate the possibility that the new release has introduced a major new bug. (For a discussion of coverage problems and regression testing, see "Avoiding the Dreaded 'Test Escape': Coverage and Regression Test Gaps" in Chapter 3.)

This problem occurs even in hardware development. It is true that motherboards, cases, and so forth have long lead times and that engineering prototypes cost a lot to produce. Nevertheless, you might still receive the BIOS du jour or the daily "gold master" hard drive. My worst experiences with what I call "churn and burn" have occurred on laptop development projects. Because of the manual nature of PC testing, you will probably have time for little more than confirmation testing on new releases if they come daily, leading to dismal test escapes.

These "incoming SCUD releases" also affect the logistics and operation of your test project. Some amount of effort is required for flashing a BIOS, installing applications, or replacing a motherboard, especially if your lab contains half a dozen test platforms. If the process requires specialized skills, such as UNIX system administration, network administration, or database administration, you must have the right person available to handle the job. Moreover, the system will be unavailable for test execution throughout the upgrade. Such abrupt, unexpected changes can also impose communication overhead and confuse testers. You must inform everyone that a new release has dropped in, circulate the release notes (assuming that they exist), give your staff time to study them, and hope that everyone can keep straight just what the latest chunk of software is supposed to do.

As you can tell, I don't like midstream releases—and I'm sure you share my concerns. Despite such aversion, it's probably wise to remember the story about belling the cat.[4] If your company's development "process" includes a system test phase composed of 18-hour days, with a spinning disk containing the allegedly final build landing on your desk hourly, you can't transform that by fiat in the test plan.

Test Cycles

In Chapter 1, I used the phrase "test cycle" rather cavalierly, but perhaps a more formal definition is in order. By a test cycle, I mean running one, some, or all of the test suites planned for a given test phase as part of that

---

4. The mice are tired of scurrying about in fear of the cat, and they convene a council to decide how to deal with the problem. One suggests that they put a bell on the cat's collar so that they can hear him coming. All agree this is a capital idea, until one young whippersnapper asks, "But who will bell the cat?" When I'm tempted to push for a change in "the way things are done around here," I recall this tale and often think better of the effort.

phase. Test cycles are usually associated with a release of the system under test, such as a build of software or a motherboard. Generally, new releases occur during a test phase, triggering another test cycle. For example, if test suites 3.1 through 3.5 are planned for a three-cycle system test phase, the first cycle could entail executing 3.1 and 3.2; the second cycle, 3.3, 3.4, and 3.5; and the third cycle, 3.1, 3.2, 3.3, 3.4, and 3.5.

Any given test phase involves at least one cycle through the test suites planned for that phase. As mentioned earlier, I often use an estimate of three cycles per phase. Each subsequent cycle generally involves a new release of one or more components in the system. This section of the test plan should spell out your specific assumptions and estimates about the number, timing, and arrangement of test cycles.

RISKS AND CONTINGENCIES

I sometimes use the title Open Issues for this section. It should address potential or likely events that could make the test plan difficult or impossible to carry out. Topics might include training needs, the availability of additional development support for debugging if an exceptional number of bugs are found, and so forth. Alternatively, you can include this kind of information when you discuss stopping criteria.

Strictly speaking, most advocates of good development processes encourage a global approach to risk management. If you work on a project in which the entire team has a single risk-management plan, you might be able to omit this section by including these concerns in that plan.

CHANGE HISTORY

This part of the document records the changes and revisions that have been made to the test plan itself to this point. Specifically, you can assign a revision number and record who made the changes, what those changes were, and when the revision was released.

REFERENCED DOCUMENTS

As a rule, a test plan refers to other documents such as specifications, requirements, the test suites, any quality-risk analysis documents, and other pertinent information. Listing these documents in this section lets you avoid extensive repetition of their contents (which can create complications when these documents change).

SELLING THE PLAN

After finishing a test plan, you'll probably want to obtain approval from the project management and your development peers. You can use the approach of attaching a formal sign-off sheet to the plan or the approach of holding a review meeting with all the involved managers—or both.

If your company tends to become mired in politics, a sign-off might be necessary to protect yourself. If such formality is rare in your company, there are other ways to document approval, such as a circulation list that you keep. In any case, use a tactful approach if you pursue a formal sign-off. Strutting around the office with a document, requiring management signatures before you proceed with the test project, is not likely to endear you to your colleagues.[5]

I am often tempted to send off the test plan via e-mail demanding that the recipients "speak now or forever hold your peace." After failing to receive any criticisms or concerns, you might assume that everyone has read your plan and agrees with it. This assumption is almost universally false. Lack of response usually means that no one has read it.

Review meetings are the best way to get people to read plans. One benefit of writing and circulating the plan is to provide a forum for discussing the test part of the project. What better way to achieve that than assembling the appropriate parties to hash out the plan?

Before I hold a review, I e-mail the test plan with a note mentioning that we'll hold a meeting to review it in the next week. (Since e-mail attachments are notoriously flaky, I offer to print a hard copy for anyone who can't open the file.) I invite every manager who is directly affected by the plan—usually the development manager, the project manager, the build/release manager, and my own manager—as well as the lead test engineer on the project. I send courtesy invitations to others who might have an interest, but I try to limit the total list to ten or fewer. I then schedule the review.

At the meeting, I provide extra hard copies of the plan for forgetful participants. As the test manager, I lead the group through the plan section by section or page by page. If anyone has concerns, we discuss—and try to resolve—them on the spot. My goal is to leave the meeting with a marked-up copy of the test plan that will enable me to produce a "final" version.

---

5. You might want to consult the discussion on test plan approval in *Testing Computer Software*, by Cem Kaner, Jack Falk, and Hung Quoc Nguyen. These authors seem to have had positive experiences using a sign-off approach.

Shortly after the review, I make the requested changes to the document and recirculate it, this time marked as "Released for Execution" or "Release 1.0," to flag the fact that we intend to proceed according to this plan.

STAYING PERTINENT: A WARNING

One of my clients refers to certain test documents as "shelfware." He has seen too many test managers and senior test engineers spend too much of their time filling enormous binders that then sit on shelves, untouched during test execution. My client's comments are a cautionary tale: veer off into a morass of documentation for its own sake—to follow a standard or to "fill in the blanks"—and you can lose focus, relevance, and credibility.

I keep my test documents practical, focused, and short, and they work well for me. This approach to planning, customized to fit your particular needs, will help you write effective test plans that you can really use.

3

Test System Architecture, Cases, and Coverage

Chapters 1 and 2 provided a practical look at the process of defining a test organization's purview, understanding the quality risks that fall within it, and drawing up an overall plan for testing the most important of those risks. Now that you have a grasp of what's involved in these initial tasks, let's turn our attention to the specifics of building the test system itself.

First we'll take a step back for a conceptual view of a complete test system and the relationships among its component parts. This section provides some essential definitions and describes the basic operation of a model system. I use the phrase "test system architecture" to emphasize the fact that solid design and implementation are just as important for test systems as they are for the systems under test.

After laying this foundation, we'll look at a method of defining test cases. This discussion presents a test case template that you might find useful, and it also examines the level of detail required when writing test cases. We'll conclude by analyzing the issue of test coverage, discussing different approaches to measuring coverage as well as appropriate steps you can take to fill the inevitable gaps.

TEST SYSTEM ARCHITECTURE AND ENGINEERING

I refer to a complete test system as "an integrated and maintainable test environment and reporting system," whose primary purpose is to find, reproduce, isolate, describe, and manage bugs in the software or hardware under test. Later chapters focus on the reporting and data management aspects of this definition; for now, let's look at the elements that constitute an "integrated and maintainable" test system. Figure 3-1 is a visual representation of such a system, a model that I find useful in thinking about and communicating the structure and mechanics of test systems.

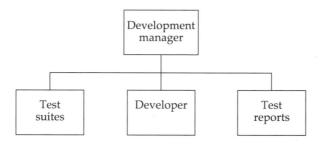

FIGURE 3-1 *A visual representation of a test system.*

To best understand the model shown in Figure 3-1, let's begin with the elements that appear at the bottom of the model. A test system usually involves one or more test tools—for example, operating systems, scripting languages, GUI test automation systems, oscilloscopes, or thermal chambers. Using these tools produces result logs, which are either created automatically from the tool or logged manually by the tester.

Because the test team uses the tools to execute test cases, these tools support the test case library. The relationship between the two elements is "many-to-many"—that is, each tool can appear in multiple test cases, and any one test case can involve the use of multiple tools. Both the test case library and the result logs feed into reporting tools, with a greater or lesser degree of automation. Test engineers assemble test suites from the test case library; the relationship between cases and suites is also many-to-many. From the test suites and the reporting tools come test reports.

At the highest level, the test architecture defines the design principles, the structure, and the tools as well as the interrelationships between the constituent pieces; it is project-independent, but it reflects the system under test. The test plans harness the test system to the project.

The "Action" Components: Definitions

Figure 3-2 on page 65 zeroes in on three elements of the test system: the test tools, the test case library, and the test suites. These are the "action" components of a test system. Figure 3-2 presents a hypothetical—and simplified—example of how these three components fit together. (In reality, you might have a dozen or so test tools, a few hundred test cases, and a score or more test suites. Also, the lines between the test tools and the test conditions they create and measure are blurrier than those shown in Figure 3-2.)

On the left side of the figure are four test tools. In the software world, these might be a GUI test tool, a batch scripting language, a load generator, and an external performance monitor. In the hardware world, imagine an oscilloscope, a thermal chamber, a vibration table, and a "keyboard tapper."[1] A test tool can be defined as any general-purpose hardware, software, or hardware/software system used during test case execution to set up or tear down the test environment, to create test conditions, or to measure test results. A test tool is also separate from the test case itself.

---

1. Undoubtedly those mechanical-life test tools for keyboards that can simulate years of typing have a more formal name, but "keyboard tapper" has always served me well.

In the center of Figure 3-2 is the test case library, which is a collection of independent, reusable test cases. Each test case consists of three parts:

◆ The *test case setup* describes the steps needed to configure the test environment to run the test case. Connecting a loopback device, making sure that a certain amount of disk space is available, and installing an application are examples of test case setup.

◆ The test case proper consists of a set of *test conditions;* the creation of these conditions actually performs the test. Some of the conditions run in parallel, and others run in series. In the software world, running a test tool to consume all the buffers while submitting transactions is a specific condition that might occur as part of a performance test. In the hardware world, each cycle of the power switch is a test condition that might occur as part of a mechanical-life test. (For brevity of expression, I sometimes refer instead to the "steps" and "substeps" of a test case rather than to its conditions. To be completely accurate, test conditions are the system states or circumstances created through the execution of the steps in a test case.)

◆ The *test case teardown* specifies the steps required to restore the test environment to a "clean" condition after execution of the test case (or test suite). Disconnecting a loopback device, deleting temporary files, and removing an application are examples of test case teardown.

Figure 3-2 also illustrates the role of test suites. Because test cases are reusable, you can incorporate each one into various suites. In fact, a test suite is simply a framework for the execution of test cases, a way of grouping cases. The advantage of a test suite is that it allows you to combine test cases to create unique test conditions. Test suite 2, for example, runs test cases 2 and 3 in parallel, which can lead to situations that neither test case could produce alone. As you can see in the figure, test suites, like test cases, can have setup and teardown activities associated with them.[2]

---

2. You can also have groups of test suites, which can sometimes contain overlapping suites. Chapter 10, which discusses distributed testing, describes groupings based on test organization.

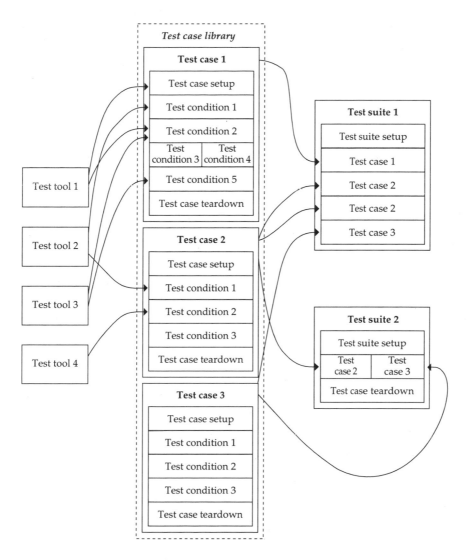

FIGURE 3-2 *An example of the relationships between test tools, a test case library, and test suites.*

IT'S NOT SAINT PAUL'S, BUT…

One of the most stately, impressive buildings in Europe is Saint Paul's Cathedral in London. With understated elegance and restrained majesty inside and out, it has reliably provided a place of worship for generations of Londoners since its completion in 1710, shortly after the Great Fire of London.

It withstood the savage Nazi bombing of South Britain in the early part of World War II as well as the fearsome V-1 and V-2 rocket attacks as the war drew to its close.[3]

Those of us who design test systems for a living could learn a lot from Sir Christopher Wren, the prolific architect who designed and built Saint Paul's Cathedral (as well as much of the rest of old London after the Fire). He built a cathedral that survived the German Blitz even though the structure was more than 200 years old at the time. How many of our test systems can withstand crunch mode on even three or four projects? The design and layout of London still work after all these years, although the city had a little trouble adjusting to the technological advance of the automobile. Do our test systems respond well to changes? Wren's works also have an elegance and simplicity that make them simultaneously powerful and obvious. Can we sit down with a typical test system and easily understand how to use it?

Frankly, all too often test systems are a mess. When you build a new system, it is imperative to consider both function and form. Careful engineering creates the functions, and pervasive design decisions produce the form. The combination of the two determines the test system architecture.

What constitutes good test system architecture? I can't offer specific statements that apply to all situations. If you use oscilloscopes, vibration tables, thermal chambers, and a hardware/software library to test PCs, you face a different set of test engineering challenges than if you need to automate the testing of a GUI application that runs on multiple operating systems. Nevertheless, some general criteria do apply.

NOT AN *OBJET D'ART*:
TEST SYSTEM CAPABILITY

Most important, a well-designed test system provides the facilities you need for your testing projects. This might go without saying except that in reality too many test systems don't meet this criterion. Developing a capable test system requires that you—like your colleagues who must develop capable software and hardware systems—focus on the tasks that the test system

---

3. The cathedral has some unusual features. It has three domes: the interior and exterior domes are parabolic, and the internal structural dome is conical. From the balcony section in the interior dome, you can hear a person whisper if that person is directly across from you on the other side of the dome. In addition, on the way to the exterior dome's observation deck, a (very thick) plate of glass allows the nonvertiginous tourist to look down at the center of the cathedral.

needs to perform. This focus must inform the initial design of the test system and persist throughout its development. Unfortunately, it's easy to get distracted by crises, minutiae, and the temptation to add bells and whistles.

Other qualities support the capability of the test system. One of the most significant is test system fidelity—that is, the degree to which a test system accurately models end user hardware, software, and interface environments and simulates end user activities. (See Chapter 1 for more details about test system fidelity.) Low-fidelity systems introduce test artifacts, which are misleading system behaviors or incorrect results reported by the test system. For example, suppose that a SpeedyWriter test fails with the result *Can't open file*. That's a bug, right? Not if your test system caused the system under test to hit its open file limit immediately before trying to open the file in question. If the tester reports this as a bug, the test system has caused a *type I error*, reporting a nonproblem as a problem.

Alternatively, test systems can also cause *type II errors*, the failure to report real problems. Suppose that the tester in charge of environmental testing for a laptop computer reports that the computer passed the drop test. But the test case specifies only a level drop on the bottom of the laptop. When the computer is dropped in the field on its edge, corner, or top, the case cracks or the LCD breaks.

Especially challenging types of fidelity and test artifact issues arise in performance, stress, capacity, error handling and recovery, and accelerated-life testing. In these types of tests, you will by necessity fake it: simulating failures by pulling power and network cables; trying to make a lifetime of use transpire by shaking, baking, sweating, pounding, and shocking a system; using scripts to generate loads; and using programs and instruments to measure cycle times. Numerous books on test case design devote attention to these topics; it's a good idea to consult the ones pertinent to your field before you spend a lot of time developing such tests.[4]

Similarly, consider robustness. In general, the failure, blockage, or skipping of one test case shouldn't prevent you from running others.[5] Imagine two orthogonal features, A and B, in a system under test. Test cases TC_A and TC_B cover these features respectively and in that order in the test system.

---

4. Two of the best discussions are found in Boris Beizer's *Software System Testing and Quality Assurance* (for software) and Patrick O'Connor's *Practical Reliability Engineering* (for hardware).

5. Of course, a test case failure can indicate a problem in the *system under test* that is blocking other tests from running—a predicament quite different from one in which the *test system* is blocking test cases.

Feature B works, but A is broken. The test system should run TC_A and report the problem in feature A. It should then proceed to run TC_B and report its results for feature B. But if TC_A's success in finding a bug renders the test system incapable of executing TC_B, the test system is not robust. Likewise, robustness is an issue if you cannot run TC_B before TC_A.

Moreover, external conditions that don't affect the operation of the system under test should not perturb or impede the operation of the test system or the results it reports. A classic example of this problem arises when you develop a test system that requires network access in order to run even though the product, which is able to access network resources, is not inherently networked. If the network goes down, you can't test. Your painful alternative is to transfer a local copy to the marooned system and modify the tests to run in a stand-alone fashion.

Test Artifact from Hell

Although it's obvious that test artifacts are bad and test system fidelity is good, desirability does not always translate into implementation. This is especially true when a test artifact appears to be a small, harmless, simplifying assumption during design but hopelessly compromises your test results during execution.

My test team and I once designed a stress and performance transaction (simulated call) generator for a telephony system. The telephony driver and utility software included a special program—a UNIX daemon—to manage communication to the telephony hardware. We chose to invoke one instance of the daemon per simulated call to make the programming easy, although the daemon was designed to support approximately 24 callers. "So what?" we thought. "As long as the operation is legal, it shouldn't matter."

It *did* matter. When we started testing, we learned immediately that the daemon was a hungry little devil, devouring about 1 megabyte of memory per invocation. Consequently, we could simulate only 300 or so calls before the daemon filled the memory. We needed to simulate approximately 800 calls, but when we tried to do this, the resulting resource contention (swapping) created a ferocious test artifact that rendered our test results meaningless. We had to reengineer the test tool to multiplex 24 simulated caller programs into one daemon.

It is also important that your test system be flexible. A minor change in the operating environment or an insignificant change in the behavior of the system under test should not topple the test system. For instance, a networked test system that can't handle outside load on the network or file server bandwidth is inflexible. Similarly, the old capture-playback test tools for command-line and GUI programs often suffer from an inability to handle changes in screen resolution, a 1-pixel shift in a window, or even changes in the date.

As a special case of flexibility, consider scalability, the extent to which the test system's parameters of operation can expand without necessitating major changes or fundamental redesign. If the system under test can support up to 60 transactions per second at its current stage, your test system must be able to hit the upper boundary and simulate 60 transactions per second. But you should design it to expand easily to accommodate 600 or maybe even 6000 transactions per second. Achieving such versatility might sound difficult, but you can often create it by devoting adequate care to design and initial implementation.

When creating any test system, but especially one that involves scalability, you should also consider test system performance. The system's performance is mostly a product of the speed of your tools, but it can also be determined by how efficiently you schedule tests. If your test system takes weeks to run, you will face a lot of hard choices about what to skip.

Flexibility, scalability, and speed are enabled by simplicity. The more bells and whistles you introduce into a test system, the wider its footprint. To stretch the metaphor a tiny bit, as objects become wider they lose the ability to fit into narrow spaces. In addition, a proliferation of test system features tends to result in tight coupling of the test system to particular operating environments and can, if you're not careful, cause interdependence between test cases as well. Generality is usually desirable, but it's a smart move to make simplifying assumptions that don't impair the capability of the test system.

That said, you'll often find a trade-off between simplicity and reusability. By making a test tool a bit more general (and thereby more complex), you might be able to get it to do double duty, saving the effort of developing another tool. In addition, two similar tools can be hard to maintain, especially if consistency of operation across the two is important.

Consistency is significant in many ways. All the tools in your test system should work in as similar a fashion as possible. If you buy various tools that must work together, be sure that they do. Remember that off-the-shelf tools, like the tools you develop, have paradigms; they are based on assumptions about what you should and shouldn't do. These assumptions will of course enable or impede certain operations.

No Test System Is an Island: Testers and the Test System

The topics of consistency and simplicity bring us to the human side of the equation. No matter how automated your test system, it does not use itself; people use it. Testers must set up the test environment, start the tests, interpret the results, reproduce anomalies manually, isolate bugs by experimentation, and tear down the test environment at the end. Indeed, the usability of the test system is the key determinant of the number of type I and type II errors your testers will make. (I must emphasize, though, that most type I and type II errors result from the test system itself, not from the work of the testers.)

In addition, the testers will usually need to maintain the test system, especially the test cases and suites. This is especially true any time development adds new features to the product being tested, changes the definition of "correct" behavior for the product, or supports new configurations or environments. Maintenance is also necessary when you decide to enhance the test system to get better test coverage. Naturally, your test team will find a well-designed test system easier to maintain than one that is a mess.

In the area of consistency, it's helpful to limit your tool set. I once developed a test system that was implemented in four languages—TCL, iTCL, C, and QA Partner/Silk—running on Solaris and Microsoft Windows NT. The complexity made the development difficult. Technical challenges arose from getting the disparate interfaces to cooperate, while human difficulties ensued from the need to have such varied skill sets in a small team. Nevertheless, we were forced to use all four languages because of the architecture of the system under test. To preserve what little consistency we had left, we rejected a tool from an outside party that had been written in Perl. Although the tool would undoubtedly have been useful, the Tower of Babel was too high to add another level.

In contrast, my test team and I on another occasion supported a test system implemented almost entirely via Korn shell scripts, with only a few localized tests and utilities written in WinBatch and AutoTester. Nonetheless the system ran on three or four variants of UNIX, AS/400 (via network), MS-DOS, PC-DOS, and Microsoft Windows 3.*x*, and it supported about ten databases. The commonality of the test system components made maintenance technically straightforward and also kept the team's skill set requirements simple.[6]

Simplicity of the test system is also essential to usability. Your system must be easy to learn and easy to use. You should also make it difficult to misuse, although you need to balance this against the costs of complexity. It shouldn't require a priesthood to operate and maintain a test system. When outside people join your team, take advantage of the opportunity to quiz them about how easy—or how difficult—it is to learn the system.

In most situations, test systems need documentation. I like to use three kinds: an operator's or user's guide ("how do I use this beast?"); a design specification ("how does this beast work?"); and a document that addresses the test system architecture ("why did you build the beast this way?").

The test system should also document itself. Largely, this happens through internal consistency. File names, result logs, and the like should be easy to read and should shed some light on their purpose. Plan to use intuitive and consistent variable names in programs and scripts, even if people won't read these files and logs during normal operation. When the test system doesn't work, a test engineer will have to figure out the problem, and obscure error messages like *SYS40: Wrong at 252.351.37.92* and files with names like TST001.TXT will make the job difficult.

On the subject of files, try to ensure that your test system software doesn't become full of junk. I once worked on a test system that tended to accrete "temporary" files with charming names like ZIT0009.PRN and other less printable garbage. To encourage cleanliness, I wrote a script that ran once a week, examining the test system and identifying every unexpected file, who created it, and when it was created. The script then mailed the list of junk files to the whole team, and I followed up with the owners of these extraneous files. If the files in fact represented new tests, I simply changed the script. Often, however, the testers had failed to clean up a test directory after running tests.

---

6. We did, however, implement a shadow version of the test system in DCL to support VAX/VMS; most of our maintenance headaches came from this version.

A well-designed test system promotes accountability. It should identify, usually through the logs and the result files, who ran specific tests. Using a generic *tester* login can cause frustration later on when you need to ask questions or investigate a problem. Testers should identify themselves when they log in so that the logs and the result files will bear date/time and owner information.

Finally, if your test organization develops special tools, you'll want to avoid two mistakes that are archetypal in software development. First, don't forget the importance of revision or version control. If the test system is software, it should be checked in, checked out, and managed just like any other software. Second, remember to test the tests. A standard test plan and suite should exist for the test system. A tester should execute the plan any time changes are made to the test system.

THE BRICKS AND MORTAR OF THE SYSTEM: A TEST CASE TEMPLATE

Let's move from the general to the specific—that is, from the architecture of the overall test system to the construction of one of its key parts, the test case. This section presents a template, shown in Figure 3-3, that I use to create test cases.[7] We'll examine each part of the template and then look at an example of its use.

GETTING IT TOGETHER: THE TEST CASE HEADER

I refer to the first 10 rows of the template, which identify and describe the test case, as the "header" section. It's a good idea to name the test case with both mnemonic and numeric identifiers. The mnemonic name is a short description, only a few words long, that conveys the essence of the test—for example, Stress, 1M Drop, or Network Performance. For the numeric identifier, I use a Dewey decimal–style notation: for instance, a test case that is

---

7. This template is compliant in content but not in format with IEEE standard 829–1983. This approach to defining test cases, together with Chapter 5's discussion of test case tracking, makes my methodology IEEE-compliant in that it captures all the same information. I have, however, changed the format entirely, aiming for a more concise approach that lends itself to automated means of summarization.

	A	B	C	D	F	G	H
1	Test Case Name:	Mnemonic identifier					
2	Test ID:	Dewey decimal–style identifier					
3	Test Suite:	Test suite(s) in which the test case is used					
4	Priority:	Based on intuition, FMEA coverage analysis, or other coverage analysis					
5	Hardware Required:	List hardware in rows					
6	Software Required:	List software in rows					
7	Duration:	Elapsed clock time					
8	Effort:	Person-hours					
9	Setup:	List steps needed to set up test					
10	Teardown:	List steps needed to return SUT to pretest state					
11							
12	ID	Test Step/Substep	Result	Bug ID			
13	1.000	Major step					
14	1.001	Minor step (substep)					
15	1.002	Minor step (substep)					
16	2.000	Major step					
17	Overall	Status					
18		System Config ID					
19		Tester					
20		Date Completed					
21		Effort					
22		Duration					

FIGURE 3-3   *A test case template.*

used in test suite 5 and that is the second test case is assigned identifier 5.002. Alternatively, you can use a pure sequential numbering, to emphasize the many-to-many relationship between test cases and test suites.[8]

The next entry in the header lists the name of the test suite (or suites) in which the test case will be used. Because a given test case might be used in multiple suites, this entry could get a bit unwieldy. But in practice most test cases are used in only one test suite, so including the name of the suite provides some useful information with only infrequent confusion.

Optionally, you might want to assign a priority to the test. Prioritizing is most useful when you need to determine how many times a given test should be run. You can assign a priority based on intuition; the opinions of the sales, marketing, technical support, and development teams; your coverage analysis; or all of these. Test coverage analysis, for example, allows

---

8. I consider numeric identifiers especially important (not only for test cases but also for test steps, bug IDs, and so on) because they allow you to generate summaries easily. Text entries are difficult to summarize unless everyone uses the same keywords. Summary reports are essential when you communicate with your management about what's happening in the test organization.

you to assign the highest priority to those test cases that cover the most important quality risks, requirements, and functions. (Later sections of this chapter discuss test coverage and the use of priority to drive test scheduling.)

The next entries in the header address resource requirements. For the first two of these entries, you should list, row by row, the hardware and software needed to run the test. You might want to restrict these lists to the nonobvious: for instance, if you are testing a Windows-based application and the standard test environment includes Microsoft Windows 98, Microsoft Office 97, Norton AntiVirus, and LapLink, you needn't duplicate that listing for every test case.

The entries for Duration and Effort specify how long it will take to run the test, in clock time and in person-hours, respectively. In creating these estimates, you have two alternatives: you can assume that the test passes, or you can make assumptions about the time impact of typical failures. (I prefer the former approach. I do reserve a small padding for failed tests— I assume that about one-quarter to one-third of test cases will fail the first time through—but I build the slack into the schedule, not the test cases.) The estimate of person-hours specifies the human resources needed to run the test. For example, do you need two people to run the test, one in front of each terminal? You would if you were testing the Death Match feature in a game such as Doom.

In the final two entries of the header, you should specify the setup procedures and the teardown procedures. Sometimes there are none, but typically two or three steps, such as installing or uninstalling an application, are needed at the beginning and end of a test. For instance, when a test is completed, you might need to delete sample files that were created during the test in order to return the system under test to its original state.

THE RUBBER MEETS THE ROAD: THE TEST STEPS

With the preliminaries out of the way, let's move on to the test case proper. A test case is fundamentally a sequence of actions, performed serially, in parallel, or in some combination, that creates the desired test conditions. The template breaks down these actions into steps and substeps.

Each step or substep has a numeric identifier. Once again using a Dewey decimal–style notation, you can number steps sequentially starting from 1 and then number their subordinate substeps decimally (1.001, 1.002, and so forth). This numbering allows you to refer to specific test steps by combining the test case's numeric identifier (from the header) with the test step identifier—for example, the second substep of step 5 in test case 9.010 can be unambiguously identified as 9.010.5.002. This method is useful in bug reports and in discussions with testers. (The bug tracking database defined in Chapter 4 includes a field that captures this value.)

To the right of the list of steps are two columns that allow testers to record the results of their testing. Following the evaluation of a test case, one of three statements will hold true for each step:

◆　The tester ran the test step or substep and observed the expected result, the whole expected result, and nothing but the expected result—in other words, the test step or substep was unproductive, a nonsuccess. The tester should record *Pass* in the Result column. (The step or substep can be deemed a nonsuccess because the objective of running tests is to locate, characterize, isolate, and report bugs. If all the test cases pass, you will not succeed in doing this.)

◆　The tester ran the test step or substep, and the outcome was, to a greater or lesser extent, unexpected. The test case was a success because the tester has identified some untoward behavior that can now be reported in your bug tracking database (more on this tool in Chapter 4). How to classify the test case? If the unanticipated result was something along the lines of a CPU catching fire or a program crashing with a General Protection Fault or a system lockup, the tester should enter *Fail* in the Result column. But what if the unexpected result is immaterial to the correct operation of the functionality under test? Development might see your team as unfair and alarmist if the tester throws this test case into the "failure" bucket. It is important, however, to keep track of the test case that did such a good job of finding a new bug, so you don't want your tester to record it as a pass. Entering *Warn* as a result is usually a good solution. A *Warn* entry can also cover some of the gray areas between abject failure and tangential failure—for example, if the functionality under test works correctly but causes an incorrectly spelled error message to be displayed.[9]

---

9. Not to split hairs too much further, but I would record a *Fail* for an incorrect message or a display that included offensive language, obscene images, or libelous statements.

◆ The tester did not run the test step or substep. If running the step was impossible—for instance, because the test was impeded by a known bug in the system or by the lack of essential resources—the tester should record *Block* in the Result column. If the tester chose not to run the test step or substep, it should be marked *Skip*. In either case, the tester should explain this omission.

If a test step is marked *Fail* or *Warn*, the tester should also indicate, in the Bug ID column, the identifier for the bug report filed as a result of the observed failure. Chapter 4 covers this topic in depth; for now, suffice it to say that you need a facility for recording bugs and that each bug report so logged needs a unique identifier.

THE BOTTOM LINE: THE TEST RESULT SUMMARY

At the bottom of the template is a summary section in which the tester in-dicates an overall assessment of the test case. The Status entry should be marked *Pass*, *Warn*, or *Fail*, depending on the success—or lack thereof—of the test case. (Remember, successful test cases find bugs.) The tester might also record *Block* or *Skip* if applicable. The tester should next note the spe-cific system configuration used for the test. (Chapter 5 introduces the idea of assigning an identifier to different system configurations.)

In the final part of the summary section, the tester should record his or her name or initials (depending on your custom), the date on which the test case was completed, the actual effort expended in terms of person-hours, and the duration. The latter three pieces of information allow you to track progress and understand variances from the plan that result from fast—or slow—test progress. Be careful, though, not to use these duration and effort numbers as a cudgel. Testers are not likely to find motivational an angry boss who yells at them for not achieving possibly unrealistic targets. Instead, they quickly learn to manipulate these numbers, which prevents you from see-ing a realistic picture of your test operation. (For an example of how *not* to use measures of effort, see the sidebar "Confessions of an Overzealous Test Manager" on page 78.)

A SAMPLE TEST CASE FOR DATAROCKET

Let's look at a brief example of how you might use the test case template. Figure 3-4 presents a test case designed to evaluate DataRocket's response to CPU and memory loads while running under Sun Solaris, Microsoft

	A	B	C	D	F	G	H	I	J
1	Test Case Name:	CPU and Memory							
2	Test ID:	2.001							
3	Test Suite:	Load, Capacity, and Volume							
4	Priority:	High							
5	Hardware Required:	One DataRocket Server							
6	Software Required:	Load, Capacity, and Volume test tool							
7		Windows NT							
8		Solaris							
9		Novell							
10	Duration:	3							
11	Effort:	4							
12	Setup:	Install Windows NT							
13		Install Novell							
14		Install Solaris							
15	Teardown:	None necessary							
16									
17	**ID**	**Test Step/Substep**	**Result**	**Bug ID**					
18	1.000	Test CPU load on Windows NT.							
19	1.001	Install Windows NT. Confirm proper install.	Pass						
20	1.002	Install LCV test tool from LCV CD-ROM. Confirm proper install.	Warn	9					
21	1.003	Run LCV test tool, CPU module, for one hour. Check log file for failures on exit.	Pass						
22	2.000	Repeat steps 1.001-1.003 for Solaris.	Fail	10					
23	3.000	Repeat steps 1.001-1.003 for Novell.	Pass						
24	**Overall**	**Status**	Fail						
25		**System Config ID**	B,A,C						
26		**Tester**	LTW						
27		**Date Completed**	7/14/99						
28		**Effort**	16						
29		**Duration**	16						
30									
31									

FIGURE 3-4 *Using the template to record results of the load and capacity test case.*

Windows NT, and Novell Netware. (This example is, of course, a bit contrived; in reality you would perform the installation for each operating system and then run all the load and capacity suites before installing the next OS.) A tester (initials LTW) has run the test case and recorded the results.

As noted in Figure 3-4, when LTW installed the test tool from the CD-ROM, the CD-ROM failed to read on the first two tries. The third try succeeded, but this ratio of two failures out of every three tries held up on subsequent retests. Because the failure doesn't materially affect the CPU or the memory subsystem, LTW classified it as a *Warn*.

Worse, however, Solaris, a key network operating system in the target market, did not install or run reliably. About half the time, the system panicked during the installation; the rest of the time, it panicked later, sometimes under load, sometimes just sitting there. This result is a *Fail*, as it obviously does materially affect the CPU and memory response to stress.

In the summary section, the overall test case result is marked *Fail* because of the failure of the Solaris installation. System configurations B, A, and C are not identified in Figure 3-4, but you can assume that a separate lookup table maps these IDs to specific systems. Also note that the Solaris bug seems to have consumed a lot of LTW's time; the Effort and Duration entries are well over the allocated times.

Confessions of an Overzealous Test Manager

I once worked at an organization where the testers, who were mostly contractors, had their billable hours capped by the planned effort of the test cases they ran. If they tried to bill more hours than the total effort allocated to their assigned test cases, the lead testers rejected their time cards. The leads had an incentive to enforce these limits because they received bonuses based on budget underruns incurred on their projects. Since this organization worked primarily with fixed bids, this method effectively aligned the test technicians with a key corporate objective: meeting or exceeding the profit margins for each project. What you measure is what you get.

Conversely, what you *don't* measure is what you *don't* get. In the absence of corresponding quality assurance pressures such as audits of test results, some testers adopted a "see no evil" attitude. Successful tests—ones that fail—take longer to analyze and complete than unsuccessful (passed) tests. Remarkably, most testers remained conscientious and spirited trackers of bugs.

In addition to the quality problems caused by linking pay to planned test effort, it was unfair to penalize the testers so heavily. Test case delays and time overruns have more to do with management decisions, the competence of support organizations, and the quality of product delivered by developers than with lackadaisical or featherbedding attitudes on the part of test technicians. Furthermore, there was nothing but downside for the test technicians, while the lead testers were motivated to hoard hours in an attempt to make their bonuses as big as possible. I admit to being an exacting enforcer of hour limits in those days, but I wouldn't make the same mistake today.

How Detailed?
Balancing Ambiguity

How much detail should you include when writing a test case? I've found that there is always a trade-off. On the one hand, an extensive, detailed, precise test case assumes less knowledge on the part of the testers, which allows you to use testers with lower levels of skill than you might otherwise require. It also supports reproducibility: if nothing is left to the judgment of an individual tester, you should see less variability in two evaluations of the same test by two different people or even by the same person at different times. In addition, if development is involved in the review process for test cases as you construct them, spelling out the details serves to communicate, clearly and unambiguously, what kinds of failures you are looking for and what behaviors you consider buggy.

On the other hand, writing a totally unambiguous test case can involve considerably more work than writing a spare one—and it's not simply twice as much work; in fact, it's usually closer to ten times as much. Obviously you have to write more, but you also must "unlearn" information that seems obvious to you and your test engineers but could mystify or confuse the test technicians. If you've ever tried to explain what testing is all about to someone with no experience in the field, you already know that this can be quite difficult. At some point, you have to assume that your test team is not staffed entirely with clueless technophobes.[10]

Beyond the effort required to write unequivocal test cases, consider the effort needed to maintain them. In our example test case, step 1.001 tells the test technician: *Install Windows NT. Confirm proper install.* The instruction *Install Windows NT 5.0. Confirm proper install* might have been better, but it would require you to update the OS version before using this test case in the future. Or suppose that you had launched into an exposition, dozens of steps long, about how to install Windows NT 5.0 and then how to confirm the proper install. As soon as Windows NT 6.0 comes out and totally changes the installation process (say), the test case will require an extensive rewrite.

Clearly there is no single "right" answer. Every test operation has different constraints in terms of the resources and time available to develop test cases, the technical and product expertise possessed by the engineers and technicians, the concern with strict reproducibility, and the effort that can be spent maintaining test cases. Decisions about level of detail, like much of management, must move on a continuum. The test case presented here is simplified, but its level of granularity is consistent with the test cases I have seen in some of the best test organizations.

---

10. Actually, there are times when you *will* want one or two clueless technophobes available for usability testing, depending on your system's target market—for example, as part of system testing for a consumer product that includes advanced computing features driven by voice commands.

Avoiding the Dreaded "Test Escape": Coverage and Regression Test Gaps

Whatever measurements your manager applies to your performance, one key criterion indicates whether you are doing your job well: the number of *test escapes*—that is, the number of field-reported bugs that your test team missed but could reasonably have detected during testing. Notice the word "reasonably." If your testers could have found the bug only through unusual and complicated hardware configurations or obscure operations, that bug is not considered a test escape. Nor does it count as a test escape if the testers found the bug during testing, but it was not fixed because of a project management decision.

Test escapes usually arise through one or a combination of the following kinds of problems:

◆ *A low-fidelity test system.* While a low-fidelity test system might cover a significant chunk of the product's features and operations, it doesn't cover the ones most important to your customers, usually as a result of poor engineering.

◆ *A regression test gap.* The test suite does contain test cases covering the operation in which the bug surfaced, but the test cases were last run before the fault was introduced in the system under test. Regression test gaps arise from schedule or resource limitations or from planning errors.

◆ *A type II error.* A type II error occurs when a tester fails to detect or report incorrect system behavior, assigns an excessively low priority or severity to the bug, or otherwise understates the significance of the problem. Type II errors are caused by the test system, the tester, or the test manager.

Chapter 6 discusses type II errors in more depth (see "When Test Fails: Minimizing Type I and Type II Errors," page 178); for now, let's look at how low-fidelity test systems and regression test gaps create test escapes. Imagine for a moment that defects are fish (not bugs), that tests are fishnets, and that testers are the crew on a fishing boat. When you have a low-fidelity test system, represented by the fishnet in Figure 3-5, the fish (the defects) are escaping by swimming through holes in the fishnets. When regression test gaps occur, the fish are swimming under a fishnet that is only half deployed, as shown in Figure 3-6. Prosperous fishing crews have an efficient fishing system. Flourishing test teams have powerful test systems and use them effectively. The following sections discuss some ways to maximize your catch. First, though, a cautionary tale to illustrate the stakes.

BAD COVERAGE DECISIONS WITH THE BEST INTENTIONS

Coverage mistakes are easy to make, even if you spend time thinking about the issue. Some years ago, I took over as a test manager in a company that had developed a neat way of automating testing, using a portable scripting language and the command-line functionality of the system under test. For two years my team and I worked with that test system, polishing it to a bright luster. We wrote an intelligent output comparison program. We had

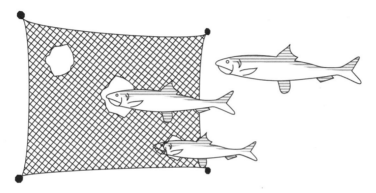

FIGURE 3-5   *Test escapes resulting from a low-fidelity test system.*

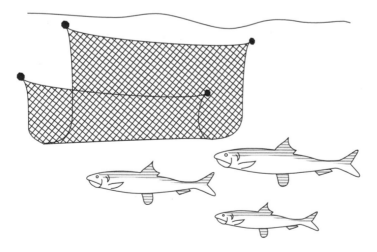

FIGURE 3-6   *Test escapes resulting from regression test gaps.*

clean, maintainable test tools, under strict revision control. The system was robust, reliable, and fast. Furthermore, we analyzed test coverage in terms of the crucial databases and operating systems supported by the system under test, and we had most of them nailed. Nevertheless we had significant test escapes, and the customers were unhappy. Accordingly, my managers were unhappy, and they made my team and me very unhappy by liquidating the test organization.

What happened? I let the test tool determine my decisions about test coverage. As Gerald Weinberg has pointed out, "The child who receives a hammer for Christmas will discover that everything needs pounding."[11] We had only two test suites that evaluated the user interface. We barely tested the utilities included with the package. We spent insufficient time understanding the unique uses and the special boundary conditions that plagued our customers.

I took a couple of lessons away from this experience. The most important was to be sure that your consideration of coverage is driven by the quality risks that matter to your customers, your end users, and your colleagues in such areas as marketing, technical support, and sales, who are close to your customers. I also learned that coverage is not a one-time consideration: be sure that you constantly revisit your coverage goals.

ARE YOU TESTING WHAT DEVELOPMENT IS BUILDING?

If you are lucky enough to get written requirements and specifications for your product, you probably already use them as a basis for test planning and test system development. You should also close the loop and ascertain the coverage. You can use a numeric approach, such as the one outlined for quality risk coverage in the following section, or you can use a cross-reference approach. To create a cross-reference document, carefully go through the requirements or specifications, and note (in a soft copy) the specific test cases that verify each requirement or specification. For those not paired with a test case, decide whether there's a good reason to skip testing in that area. If there isn't, you have found a coverage problem you need to address. Apply this approach iteratively until you are happy with your test system's coverage. You can also circulate this marked-up cross-reference to your peers, especially those in sales, marketing, and technical support, to be sure they're comfortable with what you plan to test.

---

11. Gerald Weinberg, *Secrets of Consulting*, p. 53. This book is recommended reading for consultants and contractors and is full of pithy, memorable rules of thumb like this.

You can apply this approach even if you don't have requirements or specifications documents. By listing the functional areas of the product at a general level and then subdividing them into more specific areas, you have a black-box decomposition of what the system is supposed to do. (This is analogous to building the requirements and specifications documents from the product itself, which is reverse-order but not unusual.) Then proceed as just described, using either a numeric or a cross-reference approach. Iterate until you're satisfied, and circulate the document for review.

Remember two caveats about using such a functional coverage approach, however. First, it measures testing of what the system *does*. Don't forget about what it *doesn't* do, *shouldn't* do, and *should* do—these factors are equally important to your customers. Second, if you are focused narrowly on functions, you can easily overlook factors such as stability, performance, data quality, error handling and recovery, and other such "system" problems. My mistake in the cautionary tale related earlier was, at least in part, that of depending solely on a narrow functional coverage analysis to validate my testing approach. As your coverage analyses move further away from customer requirements and more into the minutiae of system functionality, you need to augment your approach by looking at what the customers care about.

RELATING QUALITY RISKS TO TEST CASES

Chapter 1 introduced (or maybe reintroduced) you to a list of generic quality risks that apply to many computer systems, and we used that list to develop a prioritized set of quality risks for a SpeedyWriter case study. (See "What You *Should* Test: Considering Quality," page 11.) That chapter also explained the use of an FMEA approach for defining quality risks. Whichever approach you use for test case development, you will need to ensure quality risk coverage. After you have generated your list of quality risks, you can benchmark your test system against it.

To do this, list test case identifiers as column heads to the right of the FMEA chart itself. In each cell where a quality risk row intersects a test case column, enter one of three numeric values:

0 (Or leave the cell blank)	The test case does nothing to address the quality risk
1	The test case provides some level of indirect coverage for the quality risk
2	The test case provides direct and significant coverage for the quality risk

In addition to rating individual test case and quality risk intersections, you can aggregate this information. When you total the numbers by quality risk category and by test suite, you can measure, respectively, whether you are covering particular risks and whether tests are providing an adequate return on investment. Remember, though, to relate these numbers to the risk priority numbers. High coverage numbers should correspond to high risk, low coverage numbers to low risk.

Figure 3-7 shows an example of quality-risk coverage analysis for the video subsystem of DataRocket. As you can see from the rightmost column, our coverage for each risk is spartan; increased coverage for this area might be warranted.

If you were careful to capture the pertinent data in the References column of the FMEA (as explained in the Chapter 1 section "Failure Mode and Effect Analysis: A Formal Method for Understanding Quality Risks," page 30), you could also generate the coverage analyses discussed in the previous section. You could then use this cross-reference to prepare a set of documents that, because they are less information-dense than an FMEA, will allow your peers to review your coverage. It is sometimes difficult to get people outside test to review FMEA charts, but requirements, specifications, and functional decompositions are easier to digest.

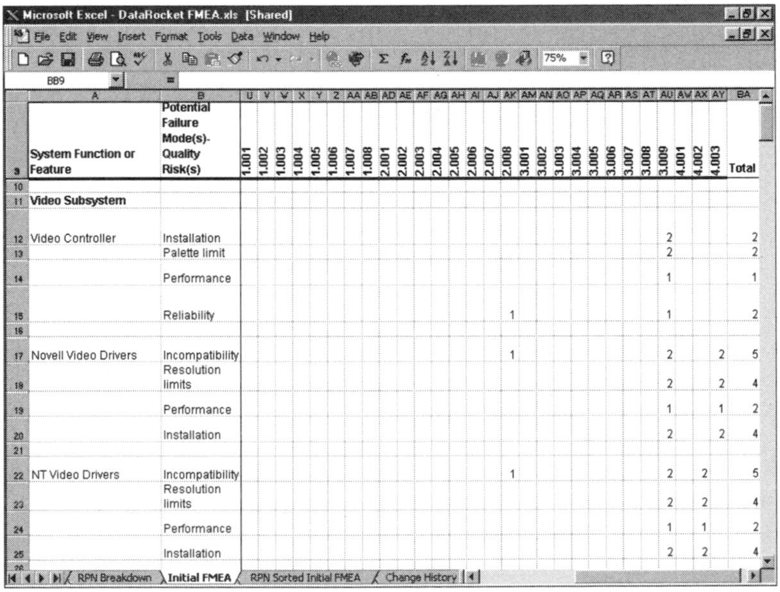

	System Function or Feature	Potential Failure Mode(s)- Quality Risk(s)	1.001	1.002	1.003	1.004	1.005	1.006	1.007	1.008	2.001	2.002	2.003	2.004	2.005	2.006	2.007	2.008	3.001	3.002	3.003	3.004	3.005	3.006	3.007	3.008	3.009	4.001	4.002	4.003	Total
11	**Video Subsystem**																														
12	Video Controller	Installation																									2				2
13		Palette limit																									2				2
14		Performance																									1				1
15		Reliability																1									1				2
17	Novell Video Drivers	Incompatibility																1									2			2	5
18		Resolution limits																									2			2	4
19		Performance																									1			1	2
20		Installation																									2			2	4
22	NT Video Drivers	Incompatibility																1									2		2		5
23		Resolution limits																									2		2		4
24		Performance																									1		1		2
25		Installation																									2		2		4

FIGURE 3-7 *Analyzing the quality risk coverage of DataRocket's video subsystem.*

Bear in mind that the rankings you use to analyze quality risk coverage are relative and subjective. No hard-and-fast rule separates a 0 rating from a 1 or a 1 from a 2. But as long as you and your engineers use the ratings consistently, and you use peer reviews to ensure agreement, the numbers have meaning. Be careful, though, to avoid bias in one direction or the other. If your team is consistently too optimistic, assigning 1s and 2s gratuitously, you overestimate your coverage. Conversely, you can also underestimate it.

CONFIGURATION COVERAGE

Let's suppose that you are testing SpeedyWriter and your manager tells you to run only the installation and file-open tests. You not only will be allowed to retain your current level of staff and resources but also will be given even more resources—an unlimited hardware budget. In return, all you have to do is test SpeedyWriter against every possible combination of client computer, platform (Web browser, operating system, and network), and I/O peripheral. Would you do it?

For purposes of illustration, let's assume twenty possible variations of each variable: twenty different client computers; twenty operating system, browser, and network combinations; and twenty combinations of printers, mice, keyboards, scanners, and video controllers. Figure 3-8 shows the "test space" created by this scenario.

As you can see from the figure, you would have to test 8000 different configurations, give or take a few hundred "impossible" configurations, such as the use of a particular peripheral with an operating system that

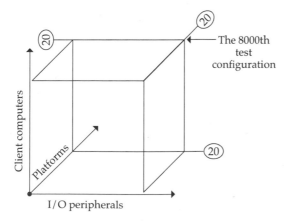

FIGURE 3-8   *An intractable configuration coverage problem.*

doesn't support it. If the two tests take about an hour, including setup and teardown time, you have about 2.75 person-years of work ahead of you. In addition to the time, imagine the expense. This simple example could easily cost $100,000 in hardware, operating systems, and server software alone.[12]

Even this discouraging example simplifies the matter. In reality, the platform and I/O peripheral dimensions are themselves multiple dimensions. In general, any time you confront the issue of configuration coverage, you are faced with a truly ugly N-dimensional matrix of configuration combinations that you have no hope whatever of covering completely.[13] What to do?

Three techniques can be effective in managing this problem. The first is to be sure that you pick the key configurations. For each configuration variable, identify a handful of hardware, software, or infrastructure items that you really care about. Factors to consider in this decision include customer usage, the risk to the product if that particular item does not work, and your gut feeling for where the bugs are. You should also consider the long-term usefulness of the item in your lab and, naturally, its price. Expect to spend some time negotiating your list with management, and be ready to justify each purchase. Also keep in mind that configuration testing is but one of the many classes of testing you must do. By trying to cover too many configurations, you might end up with too little time and money and too few staff resources to test other important quality risks.

Even if you had only five variations of each configuration variable in the SpeedyWriter example, completely covering the matrix would take three person-weeks. That's probably a significant chunk of time in your project unless configuration testing is your main quality risk. Rather than trying to cover every single cell in the matrix, you might choose a second technique, known as *shotgunning*, in which you simply distribute your tests randomly across the cells. (I'll show you another useful way to apply shotgunning later in this chapter.)

The third technique offers an opportunity to increase your test configuration coverage through careful use of test cycles. By reshuffling the configuration used with each test in each cycle, you can get even closer to

---

12. On a more realistic note, Chapter 10 discusses how to reduce the expense of covering multiple configurations by leveraging the capital expenditures of external test labs.

13. When Microsoft first released Windows 95, the need for backward compatibility with Windows 3.1 and 3.11 hardware created many of the last-minute schedule slips. This requirement opened up a truly massive configuration matrix that it took Microsoft months to cover, even with the help of beta testers.

complete coverage. Continuing our SpeedyWriter example, suppose that you had 250 test cases to run and three test cycles. You could test each configuration combination against six cases. This isn't exhaustive, but at least you've sampled each one.

BUG COVERAGE

So far we've discussed several ways to analyze coverage: by requirements or specifications, by functional areas, by quality risks, and by configurations. All these methods address the question, "Have we tested X?" But when you consider the objective of testing—to find bugs—the real question is, "What bugs *haven't* we found?" The approaches we've covered provide indirect information since bugs usually relate back to one or more of these areas. But what you really need to know about is bug coverage.

Unfortunately, you can't know what you don't know. If it were possible to know all the bugs in advance, the whole test effort would be unnecessary. Suppose, though, that you could estimate the total number of bugs in the system under test. Or perhaps you could measure the bug-finding effectiveness of your test system. The literature on testing and quality assurance suggests two techniques for solving these problems.

To estimate the total number of bugs, you might want to investigate *error seeding,* which involves the deliberate introduction of bugs into the system under test. Because the bugs are known to the people (outside the test team) who planted them, they can be removed manually at the end of the test process. Since the test team remains unaware of the seeding, the extent to which the test system reveals the known bugs allows you to infer the extent to which it found unknown bugs. Suppose that the system under test contains N bugs, and K bugs are seeded. At the end of system testing, the test team has found n unseeded and k seeded bugs. Error seeding theory asserts the following:

$$\frac{k}{K} \approx \frac{n}{N}$$

Solving for N, you find the following:

$$N \approx n\,\frac{k}{K}$$

Some important cautions apply to this technique. You must remember that these are approximations. If you have found 95 unseeded bugs and 19 out of 20 seeded bugs, you can't assume that exactly 5 bugs remain to be found. The technique simply gives you an estimate against which you can gauge a measure of effectiveness for your test system and a level of confidence in your results. Additionally, in order for this approximation to hold, the bugs seeded must be representative. The technique measures only the test system's ability to find *seeded* bugs, and you must infer its effectiveness against real bugs based on that. Also keep in mind that bugs don't exist in a vacuum. Because they often interact, the seeding itself can create test artifacts that lessen the strength of your inference.

Like error seeding, *fault injection* provides a way of measuring the effectiveness of your test system. In this technique, errors are created dynamically in the system under test by deliberately damaging, or perturbing, the source code, the executable code, or the data storage locations. For example, the fault injection process might create a so-called mutant system by flipping a bit in a data storage location immediately prior to the execution of a test case. The test results against these mutant systems allow you to make certain decisions about the quality of the system under test as well as the quality of your test system. While this technique shows promise, it currently remains in the experimental stage. The key challenges are to simplify it in such a way that a reasonable number of mutants deliver statistically meaningful results and to automate the creation of mutants.[14]

REGRESSION TEST GAPS

The concept of regression is straightforward but hard to put into words. Formally, you can say that if, as a result of a change in the system under test, a new revision of the system, S_{n+1}, contains a defect not present in revision S_n, the quality of the system has regressed. Plainly speaking, regression occurs when some previously correct operation misbehaves. (If a new revision contains a new piece of functionality that fails without affecting the rest of the system, this is not considered regression.)

---

14. If you are interested in pursuing these topics further, I recommend *Software Fault Injection*, by Jeff Voas and Gary McGraw, which provides extensive references to the pertinent research.

Usually you'll detect regression when test cases that passed previously now yield anomalies. Some regression, though, is so obvious that no test is required to find it—flaws in a system's case or a glitch in software installation, for instance. Or you can have Zen regression: if a bug crawls into the system but no one detects it, you will find this regression, like the sound of the unattended falling tree, hard to prove!

In an ideal setting, the test team would have the time needed to execute all the test suites during each cycle of each test phase. This would ensure that within days you would catch any regression in a new release. But running all the test suites in such a way that every configuration is covered could take forever, stretching test cycles into weeks rather than days. Few consumer software or hardware companies have such luxurious time frames; pesky realities such as budgets and marketing windows tend to compress test cycles.

In addition to the "do it all by tomorrow" urgency that prevails on development projects, you can become a victim of your own success. When you first start developing tests, you'll probably be able to hit only the most critical items. As your test system and your team grow and mature, however, you'll find that you have more tests to run than time to run them in.

Either (or both) of these factors forces you to select a subset of the test suites for each test cycle. Yet each test case omitted might create a regression test gap.[15] Unless you execute every test case in every test suite against every revision and configuration, you are exposed to regression test risks—to follow an earlier analogy, some fish will swim around a partially deployed fishnet. What can you do?

Is Automation a Complete Solution?

Some people suggest test automation as a solution to this problem, and it can be—at least partially. An automated test system runs more tests in a given period than a manual system, and, consequently, the regression test gap is reduced. Nevertheless, automation is not a panacea. As a test manager, you will receive lots of brochures touting (expensive) test automation tools, so bear the following in mind when you read them.

---

15. If you can drop a test case without affecting test coverage, you should consider deleting the test case from your test suite. It is probably redundant, assuming that your measurement of coverage is valid.

For a stable system, you can develop automated tests and run them again and again, with some minor modifications to one or two test cases each time. But when interfaces, major functions, or supported environments evolve and change rapidly, automated tests require significant maintenance. Because these changes occur in the course of a fast-paced development project, you will discover these problems in the thick of test execution, when you don't have the resources to fix them. This might tempt you to wait until the product is released to develop automated tests for maintenance, but systems in development run the highest risk of regression.[16] Just a cruel irony of life in a test organization, I'm afraid.

Furthermore, the efficiencies you gain in test execution come at the price of test setup overhead. Your testers can spend a significant amount of time getting the test environment configured on the system under test. Also, glitches encountered in setting up the tests usually come from the test system itself, not from the system under test. Any time spent setting up the tests or chasing down test artifacts disguised as bugs is time not spent testing.

In the hardware world, automation can help only in certain areas. For stress, capacity, and performance testing, for example, automation is essential. But when you test multiple applications—imagine compatibility testing Windows-based applications against a new desktop computer—the time needed to install the application and verify the installation can make up the bulk of the test. You can't effectively automate these operations. Even in the software world, installation of the program and its ancillary utilities, followed by configuration and verification of the install, are by necessity manual activities for most systems. You can automate the testing of the application itself, but this might save you only a few dozen hours per project. Test automation won't help if installation and configuration eat up half the time in your test cycle.

I don't mean to disparage test automation. It is useful, and it will often help to reduce regression test gaps. Despite some claims to the contrary by test automation tool vendors, however, it is not a silver bullet.

---

16. In my experience, most regression test "failures" during maintenance turn out to be unintended, but correct, consequences of other changes. Trying to anticipate these expected-result changes prior to running the tests against the maintenance release is often impractical.

Four Ways to Spread Tests Across Cycles

Test automation or no, the time will undoubtedly come when you will be forced to select only a subset of the test system for certain test cycles. When this happens, these four alternative tactics can be useful in minimizing regression test gaps:

- Assigning a priority in advance to each test suite and then running the test suites in a way that favors the higher-priority tests

- Assigning priorities dynamically to each test suite as each test cycle begins, and then running the test suites in priority order

- Shotgunning the test suites across the test cycles

- Running the entire set of test suites straight through as many times as possible (definitely more than once), which I call railroading the tests

---

Silver Bullets or Solid Engineering?

Fred Brooks, author of *The Mythical Man-Month*, has written an article entitled "No Silver Bullets," in which he argues that the quest for universal cures to the "software crisis" is counterproductive. This year's be-all-and-end-all always turns into last year's incremental improvement. RAD, object-oriented programming, 4GLs, structured programming, FORTRAN, and COBOL all have had their moment in the sun. Test automation, likewise, is useful within the limits of the problems it can solve. Nevertheless, we would do well to remember that it does not cure cancer, remove warts, feed the dog, or promote world peace.

Richard Gisselquist, a senior programmer at Silicon Graphics, makes a similar point in a 1998 article called "Engineering in Software." He writes that hot programming trends "and CASE are not engineering." He claims that solid engineering consists of managing expectations and the development team, properly designing and implementing the system (whatever the language and the CASE environment), and promoting the proper use of the system. I believe that this is just as true for testing as it is for the project as a whole.

The next few pages use a DataRocket example to illustrate each of these approaches, demonstrating practical ways of slicing and dicing the test suites in a test phase under tight—but not quite unreasonable—schedules. Of course, if you are receiving SCUD releases of software every few hours, all these means of partitioning tend to fall into the "rearranging deck chairs on the Titanic" cliché. (The most chaos-resistant technique is railroading, as you'll see.) Remember too that although these scheduling methods may appear clever and efficient, they are nevertheless only fancy ways of making compromises: you trade off added risks against saved time and resources. Any time you plan a test cycle that includes anything less than a full pass through every test suite in the current test phase, you create a regression test gap.

For our example, let's assume that you have one month to run system testing for DataRocket. During that period, you are scheduled to receive two motherboard revisions and ten BIOS releases. You plan to run ten cycles, the first and the tenth lasting one week and the intervening cycles lasting two days. The entire set of test suites for system testing takes about four days to run, depending on the number of bugs you find. Table 3-1 shows the test schedule with milestones.[17]

Cycle	Start	End	MB Rev	BIOS Rel	% Tests
1	7/1/99	7/7/99	A	X1	100
2	7/8/99	7/9/99	A	X2	50
3	7/10/99	7/11/99	A	X3	50
4	7/12/99	7/13/99	A	X4	50
5	7/14/99	7/15/99	B	X5	50
6	7/16/99	7/17/99	B	X6	50
7	7/18/99	7/19/99	B	X7	50
8	7/20/99	7/21/99	B	X8	50
9	7/22/99	7/23/99	B	X9	50
10	7/24/99	7/30/99	B	X10	100

TABLE 3-1   *A frenetic DataRocket system test schedule.*

17. This is not a recommended schedule. A four-day system test suite is probably not exhaustive, given typical staffing levels in a test organization. A two-day test cycle gives you time to hit only the high points. Nevertheless, schedules resembling Table 3-1 are hardly atypical, unfortunately.

Prioritizing

Let's start by using the priority approach. Based on a three-level division of priority, let's suppose that the high-priority subset of the test system consists of test suites STS1, STS2, STS5, and STS7 and takes two days to run. The medium-priority subset containing STS3 and STS6 takes one day. The low-priority portion containing STS4 and STS8 also takes one day. Figure 3-9 on the following page shows a road map for running these tests in priority order. (The higher-priority tests are shown with darker shading.)

Notice that the road map in Figure 3-9 starts and ends with a complete pass through the test system. The complete first pass provides a baseline for the rest of the testing and alerts development to every bug you could find in the system right from the start. The three-day hiatus from organized test suite execution allows testers to isolate all the bugs revealed by the first run of the test suites and gives the developers access to the test lab for debugging purposes.

The complete last pass gives you a chance to yell "Stop!" before your employers embarrass themselves with a buggy release. Of the two complete passes, the last pass is the most important in terms of preventing test escapes. It is also the one most likely to receive short shrift as a result of resource redirection and project fatigue. I run a complete last pass even if management declares the final cycle formally complete. Because of the ramp-up time, you still have a chance to stop a bad release before it hits the customers.

In the middle of the road map, you can spread your test suites across the other test cycles. The high-priority test suites are run seven times in total, while the medium- and low-priority test suites are run five times. This arrangement comes fairly close to totally rerunning all of the test suites in every cycle, yet it is 14 days shorter.

Of course, this road map suffers from two obvious defects. The first is that it is simplified to make a point. In the real world, you won't have eight test suites that divide into three neat groups of four, two, and two, with each suite taking exactly half a day to run. Life never works out as neatly as this example. The second defect—more "cold water of reality"—is the absence of slack except at the end. On real projects, deliverables slip as a rule rather than as an exception. (At the risk of sounding inordinately cynical, I can't remember a single project in which most of the major deliverables into test didn't miss their target dates.) This road map won't handle those slips well. Instead, you should probably hide a day of slack in each cycle or at least insist on keeping the weekends. (Think of weekends as "hidden slack" that you can draw on if you have a motivated team.)

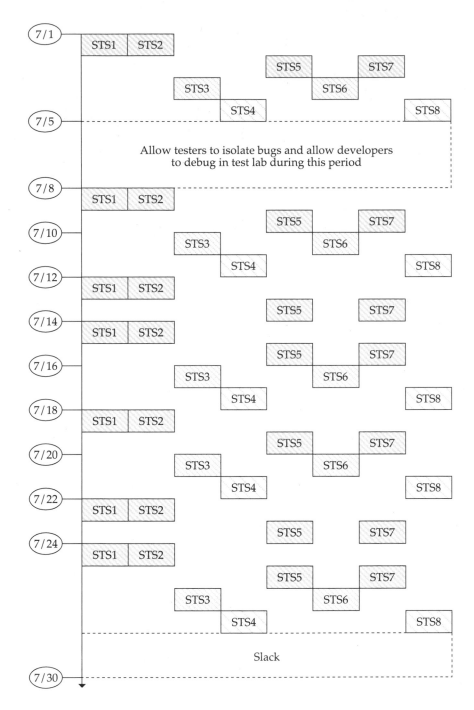

FIGURE 3-9   *A road map for test selection based on priority order.*

Dynamic prioritizing

The priority-order approach might have raised a question for you: how do you know in advance which test suites should have a high priority? You can guess, based on past experience, but the odds are pretty good that you will be proven partially or totally wrong. Suppose that you assign a high priority to DataRocket's thermal test (STS1) because an early engineering evaluation unit caught fire at one point. Also suppose that you assign a low priority to the USB, serial, and parallel port test (STS4) because development has found no problems in this area.

By the end of July 4, though, you discover that you have the priorities backward: the thermal test passes with headroom to spare, but the USB test is a target-rich environment. It turns out that the developers forgot to test the interaction of BIOS power management with USB hot plugging and hot unplugging, and the system crashes when you try this. Now, suddenly, STS4 is a high-priority suite, and STS1 is a low-priority suite.

You can handle this situation by conceding in advance that the priorities you come up with ahead of time won't mean much. With this concession, you simply plan to run four test suites, selected based on the priorities of the moment, during the second through ninth test cycles (with complete passes at the beginning and the end, as before). See Figure 3-10 on the following page for a road map of testing under this plan.

I'm not a big fan of this approach, although I know successful test managers who use it. It strikes me as dangerously close to an ad hoc, "figure it out as we go along" test methodology.[18] Maybe you can't foresee everything or assign the priorities perfectly, but refusing to plan leaves you totally crisis-driven. Caught up in the emergency *du jour*, you could easily reach the end of the test phase and find that you have spent all your time running fewer than half of your test suites. If you then run all the test suites in the last cycle (which you should) and find a slew of nasty bugs, you deliver a Hobson's choice to the project team: fix the bugs and slip the schedule, or ship the bugs and keep the schedule.

---

18. Chapter 5 discusses the use of weighted failures to estimate test suite priority. This method allows you to select the test suites that yield the most important bugs. For purposes of this discussion, I have assumed a visceral approach to test case importance, but you can apply a more rigorous technique to make this approach a lot less subjective and ad hoc.

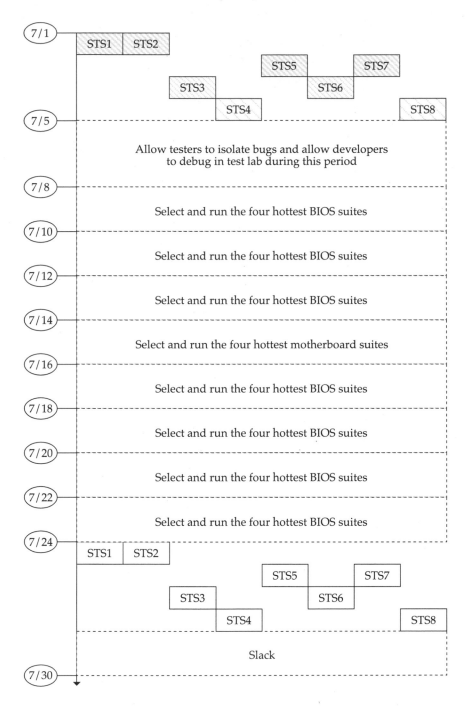

FIGURE 3-10 *A dynamically prioritized (crisis-driven) road map for test selection.*

Shotgunning

Suppose that you want to have a plan in place, to help impose some discipline, but you find the concept of selecting the priorities in advance laughable. In essence, you are considering all test suites equally important, and therefore you can simply distribute the suites randomly in test cycles 2 through 9. (Cycles 1 and 10 remain "total coverage" cycles, as always.) Figure 3-11 on the following page shows the road map for this scattering of test cases.

This shotgun approach is more robust than the others. Since you are decoupling your test suite selection from the specific test deliverables, a change in those deliverables doesn't affect your plan. What if the BIOS release doesn't show up on July 10? With the previous schedules, you might have wondered what to do next. With a shotgun road map, however, four test suites have not yet been run against the X2 BIOS release, so you can simply continue with your plan to run those tests.

Railroading

The shotgun approach looks clever on paper, but the premise may strike you as flawed. After all, if the test suites are equally important, why go to the trouble of randomizing their run order? You could just as easily use the test suite numbering—STS1 through STS8—as the sequence. In this case, the testing rolls on regardless of what's going on in the project. Figure 3-12 on page 99 shows a road map for this railroad approach.

Like the shotgun method, the railroad approach to test selection is resistant to slips in delivery dates. For example, if the X3 BIOS release arrives on July 11 instead of July 10, you needn't be concerned; you can just install the new BIOS on the test systems and run STS7 and STS8. If a deliverable slips by a long enough period, you can simply stop testing, having nothing further to test against the current revision. (In the real world, running out of things to test happens rarely indeed.)

Avoiding mistakes

Clearly, what you need to avoid is a situation in which you never get to run an entire set of tests—or in which you run the entire set only once, early on, and never return to them—because they keep getting preempted by new releases. This can happen if you run in test suite order, as in the railroad approach, but start over with the first test suite every time a new release shows up.

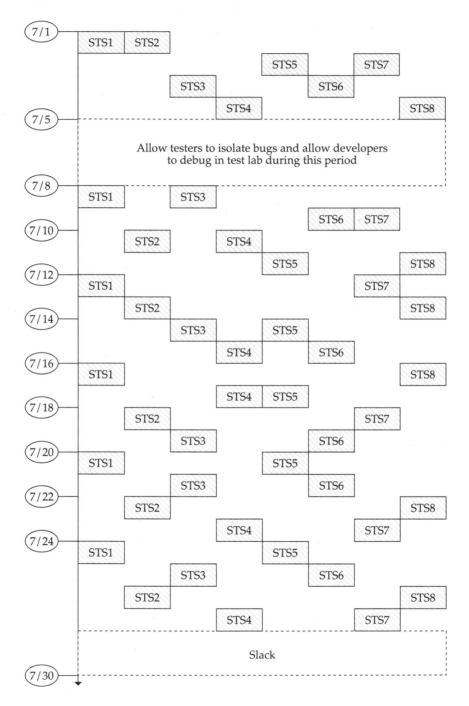

FIGURE 3-11   *A road map for test selection based on shotgunning.*

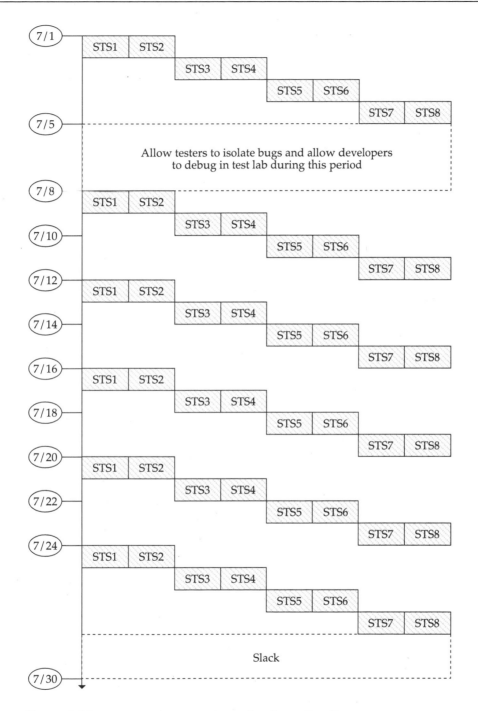

FIGURE 3-12   *A road map for test selection based on railroading.*

Figure 3-13 shows the result of this approach. Obviously, large test coverage gaps are created in the middle of the system test phase, while the test team repeats STS1 through STS4. The bill for this mistake comes due around July 27, when STS5 and STS6 are run for the first time in about 20 days. These tests, as well as STS7 and STS8, are likely to reveal significant problems that, because of the looming ship date, give management the pleasant choice of delaying the product or shipping known bugs. People will blame you for the situation, and rightly so.

Two additional points are key to good test selection. First, for every new release of software or hardware, be sure that your testers perform thorough *confirmation testing* against each bug that has allegedly been fixed in the release—and have them do this first. (Confirmation tests check for bugs related to the failure of a bug fix to address the reported issue fully, and they usually involve rerunning the test procedure and isolation steps, per the bug report.) The fixes are where the new and changed stuff lives. In software, for instance, bugs abound in new and changed code. The parts not changed, although perhaps not directly tested, at least have been subjected to incidental tests along the way. The new stuff is truly untested and unseen.

Second, take into account the inevitable ups and downs of the process. When your plan encounters reality, it should bend, not break. You should try to create robust plans that handle changes well, which is why I prefer the shotgun or the railroad approach when I have to choose. Be flexible, though, when your plan is forced to change, and remember that you can mix and match the test suite selection methods—for example, you can use the railroad approach and still preempt some of the test suites for others you feel are more important. Plans are good, but keep the goal in mind and be ready to adapt to changes as they happen. (Chapter 6 provides a tool to help you track and manage those changes effectively.)

"THERE'S A LESSON TO BE LEARNED HERE...": TEST CASE INCREMENTAL IMPROVEMENT

No matter how good a job you do on your first pass at developing test cases and suites, the test system will have holes. Budget and time pressures, along with human mistakes, will result in incomplete testing. Some test cases won't cover conditions they should, or some test suites won't include important test cases, or or the overall test system won't have all the test suites it needs.

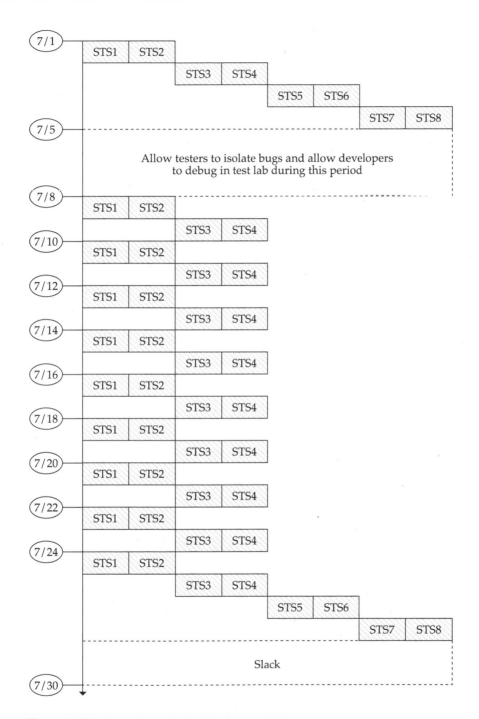

FIGURE 3-13 *A road map for bonehead test selection.*

In the case of most consumer software and hardware products, a few omissions won't prove fatal to the product, provided you are careful to test the critical features.[19] Nonetheless, you should attempt to improve your test system for each subsequent release. A few techniques for doing this involve responding to the failures in the shipping product, incorporating the practices of others into your test system, and using "error guessing" to explore for bugs.

RESPONDING TO FAILURES

One obvious way of enhancing a test system is to plug gaps that come to light when some poor customer is whacked in the forehead by a test escape. Of course, this doesn't mean that you or anyone else in your company will celebrate test escapes; you'd rather your customers were dazzled by your product's quality. But a bug found in the field is the perfect candidate for inclusion in the test system. You know that it's important to your customers, or to at least one of them, because they wouldn't bother to report it if it weren't. Assuming that development is fixing the problem, it's also important to your management. As an added bonus, the test case should be relatively easy to write: given a field report, you should have the steps to reproduce the bug and any ancillary test data at hand.

In addition to learning from your own test escapes, how about learning from someone else's? As the saying goes, any fool can learn from his (or her) own errors, but a wise person learns from the mistakes of others. Reading trade journals, keeping up on pertinent Internet newsgroups, and networking with your peers in the test profession and your niche of the computer business will allow you to learn from their blunders.

ADOPTING "BEST PRACTICES"

Beyond merely learning from others' mistakes, you also want to learn from their successes. I'm not suggesting industrial espionage, but rather research. For example, simply by reading this book you are learning new test techniques, even though the book is primarily about *managing* testing. Likewise,

---

19. The issue of test escapes takes on a different meaning when you are dealing with safety-critical systems such as traffic-light, medical, or power-plant control computers or with situations that involve people's privacy and security. This book is written for professionals who develop and test systems whose possible failure might infuriate the disappointed users but will not cause their demise or endangerment.

trade journals might print articles that evaluate your competitors' products, often including sidebars on "how we tested" that you can use to benchmark your own testing.

Training sessions, conferences, and seminars provide great opportunities to expand your test system as well as your skills. If you purchase test tools, you almost certainly have training options. Even if you believe that your team understands the use of a purchased tool, it might make sense for one person to attend the training session and bring back good ideas. Likewise, seminars are opportunities for "cross-pollinating" your test system with the best of your peers. Every presenter at a reputable conference or training session is an expert chosen by the organizers of the event to offer unique knowledge and skills.

Some practicing test professionals write off the academic world. It's true that research literature is not always practical. But today's research is tomorrow's state-of-the-art product or process. I try to read at least one or two advanced books every year as well as pertinent articles in the monthly *Journal of the Association for Computing Machinery*.

Using Ad Hoc Testing

I approach the topic of ad hoc testing (also called ad lib testing) as I would approach a South Texas rattlesnake. I worry that if I say anything good about ad hoc testing, some poor reader will assume that I am giving my blessing to "guided exploratory testing" as a primary technique.[20] Just so there's no confusion: in my opinion, testing without written test cases and documented expected results has a lot in common with the Hispanic party tradition of letting blindfolded children pummel a hanging piñata with a stick to get at the candy inside. Would you bet your job and the quality of your company's product on this methodology?

That uncharitable diatribe vented, I must admit that ad hoc testing has its place. Some people have a knack for rooting out errors, like a pig after truffles. Glenford Myers, in *The Art of Software Testing*, refers to this process as "error guessing." This might sound like a precise technique, but Myers admits that no technique exists—it's simply intuition.

---

20. Some organizations that use ad hoc testing like to apply scientific-sounding labels such as "guided exploratory testing." These labels obfuscate the fact that their testing process boils down to playing with the product to see what it does.

Your challenge as a test manager is to convince these intrepid ad hoc testers to write down their brilliant ideas. Many of these testers tend to have a problem understanding the value of documentation. You, however, know when they've come up with a particularly good test: they find a bug. Since you will be capturing defect data in your bug tracking database, you should ensure that any problems found during ad hoc testing turn into a documented test case.

YOU CAN'T DO IT ALL: DECIDING WHAT NOT TO DO

As a final note on test cases, let me revisit a point made in earlier chapters: as much as it will pain you to do so, you must make choices about what you will and will not test. With luck, you can get others to help you make those choices, thereby making your life easier and providing you with some political cover at the same time. (External support for your test goals, and the management backing it brings, is something you can't have too much of.)

Nonetheless, at times you will have to make tough decisions. Eventually someone will ask you whether, in your professional judgment, a feature needs to be tested. What they are asking you is a question about bug coverage: "Do you think we will find critical bugs in this if we test it?"

There is no magical heuristic that will prevent you from making the wrong decisions. Hard choices are hard because no solution is obvious and the stakes are high. When faced with these kinds of choices, approach them with an open mind. Question your assumptions about what "has" to be tested. Why do you feel that way? Trust your gut, but confirm your intuition. Then talk it over. Ask your test team what they feel is essential, and why. Consult peers and colleagues. Quiz your development associates on the project. Review any pertinent references in books and articles.

After going through the exploratory process with an open mind, make your decision. Document what you intend to keep and what you intend to drop. Be prepared to answer why. When you feel confident in your decision, communicate it. And be prepared to start all over again if need be.

4

Your Exciting Career in Entomology: The Bug Tracking Database

You now have a thorough test program put together. Time to relax, exchange the quadruple espressos for a few nice cold Warsteiners, and coast, right? After all, the only work that remains is executing the test plan, and surely your test technicians, with a little guidance from the test engineers, can handle that.

Definitely not. Your job as test manager remains as important as ever when you move into the stage of implementing the test plan and gathering data related to that plan.

Once test execution begins, even the most organized approach will not save you from the excitement of the project going on around you. A test plan, test cases, test tools, test architecture, measures of test coverage, and all the other program components you've developed are proactive and, when completed, relatively static objects.[1] Welcome now to the world of the reactive and the dynamic. Following a test plan diligently and using a test system properly but flexibly require continual adjustments in your priorities, meticulous attention to details both clear and subtle, and adaptation to the endless changes in the project.

You will soon find yourself awash in the data generated by your shiny new test system. This is good, for the most part. Testing is about risk management, and you can't manage risk without data. Raw test data, however, tends toward the amorphous, the confusing, and the hard to categorize.

Worse yet, remember all those commitments people made in terms of entry criteria, system delivery dates, acceptable turnaround times for test results, and so forth? Be prepared for otherwise honest and upstanding citizens to go back on their word shamelessly. This is not because they are out to get you. Eagles and sharks live at the end of the food chain, and every toxin that trickles into the ecosystem ends up sickening or killing the hapless predators disproportionately. Likewise, testing is at the end of the development schedule, and every failure, delay, and slip-up can manifest itself in the test process, concentrated along the way into a noxious slime of confusion and missed dates that can make you very ill indeed.

Clearly, you need a way to track, analyze, and present what's going on in your once-peaceful test domain. The following three chapters provide some tools and techniques that will keep you on top of the test results and help you minimize the damage from the inevitable bombshells.

As a start, this chapter introduces a tool that supports a critical and visible role played by test organizations: the documenting and tracking of product defects. The job of documenting and tracking defects is critical because, if it is done right, the bugs you find will be fixed, making test a direct contributor to increased product quality. Because bug reports provide tangible evidence of quality problems, they are visible not only to developers but often all the way up to the executive level. I have used a variety of bug tracking systems and have seen the task done well and not so well by clients, vendors, and test labs. The approach outlined here handles the nec-

---

1. This is not to say that a test system should not change. But major improvement of a test system is a matter of incorporating the lessons of a project into the system deliberately, generally at the end of the project.

essary tasks, is easy to implement, and provides information appropriate to all levels of an organization.[2]

WHY BOTHER?
THE CASE FOR A FORMAL BUG TRACKING SYSTEM

Perhaps you don't see the value in having a bug management system. You might be thinking, "Spending all that time and effort documenting bugs is too much hassle, especially with the developers right across the hall." It's true that creating, evolving, and using a bug tracking database take significant effort and discipline. But don't skip this chapter yet. I think you'll find that a systematic approach to bug tracking provides some important benefits:

◆ A bug tracking database facilitates clear communication about defects. Well-written, standardized reports tell the story much better than free-form e-mails or shouts across a hallway or to the next cubicle.

◆ Using a database allows automatic, sequential bug numbering (a useful way to keep track of and refer to bugs), and it provides a number of analysis and reporting options that are not available with a flat file. If you have never looked into the various kinds of product and process metrics that can be derived from defect information, be ready to be surprised.

◆ A bug tracking database allows the development team to fix problems based on relative and absolute importance to the project. With a more informal approach, the tester who has the best rapport with the most developers is often the one whose bugs get fixed.

◆ You can manage bugs throughout their life cycle, from the initial report to the final resolution. This ensures that bugs don't fall through the cracks, and it keeps attention focused on the important bugs that need to be fixed as quickly as possible.

---

2. For other ideas on bug tracking databases, see Chapters 5 and 6 of *Testing Computer Software,* by Cem Kaner, Jack Falk, and Hung Quoc Nguyen. I don't agree with everything these authors say, but they make some excellent points about writing good bug reports and managing bugs.

◆ As bugs progress through their life cycle, developers, testers, and managers learn new information. A well-designed bug tracking database allows you to capture this history and then refer to it later when you are looking at the status of the bugs.

◆ Every bug report that is closed in your database is a defect that might otherwise be included in a shipping product, causing support calls, bad reviews, and lost sales. Every bug report that is not closed when the product ships provides technical support with useful advance warning and proves that your testers found the bug in the event that it crops up in the field.

The following sections present a bug tracking database system that realizes these benefits. (This database complies with IEEE standard 829–1983 in terms of content, although its format differs considerably from that shown in the standard.)

So What Seems to Be the Problem? The Failure Description

The heart of any bug tracking and reporting system is the *failure description,* the part of a bug report that captures the report author's account of the problem. It is the basic message of the bug report. The failure description is the tester's first and best opportunity to communicate clearly with the development team about a problem. Done properly, it captures in simple prose the essentials of the bug. Done poorly, it obfuscates the bug and misleads the reader.

How do you write a good failure description? Let's start with an adroitly executed example. Figure 4-1 shows the failure description for a nasty bug in the SpeedyWriter product. The failure description contains three basic sections: summary, steps to reproduce, and isolation.

The *summary* is a one- or two-sentence description of the bug, emphasizing its impact on the customer or the system user. The summary tells managers, developers, and other readers why they should care about the problem. The sentence *I had trouble with screen resolutions* is a lousy summary; the sentence *Setting screen resolution to 800 by 1024 renders the screen unreadable* is much better. A succinct, hard-hitting summary hooks the reader and puts a label on the bug report. Consider it your one chance to make a first impression.

FIGURE 4-1 *A good bug report.*

The *steps to reproduce* provide a precise description of how to repeat the failure. For most bugs, you can write down a sequence of steps that re-create the problem. Be concise yet complete, unambiguous, and accurate. This information is critical for developers, who use your report as a guide to duplicate the problem as a first step to debugging it. Developers sometimes complain bitterly about bad bug reports, and their complaints almost always include poor quality of the steps to reproduce.

Reproducibility varies considerably; it is absolute only for some simple functional bugs. When repeating a test case three times reproduces the identical (incorrect) behavior three times, the bug is certainly reproducible. Nevertheless, the possibility remains that the next run of the test case will produce a different symptom or perhaps no failure whatever. Moving to a different environment—from the test lab to the development lab, for example—often affects reproducibility,[3] as can seemingly unrelated version changes. Thus it's important for the author of the bug report to verify reproducibility. Good bug reports include statements such as *I tried the above steps four times and observed the error three times.*

---

3. Chapter 7 discusses the use of a test lab to provide a controlled test environment.

Isolation refers to the results and information the tester gathered to confirm that the bug is a real problem and to identify those factors that affect the bug's manifestation. What variations or permutations did the tester try in order to influence the behavior? For example, if the problem involves reading the CD-ROM drive on DataRocket, what happens when it is set to a different SCSI ID? Did the tester check the SCSI termination? If Speedy-Writer can't print to a laser printer, can it print to an inkjet? Good isolation draws a bounding box around a bug. Documenting the isolation will assure the developers that the tester isn't simply tossing an anomaly over the wall but is instead reporting a well-characterized problem.

MORE LIKE HEMINGWAY THAN FAULKNER

Ernest Hemingway and William Faulkner allegedly hated each other. Like their personalities, their prose differs dramatically. Hemingway created a muscular style of fiction writing that used short sentences, focused on actions, and spelled out events clearly and sequentially. Faulkner, conversely, wrote long sentences, made the prose the point as much as the story, used metaphors, and changed points of view. About the only common ground they shared was a love of alcohol.

Had he tried his hand at computer testing, I suspect that Hemingway would have written great bug reports. I doubt that Faulkner would have. It's not simply a matter of style, though. Even if you write like Hemingway, it takes concentration, practice, and discipline to describe bugs well. Over the years, I have read literally hundreds of bug reports that had significant problems.

How can you write better descriptions? Most important, remember that good bug reporting starts with good testing. Testers who have an ad hoc, disorganized approach to testing tend to write rambling, confusing bug reports. Testers who follow a sequence of test steps carefully, take detailed notes, and isolate bugs using a methodical process tend to write concise, clear bug reports.

On a similar note, bug reports should be written concurrent with or immediately following testing. A tester who runs many tests, takes notes on various bugs that arise, and then waits to write reports until a dozen or so problems have piled up not only endangers the overall schedule—delaying the day the bugs are reported delays the day the bugs are fixed—but also tends to write poor reports. The tester is likely to forget pertinent details and might also lose access to the test configuration needed to repeat the test. If the test must then be rerun to gather more information on the bug, you're out of luck.

When it comes to writing a report, make sure that it's accurate, complete, and concise. A report that gets major details wrong is embarrassing at best. A report that omits important information is misleading. A report that takes four hundred words to describe a bug won't be read. After the report is written, invest a little extra time and effort in a review. As the test manager, you can either review all the reports yourself or use a peer review process. Peer review works well when everyone on the test team agrees about how reports should be written. If you're having consistency problems, though, you might want to do all the reviewing yourself.

Finally, good bug reports tell the reader what the tester found, not what the tester did. Some organizations do use a "test report" approach, documenting every step taken, every behavior observed. There's a place for this level of detail, but it's the test case description itself, not the bug report. When I write reports, I document the minimal number of reproduction steps, and I include only isolation information that yielded an interesting data point. If I run one test and see two independent bugs, I write two reports.

Figures 4-2 and 4-3 on the following page show two other versions of the failure description from Figure 4-1. The report in Figure 4-2 is vague and incomplete, with a misleading summary, missing steps, and no isolation. The report in Figure 4-3 suffers from "written diarrhea," with a rambling summary, extraneous steps, and information on isolation that doesn't help the reader understand the bug.

FIGURE 4-2   *A vague and incomplete bug report.*

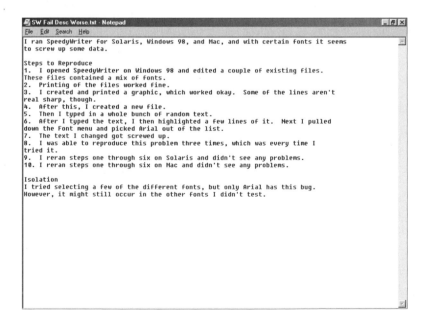

FIGURE 4-3   *A verbose and confusing bug report.*

Drawing a Line in the Sand: The Boundary Between Isolation and Debugging

Since we're on the topic, let's take a quick detour to discuss the important difference between isolation and debugging. The responsibilities of the test organization and the developers meet at this boundary. For that reason, the sharpness of the line you draw here has a lot to do with the control you have over your scarce test resources.

Any time a tester finds a potential bug—what some test experts call an anomaly—that event sets in motion a sequence of questions that move toward resolving the problem:

1. What is the exact and minimal sequence of steps required to reproduce the symptoms of the bug? How often do these steps successfully reproduce these symptoms?

2. Does the failure indicate a test bug or a system bug? In other words, does the anomalous result originate from a test artifact or a tester error, or from system misbehavior that could affect customers?

3. What external factors influence the symptoms? In the Speedy-Writer example, one way the tester looked for influential factors was by trying different fonts.

4. What is the root cause of the problem, in the code, the electronics, the network, or the environment? Root causes are internal factors.

5. How can the problem be repaired without introducing new problems?

6. Are the changes properly debugged and the unit tested?

7. Is the problem fixed? Does it now pass the same test it failed before, and does the rest of the system still behave properly?

Step 1 proves that the bug is not a fluke and refines the experiment. Steps 2 and 3 isolate the bug. Steps 4, 5, and 6 are debugging tasks. Step 7 involves confirmation and regression testing. In moving through these steps, the bug moves through and out of test (steps 1, 2, and 3), into development (steps 4, 5, and 6), and then back into test (step 7). While this flow of responsibility might seem straightforward and obvious, defining and consistently observing it, especially the boundary between steps 3 and 4, can involve a significant amount of rigor, discipline, and willpower.

In the excitement and pressure of test execution, the first four steps can get mixed up. Testers sometimes fail to characterize and isolate bugs completely, which results in uncertainty about the reproducibility, veracity, and nature of the bugs. The developers—quite correctly—then interrogate the testers as part of debugging work. The testers, who have plenty of other work on their plate, are sucked into debugging, which is a development responsibility. The developers are forced to ask the testers a lot of central questions that the testers should have answered when they wrote their reports. In short, person-hours, the most precious resource on a development project, are squandered. To me, that's unacceptable.

When you review bug reports, or when you have your staff review one another's reports, be sure that the answers to the questions in steps 1, 2, and 3 are crystal clear. This way, you can draw the line between isolation and debugging distinctly and keep your testers focused on testing.

It is true, however, that test must sometimes assist development in debugging activities, especially when test has unique hardware items tied up in the test network, when the test system—tools, scripts, and environment—requires special expertise to operate and is essential to reproducing the bug, or when a bug, for whatever reason, proves unreproducible in the development lab. Nine times out of ten, though, one or more test staff members become involved in debugging for a dysfunctional reason: because the test manager didn't adequately communicate the difference between isolation and debugging, because the tester wrote a poor report, because the developer wouldn't accept the report as complete even though it was, or because the tester found it more interesting to work with the developer on debugging than to move on to other testing. You must either limit the extent to which this happens or accept the significant drain it will impose on your resources.

FLEXIBLE REPORTING: BEGINNING TO CONSTRUCT A DATABASE

You could implement every piece of advice in the previous section in a bug reporting system that relies on e-mail or a flat file. I have seen projects that used Microsoft Excel spreadsheets or Microsoft Word files to track bugs, but the reporting options were sparse, limited to little more than a printout of the worksheet or document.[4] To store, manipulate, search, analyze, and report large volumes of data flexibly, you need a database.

This section explains how to establish a bug tracking database using what we've discussed so far. Later sections of this chapter build on this foundation to enhance the database's capabilities. I used Microsoft Access 97 for the database shown here, but you can use Paradox, FileMaker, Oracle, or any other relational database application.

Minimally, such a bug tracking database stores failure descriptions—summary, steps to reproduce, and isolation—together with identifying information such as a sequential ID number, the project name, the author of the report, and the date the report was filed. Figure 4-4 shows the design view of an Access table (*tblBugs*) that stores this basic information. I've used the memo data type in Access for the *Steps to Reproduce* and *Isolation* fields

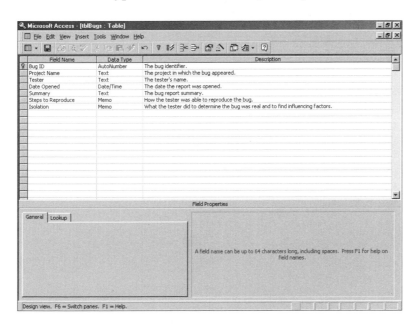

FIGURE 4-4   *The basic table for a bug tracking database.*

---

4. With Excel worksheets, you can summarize data and produce the metrics and charts discussed later in this chapter, but the text capabilities are limited. Word files have good text capabilities, but extracting metrics from them requires the use of pattern scanning tools. A database program such as Microsoft Access combines the strengths of both spreadsheet and word processing applications.

because entries in these fields can be rather long. If you want to restrict these entries to a particular size to prevent excessive verbiage, you can use a text field rather than a memo field. The *Bug ID* identifier is a sequential number assigned by the AutoNumber feature in Access. The *Date Opened* field uses the standard Access date/time data type, formatted as a short date because you don't need to capture the specific time when the bug report was filed.

Because entering text directly into an Access table is cumbersome, you can set up a form for entering bug reports. I used the Access 97 Form Wizard to create the bug entry form shown in Figure 4-5 and then entered the SpeedyWriter bug report you saw earlier in Figure 4-1.

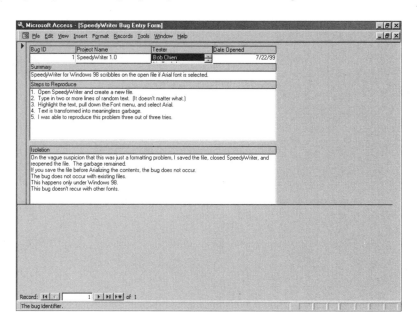

FIGURE 4-5   *A bug report in the SpeedyWriter bug tracking database, using a bug entry form.*

Once you've put a bug report into your database, you'll probably want to get it out at some point. I used the Access 97 Report Wizard (with a few design adjustments) to create two reports in about five minutes. The simplest is the bug detail report, which prints all the information about the bug; Figure 4-6 provides an example. A more compact report for management reference has the summary stand by itself, as shown in the bug summary report in Figure 4-7.

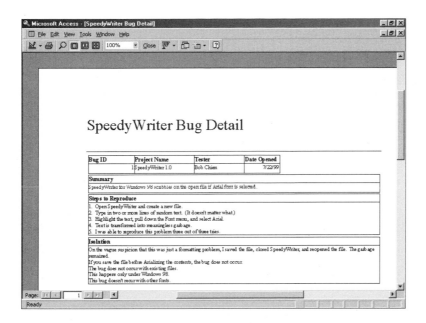

FIGURE 4-6   *A bug detail report.*

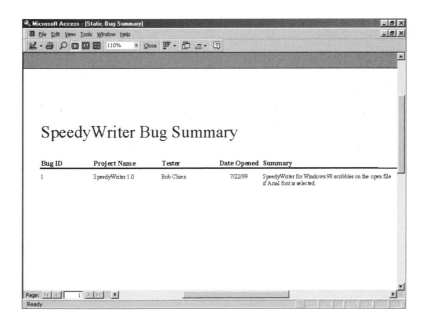

FIGURE 4-7   *A bug summary report.*

The Vital Few and the Trivial Many: Ranking Importance

This database can capture details about bugs found by test, but it suffers from what you could call a "parts is parts" problem because it doesn't yet contain a mechanism that allows you to assign levels of importance to bugs. To solve this problem, you can add two metrics of importance—severity and priority—and then aggregate them to create a third, compound, metric.

Severity

By *severity*, I mean the absolute impact of a bug on the system under test, regardless of the likelihood of occurrence under end user conditions. You can assign the problem a severity number from the following list:

1   Data loss, hardware damage, or a safety-related failure
2   Loss of functionality without any reasonable workaround
3   Loss of data or functionality with a reasonable workaround[5]
4   Partial loss of a function or a feature set
5   A cosmetic error

Priority

A measure of *priority* captures the elements of importance not considered in severity, such as the likelihood of occurrence in actual customer use and the subsequent impact on the target customer. When determining priority, you can also consider whether this kind of bug is prohibited by regulation or agreement, what kinds of customers are affected, and the cost to the company if the affected customers take their business elsewhere because of the bug. Based on the pertinent factors, you can assign a priority number as follows:

1   Highest priority. The system is practically unusable with this bug.
2   High priority. The bug will have a serious impact on the company's ability to sell and maintain this system.

---

5. The reasonableness (or lack thereof) of the workaround is important. As a wag once wrote in an Internet newsgroup, "There are perfectly good technical reasons why it is sometimes necessary to sacrifice a young goat to ensure proper SCSI chain termination." No good tester should consider this a reasonable workaround—nor would the goat!

3   Medium priority. The company will lose some money if this bug is in the system, but it might be more important to meet the schedule. Fix after release if it is not fixed before.

4   Low priority. Don't delay the release, but do fix this problem afterward.

5   Lowest priority. Fix as time and resources allow.

CAPTURING IMPORTANCE IN RISK PRIORITY NUMBERS

Priority and severity are not completely orthogonal, but it is possible to have low-priority, high-severity bugs, and vice versa. If DataRocket, for example, doesn't pass the Microsoft Windows NT certification test, the product's advertising, promotional materials, and sales pitches can't use the "Designed for Microsoft Windows NT" logo. This can be the kiss of death for a computer system since logos are often checklist items for corporate purchasers. Even if the bug that crops up in the Windows NT certification test is entirely cosmetic—a severity 5—it is a priority 1 bug if it blocks certification.

Conversely, suppose that to re-create SpeedyWriter's hypothetical bug the tester had to type one line of Arial text, followed by one line in a symbol font and then another line of Arial. The problem is a severity 1 bug because data is lost. But what are the odds of a user typing exactly three lines of text, formatting the first as Arial, the second as symbols, and the third as Arial without saving at any point in the process? Despite its severity rating, I would assign this bug a priority of 4 or 5.

What you need is a single number that captures the overall importance of a bug. We created a similar number in Chapter 1 as part of the FMEA approach to ranking quality risks: in FMEA, you multiply severity by priority by detection to create a risk priority number. For purposes of the bug tracking database, you can ignore the detection factor (since test has already detected the bug) and simply multiply severity by priority to calculate a risk priority number (RPN) for the bug. Using this approach, the RPN can range from 1 (an extremely dangerous bug) to 25 (a completely trivial bug).

ADDING MEASURES OF IMPORTANCE TO THE DATABASE

The database modifications associated with adding measures of importance are straightforward. In the initial Access table, you can add three fields: *Severity*, *Priority*, and *Risk Priority Number*. I use numeric fields of the "byte" type, not so much to save space as to emphasize the appropriate range.

Next you should make the corresponding changes in the bug entry form, adding the three fields and then automating the calculation of the risk priority number. (The automation of the calculation can be tricky, depending on your expertise with the database package you're using. Since this is a book on testing, not on programming in Visual Basic for Applications, I've omitted the details of exactly how it's done in Access, but you can look at the sample database on this book's companion CD for examples.) The expanded bug entry form appears in Figure 4-8.

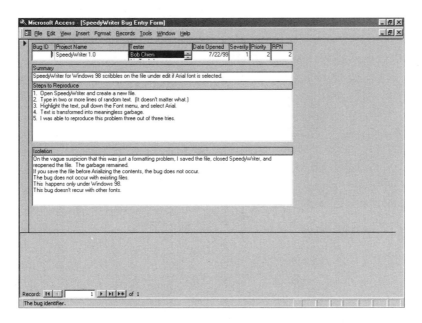

FIGURE 4-8 *A bug entry form with importance information.*

To include the measures of importance in the two reports, simply insert the appropriate fields. Of course, if you include these fields in your table from the beginning, the Report Wizard can pick them up automatically. Figure 4-9 shows an example of one of the new reports. Note that including measures of importance in the summary report helps you communicate results more effectively to management (a topic discussed in detail in Chapter 9).

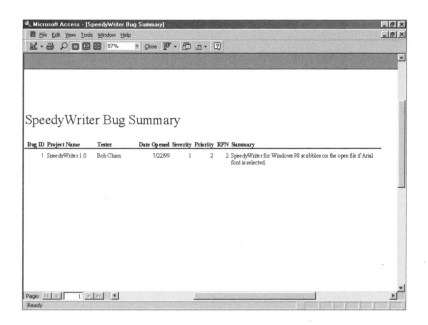

FIGURE 4-9   *A bug summary report with importance information.*

PUTTING THE TRACKING IN BUG TRACKING: ADDING DYNAMIC INFORMATION

So far you have a database that is fine for *reporting* bugs but not for *tracking* them. It still lacks a way to include dynamic information, a mechanism to trace the steps through which a bug must move on its way to resolution. Having this information available would allow you to answer questions such as these: Who is currently responsible for pushing the bug toward closure? Is the resolution process "stuck" or moving forward smoothly? When will the bug be fixed?

USING STATES TO MANAGE BUG LIFE CYCLES

The aim of reporting problems is to bring them to the attention of the appropriate people, who will then cause the most important bugs to be fixed—or will at least attempt to have them fixed. The test organization then must either confirm or rebut the possible fixes. Other possible outcomes for a particular bug report include its cancellation as a nonproblem, its closure as redundant, or its indefinite dormancy because of a lack of interest. In other words, a bug (represented at times by the bug report) goes through various states during its life cycle:

◆ *Review.* When a tester enters a new bug report in the bug tracking database, the test manager should submit it for review before it becomes active. This review can be conducted either by the test manager or by a peer, depending on the prevailing level of quality in the bug reports. (Often not only testers but also developers and other development team members report bugs.)

◆ *Rejected.* If the reviewer decides that a report needs significant rework—either more research and information or improved wording—the reviewer rejects the report. This effectively sends the report back to the tester, who can correct its deficiencies and then resubmit it.

◆ *Open.* If the tester has fully characterized and isolated the problem, the reviewer opens the report, making it visible to the world as a real bug.

◆ *Assigned.* When the development organization accepts the problem as fully characterized and isolated, the test manager assigns it to the appropriate development manager, who in turn assigns the bug to a developer.

◆ *Test.* Once development provides a fix for the problem, it enters a test state. The bug fix comes to the test organization for confirmation testing (which ensures that the prospective fix completely resolves the bug as reported) and regression testing (which addresses the question of whether the fix has introduced new problems as a side effect).

◆ *Reopened.* If the fix fails confirmation testing, the tester reopens the bug report. If the fix passes confirmation testing but fails regression testing, the tester enters a new bug report.

◆ *Closed.* If the fix passes confirmation testing, the tester closes the bug report.

◆ *Deferred.* If everyone agrees that the problem is real but project management chooses either to assign a low priority to the bug or to schedule the fix for a subsequent release, the bug is deferred. Note that a bug can be deferred at any point in its life cycle.

Figure 4-10 shows these states and the flows between them.

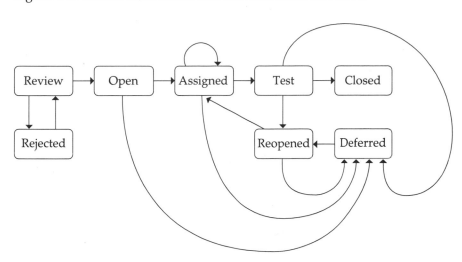

FIGURE 4-10 *Bug states and transitions.*

EMPHASIZING OWNERSHIP AND ACCOUNTABILITY

While the state of a bug gives hints about what needs to happen next, tracking the assigned "owner" of a bug as well as the intended fix date provides a rudder to keep the process sailing toward a conclusion. Emphasizing personal ownership of a problem and requesting an estimated fix date serve to cement commitments and support accountability.[6] In addition, a bug sometimes blocks forward progress on a test suite, and having some idea of its fix date allows you to plan the resumption of testing.

As the state diagram in Figure 4-10 shows, bugs can be reassigned, and such changes often shift the estimated fix date. If this is a problem in your organization, you can institute an assignment history, similar to (or part of) the status log discussed in the next section. (I haven't had that much trouble with "bouncing ball" bug reports, however, so I normally don't track at this level of detail.)

You should track not only developer ownership but also tester ownership. When a bug returns to the test organization, immediately assign a tester

---

6. Developers operate on this same assumption. Getting estimated fix dates on any but the most straightforward bugs usually requires support from the development manager, who should also enforce the dates.

to perform the confirmation and regression tests. As soon as the fix arrives in the next build or product revision, the tester verifies the fix and then closes or reopens the bug (or opens a new bug if the regression test indicates that the developer has broken something new in the course of attempting the fix). This use of ownership in the test organization ensures that fixes are tested expeditiously.

Don't Know Much About (Bug) History? Tracking Status Changes

Keeping a status log for bugs allows testers, developers, and managers to make a notation each time a bug goes through a state change. After a bug is assigned, for example, you can note to whom it was assigned, when, and under what circumstances. When the fix comes back, you might enter the comment that development believes the problem is resolved. But don't feel compelled to make a log of everything. The status entry *7/16: Muhammad assigned the bug to John* is useful; the entry *7/17: Had a five-minute discussion in the lunchroom with John about how the bug manifests itself* is not. The status log should capture significant events in the life cycle of the bug, not serve as a diary.

Putting the Dynamic Fields in Place

You can easily add all this dynamic information to your bug tracking database. You'll need to add four fields to the table and the form: *State*, *Owner*, *Estimated Fix*, and *Status*. *State* and *Owner* are text fields, with the entry selected from a list box. *Estimated Fix* (which records the intended fix date) uses a standard Access date/time data type, formatted as a short date. It's probably most useful to define *Status* as a memo field, although you can, for reasons of space, use a text field. (You could also use an external table linked through a foreign key with a separate row for each entry. Implementing such a database, however, involves Visual Basic for Applications programming, which is beyond the scope of this book.)

Figure 4-11 shows the bug entry form with the four new fields; Figure 4-12 shows the updated version of the bug detail report. I include all four of these fields in all my reports, including the bug summary report. Doing so crowds the detail report a bit, but it's worth it because I use that report as a management tool and the addition of these fields makes the report even more valuable.

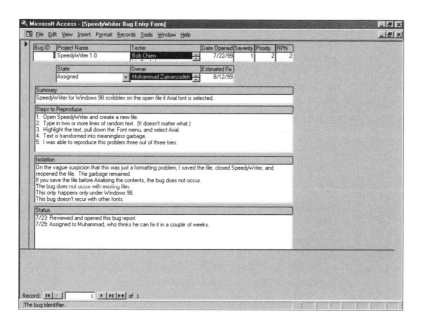

FIGURE 4-11   *A bug entry form with dynamic information.*

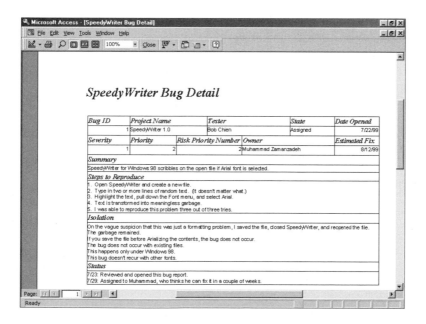

FIGURE 4-12   *A bug detail report with dynamic information.*

Finishing Touches: Focusing on the Bugs

You now have a fully adequate bug tracking database that you can use to manage bugs through their entire life cycle, to produce summary reports for management and detail reports for developers, and to keep track of who is responsible for moving bugs forward. You may want to design additional reports or make some cosmetic changes, but the database is essentially complete.

To bring bugs into sharper focus, however, I recommend that you add five more fields to the database. By using a *Subsystem* field, you can identify which areas of the system suffer from the most bugs. Including a *Configuration* field allows you to identify the setting in which a bug occurs. Adding *Close Date*, *Resolution*, and *Root Cause* fields gives you access to powerful information about why bugs happen.

Subsystem

The *Subsystem* field captures which component of the system bears the brunt of the problems caused by the current bug. In our DataRocket case study, for instance, subsystems might break down as follows:

- *Mainboard.* The CPU, the motherboard, the memory, the on-board fans, and common built-in controllers for the USB, parallel, serial, mouse, and keyboard ports.

- *Video.* The video card and, if bundled, the video cable and monitor.

- *SCSI.* The SCSI adapter, the internal cables, the external cables, the RAID hardware, the tape drive, the CD-ROM drive, and the Jaz drive.

- *Network.* The controller configuration, which can involve one or more cards.

- *Telecommunications.* The optional bundled modem(s), the ISDN terminal adapter, or the computer-telephony-integration hardware.

- *Other hardware.* The case, the power supply, the mouse, and the keyboard.

- *BIOS.* The features controlled by the BIOS, especially power management and bootup passwords.

- *Other software.* Any custom drivers, such as bundled custom network drivers, as well as any preinstalled network operating systems that might ship on the system.

For SpeedyWriter, you might choose to decompose the subsystems in this fashion:

- *User interface.* The behavior of the graphical user interface, including video, mouse, and keyboard aspects, such as screen painting, print previews, windowing behavior, and all command selection sequences.

- *Tools.* The ability to check spelling, use a thesaurus, track revisions, create tables, display graphs, insert files and other objects, draw pictures and so forth.

- *File.* Create, open, save/save as, and export and import features.

- *Edit engine.* Features such as formatting, editing, font selection, footnotes/endnotes, and so on.

- *Install/config.* The installation, configuration, reconfiguration, and upgrade processes.

- *Docs/packaging.* The documentation, help files, or packaging.

In addition to system-dependent components, you might include three catchall subsystems to deal with exceptional situations:

- *Other.* The bug affects a particular subsystem but not one that is listed.

- *Unknown.* The bug doesn't appear to have anything to do with any subsystem.

- *N/A.* No subsystem applies.

Usually a small fraction—2 or 3 percent—of the total bugs will fit into each of these three categories. If the number is larger, the Other category is probably picking up too many bugs that should have their own subsystem category.

As you've probably noticed, the division of a system into subsystems is arbitrary. In some cases, especially projects in which different teams work on each subsystem, the task is easier. Regardless, you need to establish a subsystem breakdown that is meaningful for each project because you can't categorize if everyone decides for themselves what subsystems exist in the system under test.

CONFIGURATION

Virtually no test effort (with the exception of acceptance testing) involves a single release of software or hardware running in a single hardware and software environment. Projects usually encompass multiple pieces of software and hardware, most of which go through at least a few revision changes during testing. Capturing configuration information in the bug tracking database can help you understand the setting in which failures occur.

Most often you'll want to employ multiple configuration fields. These frequently parallel the subsystem values, but it's seldom a complete overlap. For example, with DataRocket you might track the BIOS revision, the mainboard revision, the case version, and the bundled software version.

Alternatively, you can use a lookup table approach. For SpeedyWriter, you might use a combination of letters and numbers to indicate software revisions and the test environment. Suppose that the SpeedyWriter internal revisions are identified in $X.YY.ZZ$ format, such as 0.01.19. The systems in the test lab are labeled A, B, C, and D; the three networks (Novell Netware, Sun Solaris, and Microsoft Windows NT) are assigned the identifiers X, Y, and Z, respectively. A test configuration of an NT workstation connected to a Solaris server with the second major and thirty-third minor revision might thus be designated A.Y.0.2.33. Of course, you must be careful to record details about how to decode or "read" these designations; such a sequence of letters and numbers doesn't exactly explain itself.

CLOSE DATE AND RESOLUTION

The first closure detail is the date on which the bug report entered a closed or deferred state. Entering this date in the *Close Date* field is more than simply tidying up your records; you'll see how this piece of information comes into its own later in this chapter, when we discuss extracting metrics from your database.

Adding the *Resolution* field allows you to enter a short comment on how the problem was solved. (Alternatively, you could use the *Status* field for this purpose, but a separate field is more useful for reports.) You can also force completion of this field using Visual Basic for Applications or whatever automation tools your database environment provides. Any time a bug is closed, some notation should be made.

Root Cause

If you are the first test manager your company has ever had, with no exposure to root cause analysis, and your development process consists of hacking and flailing away until the product appears to work, you should probably read this section as information only. Doing root cause analysis is not a trivial undertaking. Furthermore, it requires the assistance of the developers and the support of management.

Simply put, a root cause is the underlying reason for a bug. When you are doing behavioral (black-box) testing, a bug makes its presence known through an observed behavior, a symptom, an anomalous output, data transformation, slow response time, a system crash, an inexplicable delay, or some other visible program transgression.[7] When a tester observes a bug, what the tester sees is only the symptom. Taking cough medicine to stop hacking or aspirin to lower a fever doesn't cure a cold because it doesn't address the root cause, the virus that is making you sick.

Some test experts model the connection between root causes and bugs with the sequence of events shown in Figure 4-13 on the following page. An anomaly occurs when a tester observes an unexpected behavior. If the tester's actions were correct, this anomaly indicates either a system failure or a test failure. The failure arises from a fault in either the system or the test. The fault comes from an error committed by a developer or a test engineer (while creating the test system). That error is the root cause.

This model illustrates the connection between bugs and their root causes in an elegant way, but it suffers from some flaws. First, errors, faults, and failures don't have one-to-one relationships. The trickiest bugs—stability problems, for example—often arise from complex interactions of components, any one of which is not necessarily an error. Next, the conditional language points out that while many events may, could, or might transpire, sometimes nothing happens at all. Errors don't always cause faults, faults occasionally remain hidden in programs, and failures aren't always observed.

---

7. During structural (white-box) testing, you can observe bugs that don't involve program outputs or behaviors because you have access to internal program states and other information that tells you whether something has gone awry.

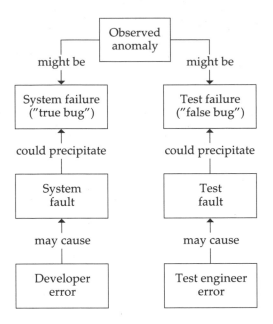

FIGURE 4-13   *A model of the connection between bugs and their root causes.*

So the model has limitations, but it does create a useful mental picture. That intellectual image—dare I use the word "paradigm"?—can help you think about root causes.

Usually the aim of performing a root cause analysis isn't to determine the exact error and how it happened. Other than flogging some hapless developer, you can't do much with such information. Instead, root cause analysis categorizes bugs into a taxonomy. For DataRocket, you might, in a root cause analysis, assign bugs to one of three categories: design, production, or material. A design bug results from the misuse of a component, a failure to understand the limitations of a chip, inappropriate air flow, or other such "should have/could have known better" failures. A production bug ensues from a failure on the production line—for example, a CPU is improperly inserted and falls out during shock and vibration testing. A material bug occurs when a component misbehaves or fails.[8] In addition to these hardware failures, you need to include at least one category for software failures arising from BIOS bugs.

---

8. Note that these categories are relative to whether your company buys or sells the failed item. A producer's design failure can cause the consumer to experience a material failure. For example, the infamous Pentium floating-point bug was Intel's design failure, but computer makers experienced a component failure.

For software, you might consider the following bug taxonomy, which is based on one originally published by Boris Beizer.[9] While retaining the essentials of the original, I have added two features to the list: explanations and examples associated with the various root causes, and a few bookkeeping categories that will help you deal with unusual cases (Duplicate, NAP, Bad Unit, RCN, and Unknown). (By doing some research, you might find other root cause breakdowns that fit your particular situation better.)

Bug Taxonomy

Functional:

- *Specification:* The specification is wrong.
- *Function:* The specification is right, but implementation is wrong.
- *Test:* The system works correctly, but the test reports a spurious error.

System:

- *Internal Interface:* The internal system communication failed.
- *Hardware Devices:* The hardware failed.
- *Operating System:* The operating system failed.
- *Software Architecture:* A fundamental design assumption proved invalid.
- *Resource Management:* The design assumptions are OK, but some implementation of the assumption is wrong.

Process:

- *Arithmetic:* The program incorrectly adds, divides, multiplies, factors, integrates numerically, or otherwise fails to perform an arithmetic operation properly.
- *Initialization:* An operation fails on its first use.
- *Control or Sequence:* An action occurs at the wrong time or for the wrong reason.
- *Static Logic:* Boundaries are misdefined, logic is invalid, "can't happen" events do happen, "won't matter" events do matter, and so forth.
- *Other:* A control-flow or processing error occurs that doesn't fit in the preceding buckets.

(continued)

---

9. This taxonomy is based on the appendix "Bug Taxonomy and Statistics," in *Software Testing Techniques*, 2d ed., by Boris Beizer. Copyright © 1990 by Boris Beizer. Reprinted by permission of the author.

Bug Taxonomy, continued

Data:

◆ *Type:* An integer should be a float, an unsigned integer stores or retrieves a negative value, an object is improperly defined, and so forth.

◆ *Structure:* A complex data structure is invalid or inappropriate.

◆ *Initial Value:* A data element's initialized value is incorrect. (This might not result in a process initialization error.)

◆ *Other:* A data-related error occurs that doesn't fit in the preceding buckets.

Code: A typo, misspelling, stylistic error, or other coding error occurs that results in a failure.

Documentation: The documentation says the system does X on condition Y, but the system does Z—a valid and correct action—instead.

Standards: The system fails to meet industry or vendor standards, follow code standards, adhere to naming conventions, and so forth.

Other: The root cause is known but fits none of the preceding categories.

Duplicate: Two bug reports describe the same problem.

NAP: The bug as described in the bug report is "not a problem" because the operation noted is correct. The report arises from a misunderstanding on the part of the tester about correct behavior. This situation is distinct from a test failure (whose root cause is categorized as *functional/test*) in that this is *tester* failure, that is, human error.

Bad Unit: The bug is a real problem, but it arises from a random hardware failure *that is unlikely to occur in the field.* (If the bug indicates a lack of reliability in some hardware component, this is not the root cause.)

RCN: A "root cause needed"; the bug report is confirmed as closed by test, but no one in development has supplied a root cause.

Unknown: No one knows—or will admit to knowing—what is broken. This root cause usually fits best when a sporadic bug doesn't appear for quite a while, leading people to conclude that some other change fixed the bug as a side effect.

Why go to the trouble of capturing this information? First, gathering root cause data allows you to apply the Pareto Principle—focus on the vital few, not the trivial many—when the time comes to try to improve your development process. For example, if most DataRocket failures result from bad components, you should revisit your choice of suppliers. Next, if you use industry-standard bug taxonomies, you can compare the root cause statistics for your projects against the averages. You can also accumulate historical data over the course of your projects that you can use for in-house comparisons. Finally, if you know where bugs are apt to originate, you can tailor your test effort to hit those areas particularly hard. By combining root cause data with subsystem breakdowns, you can get a good idea of what breaks in which parts of the system.

ADDING THE BUG FOCUS FIELDS

Let's put the bug focus fields in place in the bug tracking database. Because you will add new subsystems and configurations during the course of testing, you must first create a lookup table for each. The Access lookup table for subsystems contains these columns:

Field Name	Data Type	Description
Subsystem	Text	The subsystem experiencing the failure.
Description	Text	A description of the subsystem.

Likewise, the lookup table created for configurations contains a similar set of columns:

Field Name	Data Type	Description
Configuration	Text	The system, network environment, and SpeedyWriter revision in which the bug occurred.
Description	Text	A description of the test environment.

You'll then need to add five fields to the Access table *tblBugs* and to the bug entry form: *Subsystem*, *Configuration*, *Close Date*, *Resolution*, and *Root Cause*. The final table, with the added fields, is shown in Figure 4-14 on the following page.

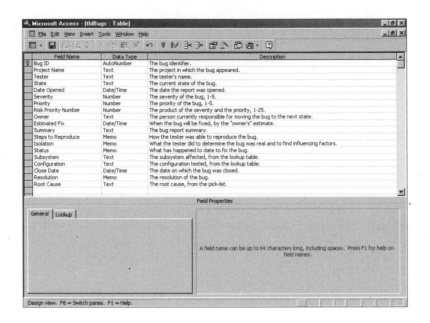

FIGURE 4-14   *The final table for the bug tracking database.*

Subsystem, Configuration, and *Root Cause* are text fields in which the bug report's author selects an entry from a list box. The list boxes for the *Subsystem* and *Configuration* fields are populated from the two lookup tables. The *Root Cause* list box is an Access value list associated with the list box through its properties. (You don't need to use a lookup table for *Root Cause* because the list of possible root causes will not change over the course of the project, unlike the lists used for *Subsystem* and *Configuration.*) I have used a single-level version of Beizer's taxonomy to create the root cause list. The *Close Date* field uses a date/time data type, again formatted as a short date. *Resolution* is a memo field.

You can see the five added fields in Figure 4-15, which shows the completed bug entry form. I typically include all five of these fields in both the bug detail report and the bug summary report.

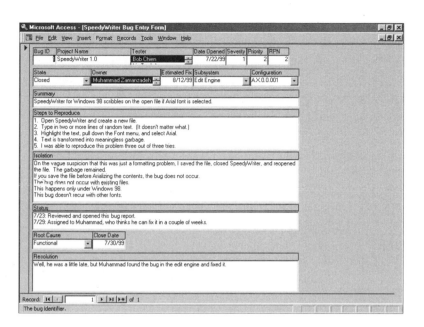

FIGURE 4-15   *A complete bug entry form.*

EXTRACTING METRICS FROM
THE BUG TRACKING DATABASE

The bug reports just described are useful in and of themselves, but the bug tracking database can be a source of even more information. Defect data—bug data—forms the basis of various quality control charts in a number of industries, and software and hardware are no exception. Using this bug tracking database, you can generate defect analysis charts that allow you to see patterns in the process of defect removal, to sort and analyze the root causes of bugs, to monitor the effectiveness of bug management, and to zero in on the parts of the product that cause the most problems. Defect analysis charts are also excellent for communicating with management because they highlight and illustrate test results that are difficult to explain with raw data.

The following sections introduce some powerful and easy-to-generate charts. The dummy data in the charts is taken from our sample SpeedyWriter database, based on the hypothetical test project outlined in Table 4-1. I've assigned pertinent data points pseudorandomly, based on my experience. The charts are representative, though cleaner and clearer than those from a real project. Although we'll examine the data with the unfair advantage of hindsight, keep in mind that these charts are at their most useful *during* a project; with practice, you'll be able to understand the trends when you see them developing.[10]

Phase	Cycle	Start Date	End Date	Bugs Found
Component test	1	7/19/99	7/25/99	25
	2	7/26/99	8/1/99	20
	3	8/2/99	8/8/99	5
Integration test	1	8/2/99	8/8/99	20
	2	8/9/99	8/15/99	15
	3	8/16/99	8/22/99	5
System test	1	8/16/99	8/22/99	10
	2	8/23/99	8/29/99	5
	3	8/30/99	9/5/99	0
First customer ship (FCS)	—	9/13/99	—	—

TABLE 4-1 *A hypothetical SpeedyWriter test project.*

HOW DEFECT REMOVAL PROCEEDS: THE OPENED / CLOSED CHART

The most basic defect analysis chart plots the cumulative number of bug reports opened against the cumulative number closed or deferred. For brevity, I refer to it as the *opened/closed* (or the *found/fixed*) chart. Figure 4-16 presents a sample chart, which offers a general view of the development project's status.

---

10. For a detailed explanation of the use of metrics, see *Metrics and Models in Software Quality Engineering*, by Stephen Kan. Also, Chapter 9 of Beizer's *Software System Testing and Quality Assurance* includes a discussion of some topics not covered in this chapter.

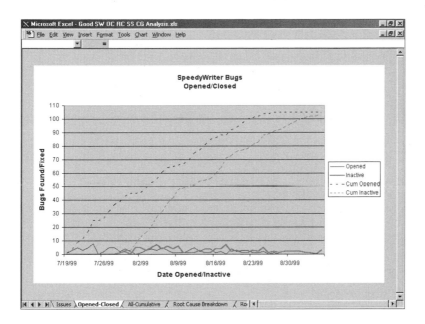

FIGURE 4-16 *An opened/closed chart for SpeedyWriter.*

This information-rich chart provides answers to a number of questions. First, are you ready to ship the product? Since the number of bugs in a given program is unknown but is essentially a fixed number once development ends, test projects eventually hit a point at which further testing produces diminishing returns.[11] When the cumulative opened curve—the top curve on the chart in Figure 4-16—levels off at an asymptotic limit, testing is

---

The Fix Date Precedes the Close Date

If you were to draw a "fix curve" based on the dates when developers actually repaired bugs, you would see that the closed curve lags behind it by a week or so. This lag results from delays incurred in getting the fix into the product, delivering that product to the test team, and testing for confirmation and regression. These various delays cause the convergence at the last day of testing shown in the sample chart in Figure 4-16.

---

11. I have, however, worked on projects in which the incidence of regression was so high that it seemed as if each fix release closed six bugs and caused a dozen new ones.

usually considered complete, at least for the phase currently under way. (The asymptote actually indicates the fading of the test system's ability to find bugs in the current phase. Given a good test system, the bugs found represent the bugs most likely to torment the customer, and the fading of the test system is consistent with customer indifference.) Conversely, a cumulative opened curve that refuses to flatten indicates that you have plenty of problems left to find. On the chart in Figure 4-16, the limit was hit around August 23: the second cycle of system testing revealed few additional bugs, and then none were found in the final round of system testing.

Next, have you finished fixing bugs? Once development winds down, developers usually start to catch up with the problems.[12] At about the same time, the opened curve starts to flatten. Consequently, the cumulative closed curve—the lower curve on the chart in Figure 4-16—begins to converge with the cumulative opened curve. (For purposes of this chart, I have aggregated closed bugs and deferred bugs; thus the designation of the lower curve as *Cumulative Inactive* in the chart.)

At a more general level, is the bug management process working? It is working well in this example: the closed curve follows right behind the opened curve, indicating that the project team is moving the bugs quickly toward resolution.

Finally, how do milestones in the project relate to inflection points, changes in the slope of the opened or closed curves? The overlapping of the phases in the example obscures this relationship somewhat, but often when you move from one test phase to the next, you will see a spike in the cumulative opened curve. Such rises are gentle in our idealized example, but these transitions can be dramatic and even downright scary on some projects. As developers move from writing new code or engineering new hardware to fixing bugs, you should see an upward turn in the cumulative closed curve. A "bug scrub" meeting, where the technical and management leaders of a project gather to decide the fate of all known bug reports, can result in a discontinuous jump in the cumulative closed curve.

---

12. Regrettably, "usually" and "always" aren't the same. On some projects, developers are spirited away to other projects before they can fix the important bugs, sometimes even before the bug find curve levels off. This usually happens when the project has gone over budget or schedule and the participants are starting to cut their losses.

To explore the use of opened/closed charts, let's look at three nightmare scenarios that represent those unpleasant projects in which all test managers eventually participate. All of these examples assume the Speedy-Writer testing schedule outlined in Table 4-1. For the first nightmare, imagine that during the system test phase the bug find rate remains high and refuses to level off. The opened/closed chart that results appears in Figure 4-17. Notice the deceptive leveling in the second cycle (8/23/99 through 8/29/99), where the opened curve appears to flatten, only to leap up sharply in the third cycle (8/30/99 through 9/5/99). If the project team ships the product on September 13 as scheduled, they can expect many failures in the field.

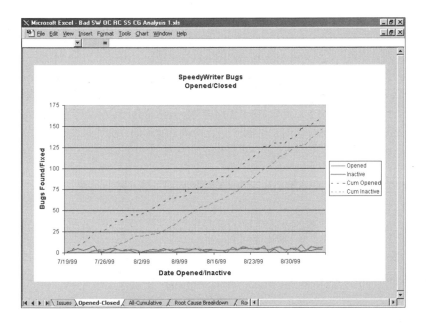

FIGURE 4-17   *The nightmare of endless bug discovery.*

For the second nightmare, which is a bit milder, let's assume that development is ignoring some of the bugs. The developers have convinced themselves that about 25 of the bugs that test has reported are beneath contempt and can be disregarded.[13] Figure 4-18 on the following page shows the

---

13. This example is based on an actual situation, which in fact was even more extreme because it involved about 500 total bugs rather than the 100 or so in our example. The development manager was able to avoid working on these bugs for literally months.

opened/closed chart for this scenario. Until about August 20, the chart in Figure 4-16 (the idealized example) and the chart in Figure 4-18 are not radically different: on that date, the opened/closed gap is about 20 in the former chart, whereas it is about 30 in the latter. Ten bug reports out of 100 one way or the other three weeks before the first customer ship is scheduled is not a catastrophe. But as the second and third cycles of system testing unfold (8/23/99 through 8/29/99, and 8/30/99 through 9/5/99, respectively), it becomes clear that the gap is not narrowing. Unless you bring the pernicious bugs to project management's attention around August 23, the development team will deliver a *fait accompli*. Overturning their decision to ignore these bugs even a week later will require a slip in the delivery date.

As a final nightmare—more of a bed sweat, actually—let's suppose that the developers and the testers are both doing the right things at a technical level, but the bug management process isn't working. The development manager doesn't notify you when bugs are fixed and ready for retesting, and you don't follow up with your testers to make sure they close bug reports that they have retested. Also, testers don't bother to report bugs when they find them but instead wait until Thursday or Friday each week. Then they enter their

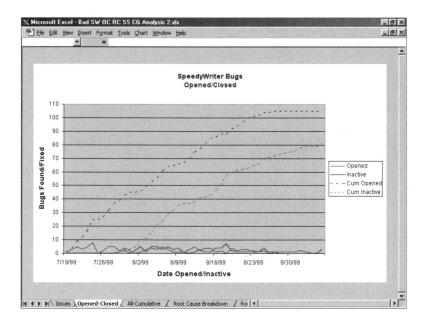

FIGURE 4-18 *The nightmare of ignored bugs.*

findings, some dimly remembered, into the bug tracking database. Figure 4-19 shows how the opened/closed chart looks in this example. The trouble here is that you can't tell whether a jump in a curve represents a significant event or simply indicates that some people are getting around to doing what they should have done earlier. If you use this chart as part of your project score-card, your vision is blurred.

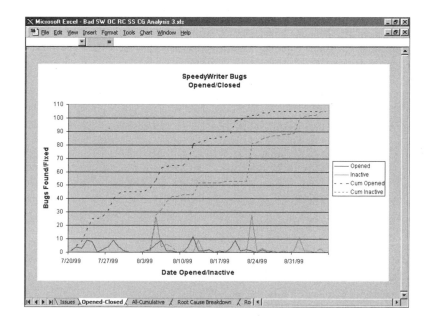

FIGURE 4-19   *The nightmare of mismanaged bugs.*

WHY BUGS HAPPEN:
THE ROOT CAUSE CHART

Root cause data is most interesting in the aggregate. Listing the closure of one bug with a specific root cause may not mean much, but seeing the breakdown for a hundred—or a thousand—bugs can convey an engaging story. Figure 4-20 on the following page presents a root cause breakdown for the SpeedyWriter example, showing the contribution of each type of error to the total number of bugs found and fixed so far. (During test execu-tion, many bugs will not have root causes assigned to them because they are still under investigation.) As discussed earlier, analyzing a breakdown of

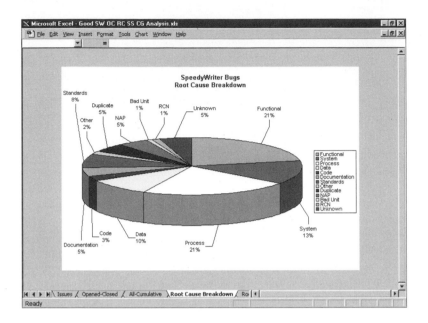

FIGURE 4-20   *A root cause breakdown for SpeedyWriter.*

root causes can serve to focus not only test efforts but also development attention on those areas that are causing the most serious and frequent problems. As you might imagine, a chart such as the one in Figure 4-20 grabs management's attention more effectively than a table.

HOW DEVELOPMENT RESPONDS: THE CLOSURE PERIOD CHART

Closure period (a.k.a. *closure gap*) is complicated to calculate, but it has a simple intuitive meaning: the closure period gauges development's responsiveness to test's bug reports. *Daily closure period* refers to the average number of days between the opening of a bug report and its resolution for all bug reports closed on the same day. *Rolling closure period* is the average for all closed bug reports, including the current day and all previous days. Figure 4-21 shows the closure period chart for the SpeedyWriter project. As you can see, the daily plot tends to "pull" the rolling plot toward it, although the ever-increasing inertia of the rolling average makes it harder to influence as the project proceeds.

It's useful to look at closure period in terms of stability and acceptability. A stable closure period chart shows a relatively low variance from one

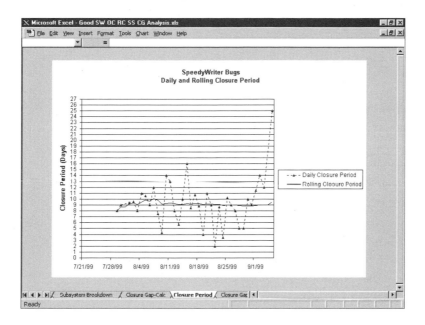

FIGURE 4-21   *A closure period chart for SpeedyWriter.*

day to another, with the slope of the rolling closure curve remaining almost constant and close to 0. In addition, to the extent that the daily closure period changes, it fluctuates randomly around the rolling closure curve, staying within a few days in either direction.

On an acceptable closure period chart, both the daily and rolling closure curves fall within the upper and lower limits set in the project or test plan for bug turnaround time.[14] Although the pressures of the typical project make it hard to believe, there is indeed a lower limit for an acceptable closure period. Bug reports deferred the day they are opened pull the daily closure curve toward 0, but the bug remains in the product. Furthermore, an acceptable daily closure curve does not exhibit a significant trend toward either boundary.

A closure period chart that is both stable and acceptable indicates a well-understood, smoothly functioning bug management process. The ideal is a low number with a downward or level trend since an efficient bug management process drives bugs through their state transitions to closure

---

14. To emphasize this, you might add these lines to the chart, but don't confuse them with the upper and lower control limits on a control chart. For more information on control charts and other statistical quality control techniques, see Kaoru Ishikawa's *Guide to Quality Control*.

with all deliberate speed. The closure period in Figure 4-21 is stable and, if management is realistic in its expectations, acceptable. Bugs tend to get fixed in about a week and a half, which is a good pace if you assume one-week cycles and don't admit experimental bug fixes into the lab during cycles. (For a discussion of the danger of midstream changes in the system under test, see the sections "Release Management" and "Test Cycles" in Chapter 2, pages 55 and 56.)

What Was Broken:
The Subsystem Chart

Like the root cause breakdown, the subsystem breakdown is a simple chart with an important message: it tells you which subsystems experience the most bugs. It's useful to format this as a Pareto chart, as shown in Figure 4-22, because usually two or three subsystems suffer the most problems.

You can use a subsystem chart in the same way you use a root cause chart, to focus process and product improvement efforts. The fact that the user interface and the edit engine account for two out of every three bugs found in SpeedyWriter, for instance, indicates that an effort to make fewer

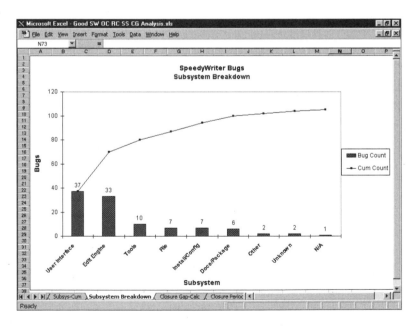

FIGURE 4-22 *A subsystem breakdown for SpeedyWriter.*

mistakes in these areas would pay off handsomely. Also, if you are dividing your test effort evenly among the six subsystems, you should consider spending most of your testers' time on these two problem areas.

This conclusion might seem counterintuitive—after all, if you didn't find many bugs in the other four subsystems, maybe you should have spent more time looking in those four categories. And you certainly should do this if postrelease field problems indicate a disproportionate number of test escapes in these four areas. But as Glenford Myers points out in *The Art of Software Testing,* where you find many bugs, you will find more bugs. Therefore you can predict from the SpeedyWriter data that most of the field bugs will also come from the user interface or the edit engine. For subsequent SpeedyWriter releases, you should spend even more time and resources looking for bugs in these subsystems.

A Note on Metrics and Charts

As you accumulate historical defect data—on both good and bad projects—you can compare charts from your current projects with charts from previous projects. Such comparisons can be enlightening. Even within a single class of projects such as laptop computer development, I have seen variances of 600 percent in the total number of bugs found. Beyond the simple totals, the shapes of the curves can also differ. If you use these four charts consistently across a few projects, you will soon recognize "virtuous" and "evil" shapes.

Avoid blind faith in your charts, though. One key assumption of the opened/closed chart is *ceteris paribus* (all things held equal). You can arbitrarily flatten any cumulative opened curve by stopping the test effort. You can cause the opened and closed curves to converge by deferring bugs rather than fixing them. You can "spoof" opened and closed dates in the database to make the opened/closed chart fit any profile you choose (as I did to create the sample charts in this section). You can easily rig the closure period chart too. Shotgun deferral of bug reports, recording phony opened and closed dates, opening new bug reports rather than reopening existing ones when fixes fail in confirmation testing, and other manipulation of the opened and closed dates will defeat your purpose. Finally, carelessness when assigning subsystems and root causes to bugs renders these charts worse than pointless. Nothing good can come of making resource allocation decisions based on incorrect data.

Similar cautions apply to any other analysis of defect or test data. For your analyses to have meaning, the underlying data must be accurate, complete, and free from gerrymandering. Only honest data yields worthwhile information.

The reports, charts, tables, and forms presented in this chapter are just starters. With a little imagination, you can extract all sorts of useful data and reports from a bug tracking database. Start with simple tasks, learn the tool, and then expand it to meet your needs. For day-to-day management, however, these four charts—or your own enhancements of them—may well suffice.[15]

MANAGING BUG TRACKING

When projects are in a test execution phase, I probably spend 10 to 20 percent of my time working with bugs, either those already reported or those about to be reported. Because testing should mitigate quality risks, and because a bug report documents the transition of a quality risk into a failure mode, I consider bug reports the most important "product" of the test effort. Time devoted to understanding and managing bug data is time well spent.

The preceding section on metrics may have given you the impression that managing bugs consists mostly of analyzing data and gleaning meaning. Would that it were so! You'll soon discover two other areas of concern. The first is staying aware of the politics and potential misuse of the bug data. The second is dealing with certain kinds of problematic bug reports that can consume a disproportionate share of your time.

POLITICS AND MISUSE OF BUG DATA

Chapter 9 deals with management considerations and the politics of the test manager's position in detail. Here, however, we should briefly examine political issues that are specifically related to bug data. From the most adversarial point of view, for instance, you can see every bug report as an attack on a developer. You probably don't—and certainly shouldn't—intend to offend,

---

15. Beizer's discussion of quantitative methods in *Software System Testing and Quality Assurance* suggests other possible metrics and emphasizes the need to manage by a limited set. Chapters 3 and 4 of Kan's *Metrics and Models in Software Quality Engineering* can help you take your metrics program to the next level once you've mastered the tools outlined in this chapter.

but it helps to remember that bug data is potentially embarrassing and subject to misuse. Candor and honesty are critical in gathering clean bug data, but developers might dissemble if they don't trust you not to slam them with the bug reports. You can think of the detailed bug information your database captures as resembling a loaded revolver: an effective tool if it's in the right hands and used with caution, but a dangerous implement of mayhem if it's treated carelessly.

Building Versus Buying

Instead of developing your own bug tracking database, you might want to consider buying one of the many excellent packages on the market. Which alternative—building or buying—is better? In J. R. R. Tolkien's *Lord of the Rings* trilogy, one character says to the protagonist, "Go not to [us] for advice, for [we] will tell you both yes and no." I'm afraid I must do the same.

On the one hand, several arguments favor purchasing a package. These packages represent the collected thoughts of many experienced testers. Most commercial software packages are professionally executed and documented. The developers have considered in advance many of the problems that you will run into later if you decide to create your own system. Buying is also a cheaper approach; a widely sold commercial package leverages the entire customer base. You might spend many hours developing your own package, and you should take into account what these hours are worth.

On the other hand, creating your own bug tracking system has its advantages. You know best what you need to track and what data is pertinent to your operation. A general-purpose package, no matter how customizable, won't be exactly what you need. Remember, too, that tools have paradigms, and test tools have embedded notions about the development process that might not fit the way your organization does business. The poorer the fit, the harder you will have to work to make the bug tracking system work for you. Finally, if you discover that your commercial system contains bugs, you must work with the vendor to get them fixed—if the vendor will fix them. When you create and control your own system, you can always fix the bugs (provided you can find the time).

The question of buying versus building is not trivial. You will have to live with the decision for some time, so be sure you consider all the angles.

Don't Fail to Build Trust

Most experienced developers will support bug tracking efforts. Neverthe-less, some individuals—especially those who have experienced highly adversarial test/development relationships—won't disclose any more infor-mation to you than required, and they may do so with an uncooperative attitude.

I once worked with a development manager who wanted to argue over every bug report. "Bug crawls" (detailed review meetings that analyze de-fect data) with this guy were a misery of semantic arguments punctuated with monotonous assertions that any bug he had succeeded in ignoring for the past three or four weeks had probably been fixed in some recent release and should be retested by my team. In his mind, our relationship was by nature purely adversarial. There was no trust.

Some situations are irretrievable. Developers who are convinced that a written bug report is one step removed from a written warning in their personnel files probably will never trust you. Most developers, though, approach testing with a cautious but open mind. How do you keep the trust and support of these developers?

◆ Don't take bugs personally, and don't become emotional about them. The times I have anointed myself the "defender of quality" and acted holier-than-thou with my colleagues are moments in my professional life that I look back on with embarrassment and regret. Even if you're right on the issue, you're doing the wrong thing because you end up alienating people with whom you need to maintain a professional and trusting relationship.

◆ Submit only quality bug reports: a succinct summary, clear steps to reproduce, evidence of significant isolation work, accuracy in classification information, and a conservative estimate in terms of priority and severity. Also try to avoid "cheap shot" bug re-ports that can seem like carping.

◆ Be willing to discuss bug reports with an open mind. No matter how convinced you are that a program or a computer is malfunc-tioning, you should listen to developers when they explain that the bug is actually correct behavior. If you make the extra effort to discuss their opinions, it goes a long way toward keeping the flow of information moving.

◆ If developers don't like the way you report bugs, be open to their suggestions for change. If they want bug reports delivered in a different fashion, advance warning before summaries are sent to management, or additional information in the reports, try to accommodate them whenever it's practical to do so.

Most of these suggestions are simple common courtesy and professionalism. You don't have to compromise your role in order to keep reasonable developers satisfied that you aren't grinding an ax. Unreasonable developers are another story, but nothing you do will satisfy them.

Don't Be a Backseat Driver

The test manager needs to ensure that testers identify, reproduce, and isolate bugs. It's also part of the job to track the bugs to conclusion and to deliver crisp bug status summaries to senior and executive management. These roles differ, though, from managing bug *fixes*. Let's be clear: managing the bug fix process is the development manager's job; ensuring that this process moves at a satisfactory pace is the program manager's job. Even if some managers encourage you, don't get sucked into doing either.

If you, as an outsider, make it your job to nag developers about when a specific bug will be fixed or to pester the development manager about how slow the bug fix process is, you are setting yourself up for a highly antagonistic situation. Reporting, tracking, retesting, and summarizing bugs are your worries. Whether any particular bug gets fixed, how it gets fixed, and when it gets fixed are someone else's concerns.

Don't Make Individuals Look Bad

It is a bad idea to create and distribute reports that make individuals look bad. There's probably no faster way to guarantee that you will have trouble getting estimated fix dates out of people than to produce a report that points out every failure to meet such estimated dates. Creating reports that show how many bug fixes resulted in reopened rather than closed bugs, grouped and totaled by developer, is another express lane to bad relationships.[16] Again, managing the developers is the development manager's job, not yours. No matter how useful a particular report seems, make sure that it doesn't bash individuals.

---

16. See Chapter 6 of *Testing Computer Software*, by Kaner, Falk, and Nguyen, for an expansive discussion of this and other ways to create bad blood between test and development using a bug tracking database.

STICKY WICKETS

Challenging bugs crop up on nearly every project. The most vexing are those that involve questions about correct behavior, "prairie dog" bugs that pop up only when they feel like it, and bugs that cause a tug-of-war over priority.

Bug or Feature?

Although a perfect development project provides you with clear and unambiguous information about correct system behavior in the form of requirements and specifications, you will seldom have such good fortune. Many projects have only informal specifications, and the requirements can be scattered around in e-mails, product road maps, and sales materials. In such cases, disagreements can arise between development and test over whether a particular bug is in fact correct system behavior.

How should you settle these differences? Begin by discussing the situation with the developers, their manager, and your testers. Most of these disagreements arise from miscommunication. Before making a federal case out of it, confirm that all the parties are clear on what the alleged bug is and why test is concerned.

Suppose that everyone understands the problem test is reporting, but the development team insists that the system is behaving properly, while you remain unconvinced. At this point, you might want to get other groups involved. Technical support, marketing, sales, and the project manager might have strong opinions. Even if consulting with other people doesn't resolve the dispute, it at least escalates the problem to the proper level of attention.

If, after all the jawboning is over, you are the lone skeptic, now what? Insisting that the bug remain assigned to the recalcitrant developer won't help. If the bug remains active, you'll be forced to rehash this discussion every time you circulate your bug list. My preference is to cancel the bug but make a notation on the record that I disagree.

"Unreproducible" Problems

This problem comes in two flavors. First, some bugs simply refuse to reproduce their symptoms consistently. This is especially the case in system testing, in which complex combinations of conditions are required to re-create problems. Sometimes these kinds of failures occur in clusters. If you see a bug three times in one day and then don't see it for a week, has it disappeared, or is it just hiding? Tempting as it is to dismiss this problem, be sure to write up these bugs. Random, intermittent failures—especially ones that result in system crashes or any other data loss—can have a significant effect on customers.

The second category of unreproducible bugs involves problems that seem to disappear with new revisions of the system, although no specific fix was made for them. I refer to these as "bugs fixed by accident," usually with sarcasm. You will find that more bugs are fixed by accident than you expect, but that fewer are fixed by accident than developers suggest. If the bug is an elusive one, you might want to keep the bug report active until you're convinced it's actually gone.

Deferring Trivia or Creating Test Escapes?

While bug severity is easy to quantify, priority is not. Developing consensus on priority is often difficult. What do you do when bugs are assigned a low priority? Bugs that will not be fixed should be deferred. If you don't keep the active bug list short, people will start to ignore it. But there's a real risk that some deferred bugs will come back to haunt you. For this reason, you should let other people make the call on priority and deferral. If a bug is assigned a low priority and then ignored, press for a clear decision about whether the bug will be fixed or deferred rather than discussing it repeatedly. What if a deferred bug pops up in the field as a critical issue? Is that a test escape? Not if you found it and then deferred it on the advice or insistence of the project manager.

After you institute a bug tracking system, including the database and metrics discussed here, you will find yourself the keeper of key indicators of project status. As I've emphasized, fairness and accuracy should be your watchwords in this role. Your peers and your managers will use your database and charts to make both tactical (day-to-day) and strategic (project-wide) decisions. If you take these activities seriously and apply the tools introduced in this chapter conscientiously, you and your test organization will provide invaluable assistance to the project team in creating the best possible product.

5

Managing Test Cases: The Test Tracking Spreadsheet

Q uick! For your three most recent test projects, try to answer the following questions, using whatever records you kept:

◆ How many test cases did you plan to run?

◆ How many test cases did you actually run?

◆ How many tests failed? Of those, how many later passed when the bug was fixed?

◆ Did the tests take less or more time, on average, than you expected?

◆ Did you skip any tests? If so, why?

◆ Did your management ever ask for a cumulative summary of test results, both passed and failed? If so, were you able to provide an accurate summary, or did you simply take a SWAG (scientific wild-ass guess)?

On any given project, I can answer these questions by checking my test tracking spreadsheet, a tool I use to manage test execution. This chapter shows you how to create and utilize this tool.

In its most basic form, the test tracking spreadsheet is a "to do" list, with the added capability of status tracking. Using DataRocket as a case study, this chapter demonstrates how to build an abbreviated test tracking spreadsheet for system testing. We'll begin our example with a minimalist, or stripped-down, model of the spreadsheet, created in Microsoft Excel. As you learn to add enhancements and to adapt this tool to fit your own needs, you should eventually be able to implement a complete hierarchical self-summarizing test system using the spreadsheet as the foundation. As you'll see, you can also integrate individual test cases constructed with the approach outlined in Chapter 3.

BUILDING A MINIMALIST
TEST TRACKING SPREADSHEET

To keep our sample worksheets relatively small, let's suppose that you have defined a simple four-suite system test phase. You intend to run the following test suites:

- Environmental

- Load, Capacity, and Volume

- Basic Functionality

- Standards

You want to track the status of each test case, the configuration against which the test was run, and who ran the test. You also want to summarize the test status numerically.

Figure 5-1 shows an example of a test case summary worksheet as it might appear halfway into the first cycle of system testing. The first column of the Excel worksheet (Test Suite / Case) contains the names of the test suites and, within each suite, the test cases. The names are short mnemonics that convey an idea of the test's purpose. In the second column (Status), you can record the status of each test case. A blank entry in this column means that

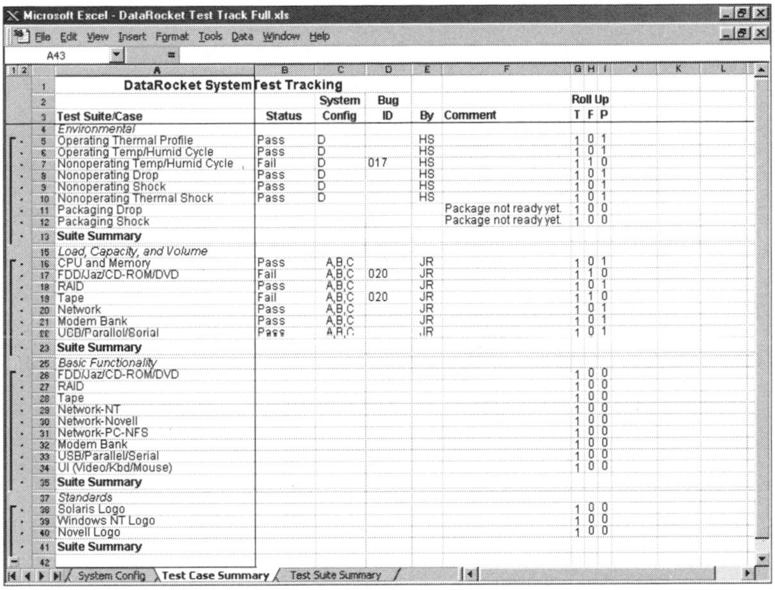

Microsoft Excel - DataRocket Test Track Full.xls

	A	B	C	D	E	F	G	H	I
1	**DataRocket System Test Tracking**								
2			**System**	**Bug**			**Roll Up**		
3	**Test Suite/Case**	**Status**	**Config**	**ID**	**By**	**Comment**	**T**	**F**	**P**
4	*Environmental*								
5	Operating Thermal Profile	Pass	D		HS		1	0	1
6	Operating Temp/Humid Cycle	Pass	D		HS		1	0	1
7	Nonoperating Temp/Humid Cycle	Fail	D	017	HS		1	1	0
8	Nonoperating Drop	Pass	D		HS		1	0	1
9	Nonoperating Shock	Pass	D		HS		1	0	1
10	Nonoperating Thermal Shock	Pass	D		HS		1	0	1
11	Packaging Drop					Package not ready yet.	1	0	0
12	Packaging Shock					Package not ready yet.	1	0	0
13	**Suite Summary**								
15	*Load, Capacity, and Volume*								
16	CPU and Memory	Pass	A,B,C		JR		1	0	1
17	FDD/Jaz/CD-ROM/DVD	Fail	A,B,C	020	JR		1	1	0
18	RAID	Pass	A,B,C		JR		1	0	1
19	Tape	Fail	A,B,C	020	JR		1	1	0
20	Network	Pass	A,B,C		JR		1	0	1
21	Modem Bank	Pass	A,B,C		JR		1	0	1
22	USB/Parallel/Serial	Pass	A,B,C		JR		1	0	1
23	**Suite Summary**								
25	*Basic Functionality*								
26	FDD/Jaz/CD-ROM/DVD						1	0	0
27	RAID						1	0	0
28	Tape						1	0	0
29	Network-NT						1	0	0
30	Network-Novell						1	0	0
31	Network-PC-NFS						1	0	0
32	Modem Bank						1	0	0
33	USB/Parallel/Serial						1	0	0
34	UI (Video/Kbd/Mouse)						1	0	0
35	**Suite Summary**								
37	*Standards*								
38	Solaris Logo						1	0	0
39	Windows NT Logo						1	0	0
40	Novell Logo						1	0	0
41	**Suite Summary**								
42									

System Config | **Test Case Summary** | Test Suite Summary

FIGURE 5-1 *A test case summary worksheet, halfway through the first cycle of system testing.*

the test case is still queued for execution. A *Pass* entry signifies that the test case did not identify any errors; *Fail* indicates that one or more bugs were found when the test was run.

The System Configuration column lists an identifier for the system configuration used in each test case. A separate worksheet that serves as a lookup table, shown in Figure 5-2 on the following page, allows you to record important details about each configuration, such as the motherboard revision, the BIOS level, the operating system, the specific network setup, and any additional software or hardware involved in the test.

Returning to the test case summary worksheet in Figure 5-1, notice the Bug ID column. For any test case that generates a failure, this column should contain the bug identifier from the bug tracking database. The By column on the worksheet contains the initials of the test technician(s) who ran the test, and the Comment column allows you to enter text to provide more information on the test case status.

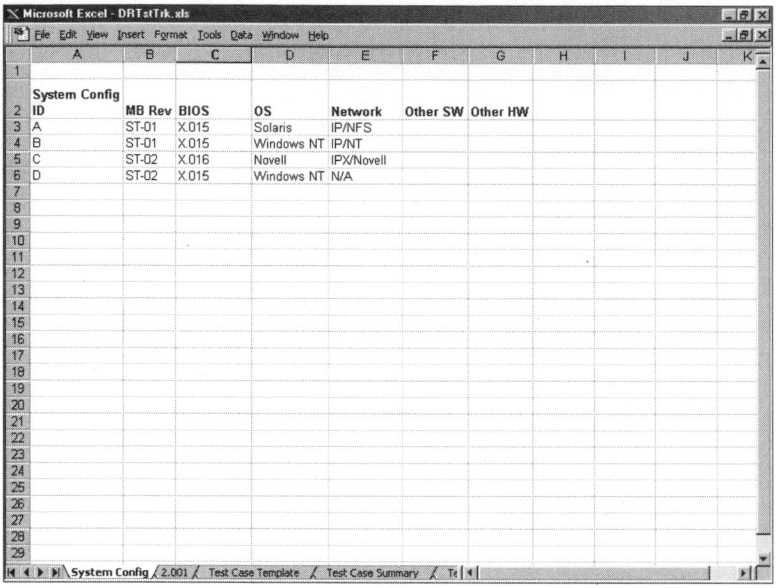

System Config ID	MB Rev	BIOS	OS	Network	Other SW	Other HW
A	ST-01	X.015	Solaris	IP/NFS		
B	ST-01	X.015	Windows NT	IP/NT		
C	ST-02	X.016	Novell	IPX/Novell		
D	ST-02	X.015	Windows NT	N/A		

FIGURE 5-2 *A system configuration worksheet that serves as a lookup table.*

The last three columns of the worksheet in Figure 5-1, which I refer to as the Roll Up columns, help you summarize the status information. Each test case can be assigned three numeric values based on its status:

- The T column contains the value 1 if the row lists a test case.
- The F column contains a formula that computes the value 1 if the test case in that row has a *Fail* status (and computes the value 0 otherwise).
- The P column contains a formula that computes the value 1 if the test case in that row has a *Pass* status (and computes the value 0 otherwise).

You can then set up a third worksheet that will count these values and summarize them for each test suite. Figure 5-3 offers an example of such a test suite summary worksheet.

At this point, you have a simple but informative test tracking spreadsheet that provides test case details, with a link to the bug tracking database for more data on failures. It offers, in the test suite summary, a management-eye view of the test execution results. The spreadsheet also contains infor-

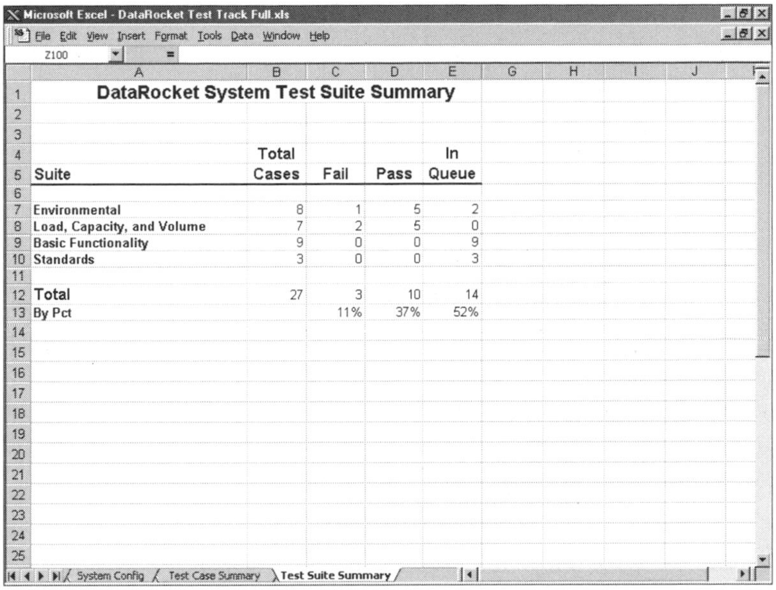

DataRocket System Test Suite Summary

Suite	Total Cases	Fail	Pass	In Queue
Environmental	8	1	5	2
Load, Capacity, and Volume	7	2	5	0
Basic Functionality	9	0	0	9
Standards	3	0	0	3
Total	27	3	10	14
By Pct		11%	37%	52%

FIGURE 5-3 *A test suite summary worksheet.*

mation about the test environment that will be useful in attempting to reproduce failures, in debugging, and in analyzing root causes. In addition, the spreadsheet identifies the tester(s) in case you need to follow up with further questions.

MAKING ENHANCEMENTS

Although the basic test tracking spreadsheet you've just seen is useful, you can certainly improve it to record and analyze even more information. The following sections describe various enhancements that I've added over the years; you might want to incorporate some of them (or come up with others on your own).

IDENTIFYING TEST SUITES AND CASES

In addition to using short names for test suites and test cases, you can assign a Dewey decimal–style ID number to each one. In a Test ID column, inserted to the left of the Test Suite/Case column, you can number each test suite, starting with 1.000, then 2.000, and so on. Each test case carries the suite number to the left of the decimal and its own sequential ID to the right of the decimal. For example, in the test case summary shown in Figure 5-1, the Load, Capacity, and Volume test suite would have the test ID 2.000, and the ID for the CPU and Memory test case would be 2.001; likewise, the test ID for the Tape test case in the Basic Functionality test suite would be 3.003.

ADDING DATE AND HOURS INFORMATION: PLAN VERSUS REALITY

Your overall schedule is based in part on projected test completion dates, and one important component of your budget is projected person-hours per test case. Adding information about completion dates and person-hours to your test tracking spreadsheet can help you perform a "reality check" if either your schedule or your budget begins to go awry.

You can add two date columns, Plan Date and Actual Date, to the test case summary. The plan date comes from the schedule, based on when you expect the test case to be completed. For simplicity, my practice is to assign every test case in a test suite the same planned completion date. Actual Date, the second date column, indicates when the tester actually completed the test.

You can also track actual and planned person-hours. If you estimated that a test case would require 5 person-hours, but instead it took 10, that bears explaining. Conversely, you might find that another test case takes less effort than predicted. By accumulating these numbers and analyzing them, you can refine your plans for test cycles, improve your test cases, and figure out which test cases are consuming the most person-hours.

GATHERING DATA FOR RELIABILITY CALCULATIONS

If you are testing hardware, you might want to gather test duration times for each test case in order to generate mean time between failures (MTBF). Adding a Test Hours column that captures the duration (clock time as opposed to effort) in the test tracking spreadsheet is a relatively straightforward way to do this.

If you are testing software, however, this technique is questionable. Software reliability is a controversial subject. Proven, statistically valid approaches exist for calculating reliability for hardware, but for software we have only hypotheses. Nevertheless, if you're motivated to dabble in these formulas, you can use the Test Hours column to tally cumulative hours. Keep in mind, though, that if you release the results, you will need to do so with appropriate caveats.[1]

INCREASING THE PRECISION OF TEST CASE STATUS

The basic test suite summary introduced earlier records three possible states of a test case: *Pass*, *Fail*, or *In Queue*. (The *In Queue* state is indicated by the lack of an entry in the Status column of the test case summary.) But you can be even more precise about the life cycle of a typical test case. Figure 5-4 shows a set of possible test case states; dotted lines indicate uncommon states or flows, while double boxes indicate states that are typically "terminal."

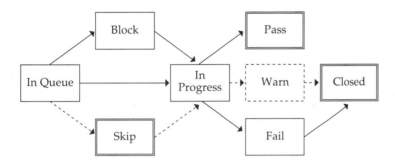

FIGURE 5-4   *A set of possible test case states.*

This diagram introduces several additional status descriptions. An *In Progress* (*IP*) status indicates that the test is running and will probably continue to do so for a while. (If a test takes less than a day or two, however, it's more efficient to simply show it as queued until it is finished rather than bothering to record *In Progress* entries.) *Block* reflects the fact that some external condition—such as a missing piece of functionality—has prevented you from executing the test. You can document this in the Comments column of the spreadsheet. Likewise, *Skip* means that you have decided— or have been told—to skip the test case (as explained in the Comments column). When a test case's status is *Closed*, the test team has confirmed that all bugs previously identified against this test case have been fixed.

---

1. For good information about software reliability, see Chapters 7 and 8 of Stephen Kan's *Metrics and Models in Software Quality Engineering*. Chapter 9 of Boris Beizer's *Software System Testing and Quality Assurance* contains an excellent discussion of techniques and problems, while Beizer's article "Software Is Different" points out the reasons such calculations are questionable.

A *Warn* status, at a level somewhere between *Pass* and *Fail*, indicates that a problem exists, although it is not serious enough to warrant flagging the test case as a *Fail*. I usually count these instances with the passes in the test suite summary rather than adding another column to the worksheet. (I consider most bugs with both severity and priority rankings of 3, 4, or 5 as qualified candidates for *Warn* status but assign a *Fail* to any bug more serious than that. I always flag incidental bugs, which are not material to the feature under test, as *Warn*.)

You can introduce even greater levels of precision into your descriptions. As Chapter 3 discussed, a test case is an amalgamation of test steps and substeps. The states shown in Figure 5-4 apply to the test steps and substeps as well as to the overall test case. Thus the state of the test case is a summary of the states of these steps and substeps—and a matter of judgment. In some instances, deciding which state applies is simple. If, in a three-step test case, two steps pass and one fails, the test case fails.

Sometimes, however, choosing the correct test status based on the state of each step is not so simple. In the three-step test case, what if step 1 passes, step 2 fails, and step 3 is blocked by the failure in step 2? Calling the case either blocked or failed omits essential information. To solve such problems, you can assign dual states such as *Block/Fail*, *Block/Warn*, *Block/Closed*, *Skip/Pass*, *Skip/Fail*, *Skip/Warn*, and *Skip/Closed*. By adding a few more formula columns in the Roll Up area of the test case summary worksheet, you can track and summarize these levels of detail. After creating the formulas—all simple variants of the two used previously—you can add columns in the test suite summary worksheet. If you use dual states, remember to be careful not to double-count test cases in this summary worksheet.

This greater precision may make your test suite summary harder to explain, however. (Conceivably, a test case can have as many states as it has steps and substeps, which certainly doesn't serve the purpose of summarizing the test case on this worksheet.) The three-state summary (*Pass*, *Fail*, or *In Queue*) has the virtue of simplicity. When you show eight to fifteen states, you have more opportunities to confuse people. The spreadsheet can become unmanageably complex, almost ludicrous. To make the spreadsheet accurate and precise yet as simple as possible, use good judgment in choosing which states to include.

CALCULATING WEIGHTED FAILURES

Our discussion of regression gaps in Chapter 3 (see "Avoiding the Dreaded 'Test Escape': Coverage and Regression Test Gaps," page 80) raised the issue of how to select test suites to be rerun in multiple-cycle situations—that is, how to select the test suites that find the most important bugs. One method of doing this, more rigorous than some of the approaches described in Chapter 3, is based on the concept of *test suite yield*. This method considers not only the number of bugs found by the suite but also the severity and priority rankings of the bugs (the risk priority numbers from the bug tracking system). By calculating a weighted failure number for each suite, you obtain a numeric yield that you can use to select test suites.

It's easy to add such a feature to your test tracking spreadsheet. Begin by inserting a column in the test case summary worksheet to store the RPN for the corresponding bug ID. Then, in the Roll Up area, insert a column named FW (for Failure Weight) that holds a formula calculating the reciprocal of the RPN in each row. Finally, add a column in the test suite summary worksheet that calculates the sum of the reciprocals for each suite. Now you have a test suite summary column that starts at 0 and increases as the yield—RPN weighted—of the test suite increases. You can now figure out at a glance which test suites in your test system are most effective.

This method raises several questions. First, what if you have multiple bug reports opened against a single test case? For such a situation, you can allot multiple rows to the test case, using only the Bug ID, Bug RPN, FW, and (possibly) Comments columns for the additional rows. I admit that this arrangement isn't very pretty; if you can come up with a more compact and elegant way of presenting this, I'd appreciate knowing about it. Fortunately, the multiple-row arrangement will apply to only a few test cases throughout an entire test project.

Second, isn't it unfair to use a sum rather than a normalized value?[2] Perhaps it is, but how would you normalize the figure? To use the number of test cases in the suite, you would need uniformity in test case effort (person-hours) and duration (clock time) for each case—usually not a safe assumption. If you use the number of hours in the suite, do you use duration or effort? When adding complexity doesn't add much value, I prefer a simpler approach. Besides, since the point of calculating test suite yield is to allow you to compare test suites, normalizing could defeat the purpose.

---

2. I use the word "normalized" in the mathematical sense of dividing by a factor that ensures "apples-to-apples" comparisons. For example, when speaking of automobile mileage, we don't talk about how many miles or kilometers are traveled per tank of gas—which varies from one vehicle to the next—but rather in terms of miles per gallon or liters per hundred kilometers.

Third, you might question my choice to add the inverse RPNs rather than, say, multiplying them, squaring the sums, or using another more exotic function. If you believe that such an approach is more appropriate, try it. I would argue that multiplying overstates the importance of RPN 1 bugs while downplaying the importance of other bugs. Is a test suite that yields one RPN 1 bug eight times better than a suite that yields three RPN 2 bugs? I would deem the latter test suite better, a conclusion that supports the additive approach. Squaring the sums also emphasizes the bugs with lower RPNs, though in a more appropriate way, but it makes the number more difficult to explain without adding much information. As always, however, follow your muse; if you have a better idea, go ahead and implement it.

RECORDING OWNERSHIP

If you have a large team or many test cases, identifying the current owner of a test case or suite can be helpful. As recorded in an Owner column in the test case summary worksheet, the owner might be the organization responsible for running the test, the engineer writing the test, or the test technician running the test. A test can have multiple owners over time; for example, a different technician might run the test in each test cycle.

RUNNING WHAT'S IMPORTANT

You might want to add a Priority column to the test case summary worksheet. This column is most useful when you are running a large test effort, or a distributed one, in which your priorities are not clear and obvious. (If the test team consists of you and two other people, there's liable to be little confusion about what's important.) Of course, the issue of priority brings us back to weighted failures. If you consider certain test cases very important, but they never yield any interesting bugs, why are they important? Perhaps a test case covers such a critical quality risk that you must run the test no matter what the circumstances.

ADDING OTHER SUMMARIES

You can create additional summary worksheets. For instance, I have seen summaries based on the work results of individual testers, on planned versus actual effort, and so forth. All sorts of interesting numbers can be generated. The test tracking spreadsheet is a flexible tool, and it lends itself to extensions. Just remember that the more bells and whistles you attach, the bigger the file gets, the slower the updates become, and the more impenetrable the data seems to many managers and developers.

You also should think twice about certain kinds of summaries—in particular those that address questions such as "Who found the most bugs?" "Who spent the most time testing?" and "Who found the most bugs per hour spent?" I find these numbers dangerous, and I don't generate them. As soon as you begin analyzing employee performance data, you take risks. If people know you are measuring them this way, they will soon figure out how to manipulate the numbers. In addition, if you use such data to rank employees for a layoff or to fire laggards, you might believe you're being fair, but you could find yourself in court responding to a lawsuit.[3]

GROUPING DATA

The test case summary worksheet shown earlier grouped data primarily by test suite. Alternatively, you could use test phases, owner, or organization as major groups.[4] The grouping can be as flat or as hierarchical as you want. If you use too many levels, you'll make the chart difficult to read. If you use too few—for example, a thousand detail rows but no grouping—the chart will be monotonous and hard to scan. If in doubt, try out a few different arrangements and see what looks most readable and accessible.

ADDING TEST CASE DETAILS

Chapter 3 provided a template for writing test cases, constructed in Excel. It has probably already occurred to you that you can integrate the test cases with the test tracking spreadsheet. By doing so, you gain automatic summaries of the test cases as you update them with test results.

Figure 5-5 on the following page reintroduces the test case template. As you might recall, the first group of rows provides introductory descriptive information about the test case; the middle section details the test case, listing the steps and substeps that create test conditions; and the last section summarizes the results.

---

3. Lest you think I'm being overly dramatic, you might want to consult *Testing Computer Software*, by Cem Kaner, Jack Falk, and Hung Quoc Nguyen, which discusses this risk. This book also devotes an entire chapter to product liability as it relates to computer testing.

4. You might want to track organizations if the developers are to run certain test suites and you have been asked to track the results in your test tracking spreadsheet. Chapter 10 discusses external organizations that can become involved in testing.

Notice that I have added a column for Bug RPN because we now have a similar field in the test case summary. You can use Excel links between worksheets to automatically transfer information such as the test ID, the test case name, and so forth from the test case template to the test case summary or vice versa.

By creating a separate worksheet for each test case, you can include all the tests, along with the summaries, from a given test phase in a single spreadsheet. By establishing links up to the test case summary and down into each test case worksheet, you can create a complete, self-summarizing test tracking system. The feasibility of building such a system depends on how many test cases you intend to run. If you have too many to fit into a single spreadsheet, you can link them across multiple files (in Excel, at least). For very large projects, however, in which you would need to tie together a great many spreadsheets, this effort might prove too complex, and the system might be too difficult to maintain.

If you decide to use this approach, you'll need to establish a process for updating the worksheets. You might want to print out the test cases, have test engineers and technicians make notes on the hard copies, and input the results yourself. This ensures that the data is more consistent, and it prevents

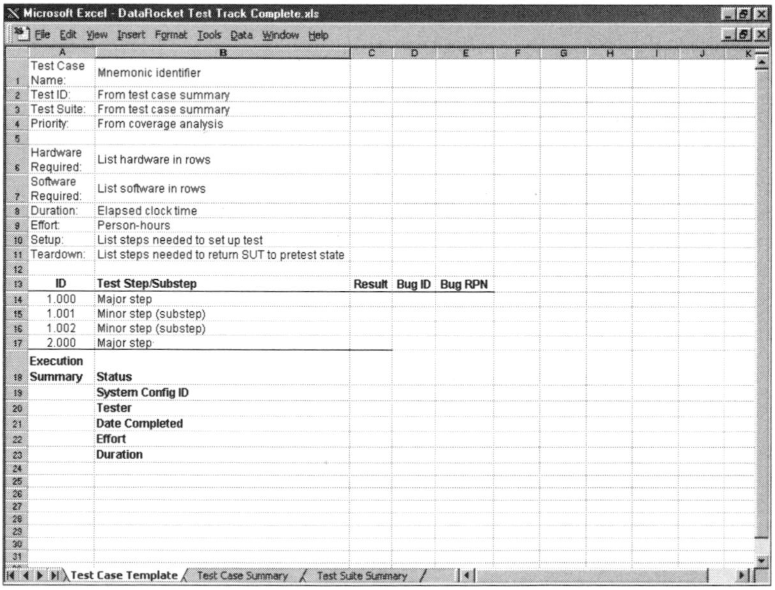

FIGURE 5-5   *A fully detailed test case template.*

mistakes in using the formulas, but it can consume a lot of your time. Personally, I find that staying intimately acquainted with test execution at a test case level makes a lot of sense. But if your management style is better suited to focusing at a higher level, let your testers update the test case worksheets, and then you can audit the test case summary and test suite summary after the updates.

Putting the Test Tracking System in Motion

To illustrate how the test tracking spreadsheet can work for you, this section presents three short case studies, using the DataRocket information shown earlier. In each scenario, assume that you are about halfway through the scheduled system test phase. The first two scenarios represent test projects in some amount of trouble, one with a minor problem and the other in serious difficulty. The third scenario describes a successful project.

Little Trouble

It's July 17, 1999. Life is pretty good on the test project. All the systems showed up on time—a small miracle—and you have yet to run into any major bugs. You sent the systems out to an external test lab named System Cookers, and most of the environmental tests finished almost a week early; this was a major stroke of luck since these tests were considered the most risky. Nevertheless, you do have a few problems, as your current test case summary worksheet (shown in Figure 5-6 on the following page) indicates.

First, and worst, the standards testing is taking longer than planned. Hitesh, the test engineer in charge, is deluged with other systems in the lab and probably won't wrap up that work for a few more days. This isn't a big deal—assuming that all the tests pass. Given the difficulty of predicting *that*, however, you're a little nervous. Second, you seem to have undersized the tests that were to be run in-house (rather than at System Cookers). All of these tests are taking longer, in person-hours, than you expected. You are incurring some overtime costs associated with your contractor, Jim, and an irritated employee, Lin-Tsu, who has had to work overtime for two weeks. Third, the packaging was given a last-minute facelift, delaying that portion of the environmental testing. Fourth, the floppy drive doesn't read 1.2-MB (Japanese) formatted disks. You mark this as a *Warn* because this problem might delay shipment in Japan, though nowhere else. Figure 5-7 on the following page shows your current test suite summary worksheet.

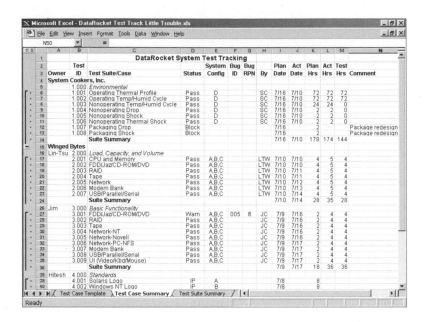

FIGURE 5-6   *A worrisome test case summary.*

Suite	Total Cases	Block	Run	Fail	Weighted Failure	Pass	IP	Skip	In Queue
Environmental	8	2	6	0	0.00	6	0	0	0
Load, Capacity, and Volume	7	0	7	0	0.00	7	0	0	0
Basic Functionality	9	0	9	0	0.17	9	0	0	0
Standards	3	0	0	0	0.00	0	3	0	0
Total	27	2	22	0	0.17	22	3	0	0
By Pct		7%	81%	0%	N/A	81%	11%	0%	0%

DataRocket System Test Suite Summary

FIGURE 5-7   *A worrisome test suite summary.*

166

The latter two problems, of course, are system-related issues, which you can't really affect. You do, however, have two lessons to learn. The first is that you should cross-train your staff to perform standards testing so that the schedule isn't held up there again because of one person's workload. The second is that you should be careful to adjust the planned person-hours for the next test project.

Big Trouble

It's July 26, 1999. You have big problems. Engineering samples showed up for testing a week late, but the project release date remains unchanged. You lost a week from your first test cycle. On top of that, Solaris, an important network operating system for your customers, won't install or run reliably with DataRocket. The system panics during installation in nearly half the tests; at other times it panics under load. This bug, which is recorded in the test case shown in Figure 5-8, blocks completion of most tests.

	ID	Test Step/Substep	Result	Bug ID	Bug RPN
		Test Case Name:	CPU and Memory		
		Test ID:	2.001		
		Test Suite:	Load, Capacity, and Volume		
		Priority:	High		
		Hardware Required:	One DataRocket Server		
		Software Required:	Load, Capacity, and Volume test tool		
			Windows NT		
			Solaris		
			Novell		
		Duration:	3		
		Effort:	4		
		Setup:	Install Windows NT		
			Install Novell		
			Install Solaris		
		Teardown:	None necessary		
	1.000	Test CPU load on Windows NT.			
	1.001	Install Windows NT. Confirm proper install.	Pass		
	1.002	Install LCV test tool from LCV CD-ROM. Confirm proper install.	Warn	9	3
	1.003	Run LCV test tool, CPU module, for one hour. Check log file for failures on exit.	Pass		
	2.000	Repeat steps 1.001-1.003 for Solaris.	Fail	10	1
	3.000	Repeat steps 1.001-1.003 for Novell.	Pass		

Execution Summary	Status	Fail
	System Config ID	B,A,C
	Tester	LTW
	Date Completed	7/14/99
	Effort	16
	Duration	16

FIGURE 5-8 *A test case showing a serious problem.*

You also have problems with the Environmental test suite. The CPU exceeded its temperature specification in the thermal profile test. The CPU vendor tells you that the chip will suffer a serious degradation in its MTBF at this temperature, making the system prone to failure in a few months. In addition, the motherboard cracked during the temperature/humidity cycle test. Although the system still ran after the test, the damage indicates that the board is improperly mounted. To add insult to injury, the cardboard box, the padding, and the system case suffered cosmetic damage during the packaging drop test, indicating a need to redesign the package. All of these difficulties are reflected in the test case summary worksheet shown in Figure 5-9.

These problems are very serious. Does it even make sense to move on to the second cycle of system testing? Probably not. You are effectively blocked until you have a fix for the Solaris bug. The environmental test—an expensive operation—will need to be rerun, but only after the mounting and

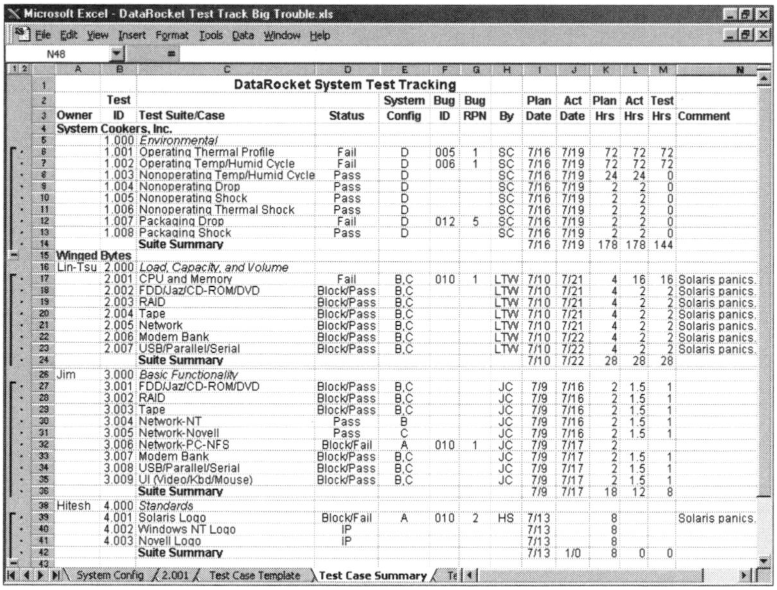

	Owner	Test ID	Test Suite/Case	Status	System Config	Bug ID	Bug RPN	By	Plan Date	Act Date	Plan Hrs	Act Hrs	Test Hrs	Comment
1			**DataRocket System Test Tracking**											
4	**System Cookers, Inc.**													
5		1.000	*Environmental*											
6		1.001	Operating Thermal Profile	Fail	D	005	1	SC	7/16	7/19	72	72	72	
7		1.002	Operating Temp/Humid Cycle	Fail	D	006	1	SC	7/16	7/19	72	72	72	
8		1.003	Nonoperating Temp/Humid Cycle	Pass	D			SC	7/16	7/19	24	24	0	
9		1.004	Nonoperating Drop	Pass	D			SC	7/16	7/19	2	2	0	
10		1.005	Nonoperating Shock	Pass	D			SC	7/16	7/19	2	2	0	
11		1.006	Nonoperating Thermal Shock	Pass	D			SC	7/16	7/19	2	2	0	
12		1.007	Packaging Drop	Fail	D	012	5	SC	7/16	7/19	2	2	0	
13		1.008	Packaging Shock	Pass	D			SC	7/16	7/19	2	2	0	
14			**Suite Summary**						7/16	7/19	178	178	144	
15	**Winged Bytes**													
16	Lin-Tsu	2.000	*Load, Capacity, and Volume*											
17		2.001	CPU and Memory	Fail	B,C	010	1	LTW	7/10	7/21	4	16	16	Solaris panics.
18		2.002	FDD/Jaz/CD-ROM/DVD	Block/Pass	B,C			LTW	7/10	7/21	4	2	2	Solaris panics.
19		2.003	RAID	Block/Pass	B,C			LTW	7/10	7/21	4	2	2	Solaris panics.
20		2.004	Tape	Block/Pass	B,C			LTW	7/10	7/21	4	2	2	Solaris panics.
21		2.005	Network	Block/Pass	B,C			LTW	7/10	7/21	4	2	2	Solaris panics.
22		2.006	Modem Bank	Block/Pass	B,C			LTW	7/10	7/22	4	2	2	Solaris panics.
23		2.007	USB/Parallel/Serial	Block/Pass	B,C			LTW	7/10	7/22	4	2	2	Solaris panics.
24			**Suite Summary**						7/10	7/22	28	28	28	
26	Jim	3.000	*Basic Functionality*											
27		3.001	FDD/Jaz/CD-ROM/DVD	Block/Pass	B,C			JC	7/9	7/16	2	1.5	1	
28		3.002	RAID	Block/Pass	B,C			JC	7/9	7/16	2	1.5	1	
29		3.003	Tape	Block/Pass	B,C			JC	7/9	7/16	2	1.5	1	
30		3.004	Network-NT	Pass	B			JC	7/9	7/16	2	1.5	1	
31		3.005	Network-Novell	Pass	C			JC	7/9	7/16	2	1.5	1	
32		3.006	Network-PC-NFS	Block/Fail	A	010	1	JC	7/9	7/17	2			
33		3.007	Modem Bank	Block/Pass	B,C			JC	7/9	7/17	2	1.5	1	
34		3.008	USB/Parallel/Serial	Block/Pass	B,C			JC	7/9	7/17	2	1.5	1	
35		3.009	UI (Video/Kbd/Mouse)	Block/Pass	B,C			JC	7/9	7/17	2	1.5	1	
36			**Suite Summary**						7/9	7/17	18	12	8	
38	Hitesh	4.000	*Standards*											
39		4.001	Solaris Logo	Block/Fail	A	010	2	HS	7/13		8			Solaris panics.
40		4.002	Windows NT Logo	IP					7/13		8			
41		4.003	Novell Logo	IP					7/13		8			
42			**Suite Summary**						7/13	1/0	8	0	0	

FIGURE 5-9 *A test case summary indicating major problems.*

temperature problems are resolved. You almost certainly won't exit the system test phase until weeks after the scheduled date, delaying first customer shipment. The severity of the problems is evident in the test suite summary worksheet shown in Figure 5-10.

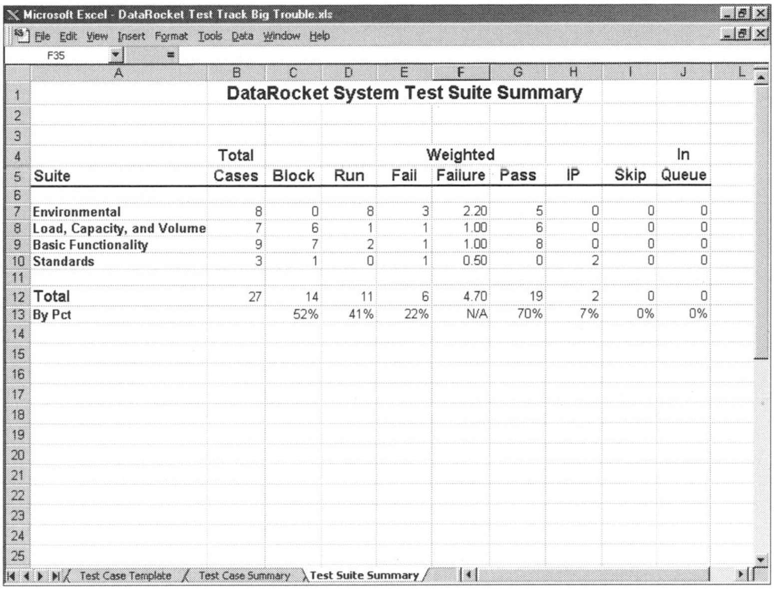

	A	B	C	D	E	F	G	H	I	J
1				DataRocket System Test Suite Summary						
2										
3										
4		Total				Weighted				In
5	Suite	Cases	Block	Run	Fail	Failure	Pass	IP	Skip	Queue
6										
7	Environmental	8	0	8	3	2.20	5	0	0	0
8	Load, Capacity, and Volume	7	6	1	1	1.00	6	0	0	0
9	Basic Functionality	9	7	2	1	1.00	8	0	0	0
10	Standards	3	1	0	1	0.50	0	2	0	0
11										
12	Total	27	14	11	6	4.70	19	2	0	0
13	By Pct		52%	41%	22%	N/A	70%	7%	0%	0%

FIGURE 5-10   *A test suite summary reporting major problems.*

No Problem!

It's July 15, 1999, and the living is easy. You received a telephone call this morning from the lab manager at System Cookers informing you that DataRocket passed all the environmental tests as of yesterday. This is only a day late, which is good, since the systems got to the lab three days late. The first cycle of system testing is now finished. The only problem found was a minor glitch during Novell standards testing, for which you just received a waiver. Your test suite summary worksheet shows that 100 percent of the tests have been run, with 100 percent passing. The test case summary worksheet (Figure 5-11) also reflects this smooth sailing.

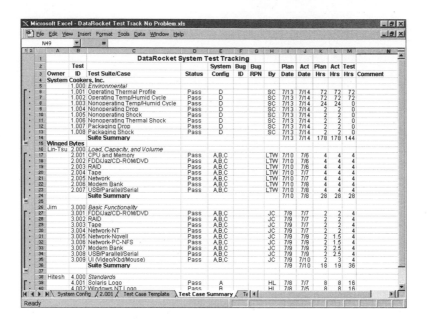

FIGURE 5-11 *A test case summary for a product that will ship soon.*

Based on these fantastic results, you have the enviable job of walking down to the project manager's office today and waiving the second and third cycles of system testing, as DataRocket now satisfies the system test exit criteria. The product will ship about a month early, provided all goes well during pilot testing.

6

Tips and Tools for Crunch Time: Managing the Dynamic

If you've been through a test project once or twice, you know that "crunch mode" is both hectic and confusing: facts are often cloudy; plans are in flux; and dependencies, once unclear, jump into sharp relief the moment they are not met. This chapter offers two new tools specifically geared toward managing the goat rodeos that can consume your life during test execution. One is a logistics database that tracks the locations, configurations, and test requirements for hardware, software, infrastructure, and staff. The other is a simple change management database that helps you respond to the inevitable course corrections, both smooth and jerky, that occur on any test project. First, though, let me offer some observations on crunch mode and some tips that might aid you in maintaining your professionalism and sanity during this high-pressure period.

DO SWEAT THE DETAILS: STAYING ON TOP OF EVERYTHING

The common thread running through all the tips in this section is the importance of remaining in control of the details swirling around you. During test execution, you will have many items to attend to, all of them urgent, but you should be sure to set aside some time to look at where the testing process is taking you. Are you on track? What risks and roadblocks loom? In that spirit, here are some suggestions that should help you survive crunch time.

MOVING FORWARD WHILE GETTING ALL THE FACTS: THE DESIRE FOR CERTITUDE, THE IMPERATIVE OF PROGRESS

Imagine that you and I have two conversations. In the first, we're standing near a brick house, and you point to the wall and say, "Look at that chameleon! It changed color to match the brick." I look, I see the lizard, I notice its red hue, and I agree. In the second, you say, "Did you know that my golden retriever Gertrude can talk?" In the absence of hearing the dog talk firsthand, I'm not likely to believe you.

Often the most interesting bug reports start out along these lines: *I did X, and everything seemed to be going fine. Then all of a sudden Y happened, and the system crashed.* Sadly, you then discover that repeating the action X doesn't repeat the consequence Y. You try it a dozen times, but you can duplicate the crash only once or twice. When you change some variables that might be related, you can't reproduce the problem. But maybe it's not gone. It's hard to tell these kinds of stories to developers without triggering incredulity.

A solid bug report is satisfying and goes a long way toward building test's credibility with developers. Certitude—"this is the truth, and I can demonstrate it"—is a good feeling. A clean, reproducible bug report is indisputable. In many cases, though, the price of certitude is too high. If you've ever had to perform a reliability test of software or hardware, you know how time-consuming such demonstrations of statistical confidence can be. If you tried to investigate every bug to the level of certitude, you'd never find half of them. It's important to keep in mind the need to progress. Testing computers, like all engineering, is not a search for truth—that's science. Engineering is about producing things, about making useful objects. Often as not, close enough must be good enough.

DEPENDENCIES, SCHEDULES, AND REMINDERS: THE IMPORTANCE OF FOLLOW-UP

One of the more daunting challenges of managing a test project is that so many dependencies converge at test execution. You can often kludge your way through test development, but you can't execute tests unless all the myriad details and external components come together at the right time. One missing configuration file or hardware device can render all your test results meaningless. You can end up with a whole platoon of testers sitting around for days.

This kind of incident is hardly the test manager's fault. You will have your hands full managing your own team, and you can't be expected to manage others. This is cold comfort, however, when you are spending a weekend in the lab with your testers. All too often, missing components show up or prerequisite tasks are completed at 5:00 on a Friday afternoon, accompanied by a pep talk from a manager who stresses that it's the responsibility of the team players in the test organization to help compensate for the schedule hit. It's true that you can't manage other groups, but you can keep an eye on project-wide events and trends that might affect the test schedule and clearly communicate the potential or pending difficulties to your management.

Beyond simply staying in the loop concerning other aspects of the project, it's essential to set reminders and milestones for yourself. A scheduling program such as Microsoft Outlook can help, or you can use a paper system such as Day-Timer. Either way, a reminder about when an external event that affects testing is scheduled to occur will alert you to follow up with the appropriate person:

> *Phone switch should be configured today. Check with John.*
>
> *Three systems due to ship from Lucky Bit today. Check with Lin-Tsu and then verify customs broker with Jack.*
>
> *Muhammad's team to deliver first cut of the XYZ software today. Follow up.*

Keeping apprised of schedule slips, feature changes, and other modifications to the plan allows you to react in advance, which gives you more options. Wouldn't you rather know at 4:00 on Wednesday afternoon that you have to line up staff for weekend coverage instead of finding out at 4:00 on Friday afternoon? By being proactive, you will earn some recovery or contingency time.

It Won't Deliver Itself:
Revisions and Release Processes

Between the completion of a hardware or software subsystem and its delivery to test lie various degrees and kinds of heavy lifting. Software must be assembled into a package of some sort, either physical or electronic. Hardware must be configured, packed up, and sent. Shipping and customs clearance might be issues. These activities are often not sexy, popular, or easy to keep straight.

Because you are on the receiving end, it behooves you to drive the definition of the process. For each subsystem or system, you should ensure that someone is on the hook for delivering usable, testable items to your test group. I'm not suggesting that you claim ownership of such tasks; far from it—you have enough to do. Often a well-worded e-mail, sent to your manager and some of the people you suspect *might* be appropriate owners, will suffice.

In extreme cases, you might need to develop and promulgate a plan yourself. Such a plan would assign ownership of various stages of the delivery process to specific individuals, based on your understanding of their roles. This is dangerous ground politically, however; be sure that you have sufficient clout before you attempt it.

As discussed in earlier chapters, you'll also face the issues of frequency and configuration management as new builds are released. Within a few weeks of initial delivery, you should seek renewed commitments from your development counterparts that they intend to adhere to the release plan previously agreed upon.

It Won't Install Itself, Either:
Configuring the Test Environment

In some cases, testing covers the process of installing software or hardware components. When you test operating systems or applications, for example, the first step of testing a new build is to test the installation or upgrade procedures, which should result in a configured test environment. Unfortunately, it often leaves you with a broken mess instead, especially with early builds, so you must have contingency plans in place whenever possible.

Contingency plans can't always be implemented, of course. Obviously, access to a stable, completely installed version of the system under test is essential for effective testing. If you can't install the software or you can't get an operating system running on the computer you're testing, the test process is blocked. Since you'll find such announcements unpopular with management, always double-check to make sure you have your facts straight.

Sometimes the task of installing and configuring the test environment is too complex for a typical tester to handle. In such instances, you have two alternatives: either have the necessary level of system administration support available within your team or have the expertise available on call from the project team, information systems, technical support, or another appropriate group.

My preference is the former. The best way to ensure that someone's priorities are aligned with yours is to have that person on your team. If you do use external system administration support, do your best to get a guarantee of response times and a clear process for escalating problem situations up the management chain to prevent them from festering. I have worked with some excellent support staff, but I have also had some negative experiences when I've relied on outside help. These problems were usually not the other team's fault. When a limited set of people must support half a dozen groups, your request will sometimes languish in a queue. That will not happen if the support resource works on your team.

"THE HOBGOBLIN OF LITTLE MINDS" IS YOUR FRIEND: AUDITING AND UPDATING TEST RESULTS

Testing can be a confusing environment. Except for the simplest of functional bugs, it's seldom clear exactly what has gone wrong when an anomaly first comes to light. Significant time might elapse between the first muttered "What the heck?" and the completion of a bug report. Of course, since a bug report is often just a description of symptoms, further discovery is usually needed. Thus a certain lack of clarity comes with the territory. Indeed, since tests are experiments, you could say that testing is about *creating* a lack of clarity, about raising questions in people's minds, about challenging "facts" people "know" that just ain't so.

When you are challenging preconceived notions, you must back up your assertions with data. This requires spending a lot of time keeping your internal data—especially bug tracking and test tracking—as consistent and current as possible. When you're asked about status, you want to provide management with clear answers.

Chapters 4 and 5 introduced two linked tracking mechanisms, for bugs and for test cases. The linkages exist in both directions: the bug reports reference test case identifiers, and the test cases—at both a detail level and a summary level—reference bug reports and their risk levels. Figure 6-1 provides a visual representation of these linkages.

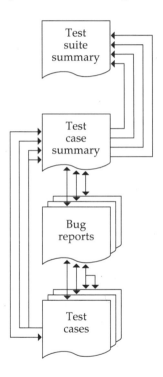

FIGURE 6-1 *Linkages between test results.*

By going through the bug reports and the test tracking spreadsheet at the same time to ensure consistency, you can keep these two mechanisms congruent. Because the status of bug reports and test cases changes over time, the two will get out of sync if you don't review the linkages regularly. This slippage can happen quickly. When test execution is running at full bore, you should audit the spreadsheet and the reports once or twice a week.

Admittedly, this can be a painstaking exercise. The truly motivated among you might decide to implement the entire system, including test tracking, in Microsoft Access or another relational database, which would allow you to automate the linkages. But reconciling the bug reports and the tests manually actually provides an interesting side benefit: by forcing yourself to crawl through the details of every active bug report and every test case that didn't pass, you become intimately aware of what's going on in the test process. The ritual can reward you by identifying a number of important issues that need to be addressed.

You might start by going through the spreadsheet. If testers are making notes about test cases on hard copy, you should enter this data in the worksheets. If testers are doing the updates themselves, you should review the results in the test case summaries and the test suite summaries. If you have questions, drill down to the test case level or across to the bug tracking database. For each test case that has identified a bug, check the status of the bug report: Is it still open? Is the risk priority number correct? Does the configuration and tester information in the bug report match the test case summary?

After checking the spreadsheet, move on to the bug reports. Although you will have already audited many of the reports as part of auditing the spreadsheet, it's a good idea to walk through the bug reports at the detail level. Seeing a bug report might remind you to follow up on an item with a colleague or to schedule a confirmation test that you somehow missed.

Avoiding the Venus Flytrap: Not Getting Stuck in Debugging

Chapter 4 emphasized the distinction between isolation and debugging. (See "Drawing a Line in the Sand: The Boundary Between Isolation and Debugging," page 113.) As test execution gets cranked up, it's a good time to remind all your testers that they should politely decline to participate in debugging activities. If management demands test involvement in debugging, either before testing starts or during test execution, insist that they make a good case for why the involvement of testers is so critical.

Many testers really enjoy participating in the debugging process, so I may sound like the grinch who stole Christmas. Why am I so adamant about keeping testers out of debugging activities?

◆ They have other work to do. Every hour a tester spends working with a developer is either an hour of overtime, an hour of testing lost, or an hour tacked onto the current test cycle. In other words, the test organization suffers a budget, coverage, or schedule hit.

◆ Debugging effort is hard to estimate. During test execution, most developers are scheduled to spend their time fixing bugs. Given access to tester debugging support, developers will use varying degrees of that support, depending on the number and types of bugs found, and the requests for that support will come at random times.

◆ Debugging work can be difficult to manage. It tends to arrive unannounced and under the radar. I once worked with a test engineer who loved debugging. I would walk into his office in the midst of a furious schedule crunch and find him bent over a keyboard with some developer. You can't manage a group if its members set their own priorities.

Nevertheless, testers do need to support debugging on occasion—typically when a bug cannot be reproduced in the development environment, when a tester has product skills (content expertise) that the developers don't have, or when a product has entered test in an unstable state, leaving you no option but to help debug or sit and wait.[1] In addition, you might find that a specific development process or culture requires testers to participate in debugging. In such cases, be sure that management knows the price they are paying. Whatever your situation, you should understand the level of debugging support that the test team will be called on to render and build the necessary time and resources into your schedule.

When Test Fails: Minimizing Type I and Type II Errors

Despite your best efforts, the test system itself sometimes produces errors. As earlier chapters explained, I categorize these problems as type I or type II errors. A type I error, the less serious of the two, occurs when a tester

---

1. Receipt of an unstable product often means that entry criteria have been violated. Nevertheless, in an attempt to stick to the given schedule, management might dictate the start of testing anyway. Once test execution formally begins, Pandora's box is open. Chapter 9 deals with this and other political issues.

reports correct system behavior as a bug, assigns an excessively high severity or priority to a bug, or otherwise overstates the significance of a problem. Although they don't jeopardize product quality, type I errors can damage the credibility of the test organization; developers and project managers tend to adopt a "boy who cried wolf" attitude toward the test team after enough false alarms. A type II error occurs when a tester fails to detect or report incorrect system behavior, assigns an excessively low priority or severity to a bug, or otherwise understates the significance of a problem. A type II error often leads to a test escape, which is a direct risk to product quality.

One cause of both types of errors is MEGO, the affliction in which my…eyes…glaze…over. A tester running a test will always notice if the system catches fire or the program causes the blue screen of death, but an inattentive tester can miss subtle signs of system failure. Likewise, a lack of attention to specifications or other system documentation during bug isolation can cause correct behavior to be mistaken for a bug.

Test automation provides a partial solution to this problem. Automated tests, unlike testers, never get too bored to notice that an error message is misspelled or a transaction takes 50 milliseconds too long. (Bill Perry and Randall Rice, in their fine book *Surviving the Top Ten Challenges of Software Testing*, make a similar point when discussing test automation.) It is, however, quite possible—indeed, all too common—for a test developer to embed type I and type II errors in automated tests.

Even if your testers don't suffer from shrinking attention spans after 12 grueling hours of running tests, they can make type I and type II errors by guessing wrong about what is supposed to happen. As noted in Chapter 3 (see "How Detailed? Balancing Ambiguity," page 78), you don't want to turn your test case library into a groaning bookshelf of totally unambiguous—and totally unmaintainable—pages stuffed into binder upon binder. Nevertheless, if you leave questions of correct behavior to the judgment of testers, they will make some mistakes. There is no perfect solution to this quandary, but appropriate automation, continual enhancement of test cases in response to test escapes, avoiding workloads that strain people beyond their limits of concentration, and careful assignment of team members for test execution all help.

On the topic of assigning testers, one of your jobs as a manager is to know the strengths and weakness of your team members. One of the most important variables in preventing errors is skill level. If, for example, you assign the Microsoft Windows logo certification test to a tester who has no experience with Windows, the poor fellow will probably not succeed in running it. If you ask a software test engineer to run a shock and vibration test on DataRocket, don't be surprised when she botches the job. I'm not arguing for career stultification; assigning new tasks keeps testers challenged and ensures a well-rounded test team. When you do cross-training, though, it's important not to set up the tester—and the project—for failure. Provide adequate instruction first and then supply support from an experienced engineer during cross-training.

In addition to skill levels, you need to consider less tangible attributes when assigning testers. If the test is complicated and somewhat tedious, can the tester focus? If the test is a group effort, do the assigned testers work well together? If you suspect that the tester will need to contact a developer at some point, will the tester be able to make that contact?

Of course, in the real world, you'll have to make many test assignments based on who's free. Like any team, yours will contain some stars and some solid but unspectacular performers. As much as you want star-quality work on all the jobs in your bailiwick, there's only so much star power to go around. Also, demand for a tester's particular skills can vary depending on the kinds of tests you need to run. When these realities force you to select a less-than-perfect tester, be sure to put safety nets such as peer reviews and the support of experienced engineers in place.

Here I must also inject a note of business reality. In some fields, type II errors are totally unacceptable. If you are in charge of testing a system such as the Therac nuclear medicine device (see the sidebar "When Test Escapes Turn Deadly"), every test engineer and technician on your team must be topnotch, experienced, and deeply knowledgeable about the system under test. In contrast, if you test a typical consumer software or hardware product, you will probably have to accept a few type I and type II errors as less dangerous (to the company) than late delivery. Perhaps at some point the business model for computer hardware and software will change if customers, legislatures, or regulatory agencies decide that buggy products are unacceptable. But the reality today is that you won't have the time, the budget, the staff, or the management focus to achieve perfect testing or perfect products.

"HAPPY DRAGON BOAT FESTIVAL...":
WHEN CRUNCH TIME, HOLIDAYS, AND CULTURES COLLIDE

Remember to consider holidays when you schedule crunch periods. Needless to say, you'll encounter major impediments to getting work done during holidays. Your testers will be both reluctant and less able to work long hours. Even if everyone on the team does come into the office on a holiday, they won't be working the 60- to 80-hour weeks that are common during crunch mode. Holidays mean time spent with family, which implies a break from 14-hour days. Even more important, those people who carry the most water for your team—the men and women who consistently pull the all-nighters when the going is tough—have a debt to repay to themselves and their families during holidays. Not coming home on an ordinary Wednesday night during a big push is making a sacrifice, but not coming home for Passover or Christmas Eve can create serious issues in a tester's family life.

Testers are not the only ones who face these problems. Chapter 9 discusses what I call "gas pedals" and "brake pedals" for test operations. One major class of brake pedals is lack of proper system administration, infrastructure, and development support. Convincing system administrators and

---

When Test Escapes Turn Deadly

If you are not familiar with the Therac story, brace yourself. The Therac 25 nuclear medicine device was designed to administer precise dosages of radiation to hospital patients. Because of a software glitch that made it to the field, the device overdosed a number of patients, some of whom died as a result. Incidents such as this have fueled efforts by some in the computer industry to institute mandatory licensing or certification programs for computer professionals.

For a complete discussion of this and other dangerous test escapes, check out Peter Neumann's book *Computer-Related Risks*. You might also want to subscribe to the online forum Risks Digest, available through the *comp.risks* Usenet newsgroup and via e-mail at *risks-request@csl.sri.com*.

developers to wear pagers and give out their home telephone numbers is difficult enough under any circumstances; during holidays, people may well refuse the request. Even if you do have contact information, it might not do you any good. A system administrator who is visiting relatives in Buffalo, New York, without a laptop compeauter isn't much help when your test server goes down at 8:00 P.M. on December 31 in San Jose, California, even if you do find that individual near a telephone and sober.

If you do business internationally, you must also consider cultural issues related to crunch periods. The most obvious is that different countries observe different holidays. Asking a Taiwanese testing lab to squeeze in a rush test job from December 22 through December 31 might not create a problem. But you might get an education about the Chinese (Lunar) New Year if you schedule a month of crunch time at the same lab in January or February.[2] Using calendar software such as Microsoft Outlook that includes support for foreign holidays can help alert you to such conflicts.

In addition, you'll find that the workaholic traditions that seem to accompany high-tech jobs in some countries do not apply the world over. Asking people to work until midnight or come in over a weekend can be a cross-cultural *faux pas*. Indeed, in France, overtime recently became illegal. I have often been struck by how extremely demanding American work habits are in comparison with the "gotta live a little" attitudes prevalent in some of the foreign countries where I've worked. Also bear in mind that in some countries formal work hours end strictly on time so that informal work—building relationships with colleagues over dinner or drinks and solving the problems of the day in a frank and relaxed environment—can occur regularly.

Before you begin to conduct business internationally, I encourage you to study the cultures and work styles of your new foreign colleagues. (One of my clients organized an off-site "culture course" for employees and

---

2. Believe me, it's better to learn these lessons in advance. I once tried to schedule a critical block of tests in Taipei during the Dragon Boat Festival. All I knew was that the holiday involved boat races. "Gee," I thought, "how important can that be?" As I learned from my Taiwanese colleagues, this festival celebrates a bureaucrat who thousands of years ago gave the emperor some important advice about good government and doing right by the citizenry. After the bureaucrat was ignored, he drowned himself to draw attention to the gravity of the matter. I mistakenly concluded that the form of the celebration (boat races) indicated a frivolous event. But this is a significant and serious holiday, observed in many cities with a large Chinese population.

consultants working in Taiwan—a valuable experience.) Such study can help you build more productive working relationships, and you will also enjoy a unique chance to immerse yourself in the culture of another country without the artificiality that comes with seeing that country as a tourist.

A SPIDER'S WEB OF CONNECTIONS: MANAGING TEST HARDWARE AND SOFTWARE CONFIGURATION LOGISTICS

If your system under test is used in a limited setting with a tightly defined list of possible hardware peripherals and software applications, the management of test hardware and software configuration is simple. I once consulted with a client who was working on a Microsoft Windows CE computer for an automobile. The system was installed in the dashboard, connected to only three or four peripherals, had a very simple BIOS, ran only one operating system, and supported a small set of applications. From the point of view of hardware logistics and software configuration management, the test organization merely needed to track BIOS levels, Windows CE releases, the hardware revision levels of the handful of peripherals, and the motherboard and chassis releases. A few very simple tables, implemented in a word processing application, were sufficient.

Not all projects are this straightforward, however. Whether you work on software or hardware development projects, you might find yourself managing a complicated and changing array of hardware devices, especially during test execution. In addition, the software installed on these devices can vary. You must allocate the hardware, make sure that the right software is deployed on it, track its movements, understand who needs it and for what, and ensure that all the appropriate connections are available.

The topic of test hardware is connected to software configuration management—which is a major issue during crunch time. Chapter 7 will expand this discussion by focusing on test lab management, but for now, using SpeedyWriter as an example, we'll take a look at a database that can help you manage hardware logistics and software configuration for your project. This database tracks the following:

◆ Hardware installation, locations, and moves

◆ Current, historical, and planned software configurations

- Hardware interconnections and networking
- Test locations
- Test infrastructure
- Test engineer assignments and locations
- Human resource deployment

THE PIECES AND HOW THEY CONNECT: AN ENTITY-RELATIONSHIP DIAGRAM

Because this database is complex, it's useful to begin with a conceptual overview of the elements and how they relate. Figure 6-2 shows an entity-relationship (E-R) diagram for the database. Those of you who have some familiarity with database design or administration probably recognize this format. But if it's new to you, don't worry; you don't have to understand database design to use this tool.

The rectangles in Figure 6-2 represent entities, which are objects of various kinds. An entity can be broken down into categories; the *Testers* entity, for example, breaks down into two categories, *Engineers* and *Technicians*.

Each entity has a set of properties, represented in the diagram by labeled lines. One (or more) of these properties, called the key, uniquely identifies an individual entity. In Figure 6-2, key properties are indicated by lines with solid endpoints, whereas nonkey properties are indicated by lines with open endpoints. For example, *Name* is a key property of the *Hardware* entity, while *Quantity* is a nonkey property of this entity.

The diamonds represent relationships between pairs of entities. Relationships can also have properties. (Not all relationships have properties; relationships are identified by the entities they associate.) There are three kinds of relationships: one-to-one, one-to-many, and many-to-many. In a one-to-one relationship between entities X and Y, any one Y can have a relationship with one and only one X, and vice versa, much like a marriage. A one-to-many relationship between X and Y would allow any one X to have relationships with multiple Ys, but each Y could have a relationship with only one X. In a many-to-many relationship, both X and Y are unrestricted.

In an entity-relationship diagram, you can tell what kind of relationship exists by looking at the parenthetical notations on the entity ends of the lines connecting the entity pairs to the relationships. These notations are referred to as *minimal and maximal cardinalities*. For example, (0,1) means that either no entity or one entity participates in that side of the relationship. If the other entity involved in the relationship also has (0,1) cardinalities with the first entity, the relationship is one-to-one. The cardinalities (1,n) imply at least one and no maximum number of participating entities. If the other entity has (0,n) cardinalities, the relationship is many-to-many, with possibly no objects paired with objects in the other entity.[3]

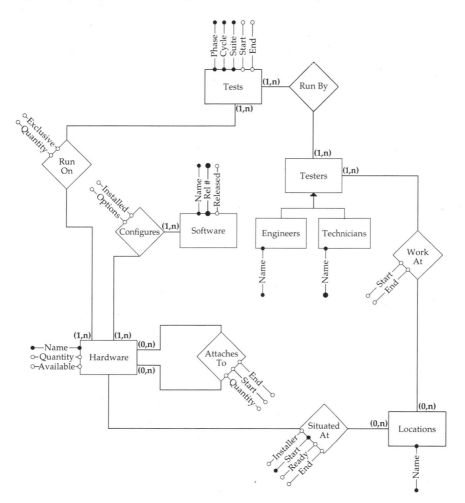

FIGURE 6-2   *An entity-relationship diagram for test execution.*

---

3. For a complete explanation of entity-relationship modeling of databases, see *Conceptual Database Design*, by Carlo Batini, Stefano Ceri, and Shamkant Navathe. This book is especially useful for beginning database users, data modelers, and business analysts.

Let's look more closely at each entity and relationship in Figure 6-2. The *Tests* entity, with five properties, appears at the center top of the chart. The value of the *Phase* property can be Component Test, Integration Test, or System Test. The value of the *Cycle* property is the sequence number of the test cycle in that phase; the value of the *Suite* property is the name of the suite. (Alternatively, you could use an ID number for the *Suite* property, although a number is less descriptive.) These first three properties taken together uniquely identify an individual test—for example, Integration Test, 2, GUI/Edit Engine. The *Start* and *End* properties indicate the scheduled run dates for that suite in that cycle.

Proceeding clockwise around the diagram, you can see that the entities *Tests* and *Testers* are linked by the relationship *Run By*—in other words, tests are run by testers. Testers can be categorized as engineers or technicians; either way, testers are uniquely identified by their names. Because each test is run by one or more testers, and each tester runs one or more tests, the relationship is many-to-many.

Testers work at locations—that is, the *Testers* and *Locations* entities are linked by the *Work At* relationship. In some cases, locations are temporary, within the time frame of the project, so the relationship includes start and end dates. Testers might work at more than one location during a given period of time. Furthermore, a single location might have no testers, one tester, or more than one tester working there at any given time. Therefore, the relationship is many-to-many.

Let's return to the top of the diagram and work our way counterclockwise and down. Tests run on one or more items of hardware, each of which in turn runs one or more tests. A test requires a given quantity of the hardware items, usually one but sometime more, and the test's relationship with the hardware can be either exclusive or nonexclusive, depending on whether the test requires dedicated use of that piece of hardware during its execution. For a hardware item, the properties of interest are *Name, Quantity,* and *Available* (the date of availability).

Software configures most hardware items—that is, the particular combination of software items installed on a piece of hardware, and the way in which they are installed, determines the hardware's functionality. The *Software* entity has three properties of interest: *Name*, *Rel #* (the release number), and *Released* (the release date). The software configures the hardware on the date on which it is installed with particular options.

In a networked or telecommunications environment, a given piece of hardware attaches to one or more other pieces of hardware. Routers, hubs, and switches attach to many devices at once; modems, keyboards, and mice attach to one computer at a time. Such attachments have start and end dates, and the quantity required is also relevant.

Finally, hardware items are situated at a particular location during certain periods of time. In the *Situated At* relationship, an installer sets up the hardware, starting on a particular date. The hardware will be ready for test on a date shortly thereafter, and the hardware will end its sojourn at that location at a later date.

From Diagram to Schemas: Implementing the Logistics Database

To implement the logistics database, I have used Microsoft Access, but you can use any relational database. Begin by creating a table for each entity. Each table should contain a field for each entity property.

Because each relationship is many-to-many, the relationships in the diagram also translate directly into tables. A table for a many-to-many relationship includes the keys from the two related tables, with the combined keys and possibly some relationship properties used as the key for the relationship table. The relationship table also contains a field for each property in the relationship.

I have not provided design details for each table, but they are not complex. Most of the fields are basic text, integer, or date fields, except for the *Exclusive* field in the *Run On* table, which is a yes/no field. Figure 6-3 on the next page shows the tables and their relationships.[4]

---

4. Database purists and data modeling professionals might not like this translation. Access, with its cascading update feature, allows me to avoid the use of surrogate keys for the joins while retaining the ability to change values in key fields without having to do extensive database updates. If you use a database without cascading update capabilities, however, you might be stuck with surrogate keys.

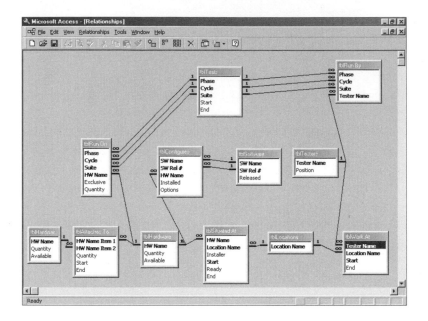

FIGURE 6-3   *Microsoft Access view of tables and relationships in the logistics database.*

BUDGETING AND PLANNING:
USING THE LOGISTICS DATABASE AHEAD OF TIME

One of most important uses of the logistics database is as a planning tool. The following sections walk through an example of how to use the database, based on a case study of SpeedyWriter test logistics. The example illustrates how you can enter data in the database's tables and then display it in simple but powerful reports. This database does not support form-based data entry, although you might want to add this and other enhancements if you choose to make the logistics database part of your standard toolkit. To keep the data minimal in this example, I have omitted test development, but you might need to allocate hardware and people for test development on most of your projects. Although this case study is a simplification, I have used this database to plan hardware, software, network, and human logistics for test projects much more complex than this.

The Work, Who Does It, and
Where It Happens: The People Side

To begin planning the SpeedyWriter test project, you can start with individual tests and who will run them. Figure 6-4 shows the table created for

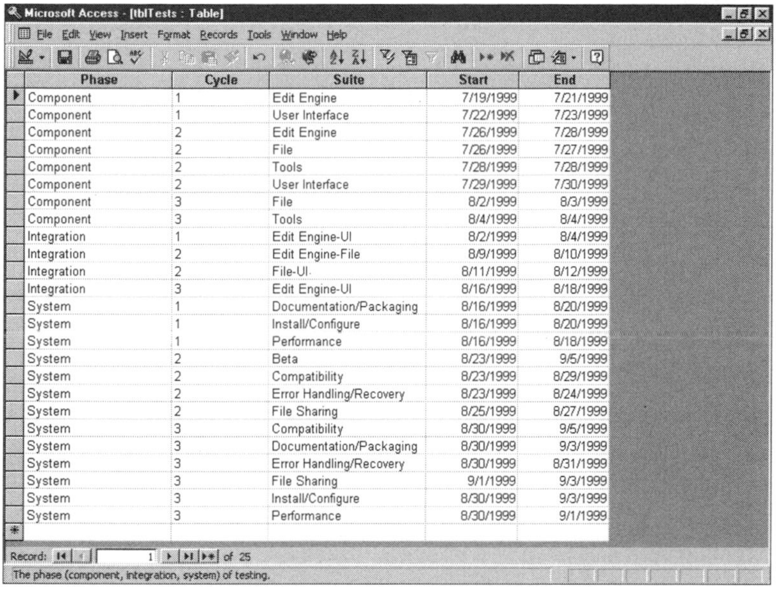

Microsoft Access - [tblTests : Table]

Phase	Cycle	Suite	Start	End
Component	1	Edit Engine	7/19/1999	7/21/1999
Component	1	User Interface	7/22/1999	7/23/1999
Component	2	Edit Engine	7/26/1999	7/28/1999
Component	2	File	7/26/1999	7/27/1999
Component	2	Tools	7/28/1999	7/28/1999
Component	2	User Interface	7/29/1999	7/30/1999
Component	3	File	8/2/1999	8/3/1999
Component	3	Tools	8/4/1999	8/4/1999
Integration	1	Edit Engine-UI	8/2/1999	8/4/1999
Integration	2	Edit Engine-File	8/9/1999	8/10/1999
Integration	2	File-UI	8/11/1999	8/12/1999
Integration	3	Edit Engine-UI	8/16/1999	8/18/1999
System	1	Documentation/Packaging	8/16/1999	8/20/1999
System	1	Install/Configure	8/16/1999	8/20/1999
System	1	Performance	8/16/1999	8/18/1999
System	2	Beta	8/23/1999	9/5/1999
System	2	Compatibility	8/23/1999	8/29/1999
System	2	Error Handling/Recovery	8/23/1999	8/24/1999
System	2	File Sharing	8/25/1999	8/27/1999
System	3	Compatibility	8/30/1999	9/5/1999
System	3	Documentation/Packaging	8/30/1999	9/3/1999
System	3	Error Handling/Recovery	8/30/1999	8/31/1999
System	3	File Sharing	9/1/1999	9/3/1999
System	3	Install/Configure	8/30/1999	9/3/1999
System	3	Performance	8/30/1999	9/1/1999

Record: 1 of 25

The phase (component, integration, system) of testing.

FIGURE 6-4 *The SpeedyWriter tests.*

the *Tests* entity, detailing the test suites to be run during the various phases, along with their constituent cycles. A table of testers appears in Figure 6-5 on the next page, and the table in Figure 6-6 represents the *Run By* relationship, which matches testers to tests. Note that some tests require more than one tester and that some testers run more than one test. Also note that two of the "testers" aren't people. STC is an external test lab (fictional but not atypical) that specializes in software/hardware compatibility testing. Sales/Marketing refers to the internal sales and marketing staff and those special users they choose to involve in testing.

Alone, the three tables shown in Figures 6-4, 6-5, and 6-6 don't do a good job of telling you who's doing what when. Why should you manually cross-reference the three tables when you can create reports based on a query that joins all three? In Figure 6-7 on page 191, for example, you'll find a report titled Tester Assignments that documents which tester performs which tests, and when. This report is organized by phase, cycle, and start date, and it also shows the overall length of time the tester is scheduled to work on the project.

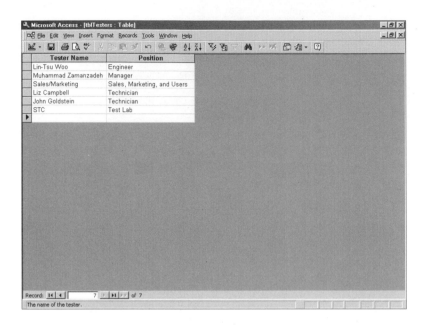

FIGURE 6-5   *The SpeedyWriter testers.*

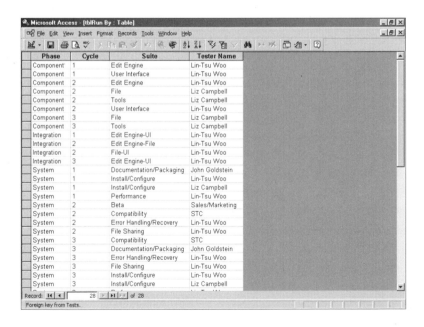

FIGURE 6-6   *The SpeedyWriter test assignments.*

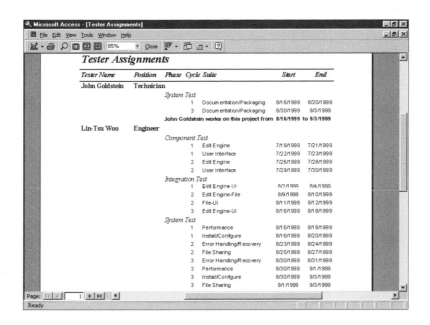

FIGURE 6-7   *The Tester Assignments report.*

An alternative view of the same information, shown in Figure 6-8, documents when and by whom each test is to be run. You might notice that in this Test Schedule report the tests run finish-to-start with no down time in between. This is fine if you have built slack into the duration of each test suite; for example, three days are scheduled for the Edit Engine test suite during the component test phase, even though this suite is likely to take only two days. But if you use a best-case estimate for each suite and pack the tests as shown here, you will find yourself either slipping the schedule or requiring lots of weekend work from your testers when expectations aren't met.

Next you need to address the question of where the test work happens. The table in Figure 6-9 indicates possible locations for the testers and the hardware. The table in Figure 6-10 represents the *Work At* relationship, which matches testers with locations. (Note the use of *1/1/1900* to indicate "as far in the past as is relevant to this project" and *12/31/9999* to indicate "for the duration of this project." Rest assured that Lin-Tsu, Liz, and Muhammad will not spend 8100 years at Software Cafeteria, although on some late nights it might feel that way.) The real globetrotter of the team, you can see, is John Goldstein, the resident technical writing evaluator. He spends the first week testing at the Engineering office, stays for a week of meetings related to

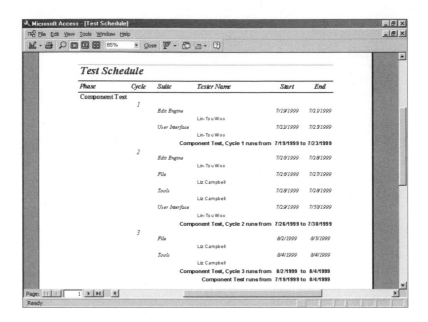

FIGURE 6-8   *The Test Schedule report.*

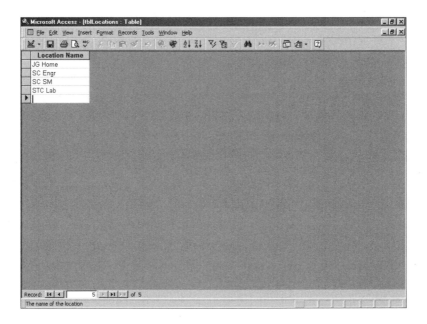

FIGURE 6-9   *The test locations.*

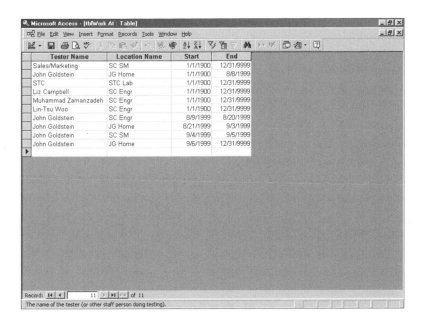

FIGURE 6-10   *The testers at their locations.*

another project, returns to his home office for what he hopes will be a final review of the documentation, and then jets off to the Sales/Marketing office to help with the product launch.

Rather than putting together a report that merely correlates testers and locations—the table is simple enough, after all—you can generate two reports that tie together tests, testers, and locations, as shown in Figures 6-11 and 6-12. The first is location-oriented, organized by place; the second is test-oriented, providing the location last. As you can see, these reports can, to a great extent, supersede some of the previous reports.

A certain amount of magic is required in the query that creates these two reports, which is shown in Figure 6-13. The database join by itself does not restrict the testing by location, since it is the date on which the tester performs the test, together with the tester's location at that time, that determines where the testing happens. Therefore the two date-matching criteria shown in the join are essential to making the query—and the reports that use it—work.

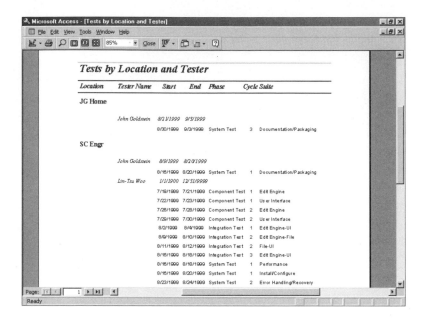

FIGURE 6-11   *The Tests by Location and Tester report.*

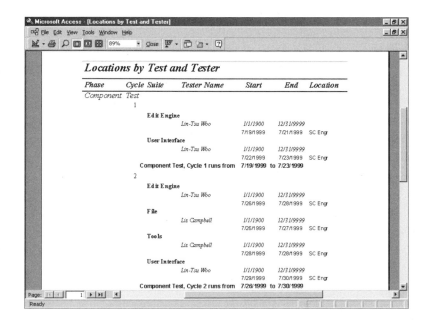

FIGURE 6-12   *The Locations by Test and Tester report.*

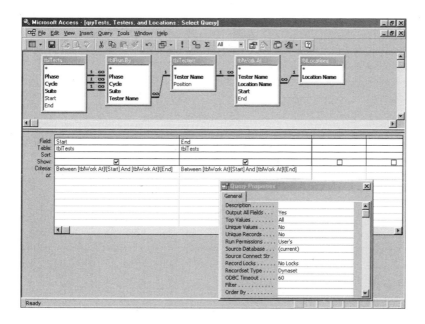

FIGURE 6-13 *A query to show locations, tests, and testers.*

The Assets, How You Use Them, and
Where They Live: The Hardware and Infrastructure Side

In a perfect world, you could simply say, "In order to do this testing, I need hardware items X, Y, and Z; and I need infrastructure M, N, O, and P; and I need software items A, B, C, D, and E." Having said that, you would receive all these items immediately and would have them available for the exclusive use of your test team throughout the entire test process. That never happens. Instead, you'll need to develop a resource allocation plan and submit detailed requests for the items you need. You'll probably get some—but not all—of the items you request, and you'll have to share many of them with other teams.

This section looks at the issue of managing hardware and infrastructure, starting with hardware. Chapter 2 introduced the idea of a hardware allocation plan. (See "Test Configurations and Environments" in that chapter, page 51.) Now you can expand this concept by using the logistics database to plan for the hardware, software, and infrastructure items you need; to organize how these items will be assigned and shared; and to track various configurations.

For the SpeedyWriter case study, hardware and infrastructure come in three flavors: clients, servers, and networking/telecommunications devices.

Let's assume that you want to cover five operating systems on the client side: Mac OS, Windows 95, Windows 98, Windows NT, and Sun Solaris. As noted earlier, SpeedyWriter testing starts in mid-July and runs through early September. Suppose that three client systems are available in the test lab during this time: a Dell desktop, a Macintosh, and a Sony laptop. By purchasing two other clients—say, a Hewlett-Packard and a Micron—you can cover all five target client platforms. Figure 6-14 shows the beginnings of your hardware collection for SpeedyWriter testing, including the operating systems run on each platform.[5]

| Dell | Macintosh | Sony laptop | Hewlett-Packard | Micron |
| (Windows 98) | (Mac OS) | (Windows 95) | (Solaris) | (Windows NT) |

FIGURE 6-14   *Client platforms to be used for SpeedyWriter testing.*

Two questions might occur to you at this point. First, why not simply plan to use the testers' workstations as test platforms? Sometimes you should do this. In our example, John Goldstein uses his PowerBook to do the documentation and packaging testing. Testers will undoubtedly install SpeedyWriter on their workstations and use these for isolation. Usually, however, your test clients should be "clean" configurations. Using an individual's workstation can create questions about bugs. For example, did the software under test corrupt the registry, or does the problem stem from the old shareware game the user installed six months ago that never would completely uninstall?

Second, could you save money by allocating only two or three systems and using partitioning and multiboot utilities to install and select multiple operating systems on each? Again, this is sometimes a good idea. When testing software, you indeed might want to be able to boot different operating systems on a single platform to determine whether bugs are hardware-related. But don't plan on saving money by getting too clever with your test hardware allocation. Do you want one bug on a single platform/operating system combination to bring other scheduled testing to a halt because you

---

5. Alternatively, you could see the operating systems as software that configures the client hardware. But the clients in this case serve primarily to host the operating systems, and the operating system loaded on a given client remains static throughout the testing.

have a platform shortage? How many wasted hours of a test engineer's time will pay for a $2,500 computer? Of course, when you're talking about $250,000 servers, the story is different, but those servers can frequently support multiple users simultaneously. A client computer running tests is generally exclusively allocated for those tests for the duration of the tests.

Let's assume that you want to cover four logical network types: Windows 95 peer-to-peer (NetBEUI), Novell (SPX and TCP/IP), Solaris (NFS with TCP/IP), and Windows NT (TCP/IP). Suppose that everything except the Windows 95 peer-to-peer server is already up and running in the building; you can then budget an inexpensive Acer system to serve as the cooperating host. The systems attach, variously, to five different physical network types: 100 Mbps Ethernet TCP/IP, 10 Mbps Ethernet TCP/IP, 10 Mbps Ethernet SPX, 16 Mbps token ring NetBEUI, and ISDN dial-up networking TCP/IP. (It's important to include different physical network types because different network connections require different drivers on the client side, which can intersect with application operations—even though they're not supposed to do so.) Figure 6-15 shows the test lab configuration with these clients, servers, and network types.

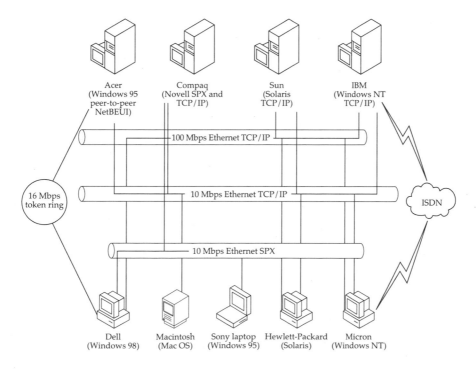

FIGURE 6-15 *The test hardware and network environment for SpeedyWriter testing.*

Although you have now defined a test network without much regard to the specific tests you will run on it, this is not a case of putting the cart before the horse. Your test network definition grew out of your coverage goals for the clients, servers, and network types. Having met these goals, you can now shotgun test suites across the various client configurations. (See the discussion of shotgunning on page 97 in "Regression Test Gaps," in Chapter 3.) Notice that by spreading the testing over the clients, you can also cover the servers and networks easily, provided you ensure that tests actually do exercise all the network connections available to the clients.

Your next task is to set up some reports. You can begin by creating tables based on the *Hardware* entity and the *Run On* and *Attaches To* relationships from Figure 6-2. In much the same way you created reports for the tests and the testers, you can create two reports for tests and hardware, including the attached hardware in this case. Figure 6-16 shows the Hardware Assignment report, organized by hardware; Figure 6-17 shows the Test Hardware report, organized by tests. The former is useful for system administrators and for preparing budgets, while the latter helps testers and test managers understand what hardware they will use to run tests (and also helps you spot missing hardware).

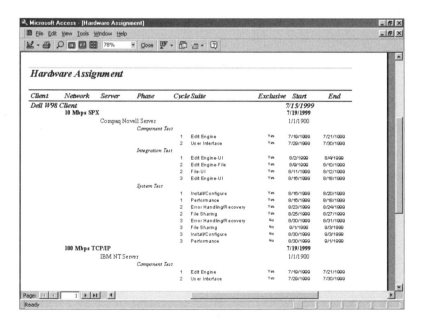

FIGURE 6-16 *The Hardware Assignment report.*

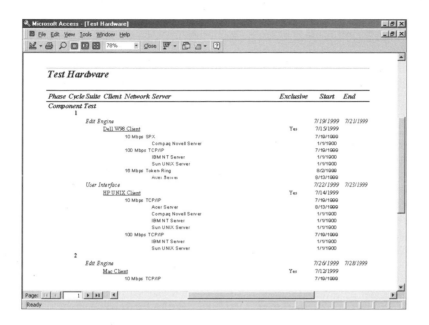

FIGURE 6-17   *The Test Hardware report.*

You will also need to situate the hardware. In the location table in this example, all the hardware is located at the Software Cafeteria Engineering headquarters in Austin, Texas. Typically I use a finer granularity for locations than this example allows, which enables me to track places such as "Second Floor Lab," "Thermal Chamber," and so forth. If you want to use this database to manage tight or limited spaces, you should consider this level of detail. In addition, you might want to include footprint areas and overall dimensions for servers and other lab equipment so that you can compare the space taken up by the hardware in a lab to the space available in the lab. (See Chapter 7 for more on this idea.)

As a final note, let me point out another simplification contained in this section. This example does not account for the hardware that the sales and marketing beta sites will provide, nor does it include the STC lab's hardware. To use this database to ascertain hardware coverage, you would certainly need that level of detail. However, I usually capture that kind of data in the test tracking spreadsheet.

What's Running Where?
Tracking Software Configurations

In general, you can use the logistics database to track all kinds of software configurations on test hardware. You can trace BIOSs, operating system versions, applications, virtual machines and interpreters, compilers, utilities, test tools, test scripts, and other software revisions. To keep our case study simple, though, this section shows only SpeedyWriter software revisions.

Unlike the hardware and human logistics planning discussed in the preceding sections, this section focuses on a dynamic aspect of the database. (After all, this chapter is about crunch mode!) In this example, software is arriving according to a release schedule but rather unpredictably within a one- or two-day window. Table 6-1 shows the planned release schedule for each flavor of SpeedyWriter (that is, for each of the five host, or target, client systems: Mac OS, Windows 95, Windows 98, Windows NT, and Solaris), with the associated test phase and cycle. In addition, releases of SpeedyWriter for each host system are planned for the same day.

The plan shown in Table 6-1 looks good, but it probably won't survive its first encounter with reality. Good tests will find bugs, which will delay releases. Some bugs hold up the releases to the point that entire revision levels will be skipped for certain cycles. Logistical problems—lack of proper build platforms, compiler glitches, and so forth—will also detain releases. Every now and then releases will come in early. And some releases might be skipped because the previous test cycle did not find any bugs in them.

Let's take a hindsight view of what actually happens. Figure 6-18 shows a snapshot of a table based on the *Software* entity. If you are using the railroad method of spreading test suites across configurations (see page 97 in "Regression Test Gaps" in Chapter 3), you can assume that delayed and even skipped releases do not affect the planned execution of tests. Figure 6-19 shows the Tested Configurations report, which cross-references tests against hardware and the software running on those platforms. (Of course, you could also produce a report that was organized by software and showed the tests run against the software configurations.) Since SpeedyWriter runs on the client side, this report does not show the networks or servers.

Revision Identifiers	Release Date	Phase	Cycle
C.1.Mac C.1.W95 C.1.W98 C.1.WNT C.1.Sol	7/19/1999	Component	1
C.2.Mac C.2.W95 C.2.W98 C.2.WNT C.2.Sol	7/26/1999	Component	2
I.1.Mac I.1.W95 I.1.W98 I.1.WNT I.1.Sol	8/2/1999	Component Integration	3 1
I.2.Mac I.2.W95 I.2.W98 I.2.WNT I.2.Sol	8/9/1999	Integration	2
S.1.Mac S.1.W95 S.1.W98 S.1.WNT S.1.Sol	8/16/1999	Integration System	3 1
S.2.Mac S.2.W95 S.2.W98 S.2.WNT S.2.Sol	8/23/1999	System	2
S.3.Mac S.3.W95 S.3.W98 S.3.WNT S.3.Sol	8/30/1999	System	3

TABLE 6-1 *Planned releases for target platforms.*

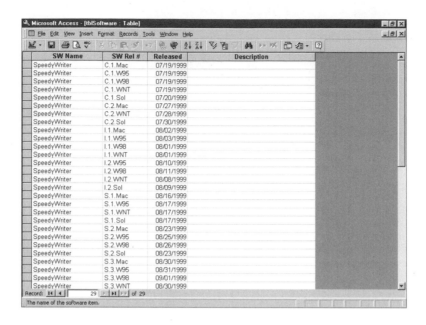

FIGURE 6-18   *Release of software for SpeedyWriter.*

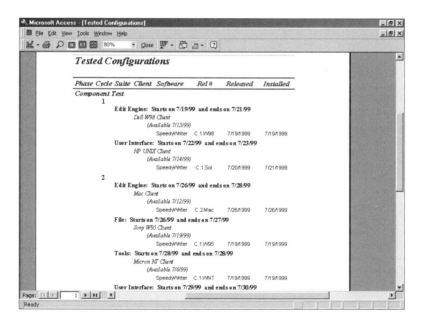

FIGURE 6-19   *The Tested Configurations report, which relates tests, hardware, and the software running on the hardware.*

You can also expand this database to track hardware changes as they occur. In order to do that most effectively, you would need to bifurcate every date field into *Planned* and *Actual* fields. You can even use "deleted" and "added" flags to indicate those records that were dropped or inserted after the initial plan was formulated. Such an approach might constitute the beginnings of a very precise change management database for testing. I prefer, however, to use the more flexible approach introduced in the following section.

EXPECT THE UNEXPECTED: A CHANGE MANAGEMENT DATABASE

No matter how well you plan, no matter how carefully you follow up, no matter how effectively you work with your testers, colleagues, and managers, you will have to respond to the unexpected. Change is unavoidable, and not all changes can be foreseen. Last-minute course corrections, external errors, and internal omissions occur on every development project.

Change is often a manifestation of the learning process. As the development team—including test—proceeds through design, implementation, and testing toward the released product, individuals, groups, and the entire team learn more about how the product should function and behave. Changes related to such acquired wisdom are opportunities to be welcomed, since they let you build a better product.

But there is no point in avoiding the reality that sometimes changes are the result of someone's mistake. A failure to plan or follow up in one group can cause problems in other groups. Because the test group is on the receiving end of many project deliverables—and also because it needs extensive infrastructure, hardware, and software resources and support—your team is probably more susceptible than other development teams to the vagaries of the unexpected. (In fact, Bill Perry and Randall Rice, in *Surviving the Top Ten Challenges of Software Testing*, identify responding to change as one of the top ten challenges facing test organizations.) Thus you may find yourself in need of a way to track and manage incoming changes that threaten to rock—if not tip over—your boat.

That said, most software development books I've read do not identify change management as a proper function of the test organization. For example, Steve McConnell recommends that the project manager or the project management team establish a change control board. This board manages—

monitors, assesses, and accepts or rejects—alterations in any portion of the project plan that is under change control, which includes the test plans and the schedule. (See Chapter 6 of McConnell's *Software Project Survival Guide* for an excellent discussion of how such a change board should work and what it should do.)

If you are fortunate enough to work on a project that has a formal change board, you can use that mechanism to track both deliberate and accidental alterations in the test plan and the schedule. But if you work in environments such as those I'm accustomed to, where change management is an unknown process, the following sections may help you find a way to track the changes that affect your team, the consequences and the impact of those changes, and the recovery plans you put in place.

So What?
Using (and Misusing) Change Management Data

By gathering data about changes, impact, and recovery plans, you can fulfill several important communication and planning responsibilities. Gathering this data provides a structured way to communicate to project management the consequences that certain decisions and events have for the test organization. Using a database also allows you to assemble persistent data that is especially helpful in postmortems or post-project analysis meetings. In addition, committing recovery plans to writing helps to ensure that you aren't simply reacting on the spur of the moment—and it can also save you from having to formally update the test plan, the schedule, and other documents in the midst of crisis conditions. (Significant unexpected changes often rule out the possibility that you can spend an hour checking out documents from the repository, modifying them, and then recirculating them for comments, sign-off, or approval.)

Bear in mind, however, that a change management database is not a place to record a laundry list of complaints. You will probably want to track only those changes that gain or cost a person-day, a calendar-day, or more. Note that you should include gains—after all, some changes are for the better: deliverables show up a day early, software is so good that test cycles are dropped, external support is beyond expectations. The database described here supports capturing the good as well as the bad and the ugly.

Simple Is Good:
The Change Management Database

This change management database is actually quite simple because the needs it serves are straightforward. Figure 6-20 shows the underlying table definition in Access, including a brief description of each field. You can insert data directly into the table using the Access datasheet view, but if you find lengthy text (memo) fields difficult to work with in this view, you can use a form such as the one shown in Figure 6-21, which presents a sample entry for DataRocket.

The *Change Type* field captures information that categorizes the changes. Your list of possible values might include categories such as these:

◆ *Late Deliverable.* Some piece of hardware or software—a part of the system under test—didn't show up on time.

◆ *Early Deliverable.* The converse of the preceding category: a piece of hardware or software showed up early.

◆ *Feature Addition.* A new feature was added to the product that will, presumably, require testing.

◆ *Feature Change/Deletion.* An existing feature was dropped or significantly changed. Any test tools, cases, or suites written primarily or partially for this feature must either change (requiring more time) or be dropped (meaning that the time already spent was wasted).

◆ *Test Addition.* An existing feature, not previously planned for testing, must now be tested. Such a reversal often results from a change in test priorities: what was once a "don't care" area suddenly became the most important feature in the product.

◆ *Test Change/Deletion.* An existing test was dropped, not because the feature was omitted but because someone decided that time or resources should be spent otherwise.

◆ *Schedule Slipped.* You have been granted more time to complete testing. Note that project schedule slips that do not move the planned ship date actually result in an opposite kind of change from the test team's point of view.

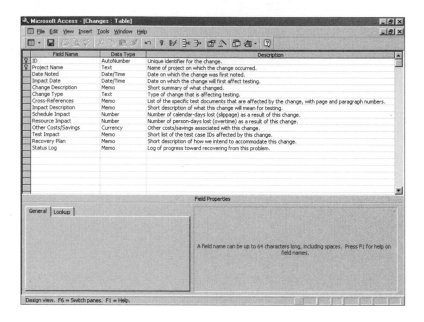

FIGURE 6-20   *A simple table for capturing test changes.*

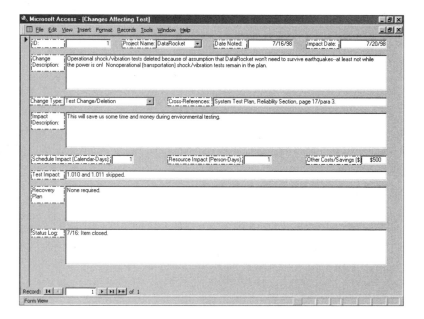

FIGURE 6-21   *A form for entering change data, with a DataRocket sample.*

◆ *Schedule Shortened.* You have less time to complete testing. This often results when you are unable to start testing on time but planned test exit dates remain unchanged.

◆ *Dependency.* Some dependency (a factor other than the system under test) was not available or did not perform as expected.

◆ *Budget Increased.* You received additional funds for testing, which, for example, allow you to purchase additional tools or hire more staff.

◆ *Budget Reduced.* You lost funds previously committed.

◆ *Quality Problem.* The system under test arrived on time but with such abysmal quality levels that the stopping criteria in the test plan must be invoked, or you might have received a late deliverable that has a quality problem.

◆ *Quality Exceptional.* The system under test arrived with such a high level of quality that you can actually skip one of the planned cycles of testing.

Because this tool is primarily text-based, it is certainly possible to use a word processing program to maintain it. But I find that I value the reporting, categorizing, and analyzing options available in a database. I can produce a report that summarizes positive and negative impacts and adds up hours gained and lost. I can also export this data to a spreadsheet for analysis by date, category of change, and so forth.

Keeping track of changes is sometimes the best you can do during crunch time. This chapter's tips and tools notwithstanding, you will probably find yourself at the mercy of events for the most part. Although you clearly have an important part to play, don't delude yourself into thinking that you, as the test manager, can guide the project team and eliminate chaos entirely. Chapters 8 and 9 discuss the "softer" management skills you will need to work with your team, your peers, and your managers. These skills will be your most valuable assets during a crunch period. Of course, personal attributes such as grace under pressure, respect for your colleagues, and an even temper will serve you well, too.

Stocking and Managing a Test Lab

In many organizations, the test manager is responsible for stocking and managing the test lab. If you are taking over an existing operation, this might not present much of a challenge; once you've seen a test lab in action, it's fairly obvious how to run one. But for a first-time test manager in a new organization, getting a test lab up and running can be something of a mystery.

Simply put, a test laboratory is a place where testing is conducted. I use the word "laboratory" deliberately to emphasize that testers must perform controlled experiments, dealing with measurements and known quantities. They must be equipped with solid tools and a skeptical outlook in their attempt to establish facts. The test lab is an engineering laboratory, of course, not a scientific research laboratory, so the testers are seeking practical knowledge. Nevertheless, like a research laboratory, the test lab should be a place where structured, methodical, calm approaches prevail, not the center of a maelstrom where chaos reigns. (Don't underestimate the psychological effect of having people put on lab coats before entering the test lab!)

A test lab is also a physical location—or locations. When you have more than one test lab, it's useful to assign a name to each lab: a designation indicating its location ("B1"), a meaningful description ("the heat lab"), or just a whimsical name ("Gretchen"). When you conduct distributed testing (more on this in Chapter 10), you might even have multiple labs spread out over several continents.

This chapter describes the process of planning, establishing, and running a test lab. We'll look at questions such as these: Do you need a test lab? How do you select and plan the physical space? How do you outfit the lab? What about security? How do you manage the configuration of the test lab? What about the human factors? Before we begin, however, let me point out several considerations to keep in mind.

First, remember that testing can be conducted in settings other than test labs. You might recall John Goldstein, the documentation tester from the SpeedyWriter example in Chapter 6, who performed tests at his home, at the engineering office, at the sales and marketing office, even on an airplane in transit. Beta testing often takes place at customers' sites. Testing is still testing when it occurs outside the lab—although a less calm and collected atmosphere often prevails in these outside settings.

Second, this chapter focuses on garden-variety test labs: labs that test hardware for environmental factors, reliability, electromagnetic radiation, sound, and software compatibility; and labs that test software for hardware compatibility, performance, system behavior, and the like. This discussion does not deal with setting up clean room environments, testing battlefield conditions, dealing with toxic chemicals, doing radiation hardness testing, or working in other such exotic or dangerous settings. If your job requires you to test in these situations, you'll need to consult other references.

Finally, note that throughout the chapter I use the phrase "test platform" to refer to any piece of hardware on which testers run tests. In the case of hardware testing, this is often the system under test, but this is not always so. For example, a hub can be a test platform when you are testing server connections to a network. In the case of software testing, the test platform is the host for the system under test (the software).

Do You Need a Test Lab?

Not every test organization needs a test lab. Some organizations need a lab only at certain times; others are immobilized without one. Because setting up and (especially) maintaining a decent test lab is an expensive proposition, you should carefully evaluate whether or not you actually need a lab.

Let's look at our two hypothetical companies. If you are the test manager for Winged Bytes, working on DataRocket and other servers, you will want a test lab. Environmental testing often requires thermal chambers and tables for shock and vibration tests. Electronic testing involves oscilloscopes, spectrum analyzers, and voltage meters. Reliability testing requires keyboard tappers and accelerated-life (environmental stress screening) test chambers. Compatibility testing calls for a library of hardware and software. These kinds of test tools—especially bulky tools such as chambers and space-consuming collections of software—require a home of their own, away from general circulation.

If you are the test manager for Software Cafeteria, however, working on SpeedyWriter, you might not need a test lab. Your setup involves only a few workstations and some operating system software in open areas. The network infrastructure and servers are probably hidden away in a server room (or at least in a wiring closet) and thus don't require a separate lab.

The following questions can help you decide whether to establish or to forgo a test lab:

◆ Do you need large test tools such as chambers? Are some of your test tools nonportable ones—an oscilloscope, for example—that need a special permanent location?

◆ Is a special environment required? If your test platforms have strict environmental requirements (as servers do) or unusual voltage needs (as telephone switches do), you will need at least a server room, if not a separate test lab.

◆ Is security an issue? For example, if you perform compatibility testing with a variety of software packages, the CD-ROMs and disks are valuable, as are the CPUs, tape drives, hard drives, and the like. Keeping them in a restricted-access test lab—especially in a locked cabinet—can save thousands of dollars in shrinkage (from loss, damage, or theft) over the years. In addition, when you are testing new software or hardware, confidentiality is a security concern. Secrets stay secret only when as few people as possible know about them.

◆ Do you need to prevent nontesters from fiddling with your test environment? You may find that some individuals from other teams can't help themselves; they insist on loading quick patches or trying to hook up some device to the test platform "just to see if it works." They then forget to undo whatever they did. If you work with people like this, the formality of a test lab might deter such well-intentioned but counterproductive hacking on your test platforms.

◆ Do you need access to the test facility for an extended period of time? Can multiple projects—concurrent, sequential, or both—leverage the cost of the lab to lower the total cost to the organization? Better yet, can you make the test lab a profit center by selling tools and services from the lab to outside, noncompetitive companies? (This is less unlikely than you might expect. For example, if you have a printer compatibility test lab for SpeedyWriter, you might sell printer compatibility test services to other companies.)

If you really need a test lab, you will be able to make a business case for it based on these (and possibly other) factors. Try preparing a budget specifically for the test lab; you'll be surprised at how much it can cost. Remember, too, that money and effort are required not only to set up a lab but also to maintain it. If the costs seem prohibitive, you almost always have alternatives. By carefully using external resources such as third-party test labs and your vendors, as described in Chapter 10, you can leverage their investments in labs and lab materiel to minimize or eliminate the need for your own.

SELECTING AND PLANNING A LAB AREA

Once you've decided that a test lab is necessary, you need to select a location for the lab and plan its configuration. As you consider the factors outlined here, try to sketch a scaled floor plan of the lab, along the lines of the example shown in Figure 7-1. Make this floor plan as large as possible if you sketch it on paper, or use software such as Visio. Either way, you should count on developing the floor plan iteratively; you might even need to start all over if you discover that the space you initially select is unsuitable.

Size. Is the potential lab space large enough? When the shape of the room is anything other than square or rectangular and wide, you must consider size in conjunction with layout—that is, you must look at the actual working space. Also consider the height of the ceiling; I have seen racks of equipment as high as 8 feet. Pay attention to the doors—everything in the lab must come in and, eventually, go out through them. Begin your sketch of the lab by drawing the lab area, including the location of the doors and the direction they open.

Lighting.   Windows can provide both aesthetic benefits and a welcome break for testers. Some of the most pleasant test labs I ever worked in had

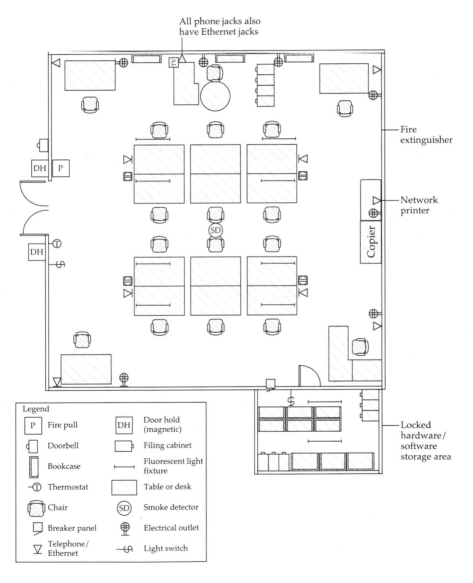

FIGURE 7-1   *An example of a floor plan sketch for a test lab.*

high-rise views, one of downtown Taipei and the other of Santa Monica. Unfortunately, these same labs were also quite unpleasant when the afternoon sun came streaming into them in the summer. Beyond the heat it generates, direct sunlight can make screens difficult to read and damage valuable equipment. All windows in your lab should be tinted and should have effective shades installed. Also note the level of the windows: if they are at ground level or close to it, they can create a security problem.

As for artificial lighting, fluorescent lights are the most common type and are probably the best. Incandescent lights, though not associated with headaches and eyestrain as fluorescents are, tend to throw light in limited areas. Spot lights, track lights, and the like look cool, but they are a better choice for conference rooms than for labs, again because of the kind of light they give off. Even and consistent lighting is important when testers are reading documents and screens or evaluating the quality of a display. On your floor plan, indicate the locations of both lighting fixtures and windows (if any).

Layout. When you select a lab space, keep in mind the kinds of tables and equipment racks you need to install. If you rack-mount most of your equipment, or if it is freestanding, a square room might work very well. If you use tables or desks, a rectangular room might be a better choice, as long as it is wide enough. Remember to leave enough open space to allow people to come and go freely. Populate your floor plan sketch with a scale layout of the chairs, desks, cabinets, shelves, tables, racks, and equipment you intend to install. To keep your floor plan less cluttered, you can use a legend to describe some of these objects.

Climate Control. The test lab must have sufficient air conditioning and heating to preserve a stable, normal operating temperature and humidity for your equipment and your testers. Although the testers might go home, the equipment doesn't—which means continuous (24-hour, year-long) climate control. Your lab might also need automated shutdown capabilities if temperature or humidity limits are exceeded. If you have multiple labs or work spaces on the same system, ensure that each lab has its own thermostat. Locate the thermostat on your floor plan.

Fire Safety and Prevention. Every workplace should have a smoke or fire detector, either battery powered or backed up by a battery, and this detector must be tested regularly. To control a fire, a test lab must have, ready at hand, portable fire extinguishers that are electrically safe and rapidly effective. If the lab contains large equipment such as mainframes or telephony switches, you will also need sophisticated, automatic fire suppression equipment that can put out a large electrical fire on its own while staff members attend to their personal safety. Include the fire detection and extinguishing equipment in your sketch, and make sure that your layout doesn't obstruct access to these devices or impede their use or flow. If objects in the lab get in the way, you should revisit your layout.

Power.   Electrical power in one form or another (120 VAC, 240 VAC, 480 VAC, 48 VDC, and so on) must be provided in all test labs, and it must be available in the right places. In addition, the incoming power must be conditioned and uninterruptible, immune from the spikes, surges, sags, brownouts, and blackouts that plague the power grid. If it isn't, you will need to provide such conditioning and backup power in the lab or be prepared to suffer the consequences. Indicate all the various power outlets on your floor plan.

Static.   If you decide to carpet your lab, you will need to take extra precautions to inhibit static. Tile, linoleum, cement, and raised floors tend not to suffer from this problem to the same degree as carpeted floors, but even clothing can generate static. The lab should contain static mats and other grounded metal objects to help testers dissipate static when they accumulate it.

Facilities.   Facilities for your staff, such as restrooms, stairways, elevators, and so forth (including handicap accessibility) are important not only because you might be legally obligated to provide them but also because they affect the productivity of the team. In addition, remember that you will need to connect the lab to the outside world using telephone lines (PSTN, BRI ISDN, PRI ISDN, T1, OC3, and so on); network cables such as category 3 Ethernet, category 5 Ethernet, token ring, or ATM; and possibly other connections. If the proposed lab site does not already have the appropriate wiring installed, you will need to build it in, possibly at considerable expense. (A raised-floor configuration can make wiring within the lab painless, but the wiring must still be brought into the lab space, either through a wall or through a crawl space above the ceiling or below the floor.) You should also identify connections for running water if your planned tests require water for cooling or heating. Indicate all facilities and connections on your drawing.

To track many of the factors listed here, you can enhance the logistics database introduced in Chapter 6. Figure 7-2 shows a Locations table that can capture descriptive data about an individual lab site. As shown in Figure 7-3, a Hardware table can track the requirements and specifications of the lab's hardware.

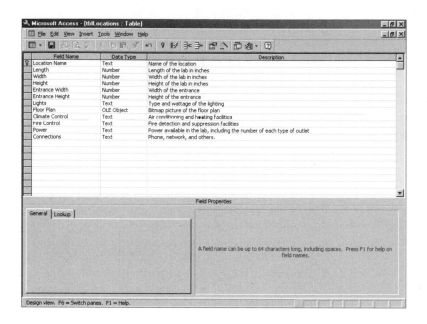

FIGURE 7-2 *Extending the logistics database to include test lab locations.*

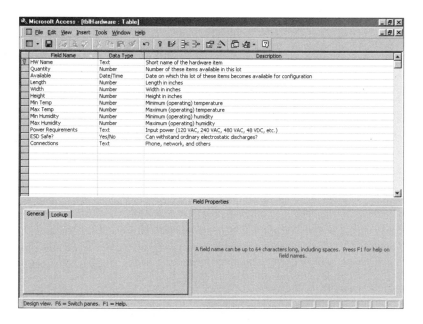

FIGURE 7-3 *Extending the logistics database to include test lab hardware.*

The Test Lab Inventory

What items will you need to operate your test lab? Every test lab has different needs, depending on the systems under test. In addition, the importance of any specific item depends on the importance of the particular tests it supports.

Suppose that you are setting up a test lab for Winged Bytes, in order to perform testing not only for DataRocket but also for the entire line of servers, desktops, and laptops produced by the company. You will use System Cookers, a third-party test lab, to do the environmental testing, so you don't need to buy thermal chambers, shock and vibration equipment, or HALT chambers.[1] Assume that your team will focus primarily on behavioral (blackbox) tests. Based on this information, let's try to put together a sample inventory list.

A Sample Inventory Checklist

The following sections might represent a first pass at your "shopping list" for equipping the Winged Bytes test lab. The list of prospective items is not exhaustive, but it illustrates what can be involved in assembling an inventory for a test lab.

I hasten to add that the presence or absence of any particular item on this checklist does not indicate my personal opinion about the vendor or the item in question. The point here is not to endorse or single out specific products—rather, my intent is to give you an idea of the amount and kind of diversity you'd want to create for such a test project.

Software

Operating Systems.   You will need a wide representation of significant operating systems, which will be used primarily for compatibility testing. The list on the following page provides an example.

---

1. HALT is an acronym for *highly accelerated life testing,* which, through a combination of software operation and extreme environmental stress, simulates an entire lifetime for a computer. You might also see this type of testing under the name of ALT (accelerated life testing) or ESS (environmental stress screen). Some computer vendors use such tests to predict the failures that will occur over the life of the product as well as the reliability of the product in general.

Sun Solaris	Microsoft Windows 2000 Pro
UNIXWare	Microsoft Windows 2000 Server
Microsoft Windows 95	Linux
Microsoft Windows 98	Novell NetWare
Microsoft Windows NT Workstation	SCO UNIX
Microsoft Windows NT Server	

Applications.   You'll want a variety of software applications for compatibility testing and also for use on tester workstations. Don't forget to obtain the requisite number of licenses for each piece of software. A typical assortment of applications might include the following:

Microsoft Office Professional Edition	Netscape Navigator
Lotus SmartSuite	Qualcomm Eudora
Lotus Notes	Visio

Test Tools and Utilities.   These items will be useful for diagnosing problems, creating simple automated tests, sending faxes and files, making system images, backing up critical data, measuring system performance, and generating background loads on systems. Your set of diagnostic and automated testing tools might look this:

Microsoft Visual Basic	Partition-It Extra Strength
Norton AntiVirus	System Commander
Symantec pcAnywhere	Norton Utilities
Procomm	CheckIt
WinFax	Nuts & Bolts
WinZip	WinDelete
Ghost	Ziff-Davis Benchmarks

Hardware

PC Cards.   PC Cards tend to expose a lot of bugs in laptop systems, especially those that arise in conjunction with power management. This list might be representative:

3COM Etherlink III	Addonics Pocket Zip
US Robotics 56K modem	Adaptec SCSI

Monitors/Video Cards.   The video subsystem is a frequent source of head-aches. Consider using a variety of monitors and video cards such as these or a similarly diverse set:

Sony Multiscan	ATI XPERT
Samsung SyncMaster	STB Velocity

Printers/Scanners.   Printers and scanners are not typically a source of hard-ware trouble, but you will find items such as the following useful for veri-fying the functionality of parallel, serial, infrared, and USB ports:

Epson FX-880	HP DeskJet
HP OfficeJet	Epson Perfection

Modems/Network Cards.   You will need a fairly wide variety of modems and network cards to test servers. For instance, the SpeedyWriter example in Chapter 6 included five physical network types (counting ISDN), four servers, five clients, and eighteen network cards or adapters. Each card should be different in order to get as much test coverage as possible. A typical set might include the following:

IBM 56K modem	D-Link Ethernet
Zoom 56K faxmodem	Intel PRO/100
3COM ISDN LAN modem	IBM Token Ring
Intel PRO/10	

Data Storage.   In addition to items such as an Iomega external Jaz drive and an HP SureStor DLT, you will need a fairly complete contingent of hard drives and other options.

Surge Protectors/UPS Units.   In a good test lab, the wall current should be conditioned and backed up, but sometimes you have to make do with what-ever power you can get. Surge protectors and uninterruptible power supply units—for example, a TrippLite Surge Suppressor and an APC UPS—can help.

Reference Platforms.   When you are conducting tests, the priority assigned to a bug often depends on whether the same failure occurs on multiple industry-standard platforms, such as Dell Inspiron, Micron Millennia, and Compaq ProLiant.

Cables.   Because cables are relatively expensive for such small items, it's tempting to skip them. But the first time an engineer wastes an hour trying to copy a group of files from one system to another because you don't have the right cable to use with LapLink, cables will start to look like a bargain. You will need cables for uses such as these:

Ethernet	Serial printer
Token ring	Serial cross-over
Parallel printer	USB
Telephone	

Networking. In order to avoid testing on the corporate network, you will need to set up temporary networks (for example, an HP ProCurve 10/100 hub or an IBM Token Ring) in your test lab.

Consumables

Be sure to have a plentiful supply of all consumables on hand. This saves time and prevents the loss of focus that occurs when your staff members become embroiled in wild goose chases searching for supplies. Remember that a missing $50 tape can cost you double that amount in an engineer's wasted time.

Computer Media. This category includes such basics as 3.5-inch floppy disks, Zip and Jaz disks, and DAT tapes.

Desk Necessities. These items are the old stand-bys: notebooks, paper, pens, pencils, transparent tape, sticky notes, staplers, and paper clips. ·

Printer Supplies. For all the printers involved in either testing or reporting results, you will need the appropriate types of toner, printer paper, printer cartridges, and ribbons.

Furnishings

Copiers and Printers. Every test lab needs its own printer; you shouldn't count on using your test printers. Having a small copier isn't a bad idea, either.

Shredder. A shredder is a good idea if you work with confidential papers.

Benches, Desks, Stools, and Chairs. It goes without saying that you will need places for your team to sit and work, but you'd be surprised how many labs have uncomfortable or inappropriate furniture.

Mouse Pads. These pads make a tester's work easier because they allow a more precise, smoother motion than trying to move a mouse across a laminated lab counter.

Static Pads. You should provide a few static pads in every lab to minimize the possibility of static-discharge damage to hardware.

Tools

Specialized Hardware. For basic electrical testing in the hardware test lab, you will need certain specialized hardware, such as a Hewlett-Packard oscilloscope or a RadioShack voltage meter.

Test Management Software. If you decide not to create your own systems for bug tracking, test tracking, estimating, and similar management tasks, you should plan to buy commercial software packages that implement such systems.

Computer Toolkit. A fully stocked computer toolkit—including screwdrivers, wrenches, chip-pullers, and so on—is a necessity in every test lab.

Reference Materials

The Classics. For every kind of testing, a small set of books defines the current best practices; be sure to have copies of these books on hand.

Standards. If industry or government standards apply to any of the systems under test, you will need to have up-to-date editions of these standards available.

Phone Books. Current phone books are useful for many reasons, not the least of which is that sooner or later you will need a late-night pizza delivery for the test team.

FURTHER THOUGHTS ON STOCKING YOUR LAB

No matter what you are testing, some general observations about your lab's inventory apply. Most important is that you must be certain to maintain some padding in your test lab budget. You can't foresee everything, and you are sure to be caught off guard by a sudden need at some stage of the project. When that need arises, it may well be urgent and unavoidable. It's easier to include $5,000 in "gravy" during budgeting than to go begging to management for another $2,500 in the middle of crunch mode—when everyone has innumerable other crises to attend to.

Also remember that the most effective test labs contain the mix of hardware, software, infrastructure, and facilities most likely to cause trouble in the field. Since it's hard to know in advance what won't work, your asset inventory must resemble that of your target customers to the extent possible. Balance your choices with considerations of cost and the likelihood of failure.

Along these lines, don't forget to budget for maintenance. Some companies will give you free upgrades to software and firmware for life, but most will not. If your hardware is three, four, or more firmware revisions out of date, and your software one or two major releases in the past, how well are you modeling the real world in your test lab? Even one revision can make a big difference in software or hardware behavior. (As a tester, you know this implicitly for your own products, but it's easy to forget that we're all in the same boat.)

Finally, as you estimate quantities for certain test equipment such as mice, keyboards, printers, and monitors, remember that these items are often shared. You must have a sufficient number on hand so that people don't waste time waiting to use them.

SECURITY AND TRACKING CONCERNS

Over time, you can spend millions of dollars outfitting a test lab. With accumulated assets worth that much, you need to protect your investment from damage, theft, and other losses. In hardware testing, for example, your assets might include some big-ticket items such as thermal chambers and oscilloscopes. A thermal chamber isn't terribly easy to steal, but one person with a car can easily make off with an oscilloscope. In software testing, you often use test platforms such as laptops that anyone with a decent-size briefcase could sneak out of the building.

No matter how honest your team and your other colleagues might be, the concept of *due diligence* requires that you, as the responsible manager, make efforts to prevent theft and the loss of valuable assets.[2] That said, however, you don't want your security system to impede your team's productivity. A happy medium might be the use of a library system, in which one or more people fill the role of asset librarian. The asset librarian assumes responsibility for ensuring that every valuable materiel asset is secured when it is not in use, possibly in a locked cabinet or safe (for small hardware and

---

2. Informally, the phrase "due diligence" refers to the requirement that responsible employees and business associates, especially managers, not be negligent of the consequences of their decisions and the attendant risks to their employers or clients. Practically speaking, you as the test manager must think of ways to protect your employer or client from harm resulting from both acts and omissions. It's important to note that the term "due diligence" has specific legal connotations; you should consult legal counsel if you need a precise definition.

software items) or a locked room (for larger items). Testers who need to use any of these items for testing can check them out from the librarian and then check them back in when the test is completed. As you'll see in the next section, a simple database can track assets as they are checked in and out.

The beauty of this system is that one person is always accountable for each article at any given time. (If you have multiple shifts, you will need one asset librarian for each shift.) Economists refer to the "tragedy of the commons" as that situation in which everyone mistreats a shared set of resources because no one has ownership. In a library system, signing out a piece of equipment indicates ownership, and the individual who has signed it out must take special care that the item doesn't turn up missing or damaged.

You should also consider the issue of insurance as the value of your lab assets increases. Even if your company has corporate insurance, you might need to declare these lab assets specifically in order to protect them. Understand the terms of coverage. For instance, if your lab is in a location that is subject to floods, are you insured against such events?

In addition to considering theft, loss, or damage to physical property, you must also worry about intellectual property. I once worked at a third-party testing company where most clients had their own separate labs, each accessible only with a card key. Each tester had an individual card key, and a printer in a locked room logged the use of that card to enter a lab. Only staff members who were actively working on a client's project had card key access. Some clients insisted on labs without windows. Locked filing cabinets held specifications and other confidential documents. Even people not directly involved in testing, such as the sales staff and the bid writers, had to clean off their desktops and lock up the contents of their desks before leaving each day.

MANAGING EQUIPMENT AND CONFIGURATIONS

The sample test lab inventory for Winged Bytes, presented earlier in this chapter, contains items that can be categorized as either consumable or durable. Most of the consumable items don't need any serious management—it's silly to try to keep track of pencils, for instance. For such items, the only management concern is ensuring an adequate supply. But durable items such as desks, hubs, software, and the like need to be managed individually.

A common approach is to use asset tags. A sticker or plaque emblazoned with a unique identifier is affixed to each valuable item. (Your company might already use this method for managing desks, chairs, and other durable office furnishings.) Such durable items can be either portable or nonportable. A desk, for instance, is fairly nonportable; once you place it, it is likely to stay put. In contrast, a laptop computer or a hub that your team uses for testing might move around. In this case, the ownership concept discussed in the preceding section becomes important. It is immaterial to you, for example, which asset tag is on the chair that Lin-Tsu sits in, but you do care which of the three copies of Microsoft Office she has at her workstation.

Note, however, that it makes sense to consider value when using this approach. Cables are a perfect example. Putting asset tags on telephone wires, and then trying to track who has them, is absurd; it'll cost you more in time than it would cost to replace the cable. In this case, I recommend that you accept some shrinkage of your cable inventory, whether from loss, damage, or even theft, rather than descend into incidents reminiscent of Captain Queeg's farcical inquisition about "who ate the strawberries" in *The Caine Mutiny*.

In addition to asset management issues, the question of asset configuration is important for some items. In the case of an oscilloscope, for example, you probably don't need to worry about revisions of the component boards. But for each DataRocket in your lab, you must know not only the revisions for all the boards but also the BIOS releases, the software installed, the disk drives present, and so forth. This is also true if you test software: because you test it on test platforms, you'll need to know exactly how each platform is configured.

You might be able to adapt the logistics database introduced in Chapter 6 to meet your configuration and asset management needs. Figure 7-4 shows the entity-relationship diagram for an adapted database. The *Hardware* entity you saw in Figure 6-2 (page 185) now becomes the *Asset* entity, with the asset tag number (*Asset ID*) as its key property. This entity also has a *Board Revisions* property, which allows you to track the board revisions in the hardware. Adding a *Project* property to the *Tests* entity enables you to manage multiple projects in this one database. With the addition of the *Assigned To* relationship, you can also track the process as your testers check hardware and software assets in and out of the library.

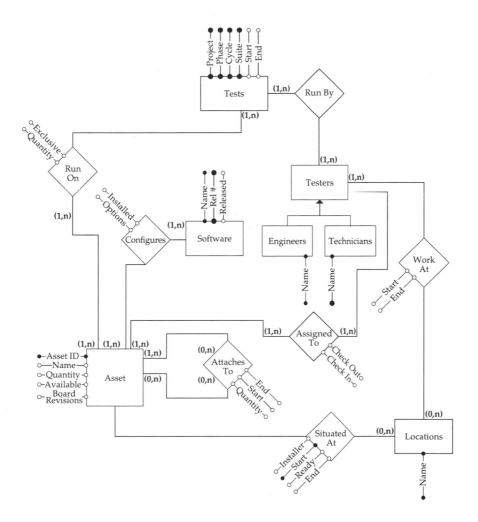

FIGURE 7-4 *An entity-relationship diagram for managing logistics and lab assets.*

Beyond software and hardware configurations, another important dimension exists for test platform configuration, as illustrated in Figure 7-5. The data dimension includes items such as databases and configuration files (the Windows 98 registry, for example, or UNIX cron tables) as well as test input, output, and log files. Data can affect the behavior of the system as much as the software and the hardware can. Moreover, data presents a unique challenge in that the data configuration of the test platform is often changed, both deliberately and inadvertently, over the course of test execution.

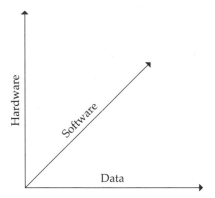

FIGURE 7-5 *The dimensions of test system configuration.*

Figure 7-6 shows the various data configuration states through which a test platform might move. These different states can be extremely complex. For each data state D_i, every byte of storage in system memory, video memory, the hard drive, networked storage, and any other secondary storage available to the test platform can be significant. In addition, the actions that cause data transformation are discrete keystrokes, mouse movements, network transactions, and so forth. Literally millions of such actions take place as part of a fairly straightforward test. Given this complexity, scaling up to, say, a 72-hour reliability test run on a network of two dozen servers and clients means that you have reached the point where capturing data configuration in any meaningful sense is impossible.

FIGURE 7-6 *Data configuration changes resulting from setup and test actions.*

Fortunately, being able to recreate any arbitrary data configuration D_i doesn't add much value. The two data states you care about most are D_0 and D_N. D_N, the final data state, is particularly important if you are testing data quality. D_0, the initial data state, is important because you must restore all three dimensions of that configuration, data included, if you want to rerun a set of test suites against a particular configuration. For this reason, it can be helpful to use tape or other secondary removable storage to take a "snapshot" of the test platform's data configuration before you begin to test. This step might add a few minutes to test suite setup time, but it is very useful if you need to reproduce a particular result.

KEEPING THE TEST ENVIRONMENT CLEAN

As I've stressed before, it's important to know precisely what is on each test system at any given time during test execution. Otherwise, bugs can become unreproducible and bug reports will be inaccurate. Although this might sound obvious, many people underestimate the importance of strict configuration management in test environments.

In my experience, the fastest way to let your test environment deteriorate into a mysterious state is to allow someone with a "hacker mentality" to work on your test systems. Just one letter altered in one configuration file, one cable disconnected, one software package installed can change the whole demeanor of a bug. Unless everyone working on your test system logs all changes to every test platform, your test environment will quickly become uncertain. The frustration engendered by bugs that change shape daily has made me a firm believer in scrupulous configuration management.

Most developers want to be able to make changes and try quick experiments when they're debugging; having to document every single step they try slows them down. Unfortunately, this often puts the goal of preserving test platform configuration in conflict with the goal of rapidly debugging a problem. From the test perspective, the best possible solution to this problem lies in preventing any debugging activities from taking place on the test platforms. In a perfect world, the development team has its own development labs—or at least development systems and networks—which reduce or eliminate the need to work in the test lab.

As a practical matter, however, some bugs will occur only in the test environment. Remember that the test environment is as "user-like" as possible, while the development environment tends to be less controlled, with a narrower range of systems available. If a SpeedyWriter bug occurs only on a PowerBook computer, and the test team has the only PowerBook in the company, the developers must use test's hardware to debug the problem. Likewise, a performance problem on a token ring network will likely have to be verified in the test lab because development networks are almost certainly Ethernet.

I'm afraid there is no simple solution here. On the one hand, dogmatically clinging to the notion that all debugging must happen outside the test lab can have a dangerous impact on a product's ship schedule. On the other hand, letting any developer who needs to track down a bug start hacking away on the test environment is an invitation to chaos. Loaning test equipment to developers isn't much of a solution, either. On occasion I have "loaned" hardware to development tiger teams for debugging, only to find it "borrowed" on a nearly permanent basis. Don't assume that there is such a thing as "test's hardware"; project management can reassign it at a moment's notice. So before you decide to let another group use your hardware "for a while," consider the possibility that "a while" might be the remainder of the project.

If you must share the test lab with the development team, and you have a workable arrangement for shifting the use of the hardware, the tape strategy mentioned earlier for capturing data configurations might be helpful. You can accumulate a library of useful tape snapshots that could accommodate both a tester who needs data state D_0 and a developer who needs states D_i and D_j. This is certainly no panacea, and conflicts will arise, but you can at least prevent chaos.

HUMAN FACTORS

Although the focus of this chapter has been on material objects and information related to them, you need to remember that *people* test in the test lab. The safety of the people who work in your lab must be of special concern to you as a manager. In addition, you need to consider the issues of how testers interact with your lab equipment (including possible damage to the equipment) and how to run the lab so that the testers are as productive as possible.

A SAFE LAB IS A PRODUCTIVE LAB

As noted earlier, I assume that you are working in a typical test lab, where no extraordinary chemical, electrical, radiological, or mechanical hazards exist. If your staff must handle, use, or store dangerous chemicals; radioisotopes; radiation-emitting devices; sharp or heavy test probes or tools; high-voltage or high-current components; mechanical presses, punches, or drills; extremely hot or cold articles; or any other compound or object that can injure, electrocute, burn, blind, deafen, sterilize, poison, genetically damage, cut, or kill, you will need to take precautions beyond those discussed in this book.

Most of the test labs I've worked in have been less dangerous than the typical garage, bathroom, or kitchen. Nevertheless, everyone working in the lab must understand basic safety considerations and practice common sense. Thoughtless or careless behavior can result in harm to personal property, injury to oneself or others, or damage to the tools, systems, or facilities in the lab.

For example, if your testers work on the interior portions of computers, with computer peripherals, or with add-on devices, you might want to have them wear lab coats. If lab coats are considered excessive, at least make sure that people do not wear billowy or very loose clothing and insist that they tuck in or bind any loose items such as ties, bandannas, and scarves. (I once ran into a colleague who was wearing a silk tie that looked as if a puppy had used it as a chew toy for a week. When I asked about it, he explained that he had been leaning over an open computer and failed to notice that his tie had become entangled in protruding pins on an ISA card. When he straightened up, the little wires shredded the end of the tie like razors.)

Hair and jewelry can cause similar problems. Beards, long hair, handlebar mustaches, and even especially long hair on forearms can, under certain circumstances, get caught in a computer or in moving parts. Moist or sweaty hair can also create a short circuit on a live board. Loose necklaces can be snagged; rings (especially if they are large or numerous) can catch on notched and hooked items. In addition, dangling earrings, nose rings, and other uncovered jewelry stuck through sensitive body parts can get snared, leading to painful or dangerous injuries.

Speaking of painful and dangerous injuries, keep in mind that the inside of a computer often has sharp edges and is certainly not sterile. I have taken more skin off my knuckles and the backs of my hands while working inside a computer than I care to recall. Gloves might help, but it is cumbersome to work on small chips, jumpers, and screws while wearing any glove thick enough to make a difference. Testers must be extremely careful and should wash cuts thoroughly and immediately.

Many test labs include eye wash stations. Drilling, machining, or filing any metal or plastic component can create shards that can lodge in the eye. Broken glass is always a possibility when working with computer monitors. A reversed capacitor, an overworked resistor, or a chip pushed beyond its specifications can smoke, snap, or even explode. Eye protection is an especially good idea when working with prototype hardware.

Earlier in this chapter I discussed the need for smoke detectors and fire extinguishers in the lab. At the risk of belaboring the point, be sure to test those smoke detectors as specified in the owner's manuals. Remember that a fire extinguisher does no good if no one knows where it is or how to use it. And you should also ensure that people know the evacuation route in case a serious fire breaks out.

As a last note on safety, keyboards and mice must be positioned to minimize the risk of repetitive stress injuries. Likewise, work surfaces, chairs, and stools need to be set up so that people can work at comfortable angles, with proper wrist support and proper posture.

DAMAGE TO LAB EQUIPMENT

Working on computers can cause injury to a person, but a person can also inflict damage on software and hardware. In a lab where I worked, someone spilled an entire cup of coffee on a keyboard. The keyboard survived, but it required a complete disassembly and cleaning. On another occasion I saw someone destroy a laptop computer by allowing a few drops of condensation to drip from the outside of a water bottle directly onto the mainboard through the keyboard. Greasy fingers can render a laptop's touchpad unreliable. If you decide to allow food in your lab, be sure that people understand the need to keep it away from the equipment, and institute rules against working on the equipment while eating or drinking.

Other objects that require caution in the lab include magnets, which can wipe out a floppy disk or a Zip disk quite easily. Paper clips, pins, and other small objects can be dropped and become lodged in a computer, which will eventually cause a short and damage the unit. Should this occur, the tester must power off the unit immediately and retrieve the lost item before powering it on again.

Shock, vibrations, and drops are also concerns. Be sure that equipment is not perched precariously in positions from which it can fall. Badly placed wires can trip and injure a tester, but they can also bring an attached component crashing to the ground or tear out a part of the system. (I seriously damaged an integrated modem in a laptop by inadvertently yanking the RJ-11 cable attached to it.) On a similar note, I once saw someone attempt to seat a recalcitrant computer board using a two-by-four and a ball peen hammer. This kind of activity, along with slapping, pounding, or kicking any delicate electronic object, is always a bad idea. And, while you can hurl a pen or pencil at a VDT in a fit of pique, doing the same to an LCD panel is likely to damage or destroy it.

When working on a computer, a technician or engineer must have the proper tools available. Trying to use a flathead screwdriver to tighten a Phillips-head screw might strip the head of the screw, leaving the component improperly seated and impossible to remove. Pliers or the wrong wrench can round the edges of a nut. Removing a chip without the proper chip-puller invites damage to a very valuable piece of equipment. If partial or complete disassembly is a possibility, you should provide trays to hold and categorize screws, jumpers, and other small components that can easily get mixed up or roll off the table.

In addition to providing proper tools, you should also train your staff to apply the carpenter's adage "measure twice, cut once"—that is, to pay proper attention to each task and double-check before taking action. When I first started working with computers, before the days of flashable EEPROMs, I installed a one-of-a-kind ROM backward in its socket. When I powered up the computer, I fried the chip and had to wait two days for a replacement. The client was not amused. Proper grounding when working on any electronic equipment is also a must, of course. Be sure to provide grounding straps and static pads liberally throughout the lab.

Finally, you need to exercise care when cleaning computers, test tools, and the like. Spraying ammonia-based window cleaners on display screens might not be a good idea, depending on what the screen is made of and where the overspray ends up. Cleaning a laptop keyboard requires special attention because excess moisture can easily work its way into the system enclosure.

PRODUCTIVITY IN THE LAB

The setup of your test lab can be an important factor in the productivity of the people working in it. Tools and workstations should be set up to minimize the need for people to move around the lab. Having all the necessary components for completing a task close at hand helps avoid breaking the tester's concentration (or the concentration of colleagues). During an intricate test, any interruption can cause the tester to lose a critical train of thought and thus to omit an important step or miss an indication of an error.

The idea of breaking one's concentration raises the issue of radios, TVs, and CD players. If all the denizens of the lab agree on a definition of "good music," allowing some low-volume background music can make for a pleasant environment. But the more people who are involved, the more likely it is that a conflict will ensue about what is tolerable. In addition, although listening to music may be enjoyable and improve morale, it doesn't necessarily improve productivity.

Radios, of course, play more than just music. Listening to talk radio might contribute to stimulating debate among those in the lab, but it is almost certainly a distraction. Even worse, a television, especially when tuned into those daytime "spectacle shows," is nothing but an electronic attention magnet; people simply aren't focused on testing if they're watching TV. In general, it's probably best that people use headphones and that the listening be confined to music.

Your lab setup can additionally contribute to productivity by ensuring that at least one network workstation is available to those working in the lab. This workstation should provide testers with access to the bug tracking database, the test tracking spreadsheet, the system configuration tracking database, and any other reporting and information resources the testers need to execute the tests and report results efficiently.

8

Staffing and Managing a Test Team

H iring, motivating, and retaining an excellent staff are among the most important tasks any manager performs. The extent to which a manager does a good or poor job at these tasks largely determines the extent to which he or she is a good or poor manager. Although these are survival issues for all managers, from those at the neighborhood steak house to corporate CEOs to successful politicians, the task of staffing and managing a test team has its own unique quirks. This chapter offers some pointers on a few of the issues that are particularly deviling:

◆ How many people do you need, what skills should they have, and what positions do they fill?

◆ Do you want to organize your staff by projects or by areas of test specialization?

◆ How do you pick good test engineers and avoid bad ones?

◆ What motivates test staff, and what demotivates them?

◆ How can you use temporary workers to help your team over the tough stretches?

Defining the Test Team: How Many Doing What?

If you were assembling a sports team, the game you intended to play would define the team: you would know how many players were required, what skills they needed to possess, and what positions they would play. When assembling a development team, you can base your decisions on certain models that indicate how many coders, engineers, architects, and so forth you will need. These various models don't all agree on every point, but you can pick an approach secure in the knowledge that someone—if only the author of the book or paper that explains the model—has successfully applied it to one or more projects. The following sections outline some workable methods of defining a test team.

Size

You can determine the size of your test team either by focusing on tasks or by focusing on the ratio of testers to developers. These two approaches are complementary in that you can use one of them to come up with an initial estimate and then use the other to "sanity check" that figure and iterate as needed. As Chapter 9 discusses, however, management doesn't exactly throw people at testing, so you will also need to tune your staffing requests to the political realities of your organization.

Let's look at an example that begins with a task-based estimate. Back in Chapter 1, Figure 1-8 (page 39) showed a Gantt chart for the SpeedyWriter project, which summarized the tasks involved in testing the product. The accompanying discussion in Chapter 1 recommended including the resources, especially the people, associated with each task as you create a project plan. If you were to assign specific people to specific tasks in the project plan outlined in Figure 1-8, you might end up with a test team that looks like the one shown in Figure 8-1. Five of the people involved are test engineers, two are test technicians, and one is the manager. As indicated in the Maximum Units column, each participant's time is allocated 100 percent for Speedy-Writer. In addition, according to the Base Calendar column, all participants are on the same work-hours, weekend, and holiday schedule.

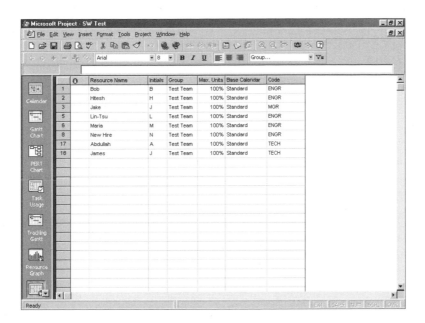

FIGURE 8-1   *A proposed SpeedyWriter test team, based on test tasks.*

Based on this plan, eight test personnel will be involved in testing SpeedyWriter. If the SpeedyWriter development team consists of twelve people, the ratio of testers to developers is 2:3, which is quite good. A 1:1 ratio or better is ideal, especially in RAD (rapid application development) environments, but ratios between 1:2 and 1:5 are common, easily defensible, and generally workable.

Deciding which ratio is right for your company depends in part on the expectations of your managers. Suppose that management responded to your plan by limiting your staff to three people, including yourself. You might be able to make this new 1:4 ratio work, but you'd have to make changes such as these:

◆   You serve as both test manager and lead engineer.

◆   You ask the developers to perform as much component testing as possible.

◆   The test team focuses on integration and system testing.

◆   You eliminate Bob, Lin-Tsu, James, Abdullah, and the proposed new hire from your team, retaining Maria and Hitesh as your assistant engineers.

◆ You reduce test coverage in system testing as a result of the 40 percent reduction in staff levels for that test phase. (The integration test phase is sufficiently staffed, and component testing is no longer your responsibility.)

This new plan will work, however, only if management has realistic expectations of what the test organization will contribute. If management anticipates dramatic, immediate improvements in product quality because of your team's efforts at this staffing level, you are in deep trouble.

Unless your company is (or intends to be) a one-hit wonder, don't forget to include other projects and activities in the test team plan. Projects will start and wind down in parallel, other tasks will come your way, test tools will need to be created, and so forth. When you put together task-based or ratio-based staffing requests, consider all the projects and developers in the organization.

If you don't receive all the staff you need the first time around, don't give up hope immediately. Your logic might not have won this time, but it may well have sensitized management to your real staffing needs. Also consider that you might be able to accomplish some of your test tasks without relying on permanent staff. The last section of this chapter ("Extending Your Talent: Using Temporary Implementers and Experts," page 260) offers some ideas on retaining temporary staff to get through busy periods, and Chapter 10 discusses external resources. Use of temporary or external resources can resolve your real problem—getting the work done—while also addressing management's concern that a test organization, once grown, will become a big, unproductive black hole.

If you do end up understaffed, try to get support from other groups in the company. For example, when I have to set up and maintain a complex test lab, I try to ensure that the MIS group is on the hook to provide system administration support for the lab (including off-hours coverage for weekend test periods).

Skills

In some cases, your test team personnel might need specialized skills. For SpeedyWriter, at least a few of the test engineers should understand Java programming to do adequate component tests. If the DataRocket test team must run signal-quality test suites, at least one engineer must understand the fundamentals of electrical engineering. In general, however, the most important tasks for testers involve the basic skills of reading, writing, and mathematics.

Testers must know how to *really* read—not in a superfical fashion, but with intense focus, meticulous attention to detail, and nearly masochistic capacity. Engineering prose is often dense, sometimes takes liberties with the mother tongue, and occasionally does a poor job of pointing out salient topics. Test case development involves a thorough reading of the specifications, the requirements, the product documentation, and myriad other detailed references. Test engineers and technicians often read hundreds of pages over the course of a project. Furthermore, these product documents often contradict one another. Whether trying to develop tests or looking for documentation bugs, testers must find and report these discrepancies, which is a painstaking process.

As e-mail becomes the primary communication channel in the high-tech world, people on a hot project—testers, developers, and managers alike—can receive dozens of project-related e-mails each day. Especially during the period of test execution, they must read these messages with care and comprehension if they are to act on them with due speed. Test execution also requires the ability to understand possibly ambiguous instructions, grasp the goals, and take the right actions. A tester can't run tests without being able to read a test case, test tool documentation, and output logs.

Test personnel must also know how to write. I'm not talking about perfect grammar and spelling, although poor use of language can certainly distract and confuse readers. The most important issue is the ability to communicate effectively in writing. When testers find a problem, they must communicate the symptoms they observe. This is the essence of testing, and it requires writing a good bug report. The bug report is the most tangible product of testing and the foundation of most quality metrics. Just as you wouldn't hire a chef who can't cook, you shouldn't hire test staff who can't write bug reports. The task of communicating blockages and breakdowns in the test process itself, often via e-mail, also requires writing ability. Poor written communications can cause you, as a test manager, some real heartburn.

Interestingly, I have found the ability to communicate clearly in writing to be nearly independent of whether the tester is using his or her native language. I've worked with some Taiwanese test engineers who were tough to communicate with in spoken English but who nevertheless wrote excellent bug reports in perfectly clear, if not always grammatically correct, English. I've also known some American test engineers whose bug reports, in English, required extensive editing. The difference lies more in the degree of care taken in expressing one's thoughts than in a deep knowledge of the language.

The application of metrics in testing, such as a reliability growth model for software or MTBF calculations for hardware, can entail a sophisticated understanding of statistics and mathematics. If your test organization uses such metrics, you will need at least one person—in addition to yourself—who understands how these metrics work. For the rest of the team, a simple understanding of some basic mathematical and statistical concepts will suffice. It's not possible to give hard-and-fast rules for which specific concepts testers need to know in all cases, but you'll usually want the engineers on your staff to be familiar with statistical concepts such as distribution functions, means and standard deviations, and the like.

POSITIONS

If you automate most of your testing, or if most of your testing involves the use of complex tools, your staff might be composed entirely of test engineers. A test engineer is the technical peer of a programmer, a mechanical engineer, or an electrical engineer. Having chosen testing as a specialty, test engineers write tests; create, customize, and use advanced test tools; and have unique skills such as test design, bug reporting, and problem isolation. (Some of the requisite skills and qualifications are explored in more detail later in this chapter; see "The Right Person for the Job: Qualifications for Test Engineers," page 243.)

If your testing involves simple manual operations such as loading floppy disks in response to a prompt, installing and checking PC Cards, and configuring systems according to a simple checklist, you should also have some test technicians on staff. Such straightforward, rote tasks tend to distract test engineers from their more challenging duties. In addition, some engineers do a poor job with tasks they find boring or "beneath" them. Having test technicians, who are less skilled, handle these easier chores may well improve the quality of your test operation. Note that in Figure 8-1 the SpeedyWriter test project has two test technicians, Abdullah and James.

Local colleges, universities, and technical schools provide good sources for test technicians. One or two postings on their job boards can often identify a few qualified computer science students. These students enjoy working in their chosen field, usually work hard, and are likely to be bright, so you'll get excellent value for the wages you pay.

Not every student is a good fit. You should try to hold out for computer science, computer engineering, or at least engineering students. The deeper level of computer knowledge these engineers-in-the-making bring to the test organization will make a difference. Watch out, however, for hacker types, who often have trouble focusing, following a process, and staying on task.[1] Worse yet, in spite of their need for guidance, these folks like to work from nine to five—but that's usually 9 P.M. to 5 A.M. For all students, monitor their work behavior for a while, especially if they have never held a job. Before turning student technicians loose on the midnight shift, make sure that they can work effectively and professionally with minimal supervision.

Speaking of late-night testing, moonlighters can be another good source of technicians who can keep your test resources utilized all night long. Most dual-job types are motivated. In addition, they might bring experiences from their day jobs that could make them better testers. Use caution with moonlighters, though. Since you don't provide their sole—or even main—source of income, and your project might not be their first priority, you should give them tasks that can slip a bit in the schedule without causing disaster. With individuals who are moonlighting expressly to build an outside consulting career, you can be a little freer about moving them into key positions, provided they have proven track records. (Regardless of who is on the night shift—seasoned test engineers, students, or moonlighters—keep a close eye on your night crew's productivity. Some people overestimate their ability to work effectively with little sleep; others get stuck or veer off track without guidance.)

Finally, keep in mind that your team might need to contain other positions in addition to test engineers and test technicians. In some cases, for example, you might have a release management or configuration management engineer in your organization. As Chapter 9 describes, a variety of nontest tasks often migrate into test organizations; see "What Else Fits? Adding Other Functions to Test," page 280.

---

1. The term "hackers" might call to mind kids who use computers with criminal intent. But I'm using the word in its original meaning: semiprofessional computer wizards who can achieve great results but tend to follow their own muse a bit too frequently.

Specialists or Project Resources? Organizational Models

In a very small company or on a dedicated project effort, everyone works on a single project, and the question of organizational models does not exactly dominate the discussion. Suppose, however, that you have two, three, or a dozen projects going at one time. Do you break your team members into groups based on the projects they are working on or based on the special skills they have?

Let's look at an example. You are the test manager at Winged Bytes. Two systems are in the test lab at the same time, the DataRocket server and the PortaByte laptop. Organization by skills assigns John to the BIOS, Hemamalini to Windows 95, Sandra to Windows NT, Gordon to PC Card and PCI add-on cards, Crystal to networks, and Shao-Lin to environmental and reliability testing, as shown in Figure 8-2. Organization by project assigns John, Hemamalini, and Sandra to the DataRocket team, while Gordon, Crystal, and Shao-Lin work on the PortaByte, as shown in Figure 8-3.

The skills-based model has a lot to recommend it, especially in the high-tech world. Instead of everyone having to keep up with many topics, each member of your test staff can focus on the quirks and subtleties of his or her own area of specialization. In some cases, the complexity of the tools and technology the tester must master demands a skills-based organization.

While the skills-based approach provides a test manager with a great deal of flexibility, project managers might not like it. As one project manager told me, "I don't want to hear about anyone working on anything other than my project." In an organization in which project managers are rewarded for delivering a quality product on time, such an attitude is consistent with the company's incentive structure. A skills-based organization deprives project managers of control over the allocation of test resources.

If you encounter such resistance, you must decide whether you can persist with a skills-based approach—and whether you *want* to persist. Don't choose a skills-based model without consideration for the feelings and interests of project managers. Maintaining a positive relationship with the project managers your test team services will boost your career and make your workday go smoothly. (Chapter 9 discusses the importance of working well with project managers in more detail.)

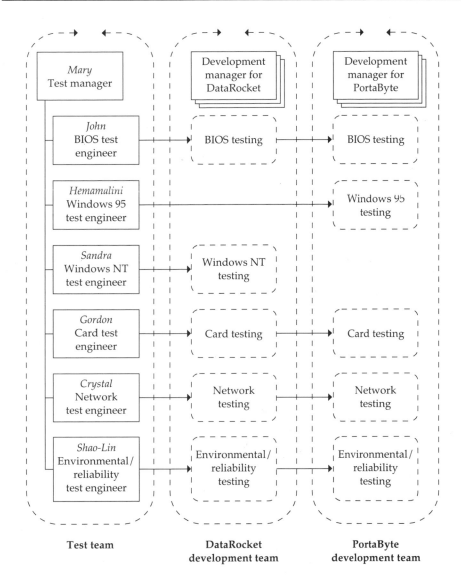

FIGURE 8-2 *A skills-based test organization.*

Besides, the second approach—a project-based organization—can have advantages for a test manager. If you have some otherwise excellent staff members who just don't focus very well, a skills-based organization might exacerbate the problem because it would force these people to jump from one project to another during the week. Assigning them to a single project, in a project-based organization, cuts down on the interruptions and shifting

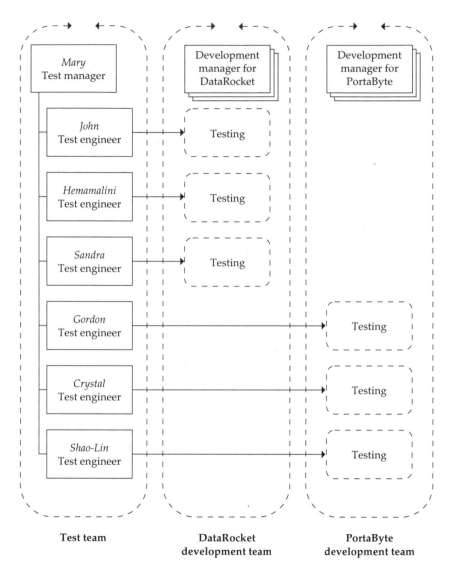

FIGURE 8-3 *A project-based test organization.*

tasks. In addition, if your company tracks hours spent on projects, having each person billing time to only one project makes your reporting job less confusing.

One risk posed by the project-based approach deserves mention, however. Although the test personnel report to you, they also, in a sense, work for the development managers. They probably have more contact on a daily basis with the development team than with you. Assuming that they can maintain positive, open working relationships with the developers, this contact reduces the need for you to micromanage the activities for each project. But development managers with a strong will or lots of political clout can sometimes prevail upon your test engineers to do things they shouldn't—closing bugs that aren't confirmed as fixed, for instance, or compromising test processes. If your test engineers don't have much experience with a formal test organization, they can easily "go native," acting more like developers than independent testers. You need to monitor this situation closely.

When first setting up a test team, few test managers can use either a skills-based model or a project-based model exclusively. Some situations require experts, especially when a task involves mastery of a tricky test tool. For example, if you use Silk or AutoTester for GUI testing, your team should include a GUI test engineer or two. Of course, your GUI test experts must understand how their expertise fits into the overall test architecture. But using a GUI tester to write API tests in C++ is probably not the best deployment of that individual's skills. Plan on using a mixed approach as your team grows. Once your organization reaches a certain size and maturity level, you will be able—and will need—to pick one approach or the other.

The Right Person for the Job: Qualifications for Test Engineers

Beyond being equipped with basic skills, the best test engineers show real commitment to testing as a specialty, have pessimistic but flexible attitudes toward any system under test, possess curious but not obsessive minds, and demonstrate an ability to focus intently. These are the traits I look for when I interview potential test engineers, and I encourage and cultivate these qualities in my team during test projects.[2]

Test Specialists Versus Content Specialists

Glenford Myers, author of *The Art of Software Testing* and a pioneer in the field, makes a case for having a test staff composed of "system test experts"—

---

2. Bill Hetzel, in Chapter 11 of *The Complete Guide to Software Testing*, identifies the "five Cs" as important characteristics of a good testing specialist: controlled (organized and systematic); competent (aware of proper test techniques); critical (focused on finding problems); comprehensive (attentive to details); and considerate (able to communicate well with development peers).

that is, people whose careers are focused on testing as a specialty. A contrary view argues that the test staff must consist of content specialists, people who understand a company's products and technologies. If the company sells database software, only database experts will do. If the company sells laptops, only laptop engineers need apply.

Clearly, a test engineer must understand how the particular system under test works. The deeper the knowledge, the better the tester's understanding of the boundary conditions, failure modes, interfaces, and weaknesses of the system. Nonetheless, I lean toward Myers's viewpoint.

Independent test organizations perform primarily behavioral (black-box) testing, with a limited amount of structural (white-box) testing. In software organizations, the unit tests and component tests are frequently the responsibility of developers. Likewise, hardware components usually enter testing after a basic level of checking has been done by hardware engineers; with some notable exceptions, testers can treat these components as opaque subsystems. Given this situation, it doesn't take smart test specialists long to learn the system under test from a user's perspective.

Another reason to prefer test specialists involves the particular skills they bring to a project. A content specialist might do a great job of functional testing but might not understand how to check system capacity and error handling, how to evaluate performance in a meaningful way, or how to track and manage bugs. On occasion I have had to explain stress testing at a beginner's level to talented and seasoned development engineers. A test team composed of content experts with such testing blind spots would end up neglecting major quality risks. It is also true that content experts sometimes feel that they have been "relegated" to the test organization, when all the exciting stuff happens in development. Unhappy people often do poor work.

I consider myself a test specialist and have worked on projects as diverse as personal computer development, PC applications, multi–operating system database utilities, laptops, mainframe operating systems, custom supercomputers, and telephony. I use my technical background as a foundation for learning the content-specific skills required and apply my knowledge of testing to each project.

Those who argue for content specialists often emphasize the need for technical training in specific areas, and I do agree that every test engineer should have a technical background. I usually look for a technical degree, whether an associate degree or a bachelor's or master's degree. I prefer candidates who have worked as programmers, engineers, system administrators, or customer support representatives. (Some test experts even recommend three to five years of hands-on programming experience, although that is probably excessive in most settings.) Test engineers should also have some level of career maturity, and their education and experience levels should be consistent with the levels of other employees who hold the "engineer" title throughout your organization.

It would certainly be wrong to discount the contributions that content specialists can make to a test project. These individuals bring an understanding of the system under test that allows them to test effectively without a lot of guidance. If you are forced to operate in an ad hoc fashion while building your test system, content specialists will probably be essential.

When I can find test specialists who have worked with—preferably tested—the system under test or similar technology, I snap them up. Test engineers who have special skills in terms of both testing and content make hiring decisions easy.

PROFESSIONAL PESSIMISM

A Pollyanna attitude is the wrong attitude on a test team. In fact, testers are professional pessimists. Management pays them to explore the dark side of the project. One development engineer told me that he "felt very depressed" after reading the FMEA chart my test staff had prepared. I find it more depressing, however, to ignore the possibility of failure during development, only to live with the reality of preventable failure after release. Testing involves anticipating the worst of all possible worlds in order to achieve the best possible situation, given realistic project constraints.

Everyone wants to release products of the highest quality. I have heard project managers comment that testing budgets are a waste of money because those development scoundrels should be building software or hardware that works in the first place. Those managers do care about quality, but they don't understand the process of software development.[3] Development

---

3. Scott Adams's series of Dilbert cartoons about testing put the following words into a development manager's mouth: "If a tree falls in the forest, and we've already sold it, does it have quality?" Actually, I've never heard anything quite that cynical. I believe that most failures to understand and appreciate the value proper testing brings to a project arise from ignorance, not apathy.

engineers, especially the good ones, want to practice a craft and to create products of elegance and quality. You will encounter very few "just a paycheck" hacks in the computer business.

Nevertheless, a test team must foresee and evaluate the ways in which a product might fail. Many books and studies have documented the reasons why this pessimistic, depressing function should live in an independent group—mostly because it *is* depressing and pessimistic, at least to developers. Having constructed a beautiful piece of software or hardware, developers can hardly be expected to turn around and beat it, torture it, subject it to cruel boundary conditions, stress it, and force it to handle "unlikely" errors.

The test organization plays this difficult and, in many ways, noble role. One computer consultant describes testing as the point in the project at which people's "depraved mind[s]...can be usefully employed."[4] A good test engineer does not mind thinking about ways the product can fail. You might hope that nothing will go wrong, but relying on this hope denies the entire history of computing. Thus the tester creates failures in a safe environment, allowing the project team to fix them. Testing requires a pessimistic mindset in the pursuit of a lofty goal: company success through better products.

That said, professional pessimism differs from obnoxious behavior. A tester should focus on catching bugs in the product, not on catching the project team member who might have introduced the bug. Furthermore, the tester must be sensitive to the possibility that a developer will see negative test results as a personal attack. Pointing out specific flaws in the product in a balanced, fair way is helpful. Attacking the product categorically and in general terms is not.

It is essential for everyone on the test team to maintain open, frank, and courteous relationships with the entire project team. If, through repeated conflicts, you reach the point where influential players on the project team refuse to listen to you, disbelieve what you say, or bear a grudge against you, the effectiveness of your test operation will suffer. Being a tester is not a license to be offensive. It is a challenge to be positive, pleasant, and the bearer of bad news, all at the same time.

---

4. Richard Conway, *An Introduction to Programming: A Structured Approach Using PL/I and PL/C.*

BALANCED CURIOSITY

During test development, a tester must spend time learning to understand the product in order to write high-yield test cases. During test execution, isolating bugs—fully identifying the factors that affect the behavior of bugs—is an essential part of creating good reports. But it's important to differentiate between a tester who takes the time needed to develop a thorough test or write a good bug report and one who goes off on a snipe hunt.

A good test engineer develops test cases the way an expert spelunker goes into a cave. Dead ends abound, but the test engineer understands the situation and writes test cases that lead to bugs. This requires curiosity. The test engineer must read the specifications, discuss "what-if" scenarios with the developers, and mentally twist and turn the system under test, examining all the angles. Without curiosity, a fascination with the goal, the engineer will write superficial test cases.

A good test engineer also knows how to chase down a problem, trying the smart variations first, with an innate sense of what levers affect the anomalous behavior. Such an engineer willingly spends an hour or two rerunning a test case with minor variations to get at the essence of a bug, if that's appropriate.[5] This same kind of curiosity leads scientists to spend time in a lab looking through a microscope or in an observatory staring at stars. A person who possesses this trait and uses it wisely is an irreplaceable asset. Curiosity is what motivates a tester to perform otherwise tedious isolation steps, to research obscure and possibly undocumented aspects of the system under test, and to sift through ambiguity for understanding.

But if a tester becomes engrossed in unlikely failure modes and spends days writing test cases to expose them, you end up with low-yield test cases. A tester who spends long hours investigating trivial bugs is squandering a precious resource—the test team's time—and is taking "curiosity" too far. In contrast, a tester who rushes to write up a serious and complex bug report after reproducing the symptom once, without additional work, probably isn't curious enough.

---

5. Myers, in *The Art of Software Testing*, refers to the ability to write high-yield test cases and to isolate bugs as "error guessing."

What divides "curious enough" from "not curious enough" and "too curious"? Good judgment. Some testers are able to balance the need to finish developing the test suite in time for execution with the thrill of writing a clever, effective test case. They can balance the pressure to move forward with the desire to know why a bug occurs.

No Space Cadets

One Saturday morning I went into the test lab and found absolutely no progress being made. A test engineer had brought everything to a standstill by pulling the three other engineers in the lab into isolating a problem. He had found a serious bug, but it didn't require the attention of four test engineers, and it really didn't need to hold up restarting the stress test, whose completion gated the product release. No one could question this engineer's dedication—he frequently spent the night in the lab, curled up in a sleeping bag—but his lack of focus put schedules in danger. He had also managed to defocus three other test engineers.

This situation exemplifies two types of focus problems. First, the engrossed engineer pursued the bug before him so narrow-mindedly that he lost sight of the more important priority. He should have realized after a few minutes that he needed to take a break, restart the stress test suite, and then continue analyzing the failure. Imagine a cook who produces perfect, lump-free gravy while the roast in the oven becomes the culinary equivalent of shoe leather. He was too focused. Second, the distracted engineers broke away from their tasks to gaze upon this wondrous bug, just for a moment. The moment passed, but they forgot what they were supposed to be doing until I arrived. They weren't focused enough.

Testers should reevaluate the appropriateness of their choice of tasks every so often. Testers need quiet, focused periods to solve difficult problems, so you don't want to encourage scatterbrained behavior. But, especially during test execution, every tester should frequently examine whether the task on the table is the most important way to spend time at the moment.

Most testers will go off on a tangent from time to time. As the test manager, you must stay on top of your staff's activities to ensure that the tester who strays is herded back quickly. Recognize that the dynamic nature of the project can lead to frequent shifts in priority, making the task that was right yesterday the wrong task today. If your whole team has problems focusing on the right tasks, ask yourself whether you are communicating priorities clearly and effectively.

Some testers need more redirection—either from the task at hand to more pressing issues, or from the chimera back to their assignments—than others do. At the least, these people shouldn't hold leadership roles in your organization because they misdirect others as well as themselves. For the most hardened offenders, you might need to consider whether they should remain in the test group. Someone who consistently makes the wrong decision about which task to focus on might not be someone you can change.

THE WRONG PERSON FOR THE JOB: DISQUALIFICATIONS FOR TEST ENGINEERS

Just as certain qualities make for a good test engineer (when not taken to extremes), other traits are bad news in any degree. The next few sections describe the sorts of people who should be disqualified from working as test engineers.

GLAMOUR-SEEKERS

Part of the problem with getting good test engineers lies in the fact that so few people choose this as a specialty. Test work is perceived as unglamorous drudgery in many companies, which creates two problems for you. First, you may end up hiring people who view the test organization as an extended "Hell Week" they must endure in order to join the fraternity of developers. These folks can work out, providing that the would-be programmer or motherboard designer is qualified for a development position, is on a career path toward that goal, and has skills you need. But this kind of situation gets ugly when it becomes obvious to everyone except the employee that a future as a developer isn't in the cards. Second, you may find that some of your test staff deal with the company's caste system by adopting an inappropriate attitude toward the development staff, who sometimes treat testers with disdain in companies that foster an exaggerated pecking order. This situation can turn into a feeding frenzy of recrimination and backstabbing that will make your life difficult and damage your team's productivity. Be sure that candidates for test positions understand their prospects and can deal with their place on the company totem pole.

SLOTHS

I worked with a test engineer who was intelligent and capable of good work but who had no drive. He would sit in the lab and read Internet news for hours, neglecting important test tasks. In response, some of his colleagues wrote a program that checked whether he was running news-related processes on the test network; if he was, the program sent a message to his screen saying, "Get back to work." In addition to his Internet vice, he had an aversion to hard work. He would work an eight-hour day, no more and often less when he could get away with it. I liked the guy personally, but he did not add a lot of value to the test organization. Eventually he quit and went into graphics work for the movie business.

We're All Geeks Together

The low-caste nature of testing, as compared to "sexy" development work, is well known among testers. I have never worked in a development organization—hardware or software—where a caste system didn't apply and where testers didn't occupy the lower rungs.

Is this situation changing? Maybe. According to a 1998 article in *Contract Professional*, a high-tech consulting and contracting magazine, "functions like hardware test engineering…were perceived as the dull cousins of sexy front-end jobs like design engineering." The article goes on to point out increasing pay rates and demand for testers but doesn't provide any evidence of an increase in "sexiness." It's nice to be well paid, but the management bromide says that although lack of money can demotivate, money itself is not a motivator. In other words, too little money can make employees miserable, but a lot of money won't make them happy about an otherwise unhappy situation.

The irony is that, from the outside, we're all geeks together. Owen Edwards, in a *Forbes ASAP* article, discusses "the Geek Tragedy"—the alleged shortage of technical workers in the United States that makes it imperative, at least in the eyes of certain high-tech executives, to admit more H1-B visa holders. Edwards writes: "It's the very fact that they can't get dates that suits them [high-tech individual contributors] for the drudgery of programming. So let's celebrate all the dauntless dorks…" Remember that the next time you start to take the company totem pole seriously!

Don't misunderstand—a test operation shouldn't be run like the Bataan death march, nor does blowing off steam by playing a video game or surfing the Web cause an immediate schedule slip. Also, people who put in eight solid hours of work at a high level of productivity and then leave the lab are not shirking. They are engaged in what is sometimes called "having a life." Some high-tech companies have a reputation for demanding ridiculous hours and slavish devotion, to the exclusion of a normal existence. In my experience, tired people do poor-quality work, and unrealistic schedules are seldom met.

Nevertheless, testing does involve hard work. Tight schedules, last-minute slip-ups, late hours, and weekend test runs call for people who will go the extra mile. If you find that a tester consistently misses deadlines, or sets individual deadlines that allow far more time than required, or evades every bit of overtime or weekend work on flimsy pretenses, you have a sloth on your hands and should set about reforming this employee if possible. Of course, if you see any indication during the hiring process that a person won't work hard, you're better off not hiring that individual in the first place. Slothful testers force their colleagues to carry their weight.

CASPER MILQUETOASTS

The flip side of the obnoxious, confrontational jerk discussed earlier is the tester who is just too mild-mannered. Rather than becoming ineffective by being in everyone's face, this tester is too retiring, too confrontation-averse. Such a person will have real difficulties in testing. In order to promote quality, a tester must advocate, argue, assert, and defend, without hesitating to bring problems to the attention of management. A tester who files a bug report and then backs down at the slightest hint of controversy can't contribute to the quality of the product.

Although it's important to avoid undue obstinance, testers must have the courage to make waves when the situation calls for it. As a colleague once said to me, "If you're not making people upset, you're not doing your job." This is different from saying, "Your job is to upset people." Rather, it means that testers necessarily cause controversy and distress when they uncover problems that have negative implications for project schedules, resource requirements, and so forth—or when they point out the possibility of those problems. A person afraid of upsetting others makes a poor tester. Testers should never go out of their way to upset people but should be willing to deliver and defend bad news in spite of the reaction it might cause.

Giving a Damn: Motivating Your Test Team

Maintaining morale and motivation on a test team takes some doing. In my experience, the traditional "team building" exercises don't work too well with test folks, since we tend to be a cynical lot. There are, however, some management styles you can adopt that will do what no amount of ersatz group bonding exercises can: convince your team members that you value their time and contributions, respect their opinions, and will stand up for them when they need you. The following sections offer tips about such styles.

Don't Let Others Use Your Team as a Doormat

As noted earlier, some people regard testing as low-caste work. You might not be able to change this perception—and often the perception is a political reality. You can, however, take some steps to minimize the extent to which this situation demotivates your team.

Stand by Me

Every now and then, someone on your staff will put a cherry bomb in a wasps' nest. The resulting swarm of angry critters, looking to sting the perpetrator, can overwhelm the lowly tester. These kinds of incidents usually arise from severity 1 bug reports, although hallway conversations about the tenuous connection between reality and the latest delivery date run a close second. These situations are even worse when your tester has in fact made a mistake. I have seen bug reports given legalistic scrutiny, and I pity the tester who mischaracterizes a bug.

When faced with angry attacks on one of your team members, never upbraid or criticize the hapless tester publicly, no matter what the mistake. You should, however, acknowledge the problem, perhaps saying something along these lines: "Yeah, we probably could have done a better job. I guess I goofed when I reviewed that report. But let's talk about this bug." This approach allows you to admit the mistake, take the blame yourself, and move to the matter at hand. (Of course, if you have staff members who habitually shoot off their mouths or write up "omigawd" bug reports without checking the facts, you must deal with this problem on a long-term basis.)

In addition, what testers do wrong should not distract attention from what they do right. If an offending bug report lacks a few isolation steps, but the bug is undeniable, don't let people lose sight of that fact. If a tester's manner is inappropriate in the course of escalating a serious problem, shift the focus back to the problem. Do this with the tester present. Visibly stand up for your employee in public, and then do whatever coaching is needed later, in private, after you both have had a chance to blow off steam and reflect calmly. You'll build real loyalty among your staff by displaying this kind of solidarity under fire and by dealing with their failures in private.

Equal Pay and More

Some years ago, a test network administrator I supervised wanted to attend a networking conference, which made good sense to me. It was appropriate for his career path, he could learn something of immediate importance, and the timing was good. We did the whole "trip request" tango, which also involved my manager.

Several development engineers had signed up for the same conference. As the date approached, a senior manager started complaining about the large number of attendees, suggesting that perhaps some attendees should cancel. Guess who made the short list of extraneous attendees? I responded reasonably, explaining the original justifications—still valid—for sending the network administrator on this trip. I became a bit less reasonable when my own manager hopped on the dog pile. I fired off an e-mail to my manager implying that my engineer was being singled out because of his position in test. I also asked pointedly whether management cared about this employee and about the effect that canceling the trip would have on his morale. My engineer attended the conference.

Make sure that your staff members get an equal crack at all the perks. The following list should help you keep an eye on the situation and restore a level playing field if need be. A word of warning, though: before you accuse anyone of stacking the deck against your test team, have your facts in order. You'll look paranoid if you can't document inequities.

Salaries.   If the pay scale for test engineers is below that of the other engineers in your company, work with the human resources department to ensure pay parity for equal levels of responsibility. The old wisdom that testers should make less than developers is just that: old. Recent (1998) salary surveys in magazines such as *Quality Progress* and *Contract Professional* show a very narrow gap between developer and test salaries. Be aware, however, that this is a tough nut to crack if you have inherited an existing test team.

Job Titles. If the ladder of job titles in development has more rungs, with more prestige, than the one in test, do whatever you can to resolve the inequity. Again, you'll probably need to enlist the cooperation of the human resources office. Argue for a parallel set of technical titles, such as Member of the Technical Staff, Senior Member of the Technical Staff, Principal Member of the Technical Staff, and so forth. If these parallel rungs already exist, but test employees hold only Member of the Technical Staff titles rather than the more senior titles, investigate whether the test employees are being given a lower rank than their history with the company, their years in the industry, and their levels of responsibility warrant.

Hours. If testers are expected to work unusual hours, or if they get stuck testing over the weekend to meet a schedule target while the rest of the development team has the weekend off, ask for compensatory time off for your staff—or just give it to them. If testers must cede test's hardware to developers for debugging during regular business hours and consequently must perform testing after hours, discuss the matter with your development manager colleagues. Point out the unfairness, and ask to work out a schedule for debugging access that "spreads the misery." If they refuse, go to your manager.

Training Sessions, Off-Sites, Seminars, and Conferences. If developers frequently attend plum events in exotic locations, while testers seldom do, find a particularly useful and particularly attractive event for your best staff person to attend, and sell it to your manager. Repeat this tactic as needed to help redress any imbalance. Budget freezes sometimes restrict the number of employees who can be sent to conferences and training seminars. If these freezes affect test attendees but not development attendees, ask your manager or the human resources office to establish a training budget for each department, including yours, with demonstrable equity.

Beware of Burnout

Hard work, unrealistic schedules, and the occasional strange hours come with the test territory. But this lifestyle burns people out. You may encounter testers whose previous employers have overworked them ferociously; not surprisingly, this usually makes them unwilling to be taken advantage of again.

To help alleviate some of the stress involved in testing, be sure to pace your team. You might be pressured to inflict undesirable work conditions on the team as soon as testing begins. Resist it. A test project is always a marathon; never start with a sprint. Testing often begins behind schedule, has too few people allocated to it, and never ends on the date originally planned. Under these circumstances, you should avoid pushing too hard too early.

Also try to break up the work whenever possible. On one of my jobs, test builds for the monthly maintenance releases usually showed up on Friday afternoon around 4:00. As the build and development teams headed out for their weekends, test staff installed these builds and started tests, sometimes working well into the evening. Next came the weekend work to keep the tests going so that we could report on test status on Monday afternoon. Everyone loved this arrangement except us. You should pay your staff back for extra effort such as this. If people work over the weekend, give them a Friday or a Monday off. Let them go early during the week after a rough session. Try to give them breathing spells between crunches.

Clearly, one reason for the feelings of stress and overload is that most test organizations are understaffed. When your best efforts to achieve a realistic staffing level fall short, you might try shifting gears by remembering that "understaffed" can be synonymous with "overtasked"—a perspective that allows you to consider other options for reducing your team's load. Try to get support from other groups in the company for chores that might not be part of your core mission but are essential to accomplishing it. For example, you might be able to use an administrative assistant to do some of the tedious data entry work, freeing up some of your testers' time.

Another problem is that test organizations often start participating in projects too late. Ideally, one or two test people should be involved in a project right from the beginning. You'll need to assign someone to start preparations for a new project up front rather than waiting until a few days before component, integration, or system test execution is scheduled to begin. As a manager, you obviously must be involved in planning the test effort, but you also need an engineer to attend to the technical details. This engineer can plan the reuse and adaptation of the existing test system (tools, cases, and suites), select whatever new tools are needed, define the changes to the test architecture, and so forth. The test engineer should also participate in technical reviews and have detailed discussions with the developers. You might not be able to spare someone full-time, but it's important enough to set aside a few hours every week. If you don't take the time to do this, you and your team will be forced into a reactive mode when test execution starts and will be chronically unable to get solid test execution under way.

Early test involvement in new projects has another benefit that feeds back into the issue of understaffing. The commencement of any new project reopens discussion of appropriate staff levels. As you demonstrate your organization's ability to add value to the delivered product, management is likely to approve more realistic staffing levels for subsequent projects.

In companies that have no experience with formal testing or with early test involvement in development projects, some care is required in implementing this up-front participation. Begin by selling the project manager on the benefits of more effective, less hectic testing. If the two of you approach management, you're more likely to succeed, especially since the project manager—as a person who will bring a saleable product to the company's portfolio—will usually have a lot more pull than you do.

A more subtle source of overload in the test organization is change. Changes in the project plan do not smite developers and test staff alike. Take scope creep, for instance. Adding a few simple APIs to a program can generate a whole slew of new test work because it will require testing other programs (and maybe even hardware devices) that use those APIs. In hardware, changing the design of a moving part—say, a PC Card bay door—might call for not only reexecuting that lengthy 10,000-repetition mechanical-life test but also reworking your fixtures and test tools.

Scope shrink is just as bad. This kind of change can make it hard to distinguish between time well spent and a perfectly good day squandered. Suppose that one of your engineers spends 12 hours implementing a particularly nifty test tool for generating network load, which seems like a good investment. Two days later, management pulls network support from the system under test as part of a decision to trim features in order to hit a marketing window. Sure, it will be nice to have that test tool in the next product cycle, but in the meantime you've let two or three other tasks languish, and those jobs are now much more important.

In addition, keep in mind that test execution occurs in the most "change-rich" portion of the project. As people begin to perceive how unrealistic the schedule is and yet make frantic efforts to adhere to it anyway, you'll see abrupt deletions in product functionality, reorganization of some or all of the project teams, dropping of entire test suites from the plan, and other such corrections. These changes aren't always constructive or carefully considered. "Do something! Do anything!" often becomes the project slogan as schedules start to slip, and schedule slip is most noticeable during test execution, simply because test happens to be the caboose on the project train.

Without exaggerating or overreacting, never let significant changes to the project go unremarked or undocumented. If the change is big, bring it to management's attention—not as a complaint but as a matter that should be understood and acknowledged. If someone suggests adding support for BeOS to DataRocket, your response should be along these lines: "Great! We anticipate that will cost $1,500 in new software for our lab, require one additional engineering sample, and consume 50 person-hours. Let's talk about how we get these new resources."

Whether the change is small or large, it must be managed. Chapter 6 introduced a simple database that can help you track changes (see "Expect the Unexpected: A Change Management Database," page 203). While best practices call for all changes to be managed at a project-wide level, you should plan on tracking and managing them yourself until your organization reaches that level of maturity.

When you are faced with too few people, too much work to handle at once, and an environment of constant change, the rush to keep up can tempt you and your team to devise kludges. A kludge is any ill-advised, substandard, or "temporary" bandage applied to an urgent problem in the (often misguided) belief that doing so will keep a project moving forward. But the reality is that these hasty little shortcuts usually serve only to transfer pain from the present to the immediate future—and add more pain to it in the bargain.

It often seems that performing an ad hoc, undocumented test on some "one-shot feature that will never come up again" almost ensures that testing this feature will become enshrined in the regular routine. Once you have a workable process in place, don't deviate from it at the drop of a hat. An engineer who devises a new test case needs to write it down. A technician who alters a test case should document the change and the reason for it. A tester who changes a system configuration must record the new setup. The cliché "more haste, less speed" is a cliché because it's true.

A final note on tester burnout: you'll find that one or two inappropriate test team members can make a tough situation untenable. I will admit to having kept some testers around long after they had demonstrated their negative impact on team morale and performance. I have learned my lesson and won't repeat that mistake. Keeping a problem employee on board does no one any good.

The rest of your staff suffers most when you keep dead weight around. The team has to compensate for this person's blunders and mistakes. Furthermore, one individual's poor work can result in a perception that the entire test team is incompetent and careless, which leads to the project team looking askance at your bug reports, metrics, and other test data. Most damaging, an individual who is not contributing usually knows it and adopts various defensive postures to camouflage the failure—for instance, denigrating the work of the other team members. In such cases, productive and motivated contributors suffer disparagement to salve the ego of the inept one. All of these outcomes are unfair to you and your team.

The person you fire might find the experience quite painful in the short run. Still, a smart person will take the opportunity to assess what went wrong and decide to do better. Presumably you took all the right steps by coaching the employee and then gradually moving up the ladder from verbal to written warnings. Once you hit the second or third written warning, it's time. You obviously aren't getting through, and after the third warning you won't be taken seriously if you don't let this person go.

TROJAN HORSES AND OTHER MISTAKES: HOW NOT TO MOTIVATE TESTERS

Test managers can be their own worst enemies when it comes to damaging the motivation of a test team. Here are some examples.

Basing Bonuses on Meeting a Schedule. Promising bonuses to staff based on whether a schedule is met is a bad idea, especially for a test team. Testing, when done properly, finds bugs, often more than expected. If the project team ignores the bugs in order to meet the schedule, the money spent on testing is wasted. But if the project team takes the time to fix the bugs, the test team's collective bonus can disappear. Project-wide, every successful test case—every case that finds a bug—reduces the odds of getting a bonus for everyone. What kind of motivation does this provide? Such obvious common sense notwithstanding, these bonus arrangements do occur.

Schedule-based bonus plans usually descend from above. If the project manager proposes a scheme like this, explain the perverse incentives it will create for the testers and the negative dynamic it will set up between test and the rest of the project team. If the development team gets a bonus for meeting a schedule, that's fine (although you should remind management of the tension this will generate as the test team succeeds in finding bugs). But the test team should have a different bonus plan, one that emphasizes the role of testers as quality advocates. How about a bonus based on a low number of test escapes for the first three months after product release? Admittedly, this arrangement will not be implemented without some effort on your part, but the path of least resistance—going along with a plan that provides an incentive for your team to do the *wrong* thing—makes no sense.

Basing Bonuses on Bugs Found. I once heard a rumor about a test contractor who got paid by the bug and by the hour, earning over $500,000 in one year from one project. This story, while apocryphal, probably contains elements of truth. But bug reports are not commodities. The importance of bugs and the quality of reports vary. If you want to generate a huge volume of bug reports—many of them lousy and many detailing unimportant bugs—you can award bonuses based on the sheer number of reports. If you want good bug reports, don't do this.

Expecting Thanks for Saturday Night's Pizza. When your team is working late nights and weekends, plan to pay for some meals during these overtime periods. Get approval to submit an expense report. And when you buy meals, remember that people get tired of pizza. Most American-style pizza is just about the least healthy food around. Vary the menu, and offer your staff options they'll find palatable. Instead of getting irritated when employees have special meal requests, remember that you are not doing them a favor by buying them a meal—they are doing you and your company a favor by giving up their own time. (Some companies foster a "macho geek chic" centered on late nights, early mornings, and pizza feasts during midnight bull sessions. What exactly is the prize for winning a sleep-deprivation or junk-food-consumption contest?)

Promoting an Us Versus Them Mentality. In my opinion, the worst motivational technique is whipping up confrontational attitudes between testers and developers. This kind of "mock duel" might inspire testers to find more bugs in the short run. But, for the same reasons that being a jerk isn't among the traits of a good test engineer, fostering mistrust and ill will between the test and development organizations won't work either.

EXTENDING YOUR TALENT: USING TEMPORARY IMPLEMENTERS AND EXPERTS

Sometimes the list of tasks that simply must be done by a given date exceeds the capability of the test team. You might need additional expertise, or you might simply need help implementing a test development or execution effort. These situations are usually transitory, and you can phase out the extra help after a period of days, weeks, or months. (For circumstances in which long-term outsourcing is appropriate, see Chapter 10.) The remainder of this chapter discusses such temporary help and its use and misuse.

ASSESSING THE ROLES OF TEMPORARY WORKERS

Let's begin by defining the kind of extra help you're likely to need. During the post–World War II era of William H. Whyte's "organization man," this would have been an easy exercise. In the rigidly bureaucratic corporate culture described by Whyte, temporary agencies supplied clerical workers and other low-level interim staff to meet rush-period needs, while academia, industry alumni, and consulting companies supplied consultants to transfer expertise into an organization.

These days, however, applying simplistic models no longer works, especially in high-tech fields. Temporary agencies still exist, but in addition to supplying data entry clerks, they now also place programmers, test engineers, and business analysts with six-figure paychecks. Some of the people who work through temporary agencies bring as much expertise to a company as those who are the more traditional "outside experts."

Correspondingly, the labels by which you could once have identified the various players have also become meaningless. "Temps" may well have experience with advanced office-automation tools and software that makes these workers quite different from yesterday's typists. Likewise, not all those who call themselves "consultants" work for consulting companies or bring dozens of years of unique experience and research to their assignments.[6]

---

6. Janet Ruhl's *The Computer Consultant's Guide*, which provides helpful tips to anyone who works as temporary staff in the high-tech world, also acknowledges the confusion that exists in the use of words such as "temp," "contractor," and "consultant."

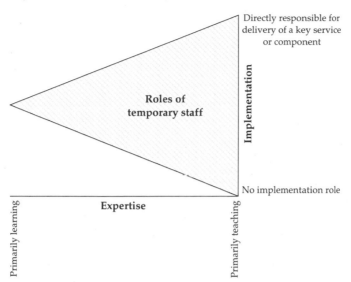

FIGURE 8-4 *The roles played by temporary staff.*

Instead of relying on labels, it's perhaps more useful to break down the contributions of temporary staff along two axes: implementation and expertise. The drawing in Figure 8-4 diagrams the kinds of assistance that temporary staff can offer your organization.

To understand what these various roles entail, you can think of moving counterclockwise around the triangle in Figure 8-4. Toward the left apex of the triangle, you find people who are best suited to be temporary test technicians. They play an important, but not critical, role in implementation. They might bring special skills to the test team, but they have no role in teaching those skills to your staff. Indeed, to the extent that knowledge is transferred, these temporary workers need to spend time learning your processes and test system.

As you move toward the lower apex of the triangle, you start to find people who might qualify as "consultants" in the traditional sense. At the midpoint of the expertise axis, perhaps, you might encounter on-site trainers who spend a few days working with your staff on a particularly tricky test automation tool, solving a few implementation problems, and then leaving. People nearest the lower apex spend their time teaching and training exclusively—for example, someone who comes on site to teach you the FMEA techniques described in Chapter 1. (These are people about whom Edwin Meese, a former U.S. Attorney General who now makes a living as an expert, quipped, "An expert is somebody who is more than 50 miles from home, has no responsibility for implementing the advice he gives, and shows slides.")

Toward the upper apex of the triangle, you find highly knowledgeable professionals who, in addition to transferring that expertise to their clients, help the clients apply the knowledge to the implementation of technology. For example, I often work side by side with my clients to implement a test program while I train the client's employee test manager to take over after I leave.

Moving back toward the left apex, you encounter temporary staff who, although they might possess great expertise, focus their efforts on implementation. The client might secure a "black box" from them—a test tool, for example—but receive little or no training in how it works internally; instead, any instruction focuses solely on how to use the tool.

Working with Long-Term Temporary Staff

Notice that, to a great extent, you can also place your permanent staff within the triangle shown in Figure 8-4. Your team members probably operate closer to the center than to the apexes, or perhaps along the upper edge (from left to right, think test technicians to test engineers). One important distinction applies, however: for temporary workers, you are not the employer—you are the client. This difference can have powerful implications for how you relate to these folks.

As mentioned earlier, many temporary workers will stay with your organization for only a few days. A trainer who teaches your engineers how to use a testing tool, for example, or a traditional consultant who counsels you on overcoming a particular challenge will probably be on site for only a week or less. Of growing significance, however, is a developing class of professionals who work on a contractual, rather than an employee, basis with companies for a few weeks, months, or even years. These workers are temporary in that they will probably leave whenever their project or assignment is over. Although they have no career path at your company, they often look and act much like typical permanent employees. To use such long-term temporary workers effectively, it's important to separate emotion and wishes from reality.

In this discussion, I'll refer to these long-term temporary workers as "contractors." By "contractor," I mean a person who works on the basis of a contract, rather than an employee agreement, for a lengthy period of time, usually working more as an implementer than as a knowledge-transfer agent or an initiator of change within the company. Contractors are paid according to units of time, whether hourly or weekly. They frequently work on site, and in a similar capacity as permanent employees, with whom they often work side by side. Contractors are generally brought in for a specific project, and their stay at the company is generally delimited by the duration of the project as well as by their contract.

It's usually the case that a contractor's idea of the perfect workplace differs from that of the average permanent employee. While every temporary worker is a human being with unique wants and needs, some generalizations do apply.

One is that money can be a different kind of motivator for temporary staff than it is for the average salaried employee. I realize that sounds crass, but the distinction is important. One implication of this is that you usually get what you pay for. If you go looking for a bargain, you might find one; perhaps a skilled contractor is new to the temporary world and doesn't know his or her own worth. More likely, though, people who have been around for a while know what they're worth. If you're paying them that much, you're not getting a bargain. If they're taking less than their usual rate because they need the money, they'll probably stick around longer than they should, but eventually they'll leave. Most contractors know that the longer they stay at a lower-paying job, the more difficult it becomes to find future work at a higher rate.

Unless your company works with temporary personnel directly as subcontractors, you should also be aware of agency fees and how they fit into the financial equation. Some agencies collect up-front fees as high as 50 percent of the billing rate. In other words, you might find a contractor's rate of $100 per hour to be steep, but the contractor might be getting only $50 of that amount. Again, you get what you pay for. The $50 per hour you pay to the agency is strictly to cover its profits and its costs of marketing, maintaining an office, and insurance, only the last of which does you any good. The only other benefit to your company is protection from tax liability should the U.S. Internal Revenue Service (IRS) retroactively reclassify your subcontractors as employees. The $50 per hour the contractor receives is for the skills that the individual brings to the job, and that's the skill level you should expect.

Suppose, however, that you are paying $100 an hour to an agency for a contractor whose skills are really worth that amount. In this case, you're actually in worse shape than in the previous example. Temporary workers talk to one another, and they either know the agency's billing rate coming in or find out about it later. Your contractor, who is not stupid, will discern the situation and will soon leave as a result of being underpaid by the agency. You'll suffer when a key resource disappears in the midst of a project because of a conflict that has nothing to do with you.

If you believe that an agency is offering you a contractor at such a low rate that the contractor will feel short-changed, you might want to consider other candidates—or at least make sure that this person won't be the linch-pin of a critical project. You should also ascertain whether the agency in question makes a practice of such behavior. If it does, this agency's place-ments will be an endless source of grief to you. The obvious solution, recti-fying the inequity to the contractor, is unfortunately quite difficult. Your management will of course assume that you have rocks in your head, or worse, if you negotiate contractors' rates upward. In addition, the agency might be happy to accept an increased rate but pass none of it on to the con-tractor. (Contracts with agencies often prohibit you from discussing contrac-tors' net pay with the affected individuals directly.) Although it might seem like simple greed for an agency to place someone at a low rate, business reasons beyond money are sometimes at work. Cheaper contractors are easier to place; and once they've moved into a higher rate, they often resist mov-ing back down.

Assuming that the pay rate is appropriate, good contractors will stick out almost any assignment, provided that you don't change the rules in the middle of the game or subject them to inhuman harassment. Because these workers don't care about advancement in the company, you don't have to worry about the usual motivators, and you might find that temporary per-sonnel will work hard on assignments that might demotivate or drive out permanent employees. Two factors, however, distinguish acceptable assign-ments from the ones contractors will fight to keep: intellectual challenges and lots of billable hours. The first applies to all employees, of course; everyone likes to learn and grow on the job. The second, though, is unique to temporary workers. Permanent salaried workers, paid by the week, will put in a certain number of hours willingly and then begin to grumble. If they're too overworked, they'll leave. But hourly contractors usually wel-come as many billable hours as you can provide.

You should structure your relationship with contractors (and their agencies) to take account of this situation. On the one hand, if your main concern is meeting a deadline, and you can hire only one contractor, make sure that person is paid hourly and is very motivated by money. To the extent that hard work and long hours can keep your project on schedule, you'll get results. On the other hand, if your main concern is staying within budget, set up a daily or weekly rate. That way, even if the contractor works seven days, you will pay for only 56 hours per week. (Unfortunately, too many managers try to have it both ways: they negotiate a daily or weekly rate and then try to have contractors work 12-hour days. This might work with some temporary staff for a little while, but, again, you get what you pay for. Eventually a sharp contractor will understand that 7 hours is closer to a full day than 12—so guess what you'll get for your money?)

Contractors' lack of concern with advancement in the company has a down side. Many of these folks pursue a bohemian work style because of their distaste for the office politics needed to "make it" in many firms. Thus they often display a real disinclination to participate in any event or exercise that smacks of office intrigue or maneuvering. Team picnics or company dinners are usually safe, but pointless meetings, "face time" with management, and pain-sharing exercises aren't. Let the contractors skip these. You'll get more work out of them, and you'll keep them happy.

Speaking of keeping contractors happy, one school of thought asks, "Why bother? After all, they're leaving eventually." Temporary workers of all stripes are used to "engagements from hell," but you'll get better work from happy people than from unhappy ones, regardless of their employment status. You will also earn whatever loyalty is possible under the circumstances, which you just might need one day.

It's also important to keep relationships with temporary workers professional and respectful. Treating contractors with disrespect or showing envy of their above-employee pay rates is a mistake. I knew of one manager who openly referred to his contractors as "software whores." He was smiling when he said it, but, needless to say, some of them found it offensive. What kind of work and commitment do you think he received from these people?

Should you try to "convert" your best contractors—that is, try to hire them as permanent employees? When I worked as an employee in management roles, I was often under pressure to convert contractors. As a contractor, I have also felt the pressure from the other side, having turned down a number of job offers. And, of course, some temporary workers sign on with a company *hoping* to get an offer.

If you want to convert someone—or if you are under pressure from management to do so—a subtle approach is best. Contractors who want job offers won't need an engraved invitation. They might even bring up the issue themselves. But some of them would consider an offer insulting and would resent any repeated efforts. These folks usually perceive a job offer as the company's way of saying, "We are paying you more than you are worth." Indeed, saving money is usually management's primary motivation in converting temporary staff. The oft-stated purpose, making sure that the contractors stay around because everyone loves their work so much, is less frequently the real reason.

If a contractor turns down a job offer, it doesn't necessarily mean that the individual is getting ready to leave your organization. Many temporary workers are happy to have serially monogamous relationships with clients. Just letting them know that they have a home for as long as they want it will minimize the odds that they will look for other work.

Hiring Contractors

Hiring a contractor is easier than hiring a person for a permanent staff position. It's a lot less difficult to get permission from management to bring in temporary help because the budget impact is less and the commitment level minimal. If you make a hiring mistake, you can quickly let the temporary worker go. That said, any hiring decision should be taken seriously.

The first step in hiring temporary help is realizing that you'll need it. If you use project management software such as Microsoft Project, for example, you'll be able to see your staffing needs during project planning. To revisit the SpeedyWriter project, suppose that you examine the time that will be required from Lin-Tsu to accomplish the tasks that have been assigned to her for this project. As you can see in Figure 8-5, she will be overallocated for three weeks in the middle of the test effort. This problem needs to be resolved, and bringing on a contractor would make sense.

Although contractors can be brought on board fairly rapidly, you do need to allocate sufficient lead time. If you need someone with basic data entry skills to sit in front of a keyboard and follow a manual test script, you can usually have this person on site in a week or less. But if you need an experienced test engineer, finding the right contractor will take at least a month—or, more likely, two months if you have exacting skill requests such as the ability to use GUI automation tools, if you need someone with an advanced technical degree, or if you require specific content expertise in areas such as security or usability.

Once you find the perfect person, establishing a business relationship between your employer and the temporary worker can be quite complex, as illustrated in Figure 8-6 on the next page. (The following information is primarily applicable to the United States; Janet Ruhl's book *The Computer Consultant's Guide* contains similar information for Canadian and British contractors.) The top two circles and the upper arrow show a test manager's relationship with the company—in this case, the manager is a permanent employee of the firm. The rest of the drawing shows the various business relationships that can be set up between temporary personnel and a client company. At least one of these relationship paths must exist before the temporary worker can do one billable minute's work for you, the test manager.

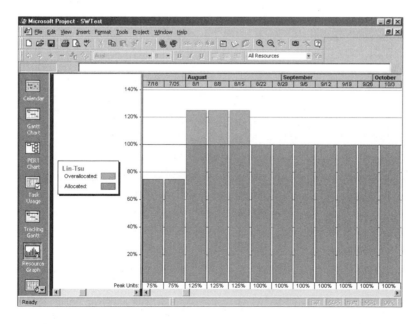

FIGURE 8-5 *An example of resource overallocation for the SpeedyWriter project.*

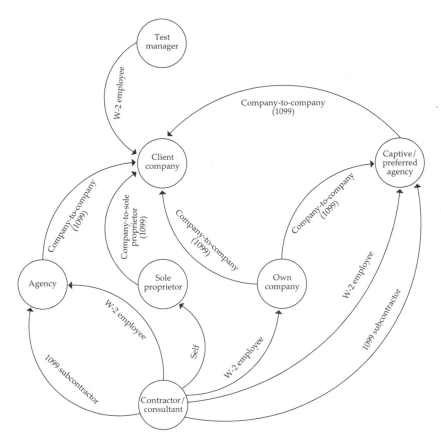

FIGURE 8-6 *Typical business relationships between a temporary worker and a client company.*

The simplest relationship appears in the center of the figure, directly below the client company. The temporary worker is self-employed as the sole proprietor of his or her own business. Your company, the client, has a direct relationship with this business. At the end of the year, your company sends the worker a 1099 federal tax form, not the W-2 form you and other permanent employees receive. Consequently, this worker is often called a "1099 subcontractor." This relationship is much like the one a homeowner might have with a house painter or the one a car owner might have with an individual (independent) mechanic.

To the immediate right of this relationship is a variation in which the temporary worker's business is incorporated. In that case, he or she works for the business as an employee. At the end of the year, your company sends the worker's business a 1099.

The indirect relationship shown in the far left of the figure is probably the most common. Here the individual works for an agency, either as a 1099 subcontractor or a W-2 employee. It's likely that the agency received your job requirements, matched them to the contractor's résumé in its database, and sent the person to see you. If you hire that worker, your company pays the agency, and the agency—after pocketing its margin—pays the worker.

You might ask, "What's the point of the middleman?"—especially when you consider that margins can run as high as 50 percent. There are several advantages for the contractors. For example, they receive marketing services: they don't have to go out looking for clients; instead, the agency finds the clients for them. Contractors can also receive other benefits such as group insurance, a 401(k) plan, and an employer-of-record, which can help with getting credit. (Especially if you have no track record, being self-employed can make buying a car or a house difficult.)

Your company also receives benefits from working with an agency, in the form of three safeguards. The first is protection from the IRS. If your company works directly with temporary personnel, the IRS can, under some circumstances, retroactively classify those people as employees and then fine your company heavily for not withholding taxes from their pay. The second is protection from the temporary personnel themselves. In the past, some of these workers have sued clients, claiming that they were really employees and thus were entitled to participate in benefit programs, especially stock option programs. The client companies have sometimes lost these lawsuits, to the tune of considerable sums of money. People who are the employees of an agency during their stint with your company have less chance of successfully bringing such a suit. The third safeguard is that the agency generally carries insurance on their contractors, which could protect you from an expensive lawsuit if an unfortunate contractor slips and breaks a bone on your company's premises. (Your own employees are likely to be covered under your workers' compensation plan and your corporate liability insurance, but contractors might not be.)

To the far right in Figure 8-6 is a variation on the worker/agency/client model. In this case, your company works only with a single, internal "captive" agency or a small set of preferred agencies. All temporary workers must be employed through these agencies, whether the worker operates as a sole proprietor or as an incorporated business. This arrangement provides all the advantages of the agency model just described, but with the added benefit of allowing your company to keep the accounts payable simple and, if desired, to control or at least curb the agencies' margins.

This arrangement has its drawbacks, however. It's usually true that people who don't have to compete for a client's business soon take it for granted. By limiting the pool of agencies, your company will pay a price in terms of service. The contractors also pay a price in that the agency, while collecting a margin from fees that arguably belong to the workers, has done little or nothing to market these people and has no incentive to keep them happy in order to place them at other companies later. Also, by limiting the pool of agencies, this arrangement limits the pool of available candidates. An agency's database is its most prized possession, and agencies do not all have access to the same pool of talent.

As if all this weren't complicated enough, you should be aware that the business relationship between the contractor and the client is often not immaterial to the contractor. Some contractors work only on a 1099 basis; others work only as W-2 employees. Some will not work through agencies at all; others work only through agencies. Sometimes workers prefer or avoid specific agencies because of positive or negative past experiences. All these factors can complicate and even scuttle your attempts to hire the best temporary help.

BRINGING IN THE EXPERTS

On occasion, you will find yourself confronted by a situation beyond your ability. You don't need extra hands to accomplish a task; rather, you need extra knowledge. At such times, you need someone who fits into the lower right-hand sector of the triangle shown in Figure 8-4: an expert, a "consultant" in the traditional meaning of the term. How do you pick the right person? How do you find someone who can actually solve your problem?

You begin by being clear about the problem you need to solve and about how you expect the consultant to help you solve it. In some cases, you want the consultant to assess your difficulties and advise you on possible solutions. Alternatively, you might want the consultant to train you or your team. For example, I work with an accountant in my consulting business, and I often call her with questions about how to stay out of trouble with the IRS. She tells me what I need to do, and I do it. This kind of activity is consulting in the original sense of the word: transferring knowledge, teaching. I also use this same accountant to do my corporate and personal taxes. In this case, she acts as a practitioner. She still brings special expertise to bear, but she applies that knowledge directly to benefit me rather than teaching me to help myself.

Similarly, a consultant on a software or hardware development project can be heavily involved in implementation or not involved at all. In my practice, most of my consulting does include implementation as well as teaching my clients. For some projects, I have come on board ostensibly to teach, only to find that I actually needed to help the client build and manage a test team. I consider myself a "consultant" regardless.

Whatever you call such an expert, the distinguishing quality is clearly the expertise. This person brings knowledge that you don't have to your relationship, and that's exactly what you want. The trick is figuring out whether this person or consulting group can bring the *right* knowledge.

Making this determination is not easy. A consultant may have as much trouble figuring out how to help you as you have trouble figuring out what help you need. (Gerald Weinberg's book *The Secrets of Consulting* can help you resolve this and other consulting paradoxes.) Obviously, a consultant wants to avoid having clients that, for some weird reason, "just didn't work out." But, from your perspective, the high fee you might pay an inappropriate consultant without any tangible benefit could doom your test operation.

Given a definition of the problem you need to solve, you can assess the kind of expertise you require. For example, if it's an implementation problem, be sure to define it that way. I once hired a consultant to work on an MTBF demonstration plan without taking this important step. He didn't expect that he would actually have to write the plan, which was exactly what I needed him to do. It was an engagement that "just didn't work out," and I had to replace him. A knowledge-transfer problem, such as training your team to use a new test tool, requires a person who not only is skilled in the use of the tool but also is an effective communicator of ideas. In contrast, an implementation problem such as building an automated test suite using a new test tool requires the same skill with the tool but less expertise in communicating.

Once the problem is clearly defined, you must extensively interview any prospective experts before signing a contract. Face-to-face interviews allow you to assess relatively intangible qualities such as teaching ability and the consultant's fit with your company's culture in addition to his or her proficiency with the relevant tools and technology. If you don't know enough about the topic at hand, you'll need to complement your interview by talking to references. If consultants provide the name and telephone number of a past client for whom they solved a similar problem, you can contact this client to satisfy yourself that the consultants can solve your problem.

Interviewing an expert may be a very different experience than interviewing a contractor or a permanent employee. Prospective consultants might want to put on a presentation, have you visit their site, or meet with some of their associates. All these are good ideas, but it's important that you stay focused on the problem, as you've defined it, and how the consultants can help.

When interviewing consultants for implementation engagements, you should also be on guard against bait-and-switch tactics. Ask the person doing the pitch, "Are you the consultant who will actually do the work?" It might not be a problem to bring someone else in, but you should reserve the right to talk directly to that person. Don't allow a situation in which the consulting business can put anyone who needs a few billable hours on your job. This might be just another project to the consulting company, but it's your livelihood.

Another danger is the overpaid neophyte. You might have seen the advertisements by a Big Six consulting firm that compare their competitors' staff to elementary school children in terms of their innocence and lack of experience. This is humorous in the abstract, but you won't find it funny if you discover one day that you are paying $200 an hour for the "expertise and experience" of someone who just graduated from college. Insist that the consultants on your project have a proven record of accomplishment in solving the kinds of problems you're facing. Again, reserve the right to interview every consultant who will work on your project.

After all, whether your staff is composed of temporary or permanent employees, technicians or senior engineers, they are part of your test team. Far from being interchangeable bit players, each of them, and all of them together, hold the success of your test organization in their hands as much as you do. While effective management cannot be discounted, neither can the importance of any participant in a team effort. Leadership is the art of getting work done through others.

9

The Triumph of Politics: Organizational Challenges for Test Managers

O ffice politics. We all use the phrase, usually to connote something negative about a co-worker, department, or company. At one time or another, you've undoubtedly made a comment such as this: "Oh, you know Jim—he's so *political*."

To some extent, I hesitate to use the term "politics"—the euphemism "management considerations" seems less negative—but the word is apt for three reasons. First, as a manager, you must be sensitive to political realities, some of which are unique to test management. Second, politics in the electoral sense is described as "the art of compromise," and that is certainly an art you must master in a typical hardware or software development organization. Finally, politics is also the art of managing relationships that involve power, authority, and responsibility.

DON QUIXOTE, CHAMPION OF QUALITY: WHAT'S YOUR JOB, ANYHOW?

Don Quixote, the immortal character created by Miguel Cervantes, is a minor Spanish nobleman who decides that he is by birth a knight-errant. Venturing forth on a quest with his "squire," Sancho Panza, he stumbles into a series of misadventures, jousting with a "giant" who is actually a windmill and defending the honor of a "maiden" named Dulcinea who turns out to be a prostitute.

I admit that I've held some quixotic positions in my career. The most notable came with the title Quality Assurance Manager. I considered myself the test manager, while everyone else drew their own conclusions about what I was to do. With the budget I had, I was lucky to do a passable job of testing. One of my development manager peers suggested that I should focus on working with the programmers to build a higher level of quality in the product, but I wasn't appropriately staffed for that role. What my managers wanted me to do, specifically, and how I would know that I was succeeding—in other words, the scope of my job—remained undefined. Not remedying this situation was a political error on my part.

I have drawn my own boundaries too widely once or twice as well. It's tempting to decide that you, the test manager, are the lone defender of product integrity. From the point at which you make this decision, it's but a short ride to the windmill and Dulcinea. Looking back on these events, I feel vaguely embarrassed that I took myself so seriously while playing Don Quixote. Again, my error was political, in that I didn't clarify with my management what purpose I and my organization were intended to serve.

The role and responsibilities of a test manager must be unambiguous. I have had the most success when I defined my role clearly and specifically with my managers and then communicated those boundaries to my peers and to my team. Whenever an issue arose that started to blur the boundaries, I reconfirmed my understanding.

The title you hold is important to drawing these boundaries. If your title is Test Manager or some variant of that designation, the boundaries are partially drawn right away. In such a situation, once you ensure clear ownership of the various phases of testing—unit, component, integration, and system, for example—you should know exactly what tasks you own. By reinforcing these perimeters in your test plans, with the use of "Is/Is Not" tables and entry, stopping, and exit criteria (as discussed in Chapter 2), you clarify what the test team will do. And, just as important, you clarify what your team will *not* do.

Be aware, though, that people sometimes use the word "test" to reach beyond the typical scope of writing and evaluating test cases against live, executable systems, hardware or software. One test authority, Bill Hetzel, defines requirements reviews, design reviews, and code reviews as tests.[1] It makes sense to investigate expectations in this regard. If your managers and peers think along the lines of Hetzel's definition, this expanded scope will have significant implications for the minimum skill set your test engineers must possess. Few test engineers, even the best ones, have expertise in business analysis. Many have the ability to lead code reviews, but they would need proficiency in the appropriate programming languages.

If your title contains the word "Quality," be careful. The title Quality Control Manager is safe, because most people understand quality control to mean testing to find defects. But the title Quality Assurance Manager leaves many questions open, as I discovered. Quality assurance (QA) is not only the location of bugs through testing—it also involves the prevention of bugs. Some might say that in addition it includes actively ensuring the continual improvement of product quality. In the strictest sense, quality control is concerned with product, quality assurance with process.

IEEE standard 610.12-1990 points out this difference. Quality assurance is defined as follows: "(1) A planned and systematic pattern of all actions necessary to provide adequate confidence that an item or product conforms to established technical requirements. (2) A set of activities designed to evaluate the process by which products are developed or manufactured" (p. 60). The first definition includes not only testing but also other activities, such as code reviews or inspections, that contribute to and measure product quality. The second definition is entirely procedural, emphasizing processes that enable quality. This definition implies that a quality assurance group has a role in ensuring conformance to best software or hardware development practices throughout an organization, often well beyond the development team itself. Conversely, quality control is defined as "a set of activities designed to evaluate the quality of developed or manufactured products," and the standard presents quality control and quality assurance

---

1. In Bill Hetzel's *The Complete Guide to Software Testing*, Chapters 4, 5, and 6 specifically discuss reviews, requirements, and designs.

as contrasting concepts. (One caveat, however: IEEE's definition of quality control includes a note stating that "this term has no standardized meaning in software engineering at this time.")

I won't make a blanket statement warning you never to take a job as a QA manager. If you accept such a job, however, be sure to work carefully with your managers and peers up front in an effort to understand and guide their expectations. In the beginning, you will probably find that their expectations are not congruent with each other's or with yours. And if you are the first QA manager the company has ever had, management's expectations of your ability to affect product quality will be inconsistent with its forecast of your budgetary needs.

Suppose that you are offered a job with the title Director of Quality or Chief Quality Officer. However you slice it, such a job entails corporation-wide management of product and service quality. To succeed, you'll require sufficient authority to dictate processes to the entire organization. You will also need sufficient staff and other resources to do a thorough, professional job of testing as well as the not insignificant amount of quality management work.[2] Don't plan on shoehorning the quality roles into the workload of your existing test engineers and technicians. Besides not having time for such tasks, they might not be qualified, either.

If you hold a title containing the word "Quality" but believe that your authority and resources support only test activities, I recommend that you try to change your title. You might need to research what a true quality management role entails, which should provide some ammunition to convince your manager that your role doesn't match this description. If your managers insist that you keep the title but don't give you the requisite authority and resources, I recommend that you consider resigning. There's rarely any point to holding a position in which you are bound to fail.

Finally, an aside on ethical implications. If you do accept a role that has wide-ranging responsibilities for quality assurance, be sure that you know enough about formal quality management. For example, I spent time in the

---

2. Occasionally you might hear it suggested that if you do a good enough job of quality assurance, you can totally eliminate independent quality control. I consider such theories dangerous and misguided in the software and hardware development worlds. Testing is a necessary precondition to achieving quality systems, regardless of how rigorous and sophisticated the development methodology is.

early 1990s studying Total Quality Management, and I stay current on the topic just in case. You will need to understand the entire development process and current best practices in your industry. Be aware, however, that a few weeks of training will not qualify you to implement a company-wide quality program. It would be, at the least, unprofessional to promote yourself as competent to perform jobs that you know are beyond your capacity. Indeed, it's a violation of the Association for Computing Machinery's Code of Ethics. This may strike you as trifling, but if your company becomes involved in a lawsuit, wearing a hat that's three sizes too big will at best make you look silly in court.

WHERE YOU FIT:
THE TEST GROUP IN THE ORGANIZATION

With the scope of your job defined, let's place the test group in its organizational context. A number of possible organizational models can apply. Figure 9-1 shows one basic model for a test group, in which the test manager reports to the development manager. In this case, a lead test engineer typically manages the team. (Test groups tend to be small when they service a single development team.) This lead engineer communicates test results directly to the development manager.

This model is a lot more common than it deserves to be. What's wrong with it? First, the notion of an independent test organization giving unbiased information to the project goes out the window when the test manager reports to the development manager. It's too much to expect that managers will pursue an agenda contrary to *their* manager's interests—but this

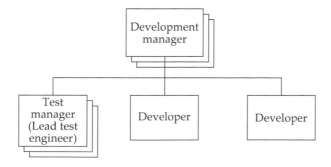

FIGURE 9-1   *The test organization as part of development.*

model requires that test managers do just that if they are to be independent in any sense. Second, testing does not receive access to the resources it needs. The development manager is often forced to choose between purchasing tools for development or for testing, between hiring developers or testers. Third, testing might not even be able to keep the resources it has. In crunch mode, testers will be pulled into debugging activities, tool creation, and even coding. Finally, the test team's clout is at an absolute minimum. Developers are often free to treat testers' bug reports as suggestions, and most testers aspire to become developers. As a practical matter, the test organization will probably disappear over time.

Nevertheless, this model makes sense in some situations. If you are working in a small startup with, say, a dozen or so engineers, other organizational models can put too many layers in place. You don't want to negate the advantages of a small organization, such as shared vision and low communication overhead, by imposing unnecessary layers of management. If your company uses the approach illustrated in Figure 9-1, just keep in mind that it will require special care to preserve a separate test team.

Figure 9-2 shows another common model, in which the test manager and the development manager both report to the project manager. This is not a perfect solution, but it is an improvement over the previous model. The test group is still not independent in a real sense, because the test manager answers to the project manager. A project manager's agenda and interests more closely resemble those of a development manager than those of a test manager. But a project manager, being less involved in the creation of the system under test, can usually bring a more dispassionate outlook to the discussion of problems than a development manager can.

Under the arrangement shown in Figure 9-2, the development and test organizations usually have separate headcounts and budgets, which reduces the resource contention encountered in the first model. You must still compete for the same pool of money, but now the development manager is a peer, not your superior. Likewise, test's "cookie jar" can't be raided without at least the project manager's blessing, thus minimizing situations in which you lose resources yet are expected to meet the original schedules. Also, the test organization has more stature, as bug reports and other test status reports go directly to project management.

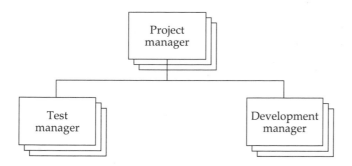

FIGURE 9-2   *The test organization as a development project resource.*

Despite these advantages, you should count on being considered a project resource and expect to participate in all the panics and crunches, even if test's involvement does not add value. For example, if the implementation falls behind schedule, your team will probably be required to commiserate with the tardy developers by suffering through the same six-day weeks, long hours, abrupt changes of priority, and all the rest. This is especially the case if your company practices the "kiddie soccer" approach to project management.[3]

Figure 9-3 shows the best model. Here the test team is truly independent. Executive management's agendas and interests promote the good of the company. (If they don't, you have bigger problems.) Therefore, management will listen to test status reports with a completely open mind. You might burst management's bubble in terms of the quality of the product, but that is the project manager's problem, not yours. Clout, budget, and staffing problems are minimized, for the most part. You have a budget based on how many projects you will be asked to support—and if your project load increases, you will be able to obtain more resources.

---

3. In real soccer, everyone plays a specific position, and the whole team plays with grace, cohesion, and a sense of trust that each player knows his or her part. When young children first play soccer, though, the whole complement of players on both sides run around in a disoriented mob, chasing the ball around the field. There are no real positions and no sense of direction. Everyone is excited and much energy is expended, but little is accomplished.

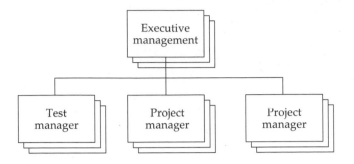

FIGURE 9-3 *The truly independent test organization.*

Of course, there is no paradise on earth. Companies make money by selling products, not by building them. Ship dates are more closely related to marketing windows than to assessments of quality, independent or not. You will be subject to project pressures, sometimes very strong ones. This third model, however, unlike the others, is at least structured in a way that does not actively undermine you.

WHAT ELSE FITS?
ADDING OTHER FUNCTIONS TO TEST

In part because testing is often a misunderstood function, you might be invited to take charge of all sorts of additional duties that are more or less peripheral to testing. Test managers, in their copious free time, sometimes discharge other duties such as these:

- Configuration management and release management

- Customer support

- Operations such as system administration and disaster recovery

- Quality management—for example, code reviews, inspections, and process

- Management of the development lab

- Creation of training data and procedures for operations staff

The list of duties that might be attached to the test function is probably endless. But does placing these functions in the test organization make sense?

In my opinion, the answer is usually—but not always—no.[4] Some of the specific situations in which I recommend against such arrangements include the following:

◆ *The test team shares some responsibility for product development or is completely integrated into the development team.* There are well-documented reasons why developers can't test their own code; in addition, they don't have the test expertise to test other developers' code at a system level. It is also true that many developers tend to dislike testing and give it short shrift when forced to do much of it.

◆ *Management assigns additional duties to the test team because the group is perceived to have the bandwidth.* This perception is nearly always wrong: I have never managed, seen, or heard of an over-staffed test group. The extra duties will assuredly weaken the team's ability to focus on testing.

◆ *Specific tasks are assigned to a member of the test team who possesses a relevant skill set.* Such assignments might make sense as temporary duties, but if the role is ongoing, your test team has been effectively downsized.

◆ *A member of the test team wants to take on additional responsibility as part of individual career growth.* This might make sense for the individual, but does it make sense for your test team? This person probably belongs in another group; perhaps now is a good time for the transition?

Even in the best-case scenario, assigning additional roles and responsibilities to the test team distracts everyone from the main mission: finding bugs. In the worst-case scenario, you might find yourself unable to fulfill test responsibilities competently, although you are still being held accountable

---

4. A specific case that seems to make sense is having a senior test engineer or the test manager serve as the project's "risk officer." Steve McConnell makes this suggestion in Chapter 7 of his *Software Project Survival Guide.*

both for testing and for the new duties. To avoid such a situation, be sure to draw your test group's organizational boundaries—your team's "Is/Is Not" table—as a first step in your tenure as test manager. If you are asked to take on additional responsibilities, be sure to clarify whether these duties are permanent or temporary and to explain their impact on your ability to test.

All that said, you may have to accept certain expansions of your test group's role in order to help the company succeed. On a purely Machiavellian basis, the last thing you want is to be branded "not a team player" or "inflexible"—unless you truly don't care about advancement or permanent tenure within the company. And it's certainly true that an arrangement in which the test team works with other teams, all under the same manager, needn't be a disaster. Such an arrangement can work well when the teams are grouped together because of synergy in the kinds of tasks they perform and the kinds of expertise each group needs, as opposed to a desire to get something for nothing or to throw undesirable duties over the wall into the test ghetto. If you are faced with the suggestion that the test team take on other responsibilities, you might consider proposing an approach like the one shown in Figure 9-4. This model illustrates the structure of a development services group in which I once worked, an organization that performed very well.

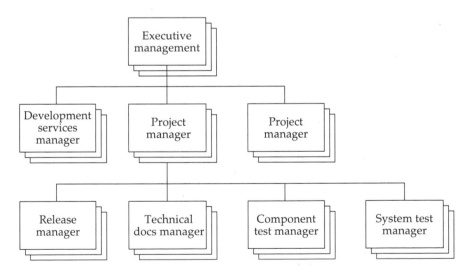

FIGURE 9-4   *A development services group.*

WORKING WITH OTHER MANAGERS: TWO MORE ASPECTS OF TEST MANAGEMENT

Test projects must be managed in three directions:

- *Inward.* Managing inward means defining your test team, hiring its members, organizing the team's structure, and supervising and motivating your employees.

- *Upward.* Managing upward means summarizing the status of the test process and escalating urgent problems to the attention of the project management team, setting expectations, responding quickly but prudently to changes in direction, participating in management meetings, and "selling" your test effort.

- *Outward.* Managing outward means communicating test results, clarifying problem reports, and discussing test needs and services with your management peers.

These three directions are represented in Figure 9-5. Chapter 8 focused on managing inward; here we'll look at the other two directions.

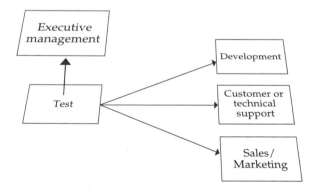

FIGURE 9-5   *The three directions of test management.*

MANAGING UPWARD

Managing upward is often a difficult challenge, especially when you are communicating to people who have only a dim understanding of what testing is all about. Managing upward requires that you spend a significant amount of time preparing reports, focusing on process, and devising an effective set of test indicators or metrics—a sort of test dashboard—that your management can use to understand test status.[5]

As part of this effort, it is critical that you learn to "manage your managers" effectively. Perhaps this concept seems strange. But it doesn't imply that you will tell your bosses what to do; rather, it means that your effectiveness in supervising your team's interactions with your superiors will determine your success as a manager in many ways. If you think about it, your ability to handle such interactions probably had a lot to do with why you became a manager in the first place.

Poor upward management leads to a perception among the upper echelons of the company that your team has "failed." As much as the paperwork and status reporting can seem tedious and disconnected from critical tasks, remember that your managers are, in a real sense, your most important customers. From your immediate supervisor on up to the corporate vice president, these are the people who must provide the funds you need to carry out testing. The better they understand what you're doing, and the more clearly you can explain the benefits, the more success you'll have in obtaining critical resources and political support.

Communicating Clearly:
Bringing Your Reality to Upper Management

One of the most important demands of your job is that you communicate with upper management clearly and effectively. Every one of your managers has an individual management style, and this style should determine exactly how you approach the task of managing upward. In general, however, it's useful to keep the following considerations in mind:

◆ Ensure that your managers do not hold you personally responsible for product quality. It should be obvious that the test organization doesn't write the code or build motherboards. But it is hardly uncommon for unenlightened senior managers and executives to blame test managers when low-quality systems under test don't complete test phases on time. Likewise, managers of customer support or sales and marketing too frequently consider every field-reported bug a test escape.

---

5. For another, similar perspective on managing upward (and outward), see Chapter 6 of Bill Perry and Randall Rice's *Surviving the Top Ten Challenges of Software Testing,* which focuses on the need to sell management on what test can contribute and to establish clear communication and reporting.

◆ Help your managers understand testing. If they lack a testing background, they might not grasp the reasons why you do (and don't do) certain things. Avoid focusing on minutiae such as boundary conditions, state machines, and load generators, which are simply a means to an end. Instead, talk about risk management and about the impact of serious test escapes on the reputation and revenues of the company.

◆ Think ROI—return on investment. Your managers will regularly go to bat for your budget with other managers (their bosses). If you can't explain to your superiors the business benefits gained by spending tens of thousands of dollars for GUI test automation tools or a thermal chamber, how will they explain the payoff to their managers?

◆ Be ready to measure your results. The charts and reports introduced in Chapters 3, 4, and 5 provide the tools you need to summarize test coverage, the status of testing, and the quality of the system under test. Being crisp and quantitative will help your managers understand and support what you're doing.

◆ Keep test data accurate and timely. Inaccurate data can damage your team's credibility, making your managers' lives—as well as your own life—more difficult.

◆ Communicate in terms of moving the project forward. Most project managers aren't interested in test theory or testing as an abstract idea; rather, they are concerned with the ways testing can advance the project. If you try to understand what your managers need to accomplish and then attempt to connect test's contributions to those goals, you can keep your communications with them relevant and on target. (A colleague once described our mutual manager as the kind of guy who, "if you told him you had a flat tire, would offer to help change your shoe." Taking actions that do nothing to promote the success of the project—or that might even actively impede it—and focusing on solving problems that are extraneous to the ones that urgently need solving will not endear you to other participants.)

◆ Be ready to participate in the dog and pony shows. I have spent many an hour putting together snazzy presentations for management meetings or searching through various CD-ROMs for a graphic to enliven a slide—even though my spiel was sometimes cancelled at the last minute. These activities are part of your managerial "selling" role, so learn to enjoy them and do them well.

◆ Address both the urgent and the important. Urgent matters require immediate action to prevent a major crisis or even the total failure of the project—for example, you are unable to install the system under test in the lab. Important matters need focused, deliberate attention. Addressing important matters usually leads to improvements in process efficiency, quality of product, clarity of communication, and order in the workplace. Often the two kinds of issues are related. On one project, we continually received builds of abysmally poor quality. We could usually install them, but they had major regressions from previous functionality. The urgent matter, repeatedly, was to get a new build to the test lab so that we could proceed with testing. The important matter, often lost in the accompanying fire drill, was that development needed to run a short regression or smoke test before delivering the product to the test group.

◆ Don't let bad news wait. If there's anything a manager dreads more than bad news, it's bad news that's two days old. The business impact of a problem almost always grows more severe as the problem festers. Nevertheless, do take the time to make sure you've gotten your story straight; reacting and managing are different behaviors.

◆ Remember that you are the interface between the test group and the project. For a tester, success means finding bugs, the worse the better. You want your team members to be diligent about finding problems and to feel a sense of accomplishment when they do. For everyone else on the project, however, news of a nasty bug is nothing to smile about. As the test manager, you must be able to play something of a dual role, displaying positive encouragement and near-celebration of bugs inside your team while understanding the negative effect bugs have outside your team. One talented test manager, Reynolds MacNary, uses the phrase "optimistic on the outside, pessimistic on the inside" to capture this dichotomy.

◆ Escalate deliberately. Before you bring a problem to your managers' attention with a request for help, ask yourself whether they can and will make the situation better, not worse. I had a client who, when informed of a problem, would immediately begin making irate phone calls to anyone he saw as responsible or culpable. Occasionally this solved the problem, but often it merely enraged those who were the targets of the phone calls. In another situation, a colleague referred to the escalation process by snorting that "escalation is just another way of saying, 'Get information to Joe [name changed to protect the guilty] so he can micromanage you.'" If you work for such managers, use caution.

Admittedly, managing upward can involve tedious activities, especially when it feels like you're trying to communicate with people who speak another language. How many presentations can you put together on the same topic, especially while your team is doing real work? Wouldn't you rather spend time managing your test engineers, who understand what you're talking about and admire your advanced knowledge and skills, instead of working with a bunch of managers who just don't get it? When you get caught up in one of these "leave me alone and let me work" funks, remember that upper management must either buy the end product—if it's in-house—or sell it to customers and clients. And these managers are the people who make what you and your team do possible. Although their different perspectives make communication challenging, they are paying for your test operation.

Like Getting Blood from a Stone:
Management's Aversion to Funding Test Groups

One important topic about which you will communicate extensively with your managers is funding. To do a decent job of testing, you must receive sufficient money, hiring requisitions, and lab equipment. But the figure you consider adequate and the figure your managers will accept seldom coincide. In a typical situation, you will have to put together an organization that is both lean and effective.

From a management perspective, even test professionals must acknowledge that testing is, to paraphrase Winston Churchill's comment about democracy, the worst possible form of ensuring quality in computer products, except for all the others. Ideally, business analysts, marketing managers, software designers, engineers, and developers could, by applying preventive techniques, produce perfect systems that would require no testing. Because this ideal is so obvious, even seasoned high-tech managers occasionally fall into the rut of complacently thinking, "Oh, what could possibly go wrong?"

Some managers never get out of this rut. When you hear of an organization in which developers do all the testing, small test groups are assigned unachievable test loads and held responsible for quality, or management doesn't read bug reports, you know that it is run by a team of senior managers who truly fail to understand the complexity of software and hardware development. Frankly, there are many lousy products on the market today, and not understanding either the need for an independent test organization or how it should function has plenty to do with that.

Even if you are fortunate enough to work in an organization whose executive managers understand the necessity of testing, don't expect them to be thrilled about paying for it. Testing is expensive. If the ratio of testers to developers is 1:3, somewhere between 15 and 35 percent of the development organization's human resources budget is going to people who, from the senior managers' bottom-line perspective, do nothing but find problems created by the people who receive the other 65 to 85 percent of the paycheck budget. In terms of resources such as hardware and software, the situation is even worse. Developers can usually work on a subset or scaled-down version of the operating environment, but to be truly effective, testing must replicate end user settings as much as possible. It's not unheard of for test labs to require resources valued at ten times those needed by the development team.

Even when senior managers understand the need for testing, they may not realize why it costs so much. It's not always simple to explain. Because I've been testing for many years, it has become paradigmatic to me that tests must run on the most "user-like" hardware configurations possible, but that principle is seldom obvious to my managers. Senior managers who understand and value the need for independent testing will give you an opportunity to justify each line item in your budget, but you will not be excused from that exercise.

Testing is about risk management, and you must explain the risks as part of selling management on your budget. Because a risk is the possibility of a bad outcome, your pitch for each budget item might sound something like this: "If you don't test A, you might have failures X, Y, and Z in the field; and I can't test A without buying C." Some salespeople refer to this technique as the creation of "fear, uncertainty, and doubt," which makes it sound pretty low. But it serves the greater good of shipping a better product, and, frankly, some managers just won't listen to you unless you use this technique to get their attention. Don't be an alarmist, though. Describe some realistic scenarios of bugs that could cost the company a ton of money but that could be caught by testing. The time you've spent understanding the important risks, using the techniques discussed in Chapter 1, should pay off here. Express those risks in terms of possible user experiences: "unable to complete a sale," "prevented from printing the file," "taking 10 seconds to respond to a keystroke." Avoid those dry and slightly mystical technical phrases like "core dump," "blue screen of death," "surface over-temp condition," and other jargon.

If you consider it crass to raise alarms, at least understand that it is not dishonest. Testing can add value only when it helps the company mitigate risk. You are tying one hand behind your back if you decide to "take the high road"—whatever that might mean in this context—and eschew discussions of what could go wrong. If at some later point you end up with so many people on your staff that everyone is playing video games half the time, then perhaps you should feel guilty.

"How About a Third Shift, and Weekends, And...": The Effects of Lateness on Test

In the high-tech world, schedule delays are a way of life. Some argue that these delays result from the incredible pace at which technology evolves and from the fact that anything new is, by nature, somewhat unknown and unknowable. Some technical staff and development managers say that delays are simply the effects of reality biting down hard on unrealistic schedules imposed by ignorant or overly aggressive managers, salespeople, and marketers, who correspondingly often blame lazy and disorganized developers and technical people. Others occupy a middle ground, holding poor planning and estimation techniques responsible. Who's right? Who cares! Although discussing culpability makes for a nice venting exercise over drinks after a long day of trying to catch up on a schedule everyone but senior management admits is unachievable, it doesn't accomplish much.

High-tech projects are almost universally late vis-à-vis the official schedule. As the test manager, your moment in the spotlight comes during test execution, at the end of the project—which means that, much of the time, you will be running tests just as the schedule's disconnection from reality becomes painfully obvious to all involved. Unfortunately, you are likely to suffer the consequences of management's rude awakening well out of proportion to the degree to which your team contributed to the delay.

As a schedule begins to slip, managers often impose a crunch mode regimen, in an attempt to make up time through sheer effort: this thinking assumes that if the schedule is off by 20 percent, making everyone work 50

What Does Testing Really Cost?

Nothing. Zilch. Nada. Zero. Quality is free—at least that's what Phillip Crosby said in his 1979 book of that name. About a decade later, J. M. Juran and F. Gryna's *Quality Control Handbook* agreed. Now, two decades after Crosby's proclamation, Sandra Slaughter, David Harter, and Mayuram Krishnan have made a similar claim for software quality in an article published in the *Communications of the ACM*.

Creative accounting strikes again, you say? Not really. To reach this rather startling conclusion, consider the costs of quality, which can be divided into two categories: the *costs of conformance* and the *costs of nonconformance*. The costs of conformance include any expenditure taken to ensure quality, which, in the test world, is the total expense associated with developing and running each test (the first time). These test expenses are called *appraisal costs*. When you must repeat a test to verify and isolate a bug, confirm a fix, or check for regression, the time and money expended represent test's costs of nonconformance arising from *internal failures*.

Costs of nonconformance also include *external failures* (what happens when a bug affects a customer). These costs include most of customer support's budget; the expenses associated with creating, testing, and deploying field fixes; product recalls and refunds; liability costs; and lost sales. Crosby, Juran, Slaughter, Harter, and Krishnan all demonstrate that, if you spend quality assurance money wisely, the costs of conformance plus the costs of nonconformance related to internal failures will be less than the costs of nonconformance related to external failures.

hours a week instead of 40 will allow them to catch up. This sounds reasonable, but I have never seen it work. In addition, test might well be chugging along just fine on a 40-hour-per-week schedule; it's often the case that only 40 hours or so of work can be done on a given deliverable, especially when quality is poor. Trying to impose extra hours on your team could actually have a negative effect in the long run, by draining energy that will be needed later.

Nevertheless, failing to participate in these exercises, or arguing openly against them, displays disloyalty to your managers and can destroy your advancement opportunities at the company. If you truly can't contribute anything by working hard, and want to conserve the test team's strength, have its weaker players put in the extra hours during the "show trial" periods of the crisis, and then bring the stronger players into the overtime mix as soon as they can be productive. If you feel absolutely compelled to dispute the intelligence of the crisis mentality, do so one-on-one with your managers; a general e-mail or a public comment that rails against management is, politically, a suicidal maneuver.

Schedule delays tend to result in scope shrink and sometimes even in product redesign. If you begin to see significant, perhaps ill-advised changes being made to the product in an attempt to meet the schedule, it is critical that you communicate the effect of these changes to your managers. Again, though, diplomacy is important. Greeting news of an alteration by telling everyone who will listen, "That's the stupidest idea yet for rescuing this hare-brained schedule," won't win you friends in high places if the change was proposed by executive management.

If the schedule slips so far that no one—not even project management—is able to pretend that it can ever be rescued, replanning often begins. This is the rational choice, but it is not painless. You'll have to participate in planning exercises all over again, which can seriously distract your attention from managing your team.

Sometimes management takes out its frustrations on the people involved. Employees can be fired, especially those perceived as malcontents or flagrant contributors to the project delay. Since testing is usually just beginning, you and your team are not likely to be pegged as responsible for the delay, but if you've spent a lot of time maligning the schedule or the management in the hallways, you are a prime candidate for malcontent status.

Along with firings, you could face a mass reorganization. A client of mine once proposed, in all seriousness, that breaking up the independent test group and having each lead test engineer report directly to the respective subsystem development manager would get us back on schedule. I had to muster a significant effort to defuse this initiative, and even then I lost about a quarter of my team to development managers who claimed to need help with the unit, component, and string testing for which they were responsible. Weird ideas become the theme as the consequences of missed schedules start to sink in.

Of course, scapegoat firings and reorganizations do not address the underlying causes of delays. Indeed, they create dysfunctional dynamics, such as fear, defensiveness, confusion, and miscommunication, that actually exacerbate the fundamental problems and produce further delays. You will gain nothing by pointing this out publicly, however. If these kinds of actions are proposed or implemented, work behind the scenes to mitigate the damage to your team.

Even more frustration can accompany a slipping schedule if senior management succumbs to the siren song of ad hoc testing. This can happen

---

Do Computer Users Need a Bill of Rights?

Perhaps you have had the all too common experience of hearing high standards of quality trumpeted at the beginning of a project, only to find that commitment is lacking when money and ship dates are at risk. This behavior highlights the fact that quality, unlike budget and schedule, is seen as both hard to quantify and of dubious business necessity.

But what if users were entitled to quality? In a 1998 article, Dr. Clare-Marie Karat, a social psychologist and user interface designer at IBM's T. J. Watson Research Center, suggested the following computer user's bill of rights (reprinted with Dr. Karat's permission):

1. *The user is always right. If there is a problem with the use of the system, the system is the problem, not the user.*

2. *The user has the right to easily install and uninstall software and hardware systems without negative consequences.*

3. *The user has the right to a system that performs exactly as promised.*

4. *The user has the right to easy-to-use instructions (user guides, online or contextual help, error messages) for understanding and utilizing a system to achieve desired goals and recover efficiently and gracefully from problem situations.*

---

5. *The user has the right to be in control of the system and to be able to get the system to respond to a request for attention.*

6. *The user has the right to a system that provides clear, understandable, and accurate information regarding the task it is performing and the progress toward completion.*

7. *The user has the right to be clearly informed about all system requirements for successfully using software or hardware.*

8. *The user has the right to know the limits of the system's capabilities.*

9. *The user has the right to communicate with the technology provider and receive a thoughtful and helpful response when raising concerns.*

10. *The user should be the master of software and hardware technology, not vice versa. Products should be natural and intuitive to use.*

When thinking like Dr. Karat's becomes the common coin of software and hardware development, those of us who make a living testing new computer products will find ourselves living in a different world, both technically and politically.

---

when managers see all forms of testing as equivalent in terms of effectiveness and value. From this mistaken context, ad hoc testing looks like a bargain: no test development is needed—just hurl a bunch of warm bodies at the product, let them bang away like monkeys, and soon enough you'll find all the bugs. In such a case, you must convince your managers that although ad hoc testing might do a decent job of finding bugs on a single release, it cannot improve product quality in the long term.

It's annoying when managers scrap "best practices" the moment schedules slip. Don't take it personally, however, and don't see it as a mark of irredeemable failure on the part of your managers. Remember that the end goal is to sell a product—that's how we all get paid—and that management may deem it necessary to cut some corners to accomplish that goal. It's unfortunate that the corners being cut are yours in this instance, but you might still be able to make a difference at your company, so don't overreact to the crisis.

"But We're Different...":
The Commonality of Solutions

In *Anna Karenina*, Leo Tolstoy observed that "all happy families are alike, but each unhappy family is unhappy in its own way." In commenting on this passage, the historian Paul Johnson disputes Tolstoy by claiming that, in reality, the sources of unhappiness in families—alcoholism, infidelity, violence, poverty—are tiresome and common and lead to tiresome, common, and sad results.[6] This may be a blessing in disguise, however, because the commonality of the afflictions allows common approaches to alleviating dysfunction, such as the twelve-step programs developed for alcoholics.

The same is true of software and hardware development companies, development projects, and test organizations. When you talk about test concepts that might help to get your organization under control, management may respond, "Oh, but we're different. That will never work here." Balderdash! In fact, many corporate dynamics are common not only among companies in similar sectors but even among organizations whose only similarities are that they are groups of people working together. As Peter Drucker writes, "The differences between managing a chain of retail stores and managing a Roman Catholic diocese are amazingly fewer than either retail executives or bishops realize...whether you are managing a software company, a hospital, a bank or a Boy Scout organization, the differences apply to only about 10% of your work. This 10% is determined by the organization's specific mission, its specific culture, its specific history and its specific vocabulary. The rest is pretty much interchangeable."[7]

I have worked with companies and clients in various areas of the computer business, from big hardware companies and small integrators to shrink-wrap software houses and custom programming shops working for huge clients. Although the level of maturity of the development process and the skill levels of the staff influenced the kinds of problems I saw, the company's particular product or service mattered not a whit. There's nothing unique about your predicaments. You are not alone, and you can apply solutions such as those you find in this book to solve your problems. Anyone who says, "Oh, but we're different..." is either uninformed or resisting change.

---

6. Paul Johnson, *Intellectuals*, pp. 121, 122.

7. Peter Drucker, "Management's New Paradigms," p. 156.

Nevertheless, you can't rush the process of change. The idealized test project models presented in this book represent organizations operating at a significant level of management maturity. The term "maturity" in this context doesn't mean that a company's senior managers are of a particular age; rather, it refers to managers who have adapted the best—or at least the better—practices of software and hardware development professionals. In other words, they have learned from the cumulative mistakes of past software and hardware organization managers.

The Software Engineering Institute's Capability Maturity Model (CMM) measures five levels of process maturity. Level 1 is characterized by an approach that is completely ad hoc, devoid of any real processes whatsoever. People work and live according to management's whim of the moment. At the first sign of a crisis, managers drop any pretense of process and simply make up something on the fly. According to the Software Engineering Institute, "in an immature organization, there is no objective basis for judging product quality or for solving product or process problems. There is little understanding of how the steps of the software process affect quality, and product quality is difficult to predict. Moreover, activities intended to enhance quality, such as reviews and testing, are often curtailed or eliminated when projects fall behind schedule."[8] Sound like any place you know?

The really pernicious aspect of a level 1 organization is that many managers who operate at that level have made a conscious choice to do so. They tend to react viscerally to suggestions that adopting a set of processes, rather than relying on intrepid improvisation, might make life better. If you work in a level 1 organization, you need first to recognize it and then to understand whether the situation results from ignorance or obstinacy.

The hypothetical examples in this book assume an organization operating at CMM level 2 or higher. To apply the approaches described here, you must be able to control the deployment of resources and the methods of work in your test group. If your organization operates at level 1, proclaiming individual heroics the only way, and managers—both those above you and your peers—insist on micromanaging your resources, it will be very

---

8. See Mark C. Paulk, Charles V. Weber, Bill Curtis, and Mary Beth Chrissis, *The Capability Maturity Model: Guidelines for Improving the Software Process*, p. 7. If you are lucky enough to work in an organization that is committed—at the highest levels—to learning better ways to make higher-quality products, you should read this book and keep it in your office as a ready reference.

difficult to improve your situation. A test manager is seldom well-positioned to be an agent of significant change to a company's processes. But the survival of the test organization depends on your ability to show tangible benefits from testing—a daunting task without some degree of formal process, both internal to the test group and at test's interfaces with other groups and managers.

Test organizations are very sensitive to abrupt changes in plan. A sudden about-face by management can blow away significant investments of time and money in test suite development, obviously undermining your return on investment. The change management database introduced in Chapter 6 can help you track the impact of such changes, but you may find that no one wants to hear explanations (a typical situation in level 1 organizations). If, after giving it the old college try, you decide that the organization will not change, and you feel as if test is treated like the poor relation of the company, you should find a job that will give you an opportunity to succeed.

MANAGING OUTWARD

Let's assume that you work in an organization such as those modeled in Figures 9-2 and 9-3 (pages 281 and 282). The development managers, and perhaps the project managers, are your peers, sitting laterally across from you on a standard organizational chart.[9] Additional peers might include the information technologies (IT), management information systems (MIS), operations, or facilities manager; the sales manager; the marketing manager; the customer support (or technical support) manager; the technical documentation manager; and the person responsible for configuration/release management, among others. These are the people who see your test group as a team of professionals who affect their work, as opposed to seeing you simply as colleagues, co-workers, or people who happen to pick up paychecks in the same office.

---

9. In this era of New Age organizational charts that show customers at the center or managers "under" their individual contributors, you might have to tweak your chart a little before the political realities become clear. Don't fall for the hype: the old pyramid organization charts represent the true power relationships.

Your Friendly Adversaries:
Development Peers

The toughest peer relationship to manage well is that between testers and developers—a relationship that is inherently adversarial. The bug reports that testers write are assertions that the system under test is not perfect. Often developers simply accept the assertions and fix the bugs. But it is also possible that they will take umbrage at the tests themselves, considering them "unfair"; that they will claim the bug reports are poorly written or unclear; or that they will consider the bugs in question too trivial to waste precious time on.

Testers and developers must also have fundamentally different outlooks to do their jobs properly. Developers must be optimistic to succeed. Why work long hours, give up weekends, and make other sacrifices to create something if you fear that the only result will be a raft of bugs? Testers, however, must pursue bugs with vigor and enthusiasm. Chapter 8 described testers as professional pessimists, who must think about ways to break the product in order to find these defects.

These differences of professional perspective can descend into rancor if you're not careful. Gloating over bugs, trying to "catch" developers, or making a point of embarrassing development colleagues will poison the well. Even though most developers and development managers do not take every bug report as a personal attack, the situation can devolve into a high degree of polarization.

Despite these potential problems, there is no peer relationship in which it is more important for you to maintain open, collegial communications. Don't forget that the test team and the development team will either succeed together or fail together. A development project is like a boat headed for a port, with the entire team aboard. If the testers waste time taking potshots at the developers, they might succeed in wounding a few, but they will primarily succeed in shooting holes in the boat and sinking it.

Don't draw the definition of "developer" too narrowly, either. Anyone who provides you with products to test is a developer. A technical writer or a release/configuration engineer is also a developer. Testing finds their mistakes, too, and you must handle these relationships with care as well.

All these developers also receive a product from you: your bug reports. Most enlightened developers entertain a well-written, clear, conscientiously researched bug report with professionalism. Like your team, though, they are affected by the quality of the product they receive. A poorly done bug report slows down the debugging process just as an unstable, buggy system under test slows down the test cycle. Unlike your team, however, developers' jobs do not involve helping you improve the quality of your bug reports. As Chapter 4 stresses, you and everyone on the test team must strive to provide high-quality bug reports to your development colleagues.

Be careful to keep your development peers honest about which test tasks they own and which tasks you own. As you begin to build an independent test organization, some development managers and staff tend to disengage from testing, assuming that your group, operating in parallel, is somehow redundant to their efforts. A colleague of mine describes this behavior as development becoming "addicted" to the new test organization, relying on you to perform tasks that in reality are the responsibilities of developers. Once development stops doing its own testing, an unfortunate scenario results in which the presence of the test organization actually worsens product quality because the structural testing at which developers excel—and which complements the behavioral testing performed by most independent test organizations—disappears from the overall test program. A dysfunctional situation, indeed, but it occurs frequently. Proactive discussions with your development management peers can keep such a misfortune from befalling your company.

The Supporting Cast:
Internal Service Providers

Some of your management peers are involved in providing services—usually some sort of logistical or administrative support—to the test organization. If you are tempted to think of these service providers as in some sense lower on the political totem pole than the test group, don't. Because you must depend on these organizations to get, maintain, and use critical resources, managing these peers effectively is essential to your success.

The logistics database introduced in Chapters 6 and 7 can help you work with your management peers who are responsible for computer equipment, networking, and facilities. Don't be the tail trying to wag the dog, however. Before you put together a complete hardware, software, infrastructure, and staffing logistics plan using this database, be sure that the IT or MIS manager will agree to execute it. The plan you devise might conflict with the manager's other priorities, or the staff might not be available to make it happen. I have occasionally found that although I could propose a detailed plan, implementing that plan was not on the MIS manager's "to do" list.

The human resources or staffing manager is another key person among your peer relationships, especially if you are building a new test organization. HR managers sometimes hold outmoded but still too common ideas about testers being low-paid button-pushers rather than skilled professionals. You will need to change this thinking before the HR manager can help you effectively. In addition, as Chapter 8 stressed, you might need the HR manager as an ally to remedy inequities that exist in your company between developers and testers.

Administrative staff and their managers are also invaluable resources. They can help with travel arrangements, procure necessary supplies for your team, and be an extra set of hands for reports, presentations, and the like. And in the more Byzantine sense of the word "politics," don't forget that administrative assistants and secretaries often know all sorts of interesting facts. I'm referring not to gossip but to pertinent questions about staffing assignments, upcoming projects, and meeting agendas.

Customer or Technical Support: Often Overlooked

A good relationship with the customer support (technical support) manager serves both preventive and corrective purposes. Effective, proactive communication with the customer support manager and team during the test design and implementation phases can add a lot of value to your tests. Most customer support managers have been on the receiving end of the fallout from a bad product, shipped way too early, with too many unknown (and even known) bugs. Every one of these field failures can be translated into a useful test case. (To get an idea of how motivated these folks are to help you do a good job in preventing field problems, imagine the churn-and-burn atmosphere of an understaffed support organization dealing with a deluge of angry customers who just spent an hour on hold in addition to suffering some critical system failure.)

The customer support manager also has a nonacademic interest in your test results. Bugs found during testing, if fixed, are bugs not reported in the field. The key phrase, of course, is "if fixed." It's important, therefore, that you work closely with the customer support manager to communicate bugs found and bugs fixed and that you set the manager's expectations properly. If you include customer support in your circulation list for bug reports and metrics, you give the manager an invaluable opportunity to sound off if it seems that the project is on track to lay an egg.

This level of interest is a two-edged sword. If you don't include customer support in discussions of bugs and test coverage, the manager might conclude, especially if significant field problems remain, that the test organization is incompetent. A manager with this opinion who is politically well connected could decide to agitate for the dissolution of the existing test team and its replacement by an organization internal to the customer support group. I have seen such moves succeed, so beware.

Sales and Marketing:
A Vital Ally

Like customer support managers, sales and marketing managers tend to have strong feelings about what you should test and what your results should be. In general, you should manage your relationship with these peers similarly. There are, however, two key differences, the first positive for your test operation, the second negative.

On the plus side, sales and marketing can provide useful support in terms of budgeting and scope. Strategically, if sales and marketing managers agree that high quality is an important brand differentiator in your market niche, and if you can then convince them that thorough testing is essential to achieve this distinction, you will have powerful backing for an effective, wide-ranging test operation, adequately staffed and funded. Tactically, for any particular product, discussing with the sales and marketing people what's in and what's out of the scope of testing (and why) could spark a reconsideration of the project plan that would allow test to have a bigger impact.

Handle these opportunities with care, though. Reciting to the sales manager a tale of woe about the sorry budget you have and the screwed-up product that will be shipped because of poor testing will, at best, come off as whining. Assuming that the sales manager is not your direct superior, it could also come across as backstabbing your boss, with predictable consequences. A diplomatic opening through a telephone call or e-mail—"Hi, I'm the new test manager, and I'd like to get your input on what we should be testing"—is much more positive. Be forthright in telling your own managers that you intend to have such a conversation to get concurrence on test priorities for the project in question. (You don't have to declare your intentions to lobby sales and marketing managers for their strategic support of your test organization, because you're going to be subtle and indirect about that, right?)

On the negative side, some sales and marketing experts, even those with considerable experience in high-tech fields, don't really understand the complexity of testing. They may not understand your bug reports unless you are careful to describe the possible impact on customers in the summary. Even if you are, not all failures lend themselves to concise, straightforward impact assessments, especially sporadic but dangerous ones. It takes a technically sophisticated person to understand why "sometimes" is worse than "always" in such cases. In addition, sales and marketing people don't always understand why testing takes as long as it does. The "how hard can it be?" mentality can easily take root in organizations that are removed from the technical realities.

To a few misguided sales and marketing types, every failure reported from the field is a test escape. No matter how obscure a customer's problem, you and your team of knuckleheads should have found it during testing. I once took considerable heat for a bug that caused a loss of network connection on a computer running Microsoft Windows 95. The failure occurred only in heavily loaded 16-Mbps token ring environments with one particular brand of PC Card adapter connecting to one type of network server. Even when I pointed out that we couldn't very well run stress and capacity tests on every single PC Card network adapter/NOS combination, since these combinations would surely number in the thousands, one salesperson continued to rail against my organization's lousy testing. The bug did cost the company a large sale, but this individual's unreasonable expectations about what it was possible to test were out in the stratosphere.

TESTING IN THE DARK: SHOULD YOU PROCEED WITHOUT DOCUMENTATION?

In order to design, develop, and run tests, you need what's often referred to as an *oracle*, something that tells you what the expected, correct result of a specific test should be. Specifications, requirements, business rules, marketing road maps, and other such documents frequently play this role. But what if you receive no formal information that explains what the system under test should do?

In some organizations with mature development processes, the test department will not proceed without specifications. Because everyone expects to provide a specification to the test team as part of the development process, you are seen as reasonable and within the bounds of the company's culture when you insist on written specs. Trouble arises, however, if you stiffen your neck this way in a company that operates in an ad hoc fashion. Depending on your company's readiness to embrace formal processes (and also on your personal popularity, tenure, and political clout), any one of a spectrum of outcomes could occur:

◆ Your management, recognizing the need to formalize processes, backs you up 100 percent and institutes specifications throughout the organization as part of the planning phase of every new development project. Industry-standard templates for internal product documentation become the norm, and consultants are brought in to train people.

◆ Your management, not knowing quite how to handle this odd demand, assumes that you must know what you're talking about. The dictate goes out to all the organization's groups to support you, but since no one has any training in formal development processes, the effort produces poor-quality documents that don't help. Furthermore, because the effort is (rightly) seen as a waste of time, people are upset with you for bringing it up.

◆ Your management listens to your demand but then explains that the company just isn't ready for such cultural and process shifts. Perhaps things will change after the next few products go out, they speculate, but right now process just isn't on the "to do" list. Besides, this product is really critical to the success of the company and taking big chances on unproven ways of doing things would be too risky. You are told to get back to work.

◆ You are fired.

The moral of this story is that you should carefully consider whether your company is ready for formal processes before you insist on specifications, requirements, and other accoutrements of mature development projects.

If you are willing to compromise, you might consider the following options for testing without specifications:

◆ If you are testing a commercial product, remember that you have the benefit of competitors. Because your customers will expect your product to behave substantially like the products of your competitors, these competitive products are, in a sense, your specs. In compatibility test labs, for example, most projects have a "reference platform"—a competitor's system against which the system under test is being positioned, in the hope of demolishing it in the marketplace.

◆ If your technical colleagues won't tell you what the product should do, perhaps your friends in sales and marketing will. In my experience, sales and marketing people live to create glitzy presentations showing where the product line is going. Although they can be general and imprecise, these documents might tell you which features and capabilities the product should support. If you're testing a product for which questions about supported features are harder to answer than questions regarding correct behavior, these documents might suffice for specs.

◆ Your colleagues in customer support might not have much information about what the product should do, but they probably know what they don't want the product to do. Since your testing stands between them and the hellish scenario outlined in the previous section, they are usually happy to tell you.

◆ Unless the product is truly unique, you can use inductive reasoning to figure out what constitutes reasonable expectations and correct behavior in many cases. The generic categories into which products fit tell you a lot about what the products are supposed to do: a word processor, a Web browser, a PC, a laptop, a server, an operating system. Some esoteric questions may arise, but a core dump, a system crash, a burning CPU, garbage on the screen, an error message in the wrong language, and abysmal performance are indisputably bugs.

◆ If in doubt, you should consider any suspect behavior buggy. Because you don't have a crisp way of determining pass and fail conditions, you will commit errors. Remember that type I errors are much less detrimental to product quality than type II errors, and be sure to file bug reports when questions arise.

Test Is Not an Island: External Effects on Your Productivity

Various organizational behaviors and attributes, which I call "gas pedals" and "brake pedals," can speed up or slow down test progress. In general, all of them exercise incremental influence on your test operation: a single tap on the brake won't bring the test project to a dead stop, just as a jab to the gas won't send the system under test rocketing through the test exit criteria in a single pass. Overall, however, to make testing proceed smoothly, your company needs to press on the gas pedals and lay off the brake pedals. Although each single incident or behavior is incremental, it can be part of a troubling trend.

Your test project can easily suffer the "death of 10,000 cuts" from many little braking events. In a reactive sense, when the project takes a significant hit, you should document it in the change management database introduced in Chapter 6. However, the broader theme of this chapter—the challenge of politics—suggests that you use your relationships and your influence with management and peers to be *proactive*. Try to recognize any trends of inhibitors that develop, in order to prevent or reduce their occurrence in the future. Likewise, you can actively promote behaviors that make your job easier. Help your peers and colleagues understand that following certain courses of action and eschewing others have important effects on your productivity.

Gas Pedals

The following organizational behaviors and attributes tend to accelerate the test process. Encourage these activities and values among your peers, and set a good example in your own work as much as possible.

Testing Throughout the Project. I use the phrase "testing throughout the project" in a three-dimensional sense. The first dimension involves time: in order to be properly prepared, and to help contain bugs as early as possible, the test team must become involved when the project starts, not simply at the end. The second dimension is organizational: the more a company promotes open communication between the test organization and the other teams throughout the company, the better the test group can align its efforts with the company's needs. The third dimension is cultural: in a mature company, testing as an entity, a way of mitigating risk, and a business management philosophy permeates the development projects.

Employing Plenty of Good Technicians. As Chapter 8 explained, you can get qualified test technicians from the computer science and engineering schools of local universities and colleges as well as from technical institutes. Try to use these employees to perform any tasks that do not specifically require a test engineer's level of expertise. Since they are a relatively inexpensive resource, you might be successful in adding two or three such employees to your staff, when management would be inclined to deny you an additional test engineer.

Automation. The more automated the test system, the less time it takes to run the tests. Automation also allows unattended test execution overnight and over weekends, which maximizes utilization of the system under test and other resources, leaving more time for engineers and technicians to analyze and report test failures. You should apply a careful balance, however. Generating a good automated test case can take many more hours than writing a good manual test case. If you don't have the running room to thoroughly develop automated test cases before test execution begins, you should focus on automating a few simple tools that will make manual testing go more quickly.

Good Test System Architecture. Spending time in advance understanding how the test system should work, selecting the right tools, ensuring the compatibility and logical structure of all the components, and designing for subsequent maintainability really pay off once test execution starts. The more elegant the test system, the more easily testers can use it.

A Clearly Defined Test-to-Development Hand-Off Process. Two closely related activities, bug isolation and debugging, occur on opposite sides of the fence between test and development. On the one hand, test managers must ensure that test engineers and technicians thoroughly isolate every bug they find and write up those isolation steps in the bug report. Development managers, on the other hand, must ensure that their staff does not try to involve test engineers and technicians, who have other responsibilities, in debugging activities.

A Clearly Defined Development-to-Test Hand-Off Process. The project team must manage the release of new hardware and software revisions to the test group. As part of this process, the following conditions should be met:

- All software is under revision control.
- All test builds come from revision-controlled code.
- Consistent, clear release naming nomenclatures exist for each major system.
- A regular, planned release schedule exists and is followed.
- A well-understood, correct integration strategy is developed and followed during the test planning stages.

A Clearly Defined System Under Test. If the test team receives clear requirements and specifications while developing tests and clear documentation while running tests, it can perform both tasks more effectively. Being told how the product is expected to behave means that you don't have to waste time trying to guess—or dealing with the consequences of guessing incorrectly. (See the preceding section, "Testing in the Dark: Should You Proceed Without Documentation?" for tips on trying to operate without clear documentation.)

Continuous Test Execution. Related to, and enabled by, test automation, this type of execution involves setting up tests so that the system under test runs as nearly continuously as possible. This arrangement can entail some odd hours for the test staff, especially test technicians, so everyone on the test team should have access to all appropriate areas of the test lab.

Adding Test Engineers. Fred Brooks once observed that "adding more people to a late software project makes it later," a statement that has become known as Brooks's Law.[10] This law does not hold true as strongly in testing as it does in most areas of software and hardware engineering, however. Brooks reasoned that as you add people to a project, you increase the communication

---

10. See Frederick Brooks's software engineering classic *The Mythical Man-Month* for this and other useful observations. Published initially in 1975, this volume still has a lot to say about software engineering and software project management.

overhead, burden the current development engineers with training the new engineers, and don't usually get the new engineers up to speed soon enough to do much good. In contrast, a well-architected behavioral test system reflects the (ideally) simpler external interfaces of the system under test, not its internal complexities, which means that a new engineer will be able to contribute within a couple of weeks of joining the team. (Structural test systems, in contrast, do require an understanding of system internals.) If a schedule crisis looms six weeks or more in your future, you can bring in a new test engineer in time to help. I have added test engineers on the day system testing started, and I once joined a laptop development project as the test manager about two weeks before the start of this phase. In both cases, the results were good. (There's no doubt, of course, that testing proceeds most smoothly when you have an appropriate level of staffing from the beginning. But that shouldn't stop you from adding more staff when necessary.)

Brake Pedals

The following project behaviors and attributes tend to decelerate the test process. Whenever possible, you should try to change or avoid them.

Getting Too Clever. Because many previously independent pieces of the product come together in testing, test schedules have myriad dependencies and single-points-of-failure. Even with the collective knowledge of the entire project team, test and project managers cannot easily identify all of these before they come whistling out of nowhere and whack you on the forehead. Avoid the temptation to "accelerate" the test schedule by piling one seemingly reasonable assumption on top of another, thereby building an insupportable house of cards. When the assumptions fail, the project is left de facto without a schedule, and chaos and improvisation ensue.

Unrealistic Project Schedules. The same kinds of problems associated with getting too clever also arise when project schedules are totally disconnected from reality. This situation occurs when management confuses business priorities with technical possibilities, and it is especially prevalent when marketing windows and bonuses are involved. When your managers start telling you that they intend to make up earlier schedule slips during test execution, something bad is about to happen, and you will be intimately involved.[11]

Failure to Provide Test Deliverables.   Such failures include shortages of hardware, the release to test of incomplete software systems, software releases that are impossible to install or that are improperly packaged, incompatibilities, releases outside strict revision control, and so forth. The frequent—and frustrating—follow-up to such delays can take the form of project management dictating that the test team must meet its original schedule, hobbled though it is.

Lack of System Administration, Infrastructure, and Developer Support.   The test lab infrastructure will often require expert system administration support. An experienced system administrator can resolve in five minutes a problem that a test engineer might take five hours to figure out. For the same reason, support from facilities management is important—for example, having people on call to unlock doors that no one expected to be locked. Developer support is necessary, too. For instance, during the early stages of testing, testers sometimes need to confirm with developers that anomalous behavior is really a bug rather than a configuration change that test forgot to make or some other trivial glitch. A test team must have prompt support available from these various sources whenever tests are being run, which usually means 24 hours a day, seven days a week, once test execution begins in earnest. Testers should have contact lists, with home, cell phone, and pager numbers (including, as a last resort, the names and numbers of managers).

"Saving Money" on Tools.   Test tools, especially test automation tools, always pay for themselves. Trying to economize by building your own tools, quashing the idea of purchasing a new tool because of budget constraints, and sending test engineers on snipe hunts for "bargain" tools waste the test team's time, thus delaying the project *and* costing more money.

---

11. Robert Glass, in his Practical Programmer column in the *Communications of the ACM*, writes of consulting with a client who had put such a schedule in place: "I said things like, 'The approach you are taking to accelerate the schedule is actually costing you long term, in that enhancements and system testing are taking such unpredictably long periods of time that it is not possible to achieve any anticipated schedule.' (Things had literally crawled to a halt in system testing, with each new bug fix generating enough new bugs that almost no forward progress was achieved)."

Unrealistic Test Schedules. Test schedules must allocate sufficient time for each test case, understanding that the discovery of bugs will increase the time needed to run the test cases. The schedules must also include sufficient cycles, in advance, for the resolution of problems found in the first cycle. I have participated in too many projects whose schedules were blown when management assumed that test would find no "must-fix" bugs. As soon as the first "must-fix" bug surfaced, these projects had no schedule.

Slow Development Response. The average turnaround time from the opening of a bug report to its resolution and closure is called the closure period. (See Chapter 4 for discussion of this and other project metrics.) Only development, by promptly debugging and fixing problems, can influence the length of the closure period. The longer development takes to resolve a bug, especially for the high-severity issues that can block test progress, the slower the test project moves.

Use of the Test Lab for Debugging. Sometimes development is forced to use the test lab equipment to reproduce bugs because the development environment is not sufficiently complex. But every minute that development uses a piece of test lab equipment for debugging is a minute that the test team can't run tests.

Buggy Deliverables. The more bugs in the system under test, the slower testing goes. The time that test technicians and engineers spend in bug identification and isolation is several orders of magnitude greater than the time it takes to kick off automated tests and collect passing results.

Violations of Test Plan Entry Criteria. Project management often justifies entering a test phase before the system under test is ready by arguing that this will accelerate testing. It usually does not. Most commonly, the test team must abort the first cycle as a result of rampant stability bugs that prevent any forward progress. During hardware testing, equipment can actually be damaged because it can't "live" in the test lab environment.

Violations of Test Plan Exit Criteria. Leaving a test phase before the bug find rate has leveled off and all other exit criteria are met just passes along an immature system to the next phase of testing. This next phase will do a less efficient and less effective job of identifying the test escapes from the previous phase, because the test system operates at a coarser level of granularity as it progresses from one phase to the next.

Scope Creep, Crawl, and Redefinition.   Changes in product scope result in changes in test system scope. Test scope itself is sometimes subject to abrupt change, usually when the schedule begins to falter. Both increases and reductions in scope can create problems. Test engineers who design the test system must make certain assumptions about the pieces of functionality that will be contained in the product. If one of these pieces later drops out, a domino effect can result that compromises the test system, partially or completely breaking it.

For example, suppose that you design test tools and cases for use in testing the stress, volume, and capacity loads of a system based on a particular driver or interface in the system, and then that driver or interface changes. What if you invest person-months of effort in building a test tool that can scale up to hundreds of simultaneous load-generating connections, only to find that the design capacity has been dropped, in response to bugs found by your team, to an order of magnitude less? Was the time spent building a tool that could scale to that capacity wasted? Maybe not, in the long run, but it will surely feel that way in the midst of a furious schedule crunch, when those two person-months could have been devoted to many other priorities.

Test Suite or Phase Cancellation.   Like product scope shrink, test scope shrink can waste time, although in this case it's usually retroactive: the time spent developing or preparing to run a test suite or phase proves to have been wasted. No bugs will be found by that testing, so the ROI is shot, but most of the heavy lifting has already been done. Fortunately, it's not impossible to see this coming. If a test phase or cycle drags on well beyond its originally scheduled exit date, start to plan proactively to shut it down and catch up the testing later, if possible.

Tester Mistakes.   Simply put, test managers, test engineers, and test technicians make mistakes. Clearly, as the test manager, you own the task of preventing this class of goofs. They include, among others, the following notable examples from my own background:

- Failing to understand the dependencies while planning
- Developing tightly coupled, unstable, unmaintainable, incompatible, or erroneous test systems
- Picking the wrong test tools
- Doing poor or inefficient bug isolation
- Wasting time on trivial matters while the critical areas fall apart

♦   Reporting bugs that aren't bugs (type I errors)

♦   Failing to report bugs that are bugs (type II errors)

♦   Running automated tests with the wrong parameters or in the wrong configurations

♦   Skipping critical test cases

PINK SLIPS: LAYOFFS AND LIQUIDATION

According to Denis Meredith, 20 to 30 percent of testing and quality assurance organizations are disbanded within two years of their formation.[12] Anecdotally, I can attest to the credibility of this statistic, having experienced multiple layoffs as a test manager. In some cases, I was asked to wield the ax; in others, I—along with most or all of my test team—got the ax.

For obvious reasons, companies don't tend to post big notices around the cube farm six months before a layoff, saying, "Get your résumés ready; here comes Chainsaw Al." In some instances, even the line managers might not know what's coming, although they usually do get a few clues. Based on my admittedly limited experience, and the shared experiences of some of my colleagues, I recount here some worrisome warning signs:

♦   Being asked to participate in an employee ranking exercise, especially if this procedure involves every manager in the company. I have never seen these rankings used for anything other than whacking the bottom rungs off the ladder.

♦   Noticing a decline in your company's revenues. In one firm, everyone knew that layoffs were coming when their biggest client stopped signing up new work and started to withdraw existing work. In another company, people were laid off from departments that still produced revenue, while the people who worked on a struggling, unprofitable product survived. Why? The company saw the success of that product as a "bet the farm" proposition; some bystanders lost that bet.

---

12. Materials prepared for Denis Meredith's training course "Software Testing: An Integrated Approach," presented September 23–27, 1991, at the University of California at Los Angeles, pp. 1–19.

◆ Noticing a sudden, unexplainable invasion of accountants or consultants, especially if they're working with the human resources department. Ask yourself whether the task at hand is figuring out severance packages.

◆ Hearing any rumors of a layoff list. It may well include you or members of your test team. A test manager I know heard from other managers that they had seen a "list of developers" slated to go. He naïvely assumed that this couldn't mean testers, without asking himself how the other managers would choose to drop him a hint if it *did* mean testers.

Test operations can sometimes bear a disproportionate burden when it comes to layoffs. If management doesn't perceive a return on investment, who can blame them? Although you can't always escape layoffs in a company that is doing poorly, the keys to keeping your test operation viable are aligning your testing with customer usage, crisply reporting the problems you find to the right people, and practicing some of the political skills described elsewhere in this chapter.

PRESENTING THE RESULTS: THE RIGHT MESSAGE, DELIVERED PROPERLY

As you run tests, you will find bugs. Also, because your test lab is the place where the product hits something like the "real world" for the first time, you will find all sorts of logistical snafus and poorly thought-out processes. This is especially the case when multiple development teams are involved.

Neither situation should take you by surprise. The bugs are actually your quarry, and when you find one, you and your team should feel satisfied. The "Laurel and Hardy" routines that ensue when people fail to think through processes and logistics are less desirable, but they are hardly your fault, either. Nevertheless, you may find yourself received with dismay when the time comes to report your findings.

In ancient times, the messenger who brought bad news was sometimes executed, suggesting a human tendency that remains to this day. When you come to a meeting or approach a developer with news of bugs or unworkable test equipment, the first response might be defensiveness, anger, denial, or attack. I had a client who, in response to all the worrisome findings by a third-party test lab, seized on a few mistakes the lab had made. Every time anyone mentioned bugs found by these folks, the client would become infuriated at the mention of the lab's name, once sending me an e-mail that said (paraphrased), "Get these [idiots] out of our life."

As dysfunctional as these behaviors are, you will have to deal with them. Even if others recognize the attacks as more appropriately directed at the problem rather than at the reporter (you), they probably won't leap to your defense. After all, they have their own problems, and getting involved in your quarrels means antagonizing people. While you can't make the attacks go away, you can take certain courses of action to make the situation better—or worse.

GOOD WAYS TO DELIVER BAD NEWS

It's critical to avoid antagonizing your project teammates when discussing bugs, missed delivery schedules, support issues, and the like. Chapter 8 advocated professional pessimism, but too much pessimism approaches paranoia. The selfless, noble whistleblower who stops the evil, corrupt project team from shipping fatally flawed systems has become a mythical figure in the engineering world. When overplayed, however, such a role makes the test group the loose cannon of the development project. Loose cannons do not roll around on the corporate deck in the tempest of development for long before they fall overboard.

Likewise, you should guard against melodramatic reporting of results. It's important to maintain a sense of perspective about how a bug will actually affect a customer, which can differ significantly from how it affects you, your testers, and your test system. Holding up the shipment of a commercial product that is as good as or better than its competitors is a bad business decision and can cause real political damage for you. As a professional tester, you must keep an open mind during reasoned discussions about the business realities of delayed ship dates.

Expressing any opinion about the progress of bug-fixing efforts is also dangerous. I once made the mistake of commenting on a marathon, all-weekend bug isolation experiment undertaken by a set of developers, saying that it was "beyond my ability to understand why anyone would think that such an effort would actually locate the bug." The fact that I was right—the undertaking was indeed fruitless—did not win me any points from the developers involved, who were quite upset with me for making the comment.

Remember Don Quixote when you're presenting your findings. Although a bug can appear quite dangerous to testers, developers often see the same bug as benign. While the truth lies somewhere between the extremes, you can easily come off as an alarmist. Worse yet, you can be accused of not being a team player if you perpetually hold the product up to unrealistically high standards of quality and rail against moving the schedule forward because the product isn't ready yet. (Sometimes you must make this argument, because it's true. But you have to recognize that it will make you very unpopular, especially when people's bonuses are tied to hitting schedule dates. I engage in this argument only when it's likely to prevail on its own merits—the "emperor's new clothes"—or when failing to do so would approach professional malpractice. As the Jesuit historian Juan de Mariana wrote, "The greatest of follies is to exert oneself in vain, and to weary oneself without winning anything but hatred.")

The Importance of Accuracy and Audience

In addition to being as reasonable as possible, you must be as correct as possible. No mistake draws more attention and ridicule than telling someone else they have done something wrong when in fact *you* are the one who is wrong. You must ensure a high degree of accuracy in the bug reports your team generates and in the data you collect and summarize. The further up the corporate ladder you intend to escalate a particular bug report, defect analysis metric, or test status summary, the more critical this accuracy becomes.

Never send out a set of reports without reading every word first. Remember that typos and jargon can render your meaning unclear, causing your message to misfire. Time spent rereading these reports and fixing the errors is time well spent. Sending out accurate reports to your peers and managers is part of managing upward and outward, two key responsibilities.

Of course, accuracy is worthless if no one reads your reports or looks at your charts. This can happen if you send the wrong level of detail to your audience. For example, senior managers who need to look at trends will want to see defect charts. They'll also need your help understanding these reports, so you should provide high-level narrative with each chart, either as a cover sheet, as part of a presentation, or as part of the e-mail to which the report package is attached. Individual developers, however, need to see detailed bug reports and might not care about the higher-level abstractions such as defect metrics. Table 9-1 suggests target audiences for the reports and charts mentioned in this book. (I assume that you will provide these items freely to your own test organization and expect your staff to understand at least the test status reports, bug reports, defect analyses, and test logistics and how these reports affect their assignments.)

In addition to keeping in mind the appropriate audience, you should also consider the frequency of updates. Sending executive managers a daily update on test status, including all the items recommended in Table 9-1, is likely to exceed their ability to absorb and cope with the material. Developers, in contrast, might need access to these reports in real time; an intranet web site, updated every few hours, might be appropriate for critical reports. Ideally, of course, you could simply give the entire company access to the tools used to generate the reports and then send out a formal update package once a week or so.

Note that "accuracy" has a different meaning to each audience listed in Table 9-1. A developer will probably tolerate jargon and poor grammar, provided that your data is solid and your premises and conclusions sound. But a senior manager is much more focused on a solid summary line for a bug report, consistency between charts, and up-to-the-minute timeliness.

"You Can Tell the Pioneers...": The Effect of Early Adoption on Test

As the saying goes, you can tell the pioneers in computer technology by all the arrows sticking out of their backsides. Whether they represent the first of a family of CPUs, a new way of connecting peripherals, a new generation of software, or a faster telecommunications process, complex software and hardware systems just never work as advertised early in their life cycles—a fact that creates major headaches for test managers.

As you might have noticed, sales and marketing staff love to have the latest technology bundled in their products. Nothing makes their hearts beat faster than to be able to say to a prospect or print in an advertisement, "We're first to market with this supercalifragilisticexpialidocious technology, and you can only get it from us!" Don't get me wrong. I appreciate sales and marketing people, without whom I would have far fewer job opportunities. And in fact they are right: being first to market with exciting new technology can make a huge difference in a product's success and, by extension, the success of the company.

Item	Target Audience
Failure Mode and Effects Analysis (FMEA) or informal quality risks analysis	Developers, development managers, project managers, sales and marketing managers, customer and technical support managers, executive management
Test project Gantt chart	Development managers, project managers, executive management
Budget	Project managers, executive management
Test plans	Development managers, project managers, sales and marketing managers, customer and technical support managers, executive management
Hardware allocation plan or hardware/software logistics database reports	IT/MIS managers, facilities managers, project managers, executive management
Test coverage analyses	Development managers, project managers, sales and marketing managers, customer and technical support managers, executive management
Defect analyses	Development managers, project managers, sales and marketing managers, customer and technical support managers, executive management
Bug detail report	Developers, development managers, project managers
Bug summary report	Development managers, project managers, sales and marketing managers, customer and technical support managers, executive management
Test case details	Developers, development managers, project managers
Test case summary	Development managers, project managers, sales and marketing managers, customer and technical support managers, executive management
Test suite summary	Development managers, project managers, sales and marketing managers, customer and technical support managers, executive management
Lab layout	Facilities managers, IT/MIS managers, project managers, executive management
Staffing plan	Project managers, human resource managers, executive management
Test organization chart	Development managers, IT/MIS managers, project managers, executive management

TABLE 9-1 *Target audiences for the charts and reports listed in this book.*

Nevertheless, there's a price to pay during test execution for trying to evaluate this stuff before it is in wide use. It should come as no surprise to any test manager that some companies release products before they are fully tested and debugged. This is just as true of your vendors as it is of your employers. New products contain bugs, some subtle, some glaring. If your company incorporates those products into its products, or relies on them to produce products, it will suffer the consequences.

In addition, a new product might be fine by itself but suffer when it is integrated into another product. I once worked on a laptop computer project that was the first to incorporate Intel 166 MHz MMX CPUs into its systems. These chips worked well, but the increased speed and functionality meant increased power consumption, which affected battery life and increased thermal radiation, which in turn affected the heat dissipation design. These were not bugs in Intel's chip per se, but rather in our usage of it.

If you concede that lots of bugs are encountered in new technology, the logical next step would be to spend a little more time testing it. This is where yet another headache for test managers kicks in. Figure 9-6 shows what the Gartner Group refers to as the "Hype Curve." When you are testing new technology during the "Bandwagon Effect" or "Peak of Expectations" period, all anyone reading the trade magazines hears about is how great this

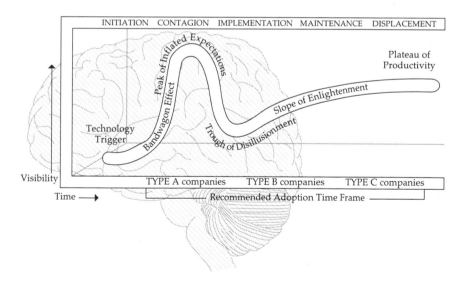

FIGURE 9-6 *The Hype Curve. (Gartner Group,* Executive Edge, *September 1998. Reprinted with permission, April 1999.)*

new technology is. Guess what that means? When you go to your management with a request for several thousand additional dollars to test the new technology in the product, you may be met with incredulity or distrust. Even some otherwise reasonable managers who have had painful past experience as early adopters can get caught up in the hype. As a result, you can end up woefully underbudgeted.

Not all companies face the risks of new technology the same way, of course. As shown in Figure 9-6, the Gartner Group identifies three kinds of organizational behaviors. Type A companies pursue new technologies aggressively, in spite of risk, to achieve predominance in a specific niche. Type B companies wait until the earliest adopters have shaken out the most serious glitches before they move in—a strategy that mitigates some risk but misses opportunities as well. Type C companies linger the longest, avoiding all the associated risk. In the high-tech world, type C behavior is even more dangerous than type A behavior: the business history of computing is rife with the corpses of once-strong companies who jumped at just one key technology just a little too late. Many other companies have had near-death experiences from the same cause. Again, keep in mind the greater good of the company. An organization that optimizes its processes for type A behavior makes your tasks more challenging, but it is less of a threat to your job security than a complacent employer who waits until everyone else has worked out the glitches.

It's critical that you, as the test manager, remain the polite pessimist, dubious about the new technology, regardless of the enthusiasm raging around you on the project. Don't get sucked into the hype. People whose jobs involve being visionaries, product architects, and implementers must buy into it to some extent; after all, the desire to achieve the nearly impossible is a useful attribute in these folks. But test managers are professional skeptics. Even if you don't get the budget and the schedule to test new technologies properly, make the request on the record, and explain your concerns. You might manage to temper the hype a bit, and you might obtain enough resources to do a passable job of testing the new technology. At the very worst, you'll have the solace of knowing that you did your best to test the new technology thoroughly, should it blow up in the customers' hands.

Ultimately, all the political advice and suggestions in this chapter come back to that theme. To feel good about your contributions as a test manager, you need to create an environment in which you and your team can do your best to find bugs. Most of the challenges are technical or managerial, and the other nine chapters of this book offer some ideas on how to surmount them. Some challenges, however, are political. Any time people get together to solve problems and create products, even in the most tightly knit teams, politics are involved. Sometimes the solution is not necessarily consistent with the technical needs of the team.

Roland Huntford, author of *The Last Place on Earth*, tells the story of two teams, one English, one Norwegian, who competed to reach the South Pole in the early 1900s. The Norwegian team was the better organized and prepared, and it prevailed. But during the expedition one of the members of the team, a man named Johansen, attacked the authority of the team leader, Amundsen. For this political offense, Johansen was excluded from the sprint to the pole and had to remain at the base camp on the Ross ice shelf, in spite of his skills and experience as a polar explorer, which might have been critical to the expedition's success. (It was by no means a foregone conclusion that the Norwegians would beat the English.) This story illustrates the inescapable fact that, even in the best of teams, under the most perilous of circumstances, political problems will arise. You can be prepared to handle them and succeed in your overarching aims, or you can try to ignore them, which will expose you, no matter how talented you are, to the possibility of failure.

10

Involving Other Players: Distributing a Test Project

Throughout this book, I've mentioned that various people and organizations within a company in addition to the test group have test-related responsibilities. Similarly, occasions arise when it makes sense to involve people and teams outside the company to help with particular test challenges. Assembling a distributed testing effort involves creating a hybrid test organization, part skills-based and part project-based, consisting of the test team, other contributors within the company, and people who work in other companies.

Distributed testing comes in four basic flavors:

◆ Your vendors (those companies who provide products that will be integrated into your products)

◆ Independent test organizations

◆ Your sales offices (especially foreign offices for localization testing)

◆ Your target customers (for beta testing)

This chapter does not discuss beta testing, which usually cannot be planned and managed in the same way you can manage people who are specifically accountable for performing particular tests. Instead, we'll focus on vendors, independent test labs, and sales offices. Distributing testing to these entities means that you have extended your test operation, with all the benefits and challenges that implies.

To distribute testing successfully, you need to perform three sequential steps:

1. Choose your test partners, based on the specific testing you need to distribute and why you need to do so

2. Plan the distributed test effort

3. Manage the external testing as if it were your own

The following sections examine each of these steps as well as suggest ways in which the tools introduced in this book can be extended to assist you.

CHOOSING YOUR PARTNERS

If you choose a Texas BBQ joint to cater your wedding, you should not be surprised when brisket and beer, rather than caviar and champagne, appear on the menu. Likewise, it helps to consider your motivations and goals when choosing your test partners. Let's start with the question of why you want to use outside test resources rather than your own team.

Typically, your reasons are related to one (or both) of these two motivations: either you are trying to leverage an external party's strength, especially one that you can't or don't want to re-create in-house; or you are off-loading work that you can't handle quickly enough. For example, suppose that you are the test manager on the SpeedyWriter project and that you have approached an external test lab, STC, about the possibility of performing localization testing. Later you decide that some compatibility testing must be done with various hardware and applications, and you want to use STC for that. As for the localization efforts, Software Cafeteria's sales partner in Tokyo is willing to do the Far East localization, and your partner in Bonn can handle European localization. Your management decides that these folks will do a better job (and for free) and tells you to use them instead of STC for this aspect of testing.

In addition, suppose that around September 9 you receive an unpleasant surprise: Maria, a key engineer for system testing, hands in her resignation. She agrees to stay through September 30 to finish developing the system test suite, but now you will need help running the suite. It's too late to bring a contractor on board, so you decide to have your STC test partners work with you during the system test phase, running the capacity/volume and network tests. See Figure 10-1 for a Gantt chart that shows test execution with these resources in place.

In the case of localization and compatibility testing, you are leveraging the strengths of external resources. Your sales partners overseas have access to multilingual people who can help you with localization. Like most external test labs, STC has access to more hardware than you want to maintain in your in-house lab. In this instance, it makes sense to use foreign sales offices and external labs for these tasks, even if you could handle the work in-house.

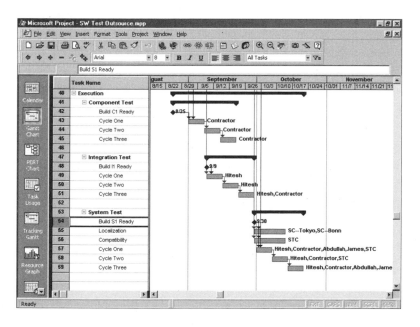

FIGURE 10-1   *A Gantt chart for test execution, showing staff resources, a contractor, foreign sales offices, and an external test lab.*

In the case of system testing, you are primarily off-loading excess work to STC. It's also true that the capacity/volume and network tests are probably good fits for an external lab, given the abundance of hardware these labs generally contain. But your principal motivation is getting the work off your plate to avoid overloading your staff. You might have chosen to use a contractor, but that would have meant trying to staff a position in three weeks and then hoping that the person could hit the ground running in a critical situation three weeks before the planned release date. Using a proven test resource like STC is a less risky approach. And since the amount of work to be off-loaded is fairly small, the cost difference between using STC and using a contractor is probably minimal.

As this example shows, you can choose to distribute testing based on the factors of strength and necessity, with each decision involving different amounts of each factor. In some cases, though, necessity can tempt you to make outsourcing decisions that are deleterious to the success of your test effort. To avoid this, you should understand the strengths and weaknesses of various prospective test partners, as the following sections discuss.

Your Vendors

If you are the test manager for DataRocket, some of the obvious participants in your distributed test effort are your vendors. The SCSI card, purchased from a Taiwanese vendor, and the LAN card, purchased from a U.S. vendor, must work properly with your motherboard, with each other, with the hard drives, with any other integrated hardware devices, and with the software—but first and foremost they must work by themselves. What assurance do you have that the vendors are selling you a product that works? And, if you believe the product works, do you need to repeat the vendors' testing?

These questions apply not only to hardware but also to software. Increasingly, software companies are outsourcing development work to third parties, some of whom are separated from the main office by thousands of miles. Whether the outsourced effort includes hardware, software, or both, you have by definition distributed the testing. The question then becomes whether you can leverage the distributed testing to play to strengths and avoid wasted effort.

Component vendors tend to focus on the testing process for their specific components. For example, I had a client who purchased custom modem subsystems from a large U.S. vendor. I audited the vendor's test process to ensure that the modem company was testing sufficiently and to determine what testing my client could omit. I found that the vendor was doing a great job of testing the modem itself. The testing was focused inward, and the modem as a modem worked well.

From the outward perspective of seeing a modem as part of an overall system, however, the testing was less complete. For instance, the vendor did thermal testing on the modem, recognizing that it would be installed in a laptop computer. But the test used an artificial case that didn't approximate the setting in my client's system very well. When I pointed this out, the vendor politely but firmly declined to alter the test specifications. I received the same response concerning questions of software compatibility: The vendor wasn't interested in modifying its testing process to include the software operating environments we intended to bundle on the hard drive. The modem vendor felt that testing the integration of the modem into the system and its behavior as part of that system was clearly my client's concern.

In the case of a component such as a modem, this limited focus might be acceptable. Because a modem's interface to the system is usually serial, software integration is through a standard interface. But if your vendor is selling SCSI cards, integration is a bigger issue for you. Compatibility issues arise between SCSI devices. You can't simply assume that connecting a hard drive, a tape drive, a removable mass-storage device, and maybe a scanner to a SCSI chain will work. Integration testing is important and should begin early.

Likewise, if you buy a significant portion of your system, such as a motherboard, from a vendor, your project's success depends on the proper functioning of the component; it's fundamental to the success of your platform. Even if some parts of the system are not quite mature, you might need to begin system testing early. A fully functional prototype—even if it's missing the "fit and finish" aspects—is required before you assume that it will work.

Most vendors take a narrow, targeted view of their testing: they might test very deeply in certain areas, but they aren't likely to test broadly. Unless your product performs only limited functions—as an ATM machine does, for instance—you probably need to complement vendors' testing with broad testing. Even if a vendor does a certain amount of broad testing, the tests are not likely to be as detailed as you need.

Figure 10-2 illustrates the three key factors that influence the extent to which you must integrate a vendor's testing efforts into your own.

- *Irreplaceability.* If a component such as a PCI LAN card or an ISA modem is a problem, you can replace it easily; a motherboard, on the other hand, may prove more essential. Likewise, if you have outsourced the writing of the back-end software for a networked application, you are entirely dependent on that software working properly.

- *Coupling.* If a vendor's component is basically stand-alone—a modem, for instance—and doesn't interact with the system in unique (and possibly far-flung) ways, the component is not tightly coupled. But if it influences the overall behavior of the system, as a BIOS does, it is tightly coupled. The coupling might be more than technical, too: marketing sometimes imposes constraints that couple your product to certain components.

- *Capability.* You can decide whether to trust a vendor's test capability by auditing the company's test operation. If you're satisfied with the quality of the testing, you can leave the vendor alone for the most part, although you might want to check in during test execution. But if the vendor's test process is entirely ad hoc and the test staff seems to be the dregs of the organization, you must plan to actively manage the vendor's work—or repeat it.

In Figure 10-2, the closer a vendor sits to the origin of these three axes, the less you need to integrate its efforts into yours. The further a vendor sits from the origin, on any of these axes, the more closely you must manage its test process as part of your own, or resign yourself to duplicating it entirely.

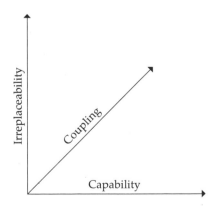

FIGURE 10-2 *Key factors dictating the need to integrate vendor/customer test efforts.*

THIRD-PARTY TESTERS

Third-party test resources include any organization that offers test services to paying clients. These services can be provided off site, on site, or both. I distinguish between a body shop, or temporary agency, and a third-party test firm based on whether the firm manages the project. A third-party test organization should provide some amount of test project planning and management. If the company merely gives you a tester to direct as you see fit, it's a temp agency, not a third-party test company.

A true third-party test organization brings several key strengths to the table. The most important is expertise in test project management and seasoned skills in technical testing. The company's skills may also be specialized, tightly focused, or unique. For example, some test consultancies do nothing but computer security work, while others have usability expertise. These skills are not common and are not mastered quickly; if you need such expertise, working with a good third-party organization might be your only choice.

Another advantage is that test companies can often begin running tests for you more quickly than you could do it yourself. Some organizations maintain a loose confederation of subcontractors who can jump in right away; others have a staff of test experts on salary. In addition, some of these companies maintain extensive hardware inventories or software libraries that you either can't afford or don't want to replicate. For example, some test labs specialize in environmental testing, which can involve large and expensive equipment such as thermal chambers and shock tables.

A common theme runs through all these strengths: for certain assets, it's better to rent than to own. If that sounds counterintuitive, consider the following example: A car rental company will, if you appear to be a stable citizen of at least moderate means, rent you a Porsche to drive for a weekend getaway. Expensive? Yes, but you've decided that you can afford it. When it comes to *owning* the Porsche, however, you probably *can't* afford it, considering the $100,000 purchase price or the tens of thousands of dollars a year it would take to finance it. If you want the Porsche only once or twice a year, renting makes sense; why pay to have it sit in your garage for the rest of the year?

That said, arrangements with third-party test labs can contain significant pitfalls. For the most part, these pitfalls are similar to the hazards encountered in hiring a consultant. When you contract with an external test organization, you are the one bearing the risk should that organization prove incapable of discharging your distributed test needs. You might sue for malpractice, but most likely a nonperforming external lab would simply walk away with one project's worth of dough and an unhappy client. You, however, could lose your job for choosing the wrong partner.

The way to avoid such a situation is for you to exercise due diligence the first time you do business with an external test team. When you hire an employee or a contractor for your own staff, you interview the individual, check references, and scrutinize the person's résumé. Retaining the right third-party test organization is not terribly different.

You begin with an interview, which is likely to be multitiered. In some cases, you'll speak to a salesperson first. This might strike you as a waste of time, but it's not. At this meeting, you can qualify (or disqualify) the company in terms of business issues such as price, turnaround time, and facilities. Remember that the salesperson is checking you out, too, gathering information about similar issues from that company's perspective.

If the results of this interview are positive for both sides, you should proceed to discussions with the project manager and the technical staff. Don't skip this step, and do insist that you talk directly to the people who will work on your project. (If the company won't commit specific individuals at this point, it might not warrant killing the deal, but you should underline to the primary contact, whoever that may be, that you must approve any and all changes in personnel.) You already know how to hire good test project leads, test engineers, and test technicians, so you can apply similar standards to the individuals involved here. In fact, in this situation your standards should be even higher: these people will cost your company more money than the salaries of your own comparable employees, so you have a right to expect a superior level of expertise.

Be aware that the hourly rate paid for services from an external test lab is linearly related but not equivalent to the rate you pay your own testers. If you pay $75 an hour for a contract test engineer, you can expect to pay two or three times as much for that same resource through a third-party test company. This might seem unreasonable, but, like renting a Porsche as opposed to owning, renting a skilled professional costs a lot more on a per-hour basis. Your level of commitment is less, and you don't pay for down time, so the test lab must be compensated for that risk. That said, don't do business with fools, or pay outrageous overhead. Your objective is to be sure that the people who claim they can do the work really can do it, that the price is reasonable to you, and that the profit is fair to the test company.

Additional considerations come into play if the work is to be performed off site. In this case, you are paying not only for people but also for facilities and access to equipment. If you hire a test lab to perform environmental testing, for example, you are renting thermal chambers and shock and vibration tables, along with the skilled professionals who operate them.

Finally, consider the facility itself. I recommend an on-site visit if you are working with a purely off-site resource. What are your security needs? Do you require a separate lab? (Do your competitors use the same facility?) Is the facility geographically convenient or inconvenient? Does its location give you access to a less expensive pool of talent than you could find locally? (For example, the lower labor costs you'll often find in an overseas test lab might make up for its lack of geographic proximity and the occasional trips you might have to make to coordinate the work.)

This might sound like quite an undertaking, but with luck you will need to do it only once. After you establish a solid working relationship with an external test organization, you can use the site repeatedly. This trusted relationship can benefit you not only at your current place of employment but again and again throughout your career. If you find a partner with whom you work well, keep the relationship going.

SALES OFFICES

If you sell a product internationally, you might have a local sales office or a sales partner (such as a distributor) in various regions. Alternatively, you might have a "virtual" sales office, with a staff member in the main sales office handling foreign sales. Either way, the sales office is singularly aware of and qualified to evaluate the unique quality risks of the foreign market.

Chapter 1's list of quality risks included localization as a major category of risk for any product sold or used internationally. (See "Localization," page 22.) In some cases, testing this quality risk at the home office is well beyond challenging. With DataRocket, for example, you might need testers fluent in Japanese, Korean, Mandarin, Thai, Cantonese, German, Dutch, French, Russian, Spanish, Italian, and Polish to vet your documentation and startup guides. How will you simulate foreign electrical power? If you include an optional modem, how about foreign dial tones? Which colloquialisms and symbols might be cultural taboos? (For instance, in certain parts of Spanish-speaking South America, the verb *coger*, meaning "to get," takes on a sexual connotation and must be avoided in polite discourse. Few besides local people are likely to be aware of such a distinction.)

As in any situation, trade-offs exist. The good news is that, as fellow employees, the staff members in a sales office have the same goals and objectives you do—they have a stake in ensuring that the test effort is successful. If the folks in your Tokyo office do a poor job of testing the Far East localization of SpeedyWriter, they will suffer as much as you will.

There are disadvantages, too. You cannot assume technical sophistication on the part of most salespeople. If you are responsible for the results of the testing and want specific items tested, you will need to spell out these details. Any test cases you give to nontechnical colleagues must be precise and unambiguous. As Chapter 3 explained, writing such test cases involves a great deal of hard work. (See "How Detailed? Balancing Ambiguity," page 78.)

You must also remember that the salespeople or sales partners probably do not work for you in any sense. Although you are responsible for ensuring the quality and completion of the testing they perform, you cannot structure their jobs, and you cannot specify standards of behavior, ways of interacting with your team, or circumstances under which you will end the relationship. As a practical matter, you might have to go to some amount of trouble to get results from them.

PLANNING A DISTRIBUTED TEST EFFORT

You need to plan distributed testing with the same level of detail you use to plan your internal effort. It should be a straightforward process, given that you have your own operation under control. The starting point is completion of the high-level test planning discussed in Chapters 1 and 2. You should also have your own test suites fairly well defined, although a few details might remain to be settled. Your test tracking and bug tracking processes should be worked out, including a plan for deploying the bug tracking system.

ASSESSING CAPABILITIES

Once you've learned enough about a potential test partner to select the organization for the project, as outlined earlier, you next need to assess that partner's specific test capabilities as part of planning your overall test effort. You should approach this exercise as you approach any business meeting: with a certain expected outcome in mind. Compile a proposed list of contributions that you can check off as you go through the assessment, focusing especially on questions related to the areas of skills, staffing, and physical setup.

For each proposed task, can the test partner produce an expert—or at least an experienced, competent person with the requisite skills—who will do the work? In many cases, you will be pleased with the skill levels of the people your test partner proposes; after all, the company *is* in the business of providing experts. But in other cases, the people you interview might not meet your expectations. This is not necessarily a reason to eliminate the

---

The Gartner Group on Outsourcing

In the September 1998 edition of *Executive Edge* magazine, the Gartner Group describes three areas of effort that are good fits for the outsourcing of information technology functions: utility functions, which are nonstrategic but necessary roles; enhancement functions, which make a strategic position better; and frontier functions, which allow a company to move into new technologies.

Although the focus of the Gartner Group's article was on in-house IT efforts for banks and the like, I find parallels with efforts to outsource testing work. For example, routine but critical test operations such as shock and vibration tests for DataRocket might fit into the utility category. Add-on testing for SpeedyWriter in areas such as broad-ranging hardware compatibility or interface usability might be considered enhancement. If your product incorporates leading-edge (frontier) technology, it's often useful to bring in an external resource such as a consultant or an outside test lab with special expertise in this area.

In my interpretation, the Gartner Group implies certain risks associated with outsourcing:

◆ Poor communication with the external organization concerning the business objectives and the reasons for outsourcing

◆ Jumping the gun on the process of selecting an external resource, perhaps in a hurried attempt to toss work over the fence

◆ Failing to manage the work, assuming that it will take care of itself

◆ Not integrating the data—in this case, test results and bug reports— back into your centralized tracking system

Distributed testing, like development outsourcing, does offer many benefits, but you must also be sure to manage these risks.

---

prospective partner from further consideration, however, especially if the people being proposed are better qualified than any other candidates you've spoken with. Holding out for the ideal set of experts at the ideal test partner may mean having no resource available in time. (As Steve McConnell notes in his *Software Project Survival Guide*, "The perfect is the enemy of the good.") If you must "settle," make a note of this to use as a bargaining chip when price comes into the picture. Also, as Chapter 8 warned concerning consultants, beware of bait-and-switch tactics, in which the company substitutes people with less skill than you have been promised.

Adequate staffing is critical. It's often tempting to see external organizations as a bottomless well of skilled test experts, especially if that's what you need. But every company has its staffing limitations. Some test labs keep client costs down by using primarily subcontractors and temporary labor, so you might find that they specialize in ramping up for test projects. Others rely on full-time staff. Assure yourself that your partner will be able to provide the entire team. It's not uncommon for a software or hardware engineering company that performs outsourced work to try to win business by overcommitting to clients in terms of the staffing resources it can bring to a project. Then, having won the business, the company is unable to execute. This is a disheartening experience for those in the company in question, but it could prove politically fatal to you if major elements of your test effort go uncompleted because you didn't fully check out your test partner.

Your assessment of your partner's physical setup should include equipment, facilities, and location. Does the company own the equipment it needs to perform the work? If not, will it be able to buy or lease it in time? Does the company have room, physically, to perform the work? Is security adequate? Is the location suitable for the tasks you are contemplating?

If the testing work will happen off site, your assessment should be performed at the test partner's facility. For foreign sales offices and the like, you should try to travel to the remote site. Contrary to accountants' wishes, on-site assessment becomes more important the further the partner is from your home office. A partner at a less remote site is less likely to try to snow you concerning test capabilities because it is easy for you to show up unannounced.

UNDERSTANDING THE COST

Before you proceed further with detailed planning, your test partner might require that you begin to pay for the project. An independent test company, of course, makes its money selling test services, not talking with prospects about test services. Your vendors might assume that further discussions are part of their deal with your company, but then again they might not. Foreign sales partners might be willing to do certain testing for free, but you can't assume that their time is worth nothing.

From vendors or third-party test companies, you can request a bid, which can be either a fixed-cost bid or a time-and-materials bid. If you receive a time-and-materials bid, you will need to estimate a weekly or monthly cost for your own budgeting purposes. Make sure that the bid includes some flexibility, not only for the inevitable changes that will occur but also to allow for alterations you will make in the next step when you create a unified test program (as the following section describes).

In addition to the fees the test partner might charge, certain expenses are necessarily associated with distributed testing itself. Later in the chapter, we'll discuss the kinds of issues that can impose some of these costs; see "Dealing with Mapping Issues," page 337. Besides these outlays, you will have other overhead such as communication and travel. Gather all these associated costs and incorporate them into your budget.

This budget work might be tedious and can slow down the process, but it's important to take care of it at an early stage to avoid getting stuck with a program you can't afford. Money always matters, and it figures significantly in distributed test efforts.

COLLATING, COORDINATING, AND PARTITIONING THE TEST PROGRAM

Your next task in distributed testing is to merge two or more test projects into a single unified test program. In general, you can think of this process as analogous to cooking and cutting up a pie. Various ingredients are involved in preparing the pie, but when the pie is served, a little of each ingredient will be on each person's plate.

Let's use another DataRocket example. Ignoring localization for the moment, assume that the players in a distributed test effort include your test team at Winged Bytes; the SCSI card vendor, Lucky Bit; and an environmental test lab, System Cookers. The goal is to produce a single set of test cases, organized into a collection of test suites, with each suite run by one of the three teams. Figure 10-3 shows the steps involved.

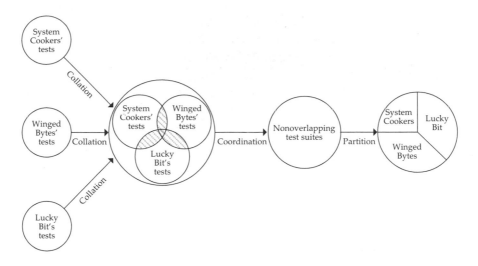

FIGURE 10-3   *Integrating three distinct test programs into one.*

The first step, collation, involves creating a single list of all the test cases that will be run. You'll need to collect each team's list of test cases and add it to your test tracking spreadsheet (discussed in Chapter 5). Use the spreadsheet's Owner column to keep track of which team is currently responsible for each test.

In the second step, coordination, you eliminate redundant test cases. For example, you notice that Lucky Bit was planning to run a thermal test on the SCSI card, but you would prefer to have System Cookers run a thermal test of the whole system with the SCSI card installed. Perhaps Lucky Bit can calculate the airflows required to keep each component operating within specifications and dispense with the test. System Cookers can attach thermal sensors to the active components and run the tests later. (Watch out, though, for partially overlapping test cases, discussed in "Dealing with Mapping Issues," page 337.)

In the test tracking spreadsheet, you can assign a *Skipped* status to each redundant test case, noting in the Comments column that the test is skipped because another team is running a preferable test. Don't forget to include the test identifiers in the comment so that people can cross-reference the other case. For example, a comment might read: *Covered by Sys. Cook. Test 3.005.*

Your third step is to partition the work, reviewing the test tracking spreadsheet and reassigning test cases to new owners. Much of this work is done by default as you coordinate the testing, since skipped test cases are removed from a team's workload and eliminated from the list. In other cases, you simply might want a different participant to run the test case. Perhaps it is better to provide Lucky Bit with a system for thermal testing than to try to get one to System Cookers, because of engineering sample limitations.

This three-step process must take into account more than just technical matters. Budget concerns will surface if you change the scope of a partner's involvement drastically. Politics and turf issues can also come into play. A vendor might be happy to have you accept most of the test burden, but the vendor's test manager could feel threatened; the test manager might want to do more testing, but that could be counter to the vendor's business interests. Independent test labs always want more work, but only if you're willing to pay.

ORGANIZING LOGISTICS

One of the advantages of distributed testing, when the test suites are partitioned properly, is that each partner plays to its strengths. This situation tends to minimize logistical problems. For example, if you use System Cookers to do your environmental testing for DataRocket, you have solved the logistical problems you would otherwise have in setting up your own thermal chambers, shock and vibration tables, and so forth. For SpeedyWriter, using STC to do compatibility testing frees you from having to stock and manage an extensive inventory of software and hardware.

In some cases, however, distributed testing creates unique logistical problems. The most difficult obstacles arise when a project includes one or more custom pieces of hardware or engineering samples. By definition, the number of such items is limited. For example, in a typical laptop project, only one or two dozen prototypes are hand-built for the first test cycle. Adding partners increases the number of engineering samples needed, thus putting an extra strain on the development organizations. Expect to have to negotiate your share of the samples, and plan on making compromises.

Since these components are engineering samples, they break more easily than production hardware. Because field support won't have any idea how to handle a damaged piece of hardware they've never seen before, a failed component must be repaired by development. This imposes an additional burden because either the item must come back to its point of origin for repair or an engineer must travel to the remote partner's location.

Speaking of traveling hardware, someone must coordinate the delivery and return of these items. Shipping is hardly an art form, but it does require planning and consideration. A test partner of mine once returned three laptop computers—irreplaceable first-stage engineering samples out of a total population of twenty-five or so—that were broken beyond repair. The person who sent them neglected to use packing foam or "peanuts" and instead placed the computers in a box, loose, and shipped them 5,000 miles. When confronted with the situation, this individual was surprised that anything had gone wrong—and expected the carrier's insurance to pay for the damage.

If computer equipment crosses an international border, you will have to deal with customs. Unlike shipping, this *is* an art form. Don't fly across the Pacific with four laptop computers in checked luggage, expecting to show up at a Taiwanese customs desk with a credit card, pay the duty, and go on your merry way, as your humble narrator once naively tried to do. Even with an experienced and competent customs broker, the process takes time and is not always transparent.

For these reasons, you'll want to keep the number of partners involved in your test project limited when you have custom hardware. In some cases, you might be able to give your test partners remote access to your custom hardware if their testing is primarily on the software side.

Even the software aspects are not without pitfalls, however. The problems in this area generally have to do with configuration and release management. For example, I participated in a project in which a remote test lab needed to have the custom software configuration of a laptop. We were forced to deliver physical disk drives because no one could come up with a workable method for delivering CD images or allowing a network download. (Such methods exist, of course, but in this case no one had the time to figure out the potentially complicated process.) If your test partners need to receive multiple software releases, you will have to spend time thinking through the delivery process.

You can use the logistics database discussed in Chapters 6 and 7 to help manage and keep track of the logistics of distributed testing. (You might recall that Chapter 6 included an example of distributed testing for Speedy-Writer, with testing being performed at Software Cafeteria's home office, at STC's lab location, and at John Goldstein's home office.) Of course, when you have remote partners, you don't need to use the lab logistics capabilities added in Chapter 7's version of this database; organizing their own lab is part of what you're paying your test partners for.

DEALING WITH MAPPING ISSUES

If every test operation worked exactly the same way—according to the model presented in this book, for example—your planning work would be finished once the test program was unified, the work was partitioned appropriately, and the logistical problems were handled. The truth is, however, that each test team uses a different approach. You can't (and needn't) make every test partner work the same way, but you do need to recognize and manage the differences. I call these "mapping issues" because you are trying to map your partners' test efforts onto your own.

The first mapping issues usually arise during coordination, as you are comparing and sorting test cases. Figure 10-4 illustrates some of the possibilities you might encounter. Some test cases are completely unrelated to one another, and you must keep them all to maintain the desired level of coverage. In other instances, truly redundant test cases exist: either two test cases serve exactly the same purpose, or one test case completely covers another's conditions (along with additional conditions). Still other test cases overlap one another partially: test case A covers some but not all of test case B's conditions, and vice versa, but you can't drop either one without compromising coverage.

When you discover partial overlap, you can sometimes drop one test case and then redesign another to cover the missing conditions. Often, however, you must resign yourself to some redundancy of coverage at the test

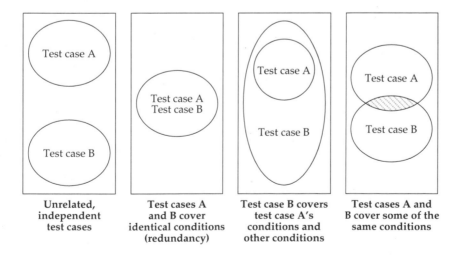

| Unrelated, independent test cases | Test cases A and B cover identical conditions (redundancy) | Test case B covers test case A's conditions and other conditions | Test cases A and B cover some of the same conditions |

FIGURE 10-4   *Examples of test case independence, redundancy, and partial overlap.*

case level. The amount of wasted time and effort is usually very low compared with the parameters of the overall project.

Test size (in terms of duration, effort, or both) can also complicate coordination and partitioning. Some test engineers write long test cases; others write shorter ones. Some test cases by nature require long duration or more effort. For example, reliability and environmental tests often run over a period of days. A test case that takes three days to execute might happen to include some but not all of a test case run elsewhere. But you can't drop the first test case unless you're willing to re-create all the work at the remote site.

You'll encounter other mapping issues during test execution, and you should plan solutions ahead of time. The most important is creating a process for getting all the bug reports into a single bug tracking system. With the database presented in Chapter 4, you can use the replication feature in Microsoft Access to distribute the database to your partners, or they can dial up and access the data on your servers. (To facilitate this, you can split the database into a front end consisting of the forms, queries, and reports and a back end consisting of the tables.) Alternatively, you or an administrative assistant can receive bug reports from partners and enter them in the database. Either approach will work, provided that you ensure minimal turnaround time.

Because multiple partners are testing, you will see more than the usual number of duplicate bug reports. Even if you do a good job of coordinating and partitioning the test cases to avoid overlap, certain bugs will manifest themselves on multiple tests. (If you do independent two-party testing, in which each party is unaware of what the other is doing, you can use the number of duplicate bug reports to estimate the effectiveness of the overall program. The more duplicates, the better.)

Language can also be a major issue when it comes to bug tracking and test tracking. You can expend a lot of effort setting up a process for sharing data electronically, only to find that the teams can't communicate anyway. Unfortunately, using a nontechnical translator or administrative assistant won't suffice, as the questions that arise are technical. Language can become an insurmountable barrier in some distributed test efforts; you should be sure to look into the matter before you set up such a program. Not every tester at every partner's site must speak a common language, however; usually, one or two people from each team can do the lion's share of communication work. I have successfully managed distributed test programs with vendors and test labs in Taiwan in which only one or two people on each test team spoke English.

Other mapping issues can stem from intercompany differences in work hours, conference calls, telecommuting policies, and the like. Technical challenges such as e-mail system incompatibilities can create difficulties. Even unexpected legal and trade barriers sometimes present challenges. For example, if you plan to encrypt sensitive documents to be shared with an overseas partner, you might end up violating U.S. trade policy restrictions on the export of munitions. (U.S. export laws classify some encryption tools as military weapons. Until quite recently, France actually prohibited the use of encryption.)

It's impossible to list every conceivable mapping issue. The fundamental point is that during the planning stages of a distributed test program, you must anticipate the differences, both formal and informal, between the processes you and your test partners follow and try to put plans in place to minimize the difficulties. Once test execution starts, you will have little time to resolve these issues on the fly.

Managing a Distributed Test Effort

Once you become accustomed to it, managing your virtual test team as the work proceeds is not that different from managing your own company's team. You will find, however, that these five areas require special attention: monitoring the test project and its findings, especially during crunch periods; communicating test status and changes in direction; handling the political realities; being sensitive to disparate cultures; and establishing and maintaining trust.

Monitoring Test Execution

Chapter 6 stresses the importance of keeping the bug tracking and test tracking mechanisms accurate and current during crunch periods. You will probably find this more challenging in a distributed test effort, even if you have done a good job of attending to the mapping issues discussed earlier. Distance, time zones, and language barriers can all get in the way. If you are updating the test tracking spreadsheet, for instance, and discover that you have questions about a set of test case failures found by your test partner, you could lose a few hours tracking down the person who can provide the information. If you need the data for an urgent presentation to management, this becomes a bigger problem.

Generally, you should plan for a certain lag in receiving results from external test partners, from a few extra minutes to as much as several days, depending on location. For example, when I worked with partners in Taiwan, our limited window for telephone conversations (early morning and early evening) meant that a miscommunication could go uncorrected for a full day. E-mail asynchronicity is convenient, but it also allows miscommunications to fester for days on end, especially when you're asking someone to carry out a task they don't really want to perform.

If you have a remote test partner whose work is on the critical path, there is no substitute for being on site. A travel budget is important: a ten-day, $3,500 trip to Tokyo or Taipei starts to look pretty affordable when a loss of momentum by your test partner risks slipping the ship date by three or four weeks.

Although this might be seen as an argument against distributed testing, don't forget that there is also an up side to your test partners' isolation. A lot of dysfunctional events can occur at the home office during test execution, and having some of your testers insulated from the effects of those events can keep them focused on the tasks at hand. I once had a client who moved the test operation from one side of the building to another at the start of a critical ten-day test period, and I've seen plenty of testers demotivated by the politics and frenzy attending crunch mode. An outside team, operating in a less crisis-driven environment, might make more headway than your own team, who is forced to react to the crisis of the moment.

COMMUNICATING STATUS AND CHANGING DIRECTION

None of your test partners can operate in a vacuum. You need a way to keep them apprised of what's going on, a way to allow them to bring problems to your attention, and a way to adjust course based on changing circumstances and test findings.

E-mail is not a bad communication channel for these purposes, but it can easily degenerate into "flame wars" and tangential discussions. If you use e-mail to communicate status, it's useful to format messages as either a status report or a list of action items. A daily update of a short (one- or two-page) document from each test partner should suffice as a status report. (To keep it from being a running report, allow old items to drop off.) Alternatively, you can keep a specific list of numbered action items, each with an owner and a due date.

The action item list is most effective when combined with a regular conference call at least once a week. During crunch mode, you'll probably find that such calls are necessary daily. A conference call should always have a structured agenda, with each partner reporting status and problems to the group in turn, followed by a review of the action items. At the end of every conference call, all the participants should agree on the current status of the test project and what is to happen next.

These conference calls are also the right place to communicate changes of direction that affect multiple partners. Changes that affect only one partner can be communicated either by telephone or by e-mail, depending on urgency. Be sure to track any alterations in plan in your change management database. Changes affecting your test partners are just as important as those affecting your own team.

I've assumed throughout this discussion that none of your test partners compete with each other directly. If they do, keep the two sides separated. In one project with some logistical exigencies, I needed to use two competing independent labs for testing, one in Taiwan, one in Los Angeles. I explained the arrangement to each lab manager, and both understood, although neither was happy about it. I had to build a "firewall" between the two in terms of conference calls, e-mail threads, and project findings to ensure that no industrial espionage or unproductive sniping could take place.

If you end up in this situation, avoid the temptation to play one side against the other. Agitating situations in which conflicting interests exist is liable to have unforeseen and negative outcomes. In addition, both of the organizations being manipulated will come to resent and dislike you. Building up reservoirs of ill will between you and people with whom you hope to do business in the future is hardly a wise move.

HANDLING POLITICAL CONSIDERATIONS

While your off-site test partners may be insulated from the turmoil and intrigue of your development project, you will inherit their political issues. Everyone in a development project must be seen as an active, positive participant. Because third-party test companies and vendors are off site, however, an image of them as noncontributive can gain currency. Also, questions of competency and diligence can arise when the inevitable mistakes are made. (Certainly such concerns arose among my client's project managers after the laptop shipping incident mentioned earlier in this chapter.)

Since you selected the test participants and planned the test effort, you have a stake in their success—not only their technical success (finding bugs and covering important test points) but also their political success (being perceived by the rest of the development team as effective, committed, and hard-working). It is up to you to champion the external test partners among your colleagues on the development team.

It sometimes happens, however, that negative perceptions of the external test partners are correct. In some cases, they are a net drag on the project. Test organizations can win contracts for which they are unqualified or understaffed. Vendors can prove unwilling to be frank about serious bugs they discover in their own products. Salespeople can turn out to be less interested in making a positive contribution to product quality than in carping about the lack of it. In these unfortunate circumstances—in which, I should point out, you may never find yourself—you need to act resolutely to mitigate the risk.

Such actions might include pulling the distributed testing back in-house—a painful solution, because you will likely discover the problem in the midst of the most pressure-filled part of the test schedule. This is not a conspiracy to make your life hell. People and organizations fail under pressure, not when the going is easy.

You might also want to shift some distributed testing to other external partners. Working with two test labs, as I described in the preceding section, did make my task of managing the project somewhat tricky. But, in addition to the logistical benefits, it also gave me a safety net. If one lab had proven unable to carry out its commitments, I could have moved its work to the other partner.

Either way, severing a relationship with a test partner is likely to prove unpleasant. Lots of money is at stake, and people get emotional under these circumstances. Since you had a hand in selecting the participants and planning the effort, you stand to lose face as well. You might also fear damaging an established relationship with the test staff of the vendor or test company. It's important, however, to keep your interests clear and consistent. Your ethical and fiduciary obligations are to your employer or client. If you handle it professionally, you can end the participation of a test partner without excessive rancor or unfairness.

Fairness in ending a relationship requires not only meeting financial considerations but also maintaining an open mind in making the decision. Move slowly on such decisions, and consider the source of derogatory information you hear about external test partners. Distributed testing, while undoubtedly a good idea under many circumstances, encounters internal resistance in most organizations; some people will resent the work being sent outside the company. These people sometimes act, both overtly and covertly, to damage the image of the distributed test program, and bashing the participants is one easy way to accomplish this. Do not disregard the concerns of such Cassandras, for they can be right, but do check out the story before making a final decision.

BEING SENSITIVE TO CULTURE CLASHES

Any time your test organization relies on an external partner, differences in corporate cultures can become an issue. This arises in part because, as discussed in Chapters 8 and 9, the perspectives held by testers differ from those held by other technical contributors.

My own background provides some examples. I changed from being a programmer and a system administrator to being a tester and test project leader when I took a job with an independent test lab. All my colleagues at the lab were testers. We worked on projects for clients who were developing hardware and software, but usually we interacted with only one or two client contacts. This all served to shield me from the political and cultural cross-currents that roil test groups in broader organizational settings.

I was forced to adapt rapidly, however, a few years later, when I became a test manager in a small custom software development shop. Chapter 9 dealt with the political realities of testing within the context of a development organization, lessons I learned to a great extent in that first test manager position. I have since relearned those same lessons, with a few variations, with subsequent employers and clients.

When you implement a distributed test program, you will experience these cultural issues writ large. Perspectives, priorities, and values differ from one team to the next even within a company, depending on the personalities of the team members, the leadership skills of the manager, the integrity of the perceived technical and moral leaders of the team (not just the manager), and, not least, the mission that team serves. When you deal with external organizations, these cultural issues are intensified by the fact that the leaders of the partner companies can instill different values. Although I always emphasize the importance of individual contributors to the success of a team, I am often reminded, sometimes shockingly, of how much the vision, ethics, and leadership skills of a handful of top managers in a company can profoundly influence the way even the most mundane tasks are performed.

In terms of distributed testing, such differences can mean that some individuals who would fail as test technicians, test engineers, or test managers in your company are seen as consummate test professionals perfectly aligned with the company culture in your test partners' organizations. For example, I place great value on cooperative relationships between testers and developers. In contrast, however, some successful organizations use an adversarial approach, with test managers encouraging testers to "catch" developers in errors. I would find it too emotionally draining to work in an organization where employees sought to undermine each other's successes, but if I worked with a test partner that used such an approach, it would hardly be within my purview to try to change that culture. Nevertheless, I might find the internecine quarrels distracting, to the extent that they spilled over into my life.

More subtle but equally challenging cultural clashes can occur. For example, I had a client who (at my recommendation) used an external lab in Taipei to handle some compatibility testing. The client's vendor was also located in Taipei. The test lab's corporate culture encouraged flexible but long hours, as my client did. The vendor involved had an "8-to-5" culture. Ironically, when we needed to institute regular conference calls, the vendor's culture and my client's culture meshed, but the time difference worked against the test lab. We had to schedule the calls for 8:30 A.M. Taipei time, which was fine for the vendor but troublesome for the project leader in the test lab, who worked from noon to midnight by choice. I resolved this particular situation by deciding to excuse him from the call, making sure that I understood the test lab's results and could represent its findings. This accommodation allowed the test manager to continue working his comfortable schedule. If I had insisted that he begin working cumbersome hours, our relationship could have been damaged.

BUILDING AND MAINTAINING TRUST

More fundamental than congruent cultures is the question of whether you can trust your test partners. Trust is an even more slippery concept than culture, but we all recognize people we trust or distrust. Even those who spend time building trust with us can lose it at a moment's notice. Suppose that you are the manager at Winged Bytes, working on DataRocket. A colleague of yours, the test manager for the SCSI card vendor, has been scrupulous about reporting any problems the vendor's test team finds, not just on this project but also on two previous projects. Suppose now that the test manager delays or conceals news of a fatal bug in the card's BIOS. That trust, built up over years, will suffer a serious, perhaps fatal, setback.[1]

All the tools and tips discussed in this chapter cannot resolve this problem. If you partition your test program to have test partners execute critical tests, you must establish a relationship of trust. You have to trust that the test lab won't skip a few tests because it's running behind schedule and fears that it will lose money on your project. You have to trust your vendor to be frank about even the most embarrassing bugs. You have to trust your colleagues in the foreign sales office to follow up with test results so that you aren't scrambling at the last minute to deal with critical bugs.

Trust also involves more than ensuring that your partners won't take advantage of you. You must look out for them, too. For example, I have helped test partners on my projects work through problems with invoices and contracts. There is, of course, a narrow path to tread in such matters, as you have fiduciary responsibilities to your employer. But assisting your chosen test partners in dealing with a nebulous contract issue or a sluggish accounts payable department shows good faith and a concern for your partners' success. When someone knows you are looking out for them, they'll usually look out for you.

As this book draws to a close, it's worthwhile to point out that trust isn't an issue only for your external test partners. It is critical for the whole project team, whether those people work at one company or at several. You have to assume that people are all pulling for the success of the project, by playing their individual roles to the best of their abilities. You must also assume that people are pulling for the success of their collaborators.

The cliché about a few bad apples spoiling the barrel applies especially to trust in an organization, but it's also true that key leaders in a firm, by setting an example of trustworthiness, can establish a company-wide standard. People who consistently apply their best efforts create passion and dedication. People who support all their colleagues and cooperate for the good of the team foster an environment of confidence and good will. No one, though, can contribute as much to a credulous company culture as a manager.

---

1. See Rajiv Sabherwal, "The Role of Trust in Outsourced IS Development Projects," for an interesting discussion of the importance of building and maintaining a trusting relationship with outsource partners. While this article addresses development resources, it could just as easily have been written about working with external test partners.

Managers who keep their commitments; who never let underlings take the fall for their own failings; who support and celebrate the successes of their star players, their team, and the company as a whole; who balance the company's needs with the personal needs of their subordinates and colleagues; and who consistently give and expect the truth from their staff, their peers, and their own managers cultivate a corporate culture of trust and integrity. As a test manager, you must participate in creating and upholding an environment of trust, both within your team and across the company. The standard you set in your team is as important as anything else you do.

APPENDIX

While this book should provide you with enough information to manage a test project, it is by no means a compendium. I encourage you to continue to augment your knowledge. The following subsections, including the bibliography of references and recommended readings, provide you with some places to go for more information. Like the book, this appendix is not complete, nor does presence or absence of a particular company, book, organization, or individual reflect my endorsement or opinion.

BIBLIOGRAPHY

This bibliography lists recommended reading for test managers. It includes the books and articles cited in the text as well as others that are especially important or helpful. In the past, there was a paucity of materials for the test professional, but that situation has begun to change. I encourage you to stay current and involved with the latest thinking and research in the field. Today's wacky idea is tomorrow's best practice, and the day after's expected minimum skill set.

Batini, Carlo, Stefano Ceri, and Shamkant Navathe. *Conceptual Database Design.* Redwood City, Calif.: Benjamin/Cummings, 1992.

Beizer, Boris. *Black Box Testing.* New York: Wiley, 1995.

Beizer, Boris. "The Black Box Vampire, or Testing Out of the Box." Closing speech at the 15th International Conference on Testing Computer Software, Washington, D.C., June 11, 1998. (Sponsor: U.S. Professional Development Institute, 1734 Elton Road, Silver Springs, Md. 20903-1724.)

Beizer, Boris. "Software Is Different." *Software Quality Professional* 1, no. 1 (1998): 44–54.

Beizer, Boris. *Software System Testing and Quality Assurance*. New York: International Thomson Computer Press, 1996.

Beizer, Boris. *Software Testing Techniques*, 2d ed. New York: Van Nostrand Reinhold, 1990.

Brooks, Frederick P., Jr. *The Mythical Man-Month*. Reading, Mass.: Addison-Wesley, 1975.

Brooks, Frederick P., Jr. "No Silver Bullets—Essence and Accidents of Software Engineering." *Computer*, April 1987, pp. 10–19.

Conway, Richard. *An Introduction to Programming: A Structured Approach Using PL/I and PL/C*. Boston: Little, Brown, 1979.

Crosby, Phillip. *Quality Is Free: The Art of Making Quality Certain*. New York: McGraw-Hill, 1979.

Drucker, Peter. "Management's New Paradigms." *Forbes*, October 5, 1998, pp. 152–76.

Edwards, Owen. "Rewriting the Geek Tragedy." *Forbes ASAP*, August 24, 1998, p. 108.

Gartner Group. "Surfing the Hype Curve." *Executive Edge*, September 1998, p. 16.

Gartner Group. "When Should You Outsource IT Functions?" *Executive Edge*, September 1998, p. 54.

Gilbreath, Robert. *Winning at Project Management*. New York: Wiley, 1986.

Gisselquist, Richard. "Engineering in Software." *Communications of the ACM* 41, no. 1 (October 1998): 107–8.

Hetzel, Bill. *The Complete Guide to Software Testing*. New York: Wiley-QED, 1988.

Ishikawa, Kaoru. *Guide to Quality Control*. Tokyo: Asian Productivity Organization, 1982.

Johnson, Paul. *Intellectuals*. New York: Harper and Row, 1988.

Juran, J. M. *Juran on Planning for Quality*. New York: Free Press, 1988.

Juran, J. M., and F. Gryna. *Quality Control Handbook*. New York: McGraw-Hill, 1988.

Kan, Stephen. *Metrics and Models in Software Quality Engineering*. Reading, Mass.: Addison-Wesley, 1995.

Kaner, Cem, Jack Falk, and Hung Quoc Nguyen. *Testing Computer Software*. New York: International Thomson Computer Press, 1993.

Karat, Clare-Marie. "Guaranteeing Rights for the User." *Communications of the ACM* 41, no. 12 (December 1998): 29–31.

Lyu, Michael, ed. *Handbook of Software Reliability Engineering*. New York: McGraw-Hill, 1996.

Mayer, John H. "Test Engineers Finally Earn Respect." *Contract Professional*, July/August 1998, pp. 22–26.

McConnell, Steve. *Software Project Survival Guide*. Redmond, Wash.: Microsoft Press, 1998.

Myers, Glenford. *The Art of Software Testing*. New York: Wiley, 1979.

Neumann, Peter. *Computer-Related Risks*. New York: Addison-Wesley, 1995.

O'Connor, Patrick. *Practical Reliability Engineering*. New York: Wiley, 1996.

Paulk, Mark C., Charles V. Weber, Bill Curtis, and Mary Beth Chrissis. *The Capability Maturity Model: Guidelines for Improving the Software Process*. Reading, Mass.: Addison-Wesley, 1995.

Perry, William. *A Structured Approach to Systems Testing*. Wellesley, Mass.: QED Information Sciences, 1988.

Perry, William, and Randall Rice. *Surviving the Top Ten Challenges of Software Testing*. New York: Dorset House, 1997.

Ruhl, Janet. *The Computer Consultant's Guide*. New York: Wiley, 1997.

Sabherwal, Rajiv. "The Role of Trust in Outsourced IS Development Projects." *Communications of the ACM* 42, no. 2 (February 1999): 80–86.

Slaughter, Sandra, David Harter, and Mayuram Krishnan. "Evaluating the Cost of Software Quality." *Communications of the ACM* 41, no. 8 (August 1998): 67–73.

Stamatis, D. H. *Failure Mode and Effects Analysis*. Milwaukee, Wisc.: ASQC Quality Press, 1995.

Voas, Jeffrey, and Gary McGraw. *Software Fault Injection*. New York: Wiley, 1998.

Walton, Mary. *The Deming Management Method*. New York: Putnam, 1986.

Weinberg, Gerald M. *Secrets of Consulting*. New York: Dorset House, 1985.

Wilson, Larry Todd, and Diane Asay. "Putting Quality in Knowledge Management." *Quality Progress*, January 1999, pp. 25–31.

Wysocki, Robert, Robert Beck Jr., and David Crane. *Effective Project Management*. New York: Wiley, 1995.

Zuckerman, Amy. *International Standards Desk Reference: Your Passport to World Markets*. New York: Amacom, 1996.

Zuckerman, Amy. "Standards Battles Heat Up Between United States and European Union." *Quality Progress*, January 1999, pp. 39–42.

HELP ON THE INTERNET

A recent Internet search under the words "software test" turned up almost 1,000 matches, and "hardware test" turned up 200. Clearly the Internet can be a powerful resource for help. As a starting point, let me suggest some sites, newsgroups, and mailing lists of general interest that will help you find the best online resources for you:

The newsgroup comp.software.testing and the FAQ sheet, located at *http://www.faqs.org/faqs/software-eng/testing-faq/*.

The newsgroup comp.software-eng and the FAQ sheet, located at *http://www.qucis.queensu.ca/Software-Engineering/*.

The newsgroup comp.risks, also available as a mailing list at risk-request@csl.sri.com.

The mailing list swtest-discuss-digest-request@rsn.hp.com.

NONPROFIT ORGANIZATIONS

You may want to consider contacting the following nonprofit organizations for more information; in some cases, you can find information on certification programs related to testing and quality. (Certification might advance your career, but, in the interest of full disclosure, I am not a certified test or quality professional.)

The Association for Computing Machinery is a professional organization that caters to academics, practitioners, and consultants. Its Web site is located at *http://www.asq.com*.

The American Society for Quality is a professional organization with computer software- and hardware-related interest groups and quality-related certification programs, and is concerned with testing, quality control, and quality assurance. They also publish two journals of interest to hardware and software test professionals, *Quality Progress* and *Software Quality Professional*. Their URL is *http://www.asq.com*.

The Institute of Electrical and Electronic Engineers is a professional organization with interest groups in the areas of hardware and software, as well as other electronics. Visit them at *http://ieee.org*.

CONTACTING ME

As I've mentioned before, I am the principal consultant at Rex Black Consulting Services, Inc. My associates and I practice test and quality assurance consulting for software and hardware development internationally. Should you have questions about the contents of this book or an interest in discussing ways in which RBCS can help your organization, please contact me at Rex_Black@RexBlackConsulting.com or at *http://www.RexBlackConsulting.com*.

GLOSSARY

Acceptance testing. A software or hardware development test phase designed to demonstrate that the system under test meets requirements. This phase is unique in all test activities in that its purpose is to demonstrate sufficiency and correctness, not to find problems. Acceptance testing is usually the last test phase before a product is released.

Ad hoc testing. Testing without written test cases, documented expected results, a checklist, a script, or instructions. Ad hoc tests often are not captured, which leads to questions about coverage and makes it impossible to do proper regression testing. Ad hoc testing can, however, be useful as a way to develop tests if records are kept. Also called *ad-lib testing.*

Behavioral tests. Tests based on what a computer system, hardware or software, is supposed to do. Such tests are usage-based and functional, at the levels of features, operational profiles, and customer scenarios. Also called *black-box tests* or *functional tests.*

Black-box tests. *See* **Behavioral tests**.

Bug. A problem present in the system under test that causes it to fail to meet reasonable expectations. "Reasonable" is usually defined by iterative consensus or management fiat if it is not obvious or defined (in the specifications or requirements documents). Notice that the test team usually sees only the failure (the improper behavior); the bug itself is the flaw that causes the failure.

Bug crawl.   A meeting or discussion focused on an item-by-item review of every active bug reported against the system under test. During this review, fix dates can be assigned, insignificant bugs can be deferred, and project management can assess the progress of the development process. Also called *bug scrub*.

Closure period.   For an individual bug that has been fixed and closed, the time between the initial bug report and the confirmation of the fix. The daily closure period is the average number of days between the opening of a bug report and its resolution for all bug reports closed on the same day, and the rolling closure period is the average for all closed bug reports. Closure period is a measure of development's responsiveness to test's bug reports.

Component testing.   A software development test phase (referred to as *subsystem testing* in hardware development) that finds bugs in the individual pieces of the system under test before the pieces are fully integrated into the system. Component testing can require support structures such as stubs or scaffolds.

Confirmation tests.   A selected set of tests designed to find ways in which a bug fix fails to address the reported issue fully. A typical confirmation test involves rerunning the test procedure and isolation steps, per the bug report.

Congruent.   A description of test system architecture in which all elements of a test system align with one another and with the objectives of the test system. In a congruent test system, each component contributes to the functioning of the test system, without contradictory or destructive interfaces, outputs, or side effects.

Debugging.   The process in which developers determine the root cause of a bug and identify possible fixes. Developers perform debugging activities to resolve a known bug either after development of a subsystem or unit or because of a bug report. *Contrast* **Isolation.**

Distributed testing.   Testing that occurs at multiple locations, involves multiple teams, or both.

Due diligence.   Informally, the requirement that responsible employees and business associates, especially managers, not be negligent of the consequences of their decisions and the attendant risks to their employers or clients. This term has legal connotations; you should consult legal counsel for a precise definition.

Entry criteria. A set of decision-making guidelines used to determine whether a system under test is ready to move into, or enter, a particular phase of testing. Entry criteria tend to become more rigorous as the test phases progress.

Error seeding. A theoretical technique for measuring the bugs remaining in the system under test and thereby measuring the effectiveness of the test system itself, by deliberately inserting known defects (hidden from the testers) into the system under test and then checking the proportion of these defects that are detected.

Escalate. To communicate a problem to a higher level of management for solution.

Exit criteria. A set of decision-making guidelines used to determine whether a system under test is ready to exit a particular phase of testing. When exit criteria are met, either the system under test moves on to the next test phase or the test project is considered complete. Exit criteria tend to become more rigorous as the test phases progress.

Experience of quality. The customers' opinion about whether a product is fulfilling their expectations and needs.

Failure mode. A particular way, in terms of symptoms, behaviors, or internal state changes, in which a failure manifests itself. For example, a heat dissipation problem in a CPU might cause a laptop case to melt or warp, or memory mismanagement might cause a core dump.

Fault injection. A theoretical technique for measuring the effectiveness of a test system, in which errors are created in the system under test by deliberately damaging, or perturbing, the source code, the executable code, or the data storage locations and then analyzing the test results.

FCS. Acronym for *first customer ship*, the point at which the first system under test, now a completely tested, finished product, ships to the first paying customer. Also called *release* or *general availability*.

Fidelity. With respect to a test system, the degree to which it accurately models end user hardware, software, and network environments and simulates end user activities.

Field-reported bug. A failure in a released, shipping product, usually reported by a customer or a salesperson, that either affects the ability of the customer to use the product or involves side effects that impair the customer's ability to use other products on the same system.

Flexibility.   The ability of a test component to handle minor changes in the behavior of the system under test without generating type I or type II errors.

FMEA.   Acronym for *failure mode and effects analysis,* a technique described by D. H. Stamatis for identifying and defining potential quality risks, ranking them by risk priority, and assigning corrective action.

Functional tests.   *See* **Behavioral tests.**

GA.   Acronym for *general availability. See* **FCS.**

Goat rodeo.   Any confused, disorganized, and chaotic group event, generally held under pressure or duress, which results in little forward progress, thus frustrating many participants.

Granularity.   Fineness or coarseness of focus. A highly granular test allows the tester to check low-level details; a structural test is very granular. Behavioral tests, which are less granular, provide the tester with information on general system behavior, not details.

IEEE.   Acronym for the Institute of Electrical and Electronic Engineers.

Integration testing.   A software development test phase (referred to as *product testing* in hardware development) that finds bugs in the relationships and interfaces between pairs and groups of components in the system under test, often in a staged fashion. This test phase occurs when all the constituent components of the system under test are being integrated.

Isolation.   Repeating the steps needed to reproduce a bug, possibly many times, with precise changes in system configuration, permission levels, background load, environment, and so forth, in an effort to understand the levers that control the bug and its behavior—in other words, to confirm that the bug is a real problem and to identify those factors that affect the bug's manifestations. Good isolation draws a bounding box around a bug. Isolation requires the tester to make intelligent guesses about the root cause of the problem. *Contrast* **Debugging.**

Kludge.   Any ill-advised, substandard, or "temporary" bandage applied to an urgent problem in the (often misguided) belief that doing so will keep a project moving forward.

Maintainable.   In terms of the test system, the extent to which a test engineer versed in the operation of the system can make changes in a test component without undue risk of damaging that component or other components.

MEGO.   Acronym for *my eyes glazed over;* refers to a loss of focus and attention, often caused by an attempt to read a particularly impenetrable or dense technical document.

MTBF.   Acronym for *mean time between failures.* Demonstrating a particular MTBF or discovering a statistically meaningful MTBF is often an important part of a hardware development project, as this figure predicts the financial impact of various warranty policies and has important implications for field defect rates and a company's reputation for quality.

MTTR.   Acronym for *mean time to repair.* Like MTBF, this figure has implications for a company's warranties and reputation. A problem that takes longer to repair is generally considered a higher priority than one that takes less time to repair, all other factors being equal.

Oracle.   Any way of determining the expected (correct) result for a test case, a test suite, or a test operation. This term is usually synonymous with *output oracle,* which, for a given input under a given set of test conditions, tells the tester what the expected output should be.

Orthogonal.   A description of the relationship between two or more variables or set members in which the value of one does not influence the values of others.

Peer review.   A quality improvement idea common in software development, in which one or more testers read and comment on a test deliverable such as a bug report, a test suite, or a test plan. The reading is followed by a review meeting in which the deliverable is discussed. Based on this discussion, the deliverable is updated, corrected, and re-released.

Pilot testing.   In hardware development, a test phase generally following or accompanying acceptance testing, which demonstrates the ability of the assembly line to mass-produce the completely tested, finished system under test. In software development, pilot testing is a test phase that demonstrates the ability of the system to handle typical operations from live customers on live hardware. First customer ship often immediately follows the successful completion of the pilot testing phase.

Product testing. *See* **Integration testing.**

Quality risk. The possibility of undesirable classes of behaviors, or failure modes, in which the system under test does not meet stated product requirements or end users' reasonable expectations of behavior; in plain terms, the possibility of a bug.

Quality risk management. The process of identifying, prioritizing, and managing quality risks, with the aim of preventing them or detecting and removing them.

Railroading. A technique that continues test execution in test suite order when a new test cycle starts. Rather than restarting the testing or moving on to a new set of suites, the testing simply continues from where it was when the test cycle began. The goal of this and similar techniques is to achieve an acceptable level of test coverage and minimize regression test gaps when coverage cannot be exhaustive.

Ramp-up. A hardware production phase that immediately follows a product release, in which the assembly line learns the process and product foibles associated with mass-producing the completely tested, finished system under test. This phase usually is accompanied by a spike in field-reported bugs.

Regression. A problem that occurs when, as a result of a change in the system under test, a new revision of the system, S_{n+1}, contains a defect not present in revisions S_1 though S_n. In other words, regression occurs when some previously correct operation misbehaves. (If a new revision contains a new piece of functionality that fails without affecting the rest of the system, this is not considered regression.) Usually you'll detect regression when test cases that previously passed now yield anomalies.

Regression test gap. For any given change or revision in the system under test, the difference between the areas of test coverage provided by the entire test system and the test coverage provided by the portion of the test system that is actually rerun. For a system release, a regression test gap is the extent to which the final release version of every component and change in the system did not experience the full brunt of the test system.

Regression tests.   A set of tests selected to find regression introduced by changes in component, interface, or product functionality, usually associated with bug fixes or new functionality. Regression is a particularly insidious risk in a software maintenance effort because there is seldom time for a full retest of the product, even though seemingly innocuous changes can have knock-on effects in remote areas of functionality or behavior.

Reporting logs.   Raw test output produced by low-level test tools, which is "human-readable" to varying degrees. Examples include text files containing test condition pass/fail results, screen shots, and diagnostics.

Reporting tools.   Special test tools that can process reporting logs into reports and charts, given some information about the context in which the log was produced.

Root cause.   The underlying reason why a bug occurs, as opposed to the observed symptoms of the bug. Root cause data is most useful in the aggregate: analyzing a breakdown of the root causes of all bugs found in a system under test can help to focus the attention of both test and development on those areas that are causing the most serious and frequent problems.

Scalability.   The ability of a test component's parameters of operation to expand without necessitating major changes or fundamental redesign in the test system.

SCUD release.   A software or hardware release, hastily prepared by development in a crisis atmosphere, that may or may not fix some number of critical bugs. Like their namesake missiles, such releases seldom hit their targets, arrive with little warning but lots of noise, cause a great deal of panic, and don't contribute much to ultimate victory.

Severity. The absolute impact of a bug on the system under test, regardless of the likelihood of its occurrence under end user conditions. I use a severity scale that ranges from 1 (most severe or dangerous) to 5 (least severe or dangerous).

Shotgunning. A technique that distributes test suites randomly across test cycles or distributes test configurations randomly across test suites throughout a test phase. Shotgunning test suites across test cycles means that the test suites are preassigned to each cycle and are run as the new cycles begin. Shotgunning test configurations across test suites means that test system configurations (combinations of hardware, software, operating system, and infrastructure) are arbitrarily selected to run specific test suites. In both cases, the goal is to achieve an acceptable level of test coverage and minimize regression test gaps when coverage cannot be exhaustive.

Spinning disk release. Like a SCUD release, a software revision that is sent by development to test so hastily that supposedly the floppy disk is still spinning.

Stopping criteria. A set of decision-making guidelines used to determine whether a particular phase of testing should be halted or suspended, usually because of poor quality of the system under test or logistical problems related to performing tests. Stopping criteria tend to become more rigorous as the test phases progress.

Straw man plan. Any lightweight or incomplete plan, such as the first draft of a test plan or a hardware allocation plan, that serves as a starting point for discussion and a framework for coalescing a more concrete plan.

String testing. A software development test phase that finds bugs in typical usage scripts and operational or control-flow "strings." This test phase is fairly unusual.

Structural tests. Tests based on how a computer system, hardware or software, operates. Such tests are code-based or component-based, and they find bugs in operations such as those that occur at the levels of lines of code, chips, subassemblies, and interfaces. Also called *white-box tests, glass-box tests, code-based tests,* or *design-based tests.*

Subsystem testing. *See* **Component testing.**

SUT. *See* **System under test.**

SWAG. Acronym for *scientific wild-ass guess;* an educated guess or estimate. SWAGs abound in test scheduling activities early in the development process.

System testing. A software or hardware development test phase that finds bugs in the overall and particular behaviors, functions, and responses of the system under test as a whole operating under realistic usage scenarios. These various system operations are performed once the system is fully integrated.

System under test. The entirety of the product, or system, being tested, which often consists of more than the immediately obvious pieces; abbreviated SUT. Test escapes can arise through misunderstanding the scope of the system under test.

TBD. Acronym for *to be determined;* a useful placeholder in test documents to indicate a work-in-progress.

Test artifacts. Behaviors arising from the artificiality of the test environment or from a test process that diverges from the way the system will behave in the field; misleading behaviors or incorrect results reported by the test system.

Test case. A sequence of steps, substeps, and other actions, performed serially, in parallel, or in some combination of consecution, that creates the desired test conditions that the test case is designed to evaluate.

Test case library. A collection of independent, reusable test cases.

Test case (suite) setup. The steps required to configure the test environment for execution of a test case or a test suite.

Test case (suite) teardown. The steps required to restore the test environment to a "clean" condition after execution of a test case or a test suite.

Test condition. A system state or circumstance created by proceeding through some combination of steps, substeps, or actions in a test case. The term is sometimes also used to refer to the steps, substeps, or actions themselves.

Test coverage. 1. The extent to which a test system covers, or exercises, the structure (the code or components) of the system under test. The metric is usually expressed as a percentage of the total count of the structural element being covered, such as lines of code or function points. 2. The extent to which a test system covers, or exercises, the behavior (the operations, activities, functions, and other uses) of the system under test. The extent is measured—albeit qualitatively—against the uses to which the customer base as a whole is likely to subject it. Thorough coverage in both respects is necessary for good testing.

Test cycle.   A partial or total execution of all the test suites planned for a given test phase as part of that phase. A test phase involves at least one cycle (usually more) through all the designated test suites. Test cycles are usually associated with a release of the system under test, such as a build of software or a motherboard. Generally, new releases occur during a test phase, triggering another test cycle.

Tester failure.   Any failure caused by a tester using the test system; human or "pilot" error. Tester failures can result in type I or type II errors, or they can simply be irritating yet immaterial.

Test escape.   Any field-reported bug that could reasonably have been caught during testing but was not. The term can also refer to a bug that makes its way into a subsequent phase of testing, although it should have been caught in a previous phase. A field-reported bug that was found during testing but that was not fixed because of a project management decision is not a test escape. A bug that could be found only through unusual and complicated hardware configurations or obscure operations is not considered a test escape, either.

Test failure.   Any failure of the test system. A test failure can result in type I or type II errors, or it can simply cause unpleasant side effects that nevertheless do not compromise the validity of the test results.

Test phase.   A distinct test subproject that addresses a particular class of quality risks. Test phases often overlap.

Test platform.   Any piece of hardware on which a test can be run. The test platform is not necessarily the system under test, especially when testing software.

Test suite.   A framework for the execution of a group of test cases; a way of organizing test cases. In a test suite, test cases can be combined to create unique test conditions.

Test system.   An integrated and maintainable test environment and reporting system, whose primary purpose is to find, reproduce, isolate, describe, and manage bugs in the software or hardware under test.

Test to fail.   The mind-set involved in designing, developing, and executing tests with the aim of finding as many problems as possible. This attitude represents the right way to think about testing.

Test tool.   Any general-purpose hardware, software, or hardware/software system used during test case execution to set up or tear down the test environment, to create test conditions, or to measure test results. A test tool is separate from the test case itself.

Test to pass.   The mind-set involved in designing, developing, and executing tests with the aim of proving compliance with requirements and correctness of operation. Such an attitude not only misses opportunities to increase product quality but also is demonstrably futile. It represents the wrong way to think about testing (except in the case of acceptance testing).

Test yield.   The degree to which a test case or a test suite finds bugs. A high-yield test suite, for example, results in many bug reports of a serious nature, whereas a low-yield test suite results in few or trivial bug reports.

Type I error.   An error that occurs when a tester reports correct system behavior as a bug, assigns an excessively high severity or priority ranking to a bug, or otherwise overstates the significance of a problem. Type I errors can have a negative impact on the test organization's credibility. These errors can be caused by the test system or the tester.

Type II error.   An error that occurs when a tester fails to detect or report incorrect system behavior, assigns an excessively low severity or priority ranking to a bug, or otherwise understates the significance of problem. A type II error, more serious than a type I error, often leads to a test escape. These errors can be caused by the test system or the tester.

Unit testing.   A software development concept that refers to the basic testing of a piece of code, the size of which is often undefined in practice, although it is usually a function or a subroutine. Unit testing is generally performed by developers.

White-box tests.   *See* **Structural tests.**

INDEX

Page numbers in italics refer to tables, figures, or illustrations.

A

B

Y

Z

REX BLACK

Rex Black has spent almost 17 years in the computer industry, with 14 years in testing and quality assurance. He is the president and principal consultant of Rex Black Consulting Services, Inc., an international software and hardware testing and quality assurance consultancy. (Visit his Web site at *www.rexblackconsulting.com*.) His clients include Dell, SunSoft, Hitachi, Netpliance, Motorola, Pacific Bell, GE Capital, Tatung, IMG, Renaissance Worldwide, DataRace, Omegabyte, Omnipoint, TeleSource, Strategic Forecasting, and Clarion. He actively participates in the planning, execution, and management of testing projects, as well as consulting with clients and providing training. Mr. Black holds a Bachelor of Science degree in Computer Science and Engineering from UCLA and belongs to the Association for Computer Machinery and the American Society for Quality.

The manuscript for this book was prepared using Microsoft Word 97. Pages were composed by Microsoft Press, with text and display type in Palatino. Composed pages were delivered to the printer as electronic prepress files.

Cover Designer
Greg Hickman

Cover Illustrator
Todd Daman

Interior Graphic Artist
Joel Panchot

Principal Compositor
Barb Runyan

Indexer
Liz Cunningham

How to be sure your
first *important project* last...
isn't your

Equip yourself with SOFTWARE PROJECT SURVIVAL GUIDE. It's for everyone with a stake in the outcome of a development project—and especially for those without formal software project management training. That includes top managers, executives, clients, investors, end-user representatives, project managers, and technical leads. Here you'll find guidance from the acclaimed author of the classics *Code Complete* and *Rapid Development*. Steve McConnell draws on solid research and a career's worth of hard-won experience to map the surest path to your goal—what he calls "one specific approach to software development that works pretty well most of the time for most projects." Get SOFTWARE PROJECT SURVIVAL GUIDE. And be sure of success.

U.S.A.	**$24.99**
U.K.	£22.49
Canada	$34.99
ISBN 1-57231-621-7	

Microsoft®

mspress.microsoft.com

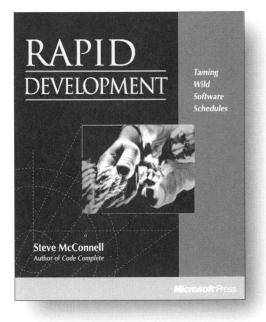

MICROSOFT LICENSE AGREEMENT

Book Companion CD

SOFTWARE PRODUCT LICENSE

The SOFTWARE PRODUCT is protected by United States copyright laws and international copyright treaties, as well as other intellectual property laws and treaties. The SOFTWARE PRODUCT is licensed, not sold.

1. GRANT OF LICENSE. This EULA grants you the following rights:

    a. Software Product. You may install and use one copy of the SOFTWARE PRODUCT on a single computer. The primary user of the computer on which the SOFTWARE PRODUCT is installed may make a second copy for his or her exclusive use on a portable computer.

    b. Storage/Network Use. You may also store or install a copy of the SOFTWARE PRODUCT on a storage device, such as a network server, used only to install or run the SOFTWARE PRODUCT on your other computers over an internal network; however, you must acquire and dedicate a license for each separate computer on which the SOFTWARE PRODUCT is installed or run from the storage device. A license for the SOFTWARE PRODUCT may not be shared or used concurrently on different computers.

    c. License Pak. If you have acquired this EULA in a Microsoft License Pak, you may make the number of additional copies of the computer software portion of the SOFTWARE PRODUCT authorized on the printed copy of this EULA, and you may use each copy in the manner specified above. You are also entitled to make a corresponding number of secondary copies for portable computer use as specified above.

    d. Sample Code. Solely with respect to portions, if any, of the SOFTWARE PRODUCT that are identified within the SOFTWARE PRODUCT as sample code (the "SAMPLE CODE"):

        i. Use and Modification. Microsoft grants you the right to use and modify the source code version of the SAMPLE CODE, *provided* you comply with subsection (d)(iii) below. You may not distribute the SAMPLE CODE, or any modified version of the SAMPLE CODE, in source code form.

        ii. Redistributable Files. Provided you comply with subsection (d)(iii) below, Microsoft grants you a nonexclusive, royalty-free right to reproduce and distribute the object code version of the SAMPLE CODE and of any modified SAMPLE CODE, other than SAMPLE CODE, or any modified version thereof, designated as not redistributable in the Readme file that forms a part of the SOFTWARE PRODUCT (the "Non-Redistributable Sample Code"). All SAMPLE CODE other than the Non-Redistributable Sample Code is collectively referred to as the "REDISTRIBUTABLES."

        iii. Redistribution Requirements. If you redistribute the REDISTRIBUTABLES, you agree to: (i) distribute the REDISTRIBUTABLES in object code form only in conjunction with and as a part of your software application product; (ii) not use Microsoft's name, logo, or trademarks to market your software application product; (iii) include a valid copyright notice on your software application product; (iv) indemnify, hold harmless, and defend Microsoft from and against any claims or lawsuits, including attorney's fees, that arise or result from the use or distribution of your software application product; and (v) not permit further distribution of the REDISTRIBUTABLES by your end user. Contact Microsoft for the applicable royalties due and other licensing terms for all other uses and/or distribution of the REDISTRIBUTABLES.

2. DESCRIPTION OF OTHER RIGHTS AND LIMITATIONS.

    • **Limitations on Reverse Engineering, Decompilation, and Disassembly.** You may not reverse engineer, decompile, or disassemble the SOFTWARE PRODUCT, except and only to the extent that such activity is expressly permitted by applicable law notwithstanding this limitation.

    • **Separation of Components.** The SOFTWARE PRODUCT is licensed as a single product. Its component parts may not be separated for use on more than one computer.

    • **Rental.** You may not rent, lease, or lend the SOFTWARE PRODUCT.

    • **Support Services.** Microsoft may, but is not obligated to, provide you with support services related to the SOFTWARE PRODUCT ("Support Services"). Use of Support Services is governed by the Microsoft policies and programs described in the user manual, in "online" documentation, and/or in other Microsoft-provided materials. Any supplemental software code provided to you as part of the Support Services shall be considered part of the SOFTWARE PRODUCT and subject to the terms and conditions of this EULA. With respect to technical information you provide to Microsoft as part of the Support Services, Microsoft may use such information for its business purposes, including for product support and development. Microsoft will not utilize such technical information in a form that personally identifies you.

- **Software Transfer.** You may permanently transfer all of your rights under this EULA, provided you retain no copies, you transfer all of the SOFTWARE PRODUCT (including all component parts, the media and printed materials, any upgrades, this EULA, and, if applicable, the Certificate of Authenticity), **and** the recipient agrees to the terms of this EULA.

- **Termination.** Without prejudice to any other rights, Microsoft may terminate this EULA if you fail to comply with the terms and conditions of this EULA. In such event, you must destroy all copies of the SOFTWARE PRODUCT and all of its component parts.

3. **COPYRIGHT.** All title and copyrights in and to the SOFTWARE PRODUCT (including but not limited to any images, photographs, animations, video, audio, music, text, SAMPLE CODE, REDISTRIBUTABLES, and "applets" incorporated into the SOFTWARE PRODUCT) and any copies of the SOFTWARE PRODUCT are owned by Microsoft or its suppliers. The SOFTWARE PRODUCT is protected by copyright laws and international treaty provisions. Therefore, you must treat the SOFTWARE PRODUCT like any other copyrighted material **except** that you may install the SOFTWARE PRODUCT on a single computer provided you keep the original solely for backup or archival purposes. You may not copy the printed materials accompanying the SOFTWARE PRODUCT.

4. **U.S. GOVERNMENT RESTRICTED RIGHTS.** The SOFTWARE PRODUCT and documentation are provided with RESTRICTED RIGHTS. Use, duplication, or disclosure by the Government is subject to restrictions as set forth in subparagraph (c)(1)(ii) of the Rights in Technical Data and Computer Software clause at DFARS 252.227-7013 or subparagraphs (c)(1) and (2) of the Commercial Computer Software—Restricted Rights at 48 CFR 52.227-19, as applicable. Manufacturer is Microsoft Corporation/One Microsoft Way/Redmond, WA 98052-6399.

5. **EXPORT RESTRICTIONS.** You agree that you will not export or re-export the SOFTWARE PRODUCT, any part thereof, or any process or service that is the direct product of the SOFTWARE PRODUCT (the foregoing collectively referred to as the "Restricted Components"), to any country, person, entity, or end user subject to U.S. export restrictions. You specifically agree not to export or re-export any of the Restricted Components (i) to any country to which the U.S. has embargoed or restricted the export of goods or services, which currently include, but are not necessarily limited to, Cuba, Iran, Iraq, Libya, North Korea, Sudan, and Syria, or to any national of any such country, wherever located, who intends to transmit or transport the Restricted Components back to such country; (ii) to any end user who you know or have reason to know will utilize the Restricted Components in the design, development, or production of nuclear, chemical, or biological weapons; or (iii) to any end user who has been prohibited from participating in U.S. export transactions by any federal agency of the U.S. government. You warrant and represent that neither the BXA nor any other U.S. federal agency has suspended, revoked, or denied your export privileges.

DISCLAIMER OF WARRANTY

NO WARRANTIES OR CONDITIONS. MICROSOFT EXPRESSLY DISCLAIMS ANY WARRANTY OR CONDITION FOR THE SOFTWARE PRODUCT. THE SOFTWARE PRODUCT AND ANY RELATED DOCUMENTATION ARE PROVIDED "AS IS" WITHOUT WARRANTY OR CONDITION OF ANY KIND, EITHER EXPRESS OR IMPLIED, INCLUDING, WITHOUT LIMITATION, THE IMPLIED WARRANTIES OF MERCHANTABILITY, FITNESS FOR A PARTICULAR PURPOSE, OR NONINFRINGEMENT. THE ENTIRE RISK ARISING OUT OF USE OR PERFORMANCE OF THE SOFTWARE PRODUCT REMAINS WITH YOU.

LIMITATION OF LIABILITY. TO THE MAXIMUM EXTENT PERMITTED BY APPLICABLE LAW, IN NO EVENT SHALL MICROSOFT OR ITS SUPPLIERS BE LIABLE FOR ANY SPECIAL, INCIDENTAL, INDIRECT, OR CONSEQUENTIAL DAMAGES WHATSOEVER (INCLUDING, WITHOUT LIMITATION, DAMAGES FOR LOSS OF BUSINESS PROFITS, BUSINESS INTERRUPTION, LOSS OF BUSINESS INFORMATION, OR ANY OTHER PECUNIARY LOSS) ARISING OUT OF THE USE OF OR INABILITY TO USE THE SOFTWARE PRODUCT OR THE PROVISION OF OR FAILURE TO PROVIDE SUPPORT SERVICES, EVEN IF MICROSOFT HAS BEEN ADVISED OF THE POSSIBILITY OF SUCH DAMAGES. IN ANY CASE, MICROSOFT'S ENTIRE LIABILITY UNDER ANY PROVISION OF THIS EULA SHALL BE LIMITED TO THE GREATER OF THE AMOUNT ACTUALLY PAID BY YOU FOR THE SOFTWARE PRODUCT OR US$5.00; PROVIDED, HOWEVER, IF YOU HAVE ENTERED INTO A MICROSOFT SUPPORT SERVICES AGREEMENT, MICROSOFT'S ENTIRE LIABILITY REGARDING SUPPORT SERVICES SHALL BE GOVERNED BY THE TERMS OF THAT AGREEMENT. BECAUSE SOME STATES AND JURISDICTIONS DO NOT ALLOW THE EXCLUSION OR LIMITATION OF LIABILITY, THE ABOVE LIMITATION MAY NOT APPLY TO YOU.

MISCELLANEOUS

This EULA is governed by the laws of the State of Washington USA, except and only to the extent that applicable law mandates governing law of a different jurisdiction.

Should you have any questions concerning this EULA, or if you desire to contact Microsoft for any reason, please contact the Microsoft subsidiary serving your country, or write: Microsoft Sales Information Center/One Microsoft Way/Redmond, WA 98052-6399.